The 1st Florida Union Cavalry Volunteers in the Civil War

The Men and the Regimental History and What That Tells Us About the Area During the War

Sharon D. Marsh

Copyright © 2017 by Sharon D. Marsh

All rights reserved. This book or any portion thereof may not be reproduced or used in any manner whatsoever without the express written permission of the publisher except for the use of brief quotations in a book review or scholarly journal.

First Paperback Edition: 2017

ISBN 978-0-9988170-0-2

Publisher: Sharon D. Marsh

The 1st Florida Union Cavalry Volunteers in the Civil War:

The Men and the Regimental History; and What That Tells Us About the Area During the War

Sharon D. Marsh

Sharon D. Marsh, Publisher

2017

Dedicated to my Mom Blannie

Her support, encouragement and love have strengthened me in the highs and lows of researching and writing this book, and throughout my life.

Acknowledgements

When it takes more than a decade to research and write a book, especially one that incorporates genealogy information on mostly unrelated men, a whole lot of people whose willingness to share family information truly becomes critical. There are too many to name, especially since there have also been two computer crashes during these years (research backed up but not email addresses and names!) But there were a number of folks I talked with and exchanged information with who were vital to this finished product. Some of these folks, like me, are related to a number of these men, some have knowledge of this time period and the events in this area and some because they were continuously supportive of this project. If I leave anyone out, please be understanding.

Bob Bryan
Dale A. Cox
Mark Curenton
Mary desVignes-Kendrick, MD, MPH
Barbara Martin
Barbara McManus
Brian Rucker
Mark J. Schaadt, MD
Don Umphrey

Preface

I came to my fascination with the 1st Florida Cavalry Union Volunteers (1st FCUV) back in the mid-1990s. I had been doing genealogy for a few years at that point and had recently discovered my first ancestor who fought in the war on the side of the South. I decided to try and identify all of my male ancestors who were between 16 and 50 during the war and determine if they too had fought. All my ancestors were already in the Deep South so I, like many people, assumed that if they fought they would have fought for the Confederacy. As much as I enjoyed and read history, I was not aware that there were a number of Union regiments in which Southern men fought during the war. I quickly developed a nice list of ancestors that I could review muster rolls for, and develop a timeline of, their experiences. But one presented a problem as soon as I started working on him. He lived in the Florida panhandle in 1860 and appeared on the rolls of the 5th Florida Infantry, Co. I but his record was very short and it appeared he had been discharged not quite two months from his muster date by a physician. But no reason for the discharge was listed. He appeared on no censuses after the war, though his wife and children did, and his wife was listed as a widow. I was thoroughly perplexed. If he didn't fight, why wasn't he buried next to his wife at Stewart Cemetery in Okaloosa Co, Florida? If he did fight, where was his records? Then a distant relative from another of my ancestral lines in the same area of Florida mentioned that he thought that was one of the men he had heard fought for the Union and was buried at Fort Barrancas.

My next vacation at home my Mom and I did a day trip to Fort Barrancas. We pulled into the cemetery and parked and went inside the visitors' station. I told the man behind the desk who and what I was trying to find out, he went to a large cabinet and in a moment pulled out a card and came back to me. Yes, James Millard Gaskin had served with the 1st FCUV and was buried in the cemetery. He had been a Master Sergeant at his death on 14 May 1865. He pointed us to the older section of the cemetery and told us James was buried at the first marker in the older section.

We walked out and across the road and I stood in front of my 3rd great grandfather's headstone. I was happy and tearful and full of questions. What did he do between his discharge from the 5th Florida Infantry and his enlistment with the 1st FCUV? Why did he decide to join the Union regiment? Did his wife agree with his decision? What happened to her when he enlisted? Who else joined the 1st FCUV and did I know any of them and more importantly was I related to them? My journey had begun.

I invested in an old microfilm reader and purchased the entire set of microfilm rolls for the 1st FCUV and began going through them. It didn't take long to realize that the same issues that exist with any other primary documents were here as well. The records weren't quite as bad as some of the Confederate records near the end of the war but they were certainly challenging. Conflicting information, incorrect information and absence of information was obvious from the start but I quickly realized I recognized more than a few of the names since I had been doing genealogy focused on the Florida panhandle for years. There were brothers of a couple of my female ancestors and one of James Millard Gaskin's brothers. There were neighbors of my ancestors, men who married into my ancestors' families, nephews and cousins of ancestors from my father's side of the family, and a number of men who were members of my ancestors' church in what was then northern Santa Rosa County. So, I began to research each man in the census and pension records.

At some point in my research I decided I should write up what I was putting together. There certainly was minimal information on the regiment other than in the Official Records and the muster rolls. Though the research has taken nearly two decades and the writing has not always been a priority, I've never stopped digging into records and compiling what I was discovering. This book is a hybrid. It is a genealogical record of each of the men who served, attempted to join or left some bit of a record that they might have been in the regiment for some period between 1864 and 1865. It is also a history of the regiment. Together they begin to give a unique perspective on the area these men came from and the men themselves.

I discovered as I went about trying to find these men and get a sense of what might have been the factors in their lives that brought them to the decision to fight for the Union that some people today on both sides of the Mason-Dixon line create myths and fallacies about this regiment and the men who served in it, assuming they know that it existed. Northerners often have no idea that there were Southerners who fought in the Union and then may discount their contribution to the War because they fought outside the main Eastern and Western Theatres. Southerners often dismiss the men who served in the regiment as Confederate deserters (they were not all deserters) or create a myth of the men just joining for the bounty money and then deserting the Union or joining to be a spy. While both of these were certainly possible motivations, it certainly does not explain the majority of enlistees. And then there is the continuing explanation that most of these men were deserters from elsewhere in the south who came to the Florida swamps and joined gangs and were sometimes used by the Union to terrorize the population. Some of these men were from elsewhere, the vast majority were not. There were gangs and possibly some of these men were members of the gangs before enlistment. There is no evidence that the Union condoned the terrorism or used it in any official capacity. A bit of real study of the regiment discounts the majority of these memes pretty rapidly. Courage can be reflected in a variety of ways, not just in fighting but not doing so, or doing so for the opposing side. As Southerners, if we wish to acknowledge our ancestors' roles in the War, we should be willing to acknowledge all roles that in total created who we are as Southerners.

While primary records are the best source of information on this or any other genealogy project, they are not always known for accuracy. Ages, birth locations and names can all be incorrect. I felt lucky when I could find a man whose muster roll and all of the other records essentially matched, with minor variations in spelling. Maybe not surprising, these were most often the men who appeared to sign their enlistment papers, were listed as having attended school on the census, and their family had property in 1850 and 1860. When all information on individual men had been reviewed at least twice I had found about 90% of the men in at least one census, before or after the war. The remaining 10% are likely the result of errors in the underlying census and the quality of the search engines or indexes at various websites, or my failure to find all possible records or see clues that were in front of my face. I do not believe there were large scale efforts by the men joining the 1st FCUV at providing false names so the men could then desert and disappear with the bounties, as one researcher suggested to me during my research.

This would be a good place to mention my research for this book. I started with the muster rolls, then searched the census before and after the war. I turned next to pension and land records and then went back through the censuses. I looked then at Ancestry for family members who had posted something on these men and when possible talked with them about their ancestor. Some were very helpful in sharing information and photographs. Finally, with information on their deaths when available I looked for them in cemeteries and at the website findagrave.com. Given all of that, it is still possible there are errors in my research. If you see something you believe is incorrect, please contact me at ptww35@gmail.com and we can share insights. Obviously, some of the information on individual men came from family members but if there was any conflict I tried to remain with the information from primary records, unless it was clearly wrong. Birth places were particularly problematic. It was common for a man to answer the question "where were you born" with the response of where they were living at the time of enlistment (how do you interpret the question "where are you from?"). If the family was in, for instance, Georgia in the census around the time of his birth and then Dale County, Alabama in 1860 and the muster role listed birth place as Dale County, Alabama, I have gone with the somewhat obvious assumption that he was not born in Dale County but somewhere in Georgia.

My hope is that each reader will discover a broader understanding of the war and its impact, specifically on south Alabama and northwest Florida. If you have a relative in the regiment, I hope you find some new information and maybe a better understanding of how they came to make the decision they made to fight for the Union. That decision had to have been a difficult one. Yes, there does appear to be some that joined briefly, maybe for the bounty that often didn't get paid immediately, and then deserted but desertion was a problem on both sides throughout the war. The war was horrible and it required a change in the relationship of man to military service that many men resisted. There were many who joined early and stayed throughout the remainder of the war or until they died from disease or wound. There were also a good number that deserted for a brief period then returned voluntarily. And some deserted after the war ended and before the regiment was mustered out in November 1865. Many of these men had their desertion charges dropped and were able to obtain pensions in their later lives. I hope this effort provides readers with some new insights and perspectives on the War and their ancestors.

Finally, I would like to take a moment to rant. Part of this research has been visiting cemeteries where many of these men are buried. Most of these men who have commemorative headstones on their Civil War service have just the Confederate service and nothing on the Union service. Many don't even have the Confederate unit they actually served in but one their records were transferred to after they deserted. In the narrative, I talk about the consolidation of regiments as the war wore on. I realize many of these markers were done by well-meaning folks in the 60s when the Southern understanding of the war was more limited than today but it would be nice to have correct information on graves and if you find one with Confederate service, please don't take that as researched and accurate. Same applies to the extra information posted at findagrave.com. If you really want to know your ancestors, honor them by attempting to get the record accurate!

Sharon, September 2016

Table of Contents

Preface vi
Introduction 1
   The United States in 1860 1
   Antebellum Northwest Florida and South Alabama 3
      Baldwin County, Alabama (contributed 32 men) 4
      Washington County, Florida (contributed 35 men) 6
      Holmes County, Florida (contributed 38 men) 7
      Dale County, Alabama (contributed 39 men) 7
      Henry County, Alabama (contributed 39 men) 8
      Covington County, Alabama (contributed 47 men) 9
      Coffee County, Alabama (contributed 53 men) 10
      Santa Rosa County, Florida (contributed 58 men) 11
      Walton County, Florida (contributed 62 men) 12
      Analysis 13
   The Area in 1861 and 1862 16
   1862 and Early 1863 21
Formation of the 1st FCUV 24
Military Engagements of the 1st FCUV 29
   Gonzales' Farm/15 Mile Station/Pollard – 7/21/64-
   7/25/64 29
      1st Florida Men Known to Participate: 30
      Summary of Events 31
   Battle of Marianna – 9/18/64-10/4/64 33
      1st Florida Men Known to Participate: 34
      Summary of events: 35

Expedition to Milton – 10/25-28/64 41
   1st Florida Men Known to Participate: 42
   Summary of events: 42
Expedition to Pine Barren Creek, FL – 11/17-18/64 44
   1st Florida Men known to Participate: 45
   Summary of events: 45
Expedition to Mitchell & Pine Barren Creek – 12/13-19/64 46
   1st Florida Cavalry men known to have participated.. 47
   Summary of events: 48
Expedition to Perdido Mills, AL – mid-February, 1865 .. 49
   1st Florida Men Known to Participate: 50
   Summary of events: 50
Sander's Detachment to Alabama 50
   1st Florida Men Known to Participate: 51
   Summary of events: 52
Mobile Campaign – March – April, 1865 56
   Raid in South Alabama – 3/21-31/65 57
   FL/AL RR – Evergreen to Brewton Station – 3/23-26/65 60
   The March to, and Siege of, Ft. Blakeley 63
Occupation of Montgomery, AL, April-May 1865 69
   1st Florida Men Known to Participate: 69
   Summary of events: 73
Conclusions 74

The Men of the 1st Florida Cavalry Union 83
    A 83
    B 88
    C 110
    D 131
    E 142
    F 145
    G 149
    H 162
    I 181
    J 182
    K 188
    L 192
    M 198
    N 219
    O 223
    P 225
    R 239
    S 249
    T 268
    V 276
    W 278
    Y 292
Known Families in the 1st FCUV 294
Appendix 320

Target Counties Military Men to Percent in 1st FCUV .. 320

Population Data for Target Alabama Counties 321

Population Data for Target Florida Counties 323

Economic Data for Nine Counties 325

Map of Route from Milton to Andalusia 1865 326

Resources 327

Index 331

Introduction

What can a combination of historical and genealogical records tell us about the area of south Alabama and northwest Florida prior to and during the Civil War? Why did so many men from this area decide to join and fight for the Union during the War? Can the combination of historical and genealogical records provide more understanding than either one separately?

The panhandle of Florida, combined with many of the southern-most counties in Alabama, fielded a Union regiment comparable to the 1st Alabama Union Cavalry in northern Alabama. The regiment was also much larger than the 2nd Florida Union Cavalry that came primarily from the eastern end of the panhandle and central and south Florida. Was this an accident of circumstances or was the population in this area more prone to Unionism than the remaining areas of Florida or central Alabama?

Because much of this area of the United States was thinly settled at the beginning of the War, good historical records are not plentiful and genealogy records must be analyzed in the aggregate to provide a community or regional view that might complement the historical records. It is possible to combine the records and gain a better insight and together these documents can begin to provide a glimpse into the communities in this area and these Southern men who chose to fight for the Union.

The United States in 1860

By 1860 the United States was anything but united. The sectional differences between North and South had grown to distort almost every interaction between the two sections of the country. It is sometimes forgotten that the various states were founded on different principles and for different purposes and those fundamental values shaped how the regions of the country developed and grew. Many of the Northern states had been settled by families who wanted religious separation from the Church of England and who believed in self-determination, small business ownership and the Puritan work ethic. Many Southern states had been initially settled by the younger sons of the English and European aristocracy and by British investors looking for a quick profit. These men acquired large land grants and brought in indentured servants, and eventually enslaved persons, to work the land to best accomplish their desires for money and profit.

In the several decades prior to the War the two sides of the Mason-Dixon Line crept ever closer to complete division. Politics would flare and some form of appeasement would ease the country back from the brink but the rancor and outright hostility remained and grew. Name-calling, beatings on the floor of Congress, and general demonization occurred on both sides as the divide widened. The issue that most deeply divided the two sections of the country centered on slavery. Many northerners resented the political power of the slaveholders through the three-fifths rule for counting the enslaved population for apportionment in Congress. They wanted Western territories to be free of slaveholders and enslaved persons and free for white men to compete for markets absent the competition of the plantation. And a much smaller percentage had come to believe that the enslavement of human beings was morally wrong.

Southerners wanted abolitionist voices to cease stirring up Northern sentiment and potentially encouraging slave rebellions, something they were quite afraid of even though they spent much effort creating the illusion of happy slaves. Slavery was legal under the Constitution and was clearly a part of each State's purview of governance. They wanted all States to recognize their special form of property and to abide by the Constitutional protection of property both in returning a runaway slave to the owner and in being allowed to take all of their property wherever they wished to go. They knew expansion of slavery would create a bond between all states that allowed slavery; therefore, their voting bloc in Congress would be maintained. Enslaved persons were not only property in the minds of plantation owners and in the Constitution; they were a significant part of the wealth of the Southern slaveholders. The plantation system was very hard on soil fertility; therefore, plantation owners needed to move and start again to continue creating wealth and to pay down the debt that many carried to maintain plantation and lifestyle. They knew they needed the outlet of western expansion to survive economically. This required, in their view, their right to move to the territories with their wealth, i.e. their slaves. And finally, as slaveholding had become a more successful venture through population growth, the slaveholders needed the western territories as outlets to sell excess slaves and to generate income since the country had ended slave importation.

Antebellum Northwest Florida and South Alabama

To begin to understand how the 1st Florida Cavalry Union Volunteers (1st FCUV) came to be and why the men who served chose to do so, we must first know where these men came from and what community influences, individual beliefs and motivations they might have brought with them in 1863 and 1864. While every county in south Alabama and northwest Florida contributed at least one man to the regiment, the location of the men in 1860 was significantly concentrated in a few of these counties (see Appendix). Eighty-one percent of the 1st FCUV men found in the 1860 census came from just nine counties. From lowest to highest total numbers they were: Baldwin County, AL; Washington County, FL; Holmes County, FL; Dale County, AL; Henry County, AL; Covington County, AL; Coffee County, AL; Santa Rosa County, FL and Walton County, FL.

The last four counties, two in Alabama and two in Florida, were adjacent to each other in 1860 and very much intertwined through trade and family relations. While some of the contribution of men was likely opportunity and proximity to Fort Barrancas and Pensacola, that does not account for very few of the men originating from Mobile County, AL; Monroe County, AL; Conecuh County, AL or Escambia County, FL. All of these four counties were closer to Fort Barrancas in Pensacola, FL than Henry or Dale Counties, AL or Washington or Holmes Counties, FL. A deeper look at these nine counties, as they existed in 1860, will begin to present a picture of the area that highlights similarities and differences between these counties and others in their respective states and in the rest of the South (See Appendix).

Baldwin County, Alabama (contributed 32 men)

Baldwin County was one of Alabama's earliest counties. It was created in 1809 from the larger Washington County that was then a part of the Mississippi Territory. Though one of the earlier counties in Alabama, it was the least populated of the 52 Alabama counties in 1860. Of the Alabama counties contributing the most men to the 1st FCUV, Baldwin County had the highest percentage of slaves to total population. Nearly half of the population of Baldwin County in 1860 was enslaved.

Slaveholders were also a slighter higher percentage of the total population here than in the other south Alabama counties providing men to the 1st FCUV, 4% versus 2-3% of the remaining Alabama counties studied. But like most slaveholding in the South, the majority of slaveholders held less than 50 enslaved persons and a sizable proportion of those held only one.

By far, Baldwin County had the fewest number of farms of the Alabama counties in question. Its farms were predominately small family farms of less than 20 acres. However, it had the largest amount of capital invested in manufacturing. It had more than the combined manufacturing worth of all of the other Alabama counties in the study area. More than one quarter of the men in Baldwin County in 1860 worked in the manufacturing sector. As we will see further in this section, this makes Baldwin County most like Santa Rosa County, FL in terms of economic structure.

But what set Baldwin County apart from the other counties in this study was its population of free persons of color and Indians. Of a total population of 7,530 in 1860, 140 (2%) of the population were free persons of color and 91 (1%) were Indians. These were larger number for both groups than in all of the other Alabama counties combined. In 1860, Baldwin County was geographically much larger than today and included a sizable population of mostly Muskogee (Creek) Indians in the northern part of the county; a section that would become part of Escambia County, Alabama after the war.

The free persons of color are not quite as easy to determine. History tells us that the French and Spanish had a different attitude toward slavery. It was more common to be able to buy or gain freedom and establish a life and livelihood in a community of mostly whites in both cultures. The area between New Orleans and Pensacola was certainly influenced by both cultures prior to the area joining the United States so that may be a factor in the number of free persons of color residing in the area. The manufacturing economic structure may also have played a role in attracting this portion of the population from the surrounding communities. It is also possible that some of these free persons of color were a mixture of Indian and white or black ancestry and not identified as Indian in the census.

Two men were listed as mulatto in the muster rolls of the 1st FCUV and eight were listed as Indian in either the muster rolls or the 1860 census. Since the census recording of free persons of color often hinged on the census takers' assessment of color and color was anything not appearing as white it is possible the two mulattoes were also Indian or an ethnic mixture. Persons of French or Spanish descent could have been classified as such whether or not also a mix with black ancestry. There do not appear to be any surnames that would indicate persons of French or Spanish descent joining the 1st FCUV but the lineage could have been from the mother's line and therefore not able to be determined by such a simplistic assessment.

Approximately 26% of the white and Indian populations in Baldwin County in 1860 were men who were, or would become, eligible to serve in the Confederate States of America (CSA) during the war. Slightly fewer than 3% of them eventually decided to serve the Union in the 1st FCUV. Seven of the thirty-two men (22%) who enlisted or attempted to enlist in the 1st FCUV, and were identified as being in Baldwin County in 1860, were Indians.[1]

Washington County, Florida (contributed 35 men)

Like most of Florida in 1860, Washington County was thinly populated. It was the second smallest county in the studied counties in Florida and in the joint study area. Washington County was formed in 1825, twenty years before Florida became a State. It was a transition county from the middle panhandle plantation counties to the primarily yeoman farmer counties of the northwest Florida panhandle. Of the three primarily agricultural counties in Florida in the study area, it had the largest number of enslaved persons and a higher percentage of slaveholders that held more than 50 enslaved persons.

Approximately 22% of the Washington County 1860 census population were enslaved persons, there were 10 free persons of color and no individuals listed as Indian. Slaveholding in Washington County was more widespread in terms of the number of slaves held per household. While in most of this area, slavery was strongly concentrated in the 1 to 5 enslaved persons per household, in Washington County the concentration was relatively evenly distributed across the categories up to 99 enslaved persons. A much smaller percentage only owned one enslaved person.

Washington County had the second largest concentration of farms of the four Florida counties in the study area. Like the other Florida counties, the most common farm acreage was 20 to 49 acres. However, in Washington County there were many more farms that were 50 to 99 and 100 to 499 acres than in the other three Florida counties in the study. This is a result of the transitional nature of the county mentioned earlier. The soil and

---

[1] University of Virginia, Geospatial and Statistical Data Center. *Historical Census Browser, 1860 census.* Accessed 2004. http://mapserver.lib.vitginia.edu/.

terrain were more suited to plantation crops and therefore to slavery.

Manufacturing was nearly non-existent in Washington County in 1860, a condition not uncommon across the South. There were 3 manufacturing establishments employing 29 men. The county was predominately rural and agricultural, thinly populated and predominately white.[2]

Holmes County, Florida (contributed 38 men)

Holmes County, Florida was the smallest of all the counties in the study area in terms of population in 1860. It was formed in 1847, so it was also one of the newest of the counties providing men to the 1st FCUV. The population was predominately white. The enslaved population was only 8% of the total population, a significantly smaller percentage than in any of the other counties. It is not surprising then that the farmers were mostly yeomen farmers with farms less than 49 acres in size.

Slaveholders accounted for only 2% of the population and nearly all of them held less than 10 slaves. There was no manufacturing in Holmes County in 1860. More than any of the other counties, Holmes was a thinly populated agricultural community of whites that did not participate extensively in the economic component of the slave economy. It may not be surprising then that 13% of the white, male 1860 population that could serve during the war, eventually served in the 1st FCUV.[3]

Dale County, Alabama (contributed 39 men)

Dale County was formed in 1825 from Covington and Henry counties and was the second largest county in the study area in 1860, surpassed slightly by Henry County in population. While much more densely populated than most of the other counties, it

---

[2] University of Virginia, Geospatial and Statistical Data Center. *Historical Census Browser, 1860 census.* Accessed 2004. http://mapserver.lib.vitginia.edu/.
[3] University of Virginia, Geospatial and Statistical Data Center. *Historical Census Browser, 1860 census.* Accessed 2004. http://mapserver.lib.vitginia.edu/.

was still agricultural and yeoman farmer in structure. The enslaved population made up about 15% of the population with no free persons of color or Indians being recorded in the 1860 census. Slaveholders accounted for 3% of the total population and the majority of the slaveholders held less than 20 enslaved persons.

Manufacturing in Dale County was composed of 8 establishments employing a total of 18 men. The capital invested in manufacturing in Dale County was as low as three of the four Florida counties, below $15,000 ($415,459 in 2015 dollars).[4] The county had the third largest dollars invested in real estate of the nine counties in the study area. It was the fourth highest in personal property value per household making it one of the wealthier counties in the study area.

Offsetting the lack of manufacturing was the largest concentration of farms of any of the nine counties studied. The majority of farms were less than 99 acres in size but about 25% of them were 100 to 999 acres in size. This would seem to indicate that Dale County was also an agricultural transitional county from the larger more prosperous Henry County (to be covered below) and the counties west and south in the study area.[5]

Henry County, Alabama (contributed 39 men)

Henry County was the largest and most prosperous county contributing men to the 1st FCUV. It was also the furthest from Ft. Barrancas. The economic structure of the county in 1860 was well distributed between farms of all sizes and manufacturing establishments. It had the highest wealth in real estate and personal property, though not in capital in manufacturing or personal property per household.

Henry County was formed in 1819, the same year that Alabama became a State. By 1860 it was relatively well developed for a

---

[4] *Inflation Calculator.* Accessed 2015. http://www.in2013dollars.com/.
[5] University of Virginia, Geospatial and Statistical Data Center. *Historical Census Browser, 1860 census.* Accessed 2004. http://mapserver.lib.vitginia.edu/.

southeastern Alabama county. Seventy percent of the population was white, thirty percent were enslaved and there were 21 free persons of color. There were no Indians listed in the 1860 census in Henry County. About 3% of the population were slaveholders with slightly over 1% of the slaveholders having 50 to 199 enslaved persons in their household. The county had the second highest number of farms, second only to Dale County and the cash value of all farms was the highest of any of the counties in the study area. The largest number of farms was in the category of 20 to 499 acres but unlike the other counties there were 23 farms in the 500 to 999 acre size and 8 in the 1000 plus acreage size.

There were 27 manufacturing establishments listed in the 1860 census but capital investment in those establishments was considerably less than the amount invested in the 34 establishments in Baldwin County. That may have meant that the manufacturing economy was in its early stages or was closer to family-sized businesses than large-scale manufacturing.[6]

Interestingly, Henry County, along with Pike County, AL, produced the most men born in any one county. Each produced 38 men. More than half of them were still in Henry County by 1860 while Pike County exported almost all of their men to other Alabama and Florida counties. It would appear to have been a stable county, both economically and socially.

Covington County, Alabama (contributed 47 men)

Covington County, located in the central part of the southern tier of Alabama counties was formed in 1821 from Henry County. In 1860 it had the largest percent of white population, 87%, with 13% of the population enslaved persons and 17 persons listed as free persons of color. Covington County was thinly populated given its geographical size in 1860 and predominately agricultural.

---

[6] University of Virginia, Geospatial and Statistical Data Center. *Historical Census Browser, 1860 census*. Accessed 2004. http://mapserver.lib.vitginia.edu/.

The cash value per farm was the lowest of the five Alabama counties and the majority of farms were 49 acres or less, indicating more small family subsistence farms rather than cash crop farms. Approximately 2% of the population were slaveholders with the majority having less than 14 enslaved persons in their household. Covington County also had the lowest number of manufacturing establishments of the five Alabama counties and was third from the lowest when considering all nine counties. Finally, it had the lowest personal property value per household of the five Alabama counties and was the fourth lowest in the nine counties.[7]

Coffee County, Alabama (contributed 53 men)

Coffee County had 53 men that would eventually join, or attempt to join, the 1st FCUV. That would have been about 3% of the 1860 white male population of the appropriate age for enlistment. Coffee County was formed entirely from Dale County in 1841, making it one of the youngest counties of those in the study area. It also had the second largest number of men born in the county with 34 men listing Coffee as their county of birth, just behind Henry and Pike with 38.

In terms of total population, it was the third largest in the study area, behind Henry and Dale. A bit over 85% of the population were free white persons and 15% were enslaved persons. Approximately 2% of the population were slaveholders in 1860, with the majority of slaveholders holding less than 20 enslaved persons and slightly more than 25% of the slaveholders only having one. The cash value per farm in Coffee County was only $1,211 ($33,541 in 2015 dollars),[8] the second lowest per farm cash value in the study area.

More than half of the farms in 1860 were less than 49 acres, indicating a predominance of yeoman farmers. Not surprisingly

---

[7] University of Virginia, Geospatial and Statistical Data Center. *Historical Census Browser, 1860 census.* Accessed 2004. http://mapserver.lib.vitginia.edu/.
[8] *Inflation Calculator.* Accessed 2015. http://www.in2013dollars.com/

there were only 6 manufacturing establishments with capital invested of only $14,550 ($402,995 in 2015 dollars).[9] These establishments employed 16 males and no females. Personal property was an average of $1,635 ($45,285 in 2015 dollars)[10] per family, again indicating poorer, yeoman farmers as opposed to the wealthier counties of Henry and Baldwin.[11] ($3,764 and $7,361 respectively, $104,253 and $203,880 in 2015 dollars)[12].

Santa Rosa County, Florida (contributed 58 men)

Santa Rosa County was formed in 1842 from the adjacent counties of Escambia and Walton. Bordered on three sides by major bodies of water (Escambia Bay & River, Blackwater Bay & River and the Gulf of Mexico), the county rapidly grew to challenge Escambia County, FL in the strength and diversity of its economy. In 1860, Santa Rosa County was the most industrialized county of all counties in Florida and was second only to Baldwin County, AL in the study area for the amount of capital invested in manufacturing.

Of the Florida counties in the study area, Santa Rosa County had the smallest number of farms, just 66 with approximately 34% of its total acreage improved for cultivation. The cash value of farms was also the lowest in both the Florida counties and in the overall study area. Nearly all of the farms were less than 49 acres in size.

Santa Rosa County had the highest number of enslaved persons in the Florida counties in the study and the highest percentage of enslaved persons to total population at 25%. That might at first glance appear to contradict the economic data but in actuality Santa Rosa had a high concentration of skilled enslaved persons that were not on plantations. It also had a high concentration of free persons of color compared to the rest of the counties in the

---

[9] *Inflation Calculator*. Accessed 2015. http://www.in2013dollars.com/
[10] *Inflation Calculator*. Accessed 2015. http://www.in2013dollars.com/
[11] University of Virginia, Geospatial and Statistical Data Center. *Historical Census Browser, 1860 census*. Accessed 2004. http://mapserver.lib.vitginia.edu/.
[12] *Inflation Calculator*. Accessed 2015. http://www.in2013dollars.com/

study area, being surpassed only by Baldwin County in total numbers. Many of Santa Rosa County's enslaved persons worked in shipbuilding around Milton, the cotton mill at Arcadia, and were hired out to the Navy in Pensacola for carpentry and brick-laying work. These skilled enslaved persons sometimes had slightly more personal freedom, were allowed to earn money by working beyond their daily quotas and may have lived away from their owners for extended periods of time while performing contract labor. Not surprisingly the higher numbers of enslaved persons also brought a higher number of slaveholders and more slaveholders with enslaved populations over 100.

Even with this much invested interest in the slave economy, Santa Rosa County provided nearly 6% of its 1860 male population in the military service age range to the 1st FCUV. One reason for this may be the more business versus plantation structure and the strong presence of the Whig Party before its demise a few years earlier (ex-Whigs tended toward opposition to secession, though not necessarily slavery). Another reason might be the small yeoman farms with little substantial economic connection to the slave economy. Proximity may also be a factor here, since Santa Rosa County was adjacent to Escambia County and the naval yard and base where the 1st FCUV was stationed during the war.[13]

Walton County, Florida (contributed 62 men)

Walton County, formed in 1824 as one of five counties in the new territory of Florida, was still primarily rural in 1860. It had the largest number of farms in the Florida counties in the study area and ranked fifth in the overall study area in number of farms. It was also the largest of the four counties in Florida in the study area, with about 28% of its total acreage improved for agriculture. While having the largest number of men who joined the 1st FCUV at 62, it was second in percentage of men who joined compared to the white male population in 1860. At 11% of its 1860 male

---

[13] University of Virginia, Geospatial and Statistical Data Center. *Historical Census Browser, 1860 census*. Accessed 2004. http://mapserver.lib.vitginia.edu/.

population eventually joining the 1st FCUV it was just barely behind Holmes County with 13%.

The county's economic basis was agriculture, with only 7 manufacturing establishments in 1860 and only $13,425 ($371,836 in 2015 dollars)[14] invested in these establishments. It also had the highest average cash value of each farm at $532 ($14,735 in 2015 dollars)[15] per farm in the Florida counties. As with most of the counties in the study area, the majority of farms were less than 49 acres. Enslaved persons constituted 15% of the total population, with 12 free persons of color and no Indians listed in the population. Slightly fewer than 4% of the population owned the 441 slaves in the county, with the majority of slaveholders having less than 15 enslaved persons per household.[16]

Walton County was the only county in Florida in which both delegates to the secession convention voted against secession. While it appears the population initially rallied behind the cause of secession, if for no other reason than to not create too much internal dissent as the southern states seceded, a fair portion of the men living in Walton County in 1860 eventually determined that the best course of action for them and their families was joining the Federals at Ft. Barrancas.

Analysis

These nine counties probably have more in common with each other than with the remainder of their respective states. That was as true in 1860, as it is today. They were primarily agricultural and generally were more yeoman farmer than plantation owner. About 45% of both state populations were enslaved persons, but only one of the counties in the study area was near that number and that was Baldwin County which also had the highest number of

---

[14] *Inflation Calculator.* Accessed 2015. http://www.in2013dollars.com/
[15] *Inflation Calculator.* Accessed 2015. http://www.in2013dollars.com/
[16] University of Virginia, Geospatial and Statistical Data Center. *Historical Census Browser, 1860 census.* Accessed 2004. http://mapserver.lib.vitginia.edu/.

Native Americans and Free Persons of Color in the study area. As has been previously noted, about 22% of the men from Baldwin County were Native Americans, most likely Muskogee (Creek).[17]

While at first blush it might be assumed that the men would be from the areas closest to Ft. Barrancas and radiating out with ever decreasing numbers, in reality the center of the bull's eye of successful recruitment was in northern Walton County (in what is now northern Okaloosa and Walton Counties), well over 150 miles from Ft. Barrancas. That would have been a significant distance in 1864, especially since the Confederate military had small encampments of men throughout the area around Pensacola. It appears that men and families began to appear in Pensacola for protection and asylum not long after the Union re-occupied Pensacola in 1862. Once the 1st FCUV was formed in late 1863, a recruiting station was established at East Pass, Florida (at the distal end of Santa Rosa Island) to assist men attempting the treacherous trip across the panhandle of Florida to Pensacola and efforts were made to go upriver to pick these men up and bring them down to the Fort.

If we use the above information to draw some conclusions about these men who enlisted with the 1st FCUV we might make the following observations:

1. Many of these men came from counties that were heavily rural but not heavily populated with plantations. Most of the area contributing the men was populated by yeoman farmers and therefore not as invested in slavery as the economic engine it was for the entire South. This would not necessarily indicate a lack of racism or an unwillingness to support a slave-enabled society as long as it did not require putting your life, or your family's life, on the line for an extended period.

---

[17] University of Virginia, Geospatial and Statistical Data Center. *Historical Census Browser, 1860 census.* Accessed 2004. http://mapserver.lib.vitginia.edu/.

2. Several of these counties had not voted for secession in their respective states or had wanted to wait (cooperationists). There is some evidence that some of the delegates to the conventions, at least in Florida, were elected as Unionist representatives but then gave in at the conventions to a Democratic party filled with fire-eaters and ready to push for secession with emotional rhetoric.[18] This could indicate a population a bit more inclined to be "Unionists" or at least not enthusiastic about secession at the time of their respective conventions.

3. The area had some examples of slavery that were not the traditional plantation gang labor. There was a slightly larger enslaved population that was skilled labor that worked in contract and manufacturing situations. Some were allowed to retain some money made and they worked on the task system of labor, not the gang labor system. This may have impacted how slavery was viewed by the majority white population though may have had little impact on racist sentiments and may not have necessarily improved the view of slavery as an economic institution.

4. While communities surrounding these men may have impacted their decisions initially or later when they joined the 1st FCUV; it is important to remember that while community values and expectations can impact decisions, ultimately decisions are individual assessments of what is in the best interest of the decision-maker and their families. Their community and family may have laid the ground work on whether they were weak or strong advocates of secession and slavery but the decisions, especially if they were already in the Confederate Army and deserting, were based on their interpretations of the justness of the war, the conduct of

---

[18] Buker, George E., *Blockaders, Refugees, & Contrabands: Civil War on Florida's Gulf Coast, 1861-1865.* (Tuscaloosa, AL: The University of Alabama Press, 1993), pp 10-14.

the war, whether their families were being adequately protected or whether they were just sick and tired of having to fight in extremely bloody battles. Regardless of the individuality of the decisions, it would appear that several of the communities in the study area were over-represented in the 1st FCUV recruits. Community and family would seem to have influenced the decision-makers to some extent.

It can be very difficult to draw solid conclusions about community sentiments in the months leading up to the war. The fire-eaters had been laying the ground work with the general population for years. While many business people and some large plantation owners were not eager to secede because of the potential repercussions on their personal wealth, the strong emotions on the side of those wanting secession encouraged many cooperationists and weak Unionists to decide to go along with the wave of secessionist fervor. And for the average panhandle Floridian or south Alabamian that did not hold enslaved persons, they may have been comfortable with the slave-based society that may have been all they had ever known but were not so economically tied to the system that they were enthusiastic about dying for the cause. Only a few continued to speak out against secession after the vote. Once the war started, speaking out became increasingly unsafe but as will be seen, regardless of the reasons for non-support of the Confederacy throughout the war, average men began making the decision to actively support the Union with their military enlistment with the Union Army.

The Area in 1861 and 1862

This area of the south was both different and similar to the rest of the lower south in 1860. As presented in the previous section these nine counties that provided the vast majority of men to the 1st FCUV were predominately rural with yeoman farmers significantly outnumbering plantation owners. This was a factor more of the topography, climate and soil than the likely inclinations of the people at the time. Slavery was certainly present but tended more toward use in households or in small and large scale industrial work than on traditional plantations. The exceptions to that were the east end of the area in both Alabama and Florida where plantations and larger enslaved populations were present and Baldwin County, AL at the far western end of the area.

This, however, did not translate to not being supportive of slavery as an economic system using people often seen by many Southerners as inferior to the dominant white population. Even those men who did not want either state to secede during their respective conventions were not anti-slavery; they were anti-secession, at least at the moment of the secession vote. Once secession occurred in both states, the vast majority of people went along with the creation of the Confederate States of America. And those that were not supportive of secession primarily remained quiet because the community pressure was substantial to be a good Southern citizen.

Pensacola was the largest city in the study area, and in the state of Florida in 1860, with smaller towns in the area including Milton, FL in Santa Rosa County; Andalusia, AL in Covington County; Pollard and Evergreen, AL in Conecuh County and Elba, AL in Coffee County. Just outside the area was Mobile, AL in Mobile County; and Marianna, FL in Jackson County. Pensacola was the site of major, though minimally garrisoned, naval and army facilities that were immediately the target of Confederates, even while the secession conventions were deciding on the course of action for the States.

Florida seceded on January 10, 1860 and two days later a combination militia of Florida and Alabama men took possession of Fort Barrancas and Fort McRee. Adam Slemmer, the senior Army Officer at Pensacola in 1860 had decided to consolidate his small force at Fort Pickens across the bay from Fort Barrancas and McRee so the two sides settled down to oppose each other through 1861 and early 1862. Though the Alabama men had arrived with the intention to ensure all of the military facilities would be taken by the seceded states, the situation never changed in the first 15 months of the war. First, the hesitancy of Colonel Chase in the prospect of a frontal assault on Fort Pickens; then, the joint decision of the seceded states' Senators in Washington to wait; and finally, by the early Confederate government to not draw the first blood before the new country was established ensured the situation slowly settled into the Confederacy holding Fort Barrancas and Fort McRee and the Federal government holding Fort Pickens.[19]

Within a month of the establishment of the Confederate States of America in February 1861, the new Provisional Congress of the Confederate States ordered Brigadier General Braxton Bragg to Pensacola to take command of all Confederate forces in the City and surrounding area. The Confederate government was adamant that all property that had been a part of the Federal government must be taken over by the Confederate government, peacefully or by force. But once in Pensacola, Bragg evaluated the situation and allowed the stand-off to continue with little change. The Confederate government initiated a Navy and Army and called up about 11,000 men across the southern states with plans to send about 5,000 of them to Pensacola.[20]

As with much of the rest of the south, most folks in Pensacola and Escambia County were supportive of the Confederate government initially and demonstrated a fair amount of anger toward the Federal government though that did not translate into not continuing to sell food and water to the Federal troops at Fort Pickens. That enterprise was significantly slowed when Bragg realized it was occurring and issued General Order No. 4 forbidding the traffic of goods to Fort Pickens. But economics being what it is in the life of humans, there is evidence that the

---

[19] Driscoll, John K., *The Civil War on Pensacola Bay, 1861-1862*. (Jefferson, NC: McFarland & Co, Inc., 2007), pp 20-78.
[20] Driscoll, John K., *The Civil War on Pensacola Bay, 1861-1862*. (Jefferson, NC: McFarland & Co, Inc., 2007), pp 66-78.

"trafficking" continued at some level or at least was attempted with records indicating confiscation of some supplies in route.[21]

While Bragg was busy in his first month or so in Pensacola, the Federal government was busy as well. The Confederate government was new and trying to get systems in place and discussing strategy to avoid confrontation until they were ready. The Federal government, on the other hand, was stumbling over its own feet, giving out lots of conflicting information on both Fort Pickens and Fort Sumter and generally seeming like a deer in the headlights. Meanwhile the men at Fort Pickens and the ships that were stationed near the Fort were beginning to run low on both food and water and they remained concerned with the possibility of a Confederate assault on the Fort;[22] notwithstanding the agreement for both sides not to attack that was put in place right after Forts Barrancas, McRee and the Navy Yard were taken.[23]

In early April, Lincoln finally made decisions to re-supply Fort Sumter with reinforcement only if they were fired on and to reinforce Fort Pickens regardless of the agreement that had been in place since the Buchanan administration. Ships left New York heading for both locations in the first few days of April 1861. It was just a matter of which was closest and likely to challenge the Confederates first and start the conflict. That turned out to be Fort Sumter.

Unfortunately, the orders carried by the commander of the reinforcements sent to Fort Pickens were from the Army so the commanding naval officer refused to abide by them, choosing instead to continue with the non-reinforcement agreement put in place by the Buchanan administration. This went on for some time until he received the necessary orders from the Navy. The troops landed and began working to truly prepare Fort Pickens for what

---

[21] Driscoll, John K., *The Civil War on Pensacola Bay, 1861-1862*. (Jefferson, NC: McFarland & Co, Inc., 2007), pp.94-95.
[22] Pearce, George F., *Pensacola During the Civil War: A Thorn in the Side of the Confederacy*. (Gainesville, FL: University Press of Florida, 2000), pp. 48-67.
[23] Driscoll, John K., *The Civil War on Pensacola Bay, 1861-1862*. (Jefferson, NC: McFarland & Co, Inc., 2007), pp. 50-78.

they considered a likely assault. But it did not come. For most of 1861 the two sides faced off and prepared for the pending attack from the other side. At one point Braxton Bragg had close to 8,000 men to a couple of thousand at Fort Pickens but the geography, the raw recruits and both sides being unclear on what was expected of them from the politicians kept them on their respective sides of the bay.[24]

That changed in October when Bragg decided to send about 1,000 troops consisting of men from the 9th Mississippi, the 1st Alabama, the Louisiana Battalion, the 5th Georgia, the Georgia Battalion, and the 1st Florida Infantry over to attack the camp east of the Fort manned by the 6th New York and to destroy the artillery batteries east of the Fort. The Confederates were discovered by the pickets from the 6th New York, firing occurred and the Union troops were quickly in an engagement with the Confederates. Both sides lost men and a number of Union troops were captured. The Confederates managed to get away, though barely. This opened the window for a number of exchanges that occurred over the last few months of 1861 against McRee and against the Naval Yard.[25]

Relatively early in the war, Pensacola lost its importance to both sides. Reinforcements ended and men began to be transferred from Bragg's command to Tennessee and Virginia. President Lincoln also issued the blockade proclamation and the Union Navy began to increase all along the Upper Gulf Coast from Florida to Louisiana. By March 1862, Bragg was transferring the majority of his men to Tennessee, going there to take direct command and left Brigadier General Samuel Jones in charge of the Department of Alabama and West Florida with the orders to destroy anything that might be of use to the Union and to abandon Pensacola.[26] This destruction was a scorched earth policy that

---

[24] Driscoll, John K., *The Civil War on Pensacola Bay, 1861-1862*. (Jefferson, NC: McFarland & Co, Inc., 2007), pp 125-158.
[25] Driscoll, John K., *The Civil War on Pensacola Bay, 1861-1862*. (Jefferson, NC: McFarland & Co, Inc., 2007), pp 179-196.
[26] Driscoll, John K., *The Civil War on Pensacola Bay, 1861-1862*. (Jefferson, NC: McFarland & Co, Inc., 2007), p 208.

impacted much of the industry in the areas of Pensacola and Milton, the grist mills in the area used by citizens to produce corn meal and all of the public property, as well as some private property. Complaints were loud and the citizenry were angered by this "wanton and atrocious vandalism" as described by A. C. Blount in a letter to Governor John Milton of Florida.[27] The Union moved in and raised the flag over the Naval Yard and Fort Barrancas the same day the Confederacy left. Pensacola remained in Union hands for the rest of the war.

1862 and Early 1863

Early 1862 found much of the southern population still in support of secession and the formation of the Confederate States of America but it would not be long before some began to sour on how the concept was developing in reality. In Pensacola, one of the first disappointments for the general population came in March 1862 when the majority of the Confederate Army withdrew from Florida and transferred to Tennessee and Virginia. While the state was still forming militia for the state's defense, it would soon become much harder. Within a short period the Confederate Army began taking these battalions and regiments and mustering them into national service and removing them from the state. This essentially left Florida to the federal army and navy and created a backcountry battleground between the Union forces and the few remaining Confederate and militia troops that left the population caught in the middle.

The withdrawal from Pensacola, as mentioned in the previous section, resulted in a scorched earth policy that angered the remaining population. The burning included public property, economic enterprises and facilities needed to produce food for the local population, such as the grist mills in Pensacola and Milton.[28]

---

[27] Blount, A. C. 1862. "Letter to Governor John Milton." Vols. Milton Letterbook, Box 1, Folder 10. Pensacola, FL: *Florida Memory: State Library & Archives of FL*, April 9th. https://www.floridamemory.com/items/show/265931.
[28] Blount, A. C. 1862. "Letter to Governor John Milton." Vols. Milton Letterbook, Box 1, Folder 10. Pensacola, FL: *Florida Memory: State Library & Archives of FL*, April 9th. https://www.floridamemory.com/items/show/265931.

It created more hardship for the local population than it did for the Union troops at the three forts and the naval yard. Families remaining in the area increasingly found it difficult to feed and defend themselves from the two armies and the increasing numbers of men who were deserters and draft dodgers. These men formed gangs, hid out in the dense woods and swamps, and took what they wanted from the population. This would lead men who had enlisted and left with their regiments to receive painful letters from home concerning the starvation of their families.

Following on the heels of the withdrawal of Confederate troops from Pensacola was the first Confederate Conscription Act, a necessary decision by the Confederacy, but one that was deeply unpopular especially for the poorer economic classes. The Act applied to all white men between the ages of 18 and 35 and provided for the ability to hire a substitute who would have normally been exempt and for exemptions for certain occupations (railroad and river workers, telegraph operators, teachers and ministers, miners, civil officials and druggists). It also extended the 12 month enlistees to 3 years or the war to retain the men in the 148 regiments that had formed early with 12 month enlistments. A thirty-day grace period was allowed for men to volunteer into service and elect their officers before being drafted.[29]

As with all drafts, this one was subject to abuse. The wealthy were able to avoid service by hiring a substitute and in October, when the draft was amended, were able to stay home if they owned twenty or more slaves. Since men had to pass a physical before being drafted, a system quickly developed by those who were opposed to the war to provide hand signals and acknowledgments that led to some men being exempted for physical ailments that may or may not have existed.

While the war in 1862 went reasonably well for the Confederates in the Eastern Theatre where they were winning more than they

---

[29] Moore, Albert B., *Conscription and Conflict in the Confederacy.* (New York, NY: The Macmillan Company, 1924), pp 12-26.

lost, that was not the case in the Western Theatre where many of the men who had been stationed in Pensacola were sent. Braxton Bragg was unpopular and often vacillated between hesitancy and rashness as a commander. His orders were sometimes open to confusion or misinterpretation which led to blunders on the battlefield. He and his subordinates would sometimes get into conflicts and finger-pointing that had to have impacted the men under them. So, many of the Florida men not only had bad news from home but difficult battlefield conditions to endure.

By 1863 the Confederate army was hungry and poorly clothed. They had their military high water mark at the Battle of Fredericksburg, handily winning after a grueling day of fighting. Their leaders began planning to take the fight into Union territory. But at home the blockade of southern ports, the lack of manpower to plant and harvest crops and the confiscation of family food stores by the Confederate agents throughout the south was particularly hard on the women and children. The year 1863 saw several protests/mob actions by women wanting better access and cheaper food, most notably in Richmond and Mobile. In the Pensacola area, there was not only the impressment agents from the Confederate government but there was the Union presence that continued to wreak havoc on any production facilities and on supplies held by Confederate families. Letters to the men in the army had to weigh heavily on them and it showed with a rising desertion rate across the southern armies.

The Confederate government had promised these men that their families would be taken care of while they were off fighting but the promises never quite reached the level that reality needed them to reach. Many plantation owners continued to grow cotton and sugar and not enough food to feed hungry families. Transportation was a problem in the South before the war and the ill-planned and mismatching rail lines exacerbated the war effort in trying to move food and men. The Armies were a priority, making food on the home front even more scarce, but it wasn't necessarily much better with the troops. As the policy of parole and exchange changed over 1863 there was also the increasing need to feed prisoners of war. And finally, 1863 saw the Union split the south in two by the taking of the Mississippi river passage from New Orleans past Tennessee and this decreased the availability of Texas cattle and foodstuffs. The major clashes between the armies in the eastern theatre throughout the Shenandoah Valley significantly decreased food production from that area. Food was scarce and the women simply could not produce enough to feed their families and supply the ever-present impressment agents and opposition forces. Given this, it isn't surprising that the desertion rate began to skyrocket in 1863 and reached its zenith in the Fall of 1864.[30]

Once Lee's army in the east invaded Gettysburg and had to withdraw with major losses to his already bedraggled army, the desertions from both western and eastern theatres into the woods of the Florida panhandle and southern Alabama were a steady stream. Many of the men who eventually fought with the 1st FCUV joined or were drafted in 1862 or 1863 and deserted within a year. Efforts were made to find them and some of those efforts were brutal to the women who were the targets of the militia trying to locate their husbands. It was a situation ripe for a new approach in the Pensacola area and that would be provided by the new Army Commander at Pensacola, Brigadier General Alexander Asboth.

Formation of the 1st FCUV

Alexander Asboth was born in Hungary and served in the Hungarian army before immigrating to the United States in 1851. He joined the Union early in the war and served in the Western Theatre until being transferred in Special Order #252 to the command of the District of West Florida on 8 October 1863. In that same month on the 29th, Brigadier General Charles P. Stone, who was the Chief of Staff of the Department of the Gulf,

---

[30] Lonn, Ella., *Desertion During the Civil War* Bison Books. (Lincoln, NE: University of Nebraska Press, 1998), pp 21-37.

instructed Brigadier General Asboth to take immediate steps to raise and enlist a regiment of men from the area.[31]

Upon reaching Pensacola, Brigadier General Asboth wrote to Brigadier General Stone that the Confederates were encamped in a number of places around the Pensacola area: at Pollard, Alabama; at Camp Hunter, Florida (9 miles from Pollard on the Mobile Railroad) and three advance camps – one near Pensacola between the Escambia and Perdido Rivers, one east of the Escambia River about 7 miles above Floridatown and one west of the Perdido River near Nueces Ferry on the Blakeley road. He indicated that the advanced encampment above Floridatown consisted of 120 to 140 cavalry and had pickets at Milton, Bagdad, and Partes (unknown location today) to prevent both white and black refugees from joining the Union forces. He asked for additional men and two side-wheel steamers to help clear the Escambia and Perdido Rivers of Confederates hindering Union movements.[32]

On 5 December 1863, Asboth made his first reference to what would become the 1st FCUV. In his report, he goes into some detail on his visit to the town of Pensacola and the general sympathy of the few residents for the "rebellion". He also indicated that the Confederates were fortifying Fifteen Mile Station on the Pensacola Railroad. He then stated that "(d)eserters are constantly coming in, taking the oath of allegiance" and that fifteen men had already enlisted. He finished by stating that several contrabands (runaway slaves) were added to the Fourteenth Regiment, Corps d'Afrique and that he had suspended the practice of allowing citizens to cross back and forth across the

---

[31] *The War of the Rebellion: A Compilation of the Official Records of the Union and Confederate Armies.*, 1997, [CD-ROM], Carmel, IN: Guild Press of Indiana, 1997, Series I, Vol. XXVI/1 [S#41], pp 780-781.
[32] *The War of the Rebellion: A Compilation of the Official Records of the Union and Confederate Armies,* 1997, [CD-ROM]. Carmel, IN: Guild Press of Indiana, Series I, Vol XXVI/1 [S#41], 817-818.

Union lines with provisions and confiscated a schooner coming from Milton for the same purpose.[33]

On 27 December 1863, he started his report by indicating that he was convinced that not one but several regiments could be raised in West Florida "by offering to all those who are anxious to enlist into the Union Army proper assistance to come within our lines." And then he went on to indicate that two side-wheelers would be necessary so that he could clear the rivers of Confederates and collect the refugees and deserters "secreted in the woods and islands." It is here that he also requested instructions and orders regarding the payment of bounties to the men enlisting for three years. A survey of the militia rolls indicates that the bounty payments were never adequately available upon enlistment and many were still unpaid and due at the time the men mustered out. Since he still did not have his requested two side-wheelers he indicated that he had made use of a private schooner captained by a "high-minded Union man" to make a trip to East Pass (eastern end of Santa Rosa Island) where they collected twenty-five able-bodied men who enlisted at once and thirty-three more who had made the run through the pickets, eighteen of whom had enlisted with Company M, Fourteenth New York Cavalry and 40 enlisted with the 1st FCUV. He finished his report with the news that the two companies of cavalry reported encamped above Floridatown had been withdrawn as they had been preparing to desert in mass.[34]

In January of 1864 Asboth reported that the 1st FCUV recruits had surpassed 120 men even though the small steamer he wanted to use to bring men down to Pensacola had been disabled. He also reported that 75 Confederate men who had been stationed at Fifteen Mile Station had laid down their arms and were arrested and sent to Pollard, Alabama. He indicated that he was sending

---

[33] *The War of the Rebellion: A Compilation of the Official Records of the Union and Confederate Armies*, 1997, [CD-ROM], Carmel, IN: Guild Press of Indiana, Series I, Vol XXVI/1 [S#41], pp 833-834.
[34] *The War of the Rebellion: A Compilation of the Official Records of the Union and Confederate Armies*, 1997, [CD-ROM], Carmel, IN: Guild Press of Indiana, Series I, Vol XXVI/1 [S#41], 886-887.

a private schooner and a steamer up Santa Rosa Sound to the Choctawhatchee Bay to bring down refugees to enlist, to capture and bring to Fort Barrancas a Confederate schooner preparing to run the blockade, and to capture and bring any other vessel not already taken by the Union back to Fort Barrancas. He ended by asking for cavalry horses and equipment to mount the Florida recruits.[35] The response back to Asboth from Brigadier-General Stone was that only 30 or 40 horses could be sent to Pensacola but that more would be forthcoming.[36]

By February 1864 he reported the number of recruits in the 1st FCUV to be 207 with 30 more on their way down Santa Rosa Sound. He stated that the inability to pay the bounty money was slowing down recruitment. He called attention to a battalion of Florida Cavalry at Marianna who he said were "inclined to desert" but "controlled by three companies of cavalry". These cavalrymen were moving frequently in Washington and Walton County and hunting deserters "with bloodhounds which have torn to pieces several women and children, creating indignation among the people".[37] A few days later he followed up his report with additional information on Confederate movements in the area of northwest Florida and south Alabama and the continuing arrival of refugees and deserters into the Union lines. He reported on the situation in Pollard, Alabama with some of the men in Clanton's Brigade plotting to desert in mass.[38] The Confederate government moved some of the command at Pollard further north to Kentucky and Tennessee and arrested many of the men and put them on trial. In a report from Major General Maury to Confederate

---

[35] *The War of the Rebellion: A Compilation of the Official Records of the Union and Confederate Armies*, 1997, [CD-ROM], Carmel, IN: Guild Press of Indiana, Series I, Vol XXXV/1 [S#65], pp 453-454.

[36] *The War of the Rebellion: A Compilation of the Official Records of the Union and Confederate Armies*, 1997, [CD-ROM], Carmel, IN: Guild Press of Indiana, Series I, Vol XXXV/1 [S#65], pp 459-460.

[37] The War of the Rebellion: A Compilation of the Official Records of the Union and Confederate Armies, 1997, [CD-ROM], Carmel, IN: Guild Press of Indiana, Series I, Vol XXXV/1 [S#65], pp 470-471.

[38] *The War of the Rebellion: A Compilation of the Official Records of the Union and Confederate Armies*, 1997, [CD-ROM], Carmel, IN: Guild Press of Indiana, Series I, Vol XXXV/1 [S#65}, pp 479-480.

Secretary of War Seddon in January 1864, Maury indicated that the "organized plan for desertion" was widespread in Clanton's troops and included organized opposition to the war and a secret association formed within the army seeking peace on any terms.[39]

Asboth mentioned a regiment of cavalry and one of infantry encamped at Canoe Station (in Alabama east of present day Atmore, AL) as part of the movement of Confederate troops in the area. And finally, he indicated that the companies between the Escambia and Blackwater Bay were also exchanged for Kentucky troops, as were the ones that had been stationed above the head of the Choctawhatchee Bay in Washington and Walton Counties. According to Asboth this was to further impair the ability of refugees and deserters to make it into the Union lines.[40]

Ten days later he reported that there were 3,000 Tennessee troops at Pollard and 500 at Milton, Blackwater Bay and Floridatown that were guarding the line from Floridatown along Pond Creek, Bagdad Factory, Crigler's Mill and along the Yellow River. According to Asboth these troops are "far more severe" than the Florida troops they replaced (some had actually been Alabama troops) and refugees and deserters could no longer get through to Federal lines. He also indicated that Confederate cavalry were stationed at Euchee Anna in Washington County to force all sixteen to fifty-five-year-old men to join the service and to take "everything from people sympathizing with and joining the Yankees".[41]

In May 1864 Asboth reported that 20 more Florida men were on their way down Santa Rosa Sound and that these men would fill the sixth company of the "First Regiment Florida Cavalry". He

---

[39] *The War of the Rebellion: A Compilation of the Official Records of the Union and Confederate Armies*, 1997, [CD-ROM], Carmel, IN: Guild Press of Indiana, Series I, Vol XXVI/2 [S#42], 551-552.
[40] *The War of the Rebellion: A Compilation of the Official Records of the Union and Confederate Armies*, 1997, [CD-ROM], Carmel, IN: Guild Press of Indiana, Series I, Vol XXXV/1 [S#65], pp 479-480.
[41] *The War of the Rebellion: A Compilation of the Official Records of the Union and Confederate Armies*, 1997, [CD-ROM], Carmel, IN: Guild Press of Indiana, Series I, Vol XXXV/1 [S#65], pp 489-490.

finished his report by indicating an absence of arms and horses for these men "who most anxiously desire to be led against the rebels and avenge the many wrongs inflicted upon them and their families by a barbarous foe".[42]

In the span of seven months, enough local men had made it into the Federal lines and joined the 1st FCUV to fill six companies (generally 100 men per company). By the end of the war the regiment would have enlisted just slightly more than seven hundred men, with the vast majority of them from northwest Florida and southeast Alabama. While these numbers would not have been a large percentage of the white males in the area (see Introduction on the area providing the men of the 1st FCUV and the Appendix) they were sufficient to give the Union an edge in this area of the Gulf Coast.

Military Engagements of the 1st FCUV

Gonzales' Farm/15 Mile Station/Pollard – 7/21/64-7/25/64

1864 Locations: Gonzales Farm and Fifteen Mile Station in Florida and the Confederate camp called Fort Hodgson in Pollard, Alabama.

Current Locations: Town of Gonzales, Florida north from Pensacola along railroad to area of Highway 184. The current Highway 29 follows the original road fairly closely. Town of Pollard, Alabama just south of Brewton, Alabama off Highway 29/31

Union Regiments Participating (under Brig. Gen. A. Asboth):

Colonel W. C. Holbrook, commanding:
       7th Vermont Veteran Volunteers – 4 companies

---

[42] *The War of the Rebellion: A Compilation of the Official Records of the Union and Confederate Armies*, 1997, [CD-ROM], Carmel, IN: Guild Press of Indiana, Series I, Vol XXXV/1 [S#65], pp 398-399.

82nd U.S. Colored Infantry – 8 companies
86th U.S. Colored Infantry - 6 companies
Colonel E. von Kielmansegge commanding:
    1st FCUV (unmounted) – 4 companies
    14th New York Cavalry, Co. M
    1st Florida Battery

Confederate Regiments Participating:

Colonel Joseph Hodgson, commanding:
    Co. G, E and I, 7th Alabama Regiment Cavalry

Victor: Union

1st Florida Men Known to Participate:

Mentioned in each Man's Muster Roll or in Official Records:

Robert A. Alsobrook, Co B, Corporal
Seaborn S. Baggett, Co F, Corporal
George W. Brown, Co C, Private
Simeon Wilder Burleson, Co A, Corporal
Constantine Butler, Co A, Private
Henry H. Creamer, Co A, Corporal
William R. Crider, Co A, Private
Henry H. Dixon, Co A, Corporal
James D. Donaldson, Co A, Corporal
James Dyson, Co A, Private
Albert Gill, Co A, Private
Lorenzo D. Gill, Co A, Private
Joseph B. Hewett, Co A, Corporal
John G. R. Hudson, Co A, Private
Andrew Jackson Johnson, Co A, Private
Francis Lyons, Co E, Captain
Andrew J. Nobles, Co C, Private
George W. Parker, Co C, Private
Richard P. Parker, Co C, Private
Soverign Frederick Ray, Co A, Sergeant
Benjamin F. Stearns, Co A, Sergeant
Joseph H. Wickliffe, Co C, 1st Lieutenant

Mentioned in Official records at Fifteen Mile House:

Allen Holman (unclear which Holman this is)
William Parker, Co F, Private
Jesse Ray, Co A, Private

Summary of Events

On 20 July 1864, Brigadier General Alexander Asboth, commander of the Union Army troops stationed at Fort Barrancas, received a dispatch instructing him to watch out for raiders sent from William T. Sherman's Army to target Confederate supply and munitions depots in central Alabama. The raiders were to destroy the supplies and munitions and report back to Sherman's Army descending into Georgia. If it became impossible for the raiders to return, they were to head to Pensacola.

Asboth immediately mobilized a force of 1,100 men and moved out on the 21st in the afternoon and probably marched up along the railroad connecting Pensacola to Pollard in a continuous night march. They arrived at Fifteen Mile House at daybreak on the 22nd and were immediately fired on by Confederate pickets near the Gonzales Farm where the Confederates had established a camp just right of the railroad track. The Seventh Vermont and the 82nd U.S. Colored Infantry were drawn up in line for battle with four companies functioning as skirmishers. The 86th was held in reserve. The Florida Battery (artillery regiment) was placed on the crest of the hill on the road, which would have been to the southwest of the Confederate camp and the line of battle. The 14th New York Cavalry and the 1st FCUV formed the left flank, just east of the railroad, and supported the artillery. Two companies were deployed as skirmishers.

After several exchanges of gunfire between the Confederates and the skirmishers from the Union regiments, the Confederates began falling back north to their new camp, Fort Hodgson, completed the day before and named in honor of their colonel. Heavy fire and cannon shot ensued and the Confederates soon withdrew from the fort and camp and retreated further north toward Pollard; abandoning official papers, muster rolls, a battle flag, commissary and quartermaster stores, arms, ammunition, horses, cattle and 7 comrades who were taken as prisoners.

In questioning, some of the men taken prisoner, Asboth discovered that the raiders had successfully accomplished their mission into Alabama and had returned to Sherman's Army. Disappointed in losing the possibility of working with them, Asboth decided he would continue his advance north toward Pollard. The next morning, he sent one wagon with captured ordinance and the sick and wounded back to Fort Barrancas, leveled Fort Hodgson and proceeded north. Rebel pickets began firing at the advancing army near the Pollard and Perdido Railroad Station, approximately six miles further along the road to Pollard. A cavalry engagement ensued between Company M of the 14th New York Cavalry and the 7th Alabama Cavalry. Three more prisoners were taken by the Union and these told Asboth that the bridge over Pine Barren Creek, two miles north, had been destroyed and the Confederates had placed four pieces of artillery on the opposite bank of the creek.

Asboth sent the 14th New York Cavalry under Captain Schmidt out toward Pine Barren Bridge to demonstrate (make a good show of advancing toward the enemy to keep them penned down) while he took the remainder of the men along the Perdido Station road. His goal was to cut the telegraph and strike the railroad, destroy the trestle work below the Perdido Station and descend between the Perdido River and Mobile Bay. In addition, he planned to destroy the Bonsecours Bay Salt works and Camp Withers and Powell, Confederate camps in Baldwin County and re-cross the Perdido at Nueces' Ferry (*note: spelled Nuenece by Asboth in his reports), where the Styx and Perdido River join just east of current day Seminole, Alabama. He sent a dispatch to that effect to the district quartermaster, instructing him to have transportation ready for the army on the 26th at Nueces Ferry.

Asboth had marched about seven miles when according to his official report he received information from three different sources that the Confederate Army had begun mobilizing along the railroad to confront him. He changed his mind on moving through Baldwin County and started back to Pensacola the following morning, arriving on the 25th.[43]

This was the first major engagement for the 1st FCUV, though they were unmounted and functioning as infantry. While the muster rolls and official records only specifically mention a handful of men, it is possible that more of the men already mustered in Companies A, C and F were involved based on the companies of the men mentioned in the record.

Battle of Marianna – 9/18/64-10/4/64

1864 Locations: The march occurred from Navy Cove & Live Oak plantation on Santa Rosa Island east & north to Euchee Anna, Cerro Gordo, Marianna and Vernon, all in Florida.

Current Locations: Highway 98 in south Santa Rosa County, Florida; around the northern side of Choctawhatchee Bay from Ft. Walton Beach to Freeport; what remains of Euchee Anna is located on Highway 280 east in Walton County; what remains of Cerro Gordo is located off Highway 179A in Holmes County; Marianna is in Jackson County along Highway 90; Vernon is on Highway 79 in Washington County.

Union Regiments Participating (under Brig. Gen. A. Asboth):

Lt. Colonel A. Spurling, commanding:
    2nd Maine Cavalry (3 battalions)
    7th Vermont Veteran Volunteers
Major Albert Ruttkay, commanding:
    1st FCUV (companies A, D, E & F)
Colonel L. L. Zulavsky, commanding:
    86th U.S. Colored Infantry (1 company)
    82nd U.S. Colored Infantry (1 company)

---

[43] *The War of the Rebellion: A Compilation of the Official Records of the Union and Confederate Armies*, 1997, [CD-ROM], Carmel, IN: Guild Press of Indiana, Series I, Vol XXXV/1 [S365}, pp 413-416.

Confederate Regiments Participating:

Colonel Alexander B. Montgomery, commanding:
    Confederate Cavalry (about 300 men)
        1 Co commanded by Capt. Chisolm
        1 Co commanded by Poe
Home Guard (about 200 men)
    1 Co commanded by Henry Robinson
    1 Co commanded by Capt. Alexander Godwin
    Capt. Jesse Norwood, commanding Town men

Victor: Union

1st Florida Men Known to Participate:

Eldred Benjamin Allen, Co E, Private
Seaborn S. Baggett, Co F, Corporal
Curtis G.H. Bagwell, Co F, Private
Charles P. Bell, Co E, Private
Simeon Wilder Burleson, Co A, Private
Bethel Haines Callahan, Co E, Private
James W. Carmichael, Co C, Private
Jasper J. Carter, Co F, Private
William Giles Caswell, Co E, Private
William R. Crider, Co A, Private
Daniel Monroe Dansby, Co F, Private
Emanuel George W. Dansby, Co F, Private
Hiram D. Dansby, Co F, Private
Franklin J. Davis, Co E, Sergeant
William S. Davis, Co E, Bugler
Henry H. Dixon, Co A, Corporal
James D. Donaldson, Co A, Corporal
Marion W. Franklin, Co A, Private
Joseph Garrett, Co E, Private
Albert Gill, Co A, Private
Lorenzo D. Gill, Co A, Bugler
Emanuel R. Grubbs, Co E, Bugler
Wiley F. Harrison, Co A, Sergeant
James Marcus Lafayette Hathaway, Co E, Private
Joseph B. Hewett, Co A, Private
Godfrey Lee Holley, Co E, Corporal
Adam Cornelius Hollinger, Co E, Sergeant

John G. R. Hudson, Co A, Private
Andrew Jackson Johnson, Co A, Private
George H. Johnson, Co E, Private
Alexander C. Levins, Co D, Private
Francis Lyons, Co E, Captain
Griffin Melvin, Co E, Corporal
Warren Mills, Co E, Private
Michael M. Moniac, Co E, Corporal
Jonathan Paulk, Co E, Private
Thomas Pullum, Co E, Sergeant
Soverign Frederick Ray, Co A, Sergeant
Benjamin Roberson, Co E, Corporal
Daniel L. Roberson, Co E, Private
Benjamin F. Stearns, Co A, Sergeant
George W. Stewart, Co E, Bugler
James H. Stewart, Co E, Sergeant
Reason Strickland, Co E, Corporal
Dawson T. Tramell, Co E, Sergeant
Jordan L. Waters, Co A, Bugler
William H. Waters, Co A, Sergeant
Burton H. Watson, Co A, Private
John W. Watson, Co A, Private
Richard B. Wright, Co E, Corporal

Summary of events:

On 4 July 1864, Brigadier General Asboth sent a report to the headquarters of the Division of West Mississippi providing a summary of his knowledge of Confederate deployments in the area surrounding Fort Barrancas and Pensacola and suggesting a cavalry raid as far north as Columbus, GA. His march would go by way of St. Andrew's Bay and Marianna, FL and march up through Georgia along the Georgia and Alabama border. By 11 September 1864 he was adding to his information on the deployment of Confederate troops and indicating in his report that there were several hundred prisoners being held at Marianna. He was given permission to conduct a raid into the northeastern portion of West Florida. His objectives were to 1) capture the Confederate cavalry and infantry in Jackson and Washington counties, 2) liberate the Union prisoners held at Marianna, 3) collect white and black recruits, and 4) secure as many horses and mules as possible.[44]

A small detachment of the 82nd U.S. Colored Infantry left Barrancas on the 15th and a smaller detachment of the 86th U.S. Colored Infantry and the 2nd Maine Cavalry left on the 16th as the advance guard for the movement east. Asboth and the main Army departed Fort Barrancas on 18 September, first crossing Pensacola Bay and landing at Navy Cove at Live Oak Plantation then marching 50 miles along the Old Military Road to Rodger's Gap on the narrows of Santa Rosa Island and 6 miles west of East Pass. Samuel Doble, a member of the 2nd Maine Cavalry, reported in his diary that it rained all night the 17th and almost continuously through the 20th.[45] Once all was across, Asboth received rations from the steamer Lizzie Davis.[46]

On the 20th the Army turned north and ascended Ridge Road, marching 134 miles into the heart of Walton County. This march took two days with the next key engagement point being just south of present day DeFuniak Springs in the community of Euchee Anna. The Army arrived there at daybreak on the 23rd. There they attacked the courthouse, defended by about 30 men from the 15th Confederate Cavalry and Chisholm's Alabama militia from Pollard, AL resulting in forty-six horses with equipment, eight mules and twenty-eight stands of arms being taken.[47] The nine prisoners of war included W. H. Terrence militia colonel and 1st Lt. Francis M. Gordon of the 15th Confederate Cavalry. The six political prisoners included wealthy cattleman and Confederate

---

[44] *The War of the Rebellion: A Compilation of the Official Records of the Union and Confederate Armies*, 1997, [CD-ROM], Carmel, IN: Guild Press of Indiana, Series I, Vol XXXV/2 [S#66], pp 165-166 and pp 285-286.
[45] Doble, Samuel Wood, *A Civil War Diary: Skirmishes Along the Southern Coast, 1864-1865*, (Lexington, KY, January 2010), pp 52-54.
[46] *The War of the Rebellion: A Compilation of the Official Records of the Union and Confederate Armies*, 1997, [CD-ROM], Carmel, IN: Guild Press of Indiana, Series I, Vol XXXV/1 [S#65], pp 443-444.
[47] *The War of the Rebellion: A Compilation of the Official Records of the Union and Confederate Armies*, 1997, [CD-ROM], Carmel, IN: Guild Press of Indiana, Series I, Vol XXXV/1 [S#65], pp 443-444.

leader William Cawthon and his son-in-law Allen Haze Hart, a Confederate beef contractor.[48]

The Army stayed the night in Euchee Anna, leaving for Cerro Gordo (then county seat of Holmes County) the following morning after destroying Douglas' Ferry. The ferry was where the main road from Vernon, Hickory Hill and Euchee Anna ran east to Marianna. Two companies of the 1st FCUV were sent back as escorts for the prisoners and freed enslaved persons to Four-Mile Landing (La Grange) on the Choctawhatchee Bay. The records do not state which two companies went back to La Grange and which two stayed with Asboth. It was likely early in this march that the Army was observed by a young man who reported his sighting to Colonel Montgomery of the Confederate Army. Unfortunately for the Confederates, Asboth destroyed the ferry and took an alternate route.[49] This maneuver and the entire march deep into the Florida back country demonstrate the usefulness of the men of the 1st FCUV to the Union effort in Florida and south Alabama. It is unlikely that Asboth would have known about alternate routes without the aid of men from the area. Union maps of the area at the time were basic and not always accurate.

The army moved quickly through Holmes County with no encounters with the home guard. By mid-day on the 26th the men had reached Holmes Creek. Once into Jackson County they marched toward Campbellton, plundering and looting homes as they moved east. It was here that Captain Alexander Godwin's cavalry, a home guard of men whose farms were in the area, began harassing the Federal column and several men were captured in the process. Godwin also sent a message to

---

[48] *The War of the Rebellion: A Compilation of the Official Records of the Union and Confederate Armies*, 1997, [CD-ROM], Carmel, IN: Guild Press of Indiana, Series I, Vol XXXV/1 [S#65], pp 443-444.
[49] *The War of the Rebellion: A Compilation of the Official Records of the Union and Confederate Armies*, 1997, [CD-ROM], Carmel, IN: Guild Press of Indiana, Series I, Vol XXXV/1 [S#65], pp 444-445 and Cox, Dale, *The Battle of Marianna, Florida,* (Ft. Smith, AR: Dale Cox, 2007), pp 36-38.

Marianna to warn Montgomery that the Union army was at Campbellton.[50]

Immediate efforts were made to call in the various army units surrounding Marianna but the local home guards were not yet called out. Montgomery then led the available men from Poe's and Chisholm's companies toward the northwest on the Campbellton Road. He didn't wire for reinforcements from Quincy or Tallahassee before leaving Marianna. As night approached Asboth decided to camp for the evening in Campbellton. While the Army was settling in, Montgomery and Godwin made contact and Montgomery began to realize the seriousness of the threat. This was not the usual small raiding party that attacked and withdrew. Still, even though the situation was serious it was difficult to determine the intended destination because Campbellton was a crossroads to several potential targets. Roads led north to Georgia and Alabama and southeast and west to Hickory Hill and Marianna. This lack of knowledge on Asboth's intended target may have kept Montgomery from consolidating his forces according to Dale Cox.[51]

On the morning of 27 September, Colonel Montgomery was watching as Asboth's Army saddled up and turned south onto the Marianna road. Marianna was confirmed as the destination a short time later when the army approached the intersection of the Marianna road and the Old Fort road and pushed south to the plantation of John R. Waddell. Montgomery sent a courier back to town to alert them and to call out the home guard. It is not known how strong this force was that assembled at the Marianna courthouse. Dale Cox has identified at least seventy men who fought with Captain Norwood. It included the home guard, some men home recuperating and every other male that could be identified. During the morning, they were joined by a company of cavalry from nearby Greenwood under the command of Captain

---

[50] Cox, Dale, *The Battle of Marianna, Florida*. (Ft. Smith, AR: Dale Cox, 2007), pp 39-42.
[51] Cox, Dale, *The Battle of Marianna, Florida*. (Ft. Smith, AR: Dale Cox, 2007), pp 43-48

Henry Robinson. Also arriving in Marianna the morning of the 27th, was some men from Captain George Robinson's home guard from eastern Jackson County. These men fought with Captain Norwood's company. In addition, they were able to round up a few conscripts from the nearby training camp and some sick and wounded from the Marianna Post Hospital. Together these combined companies and individuals were likely no more than 150 men according to Cox.[52]

Asboth's Army passed, stopped at and/or raided farms as they moved toward Marianna. After leaving the Waddell Plantation they arrived at the Joseph W. Russ farm and remained in line as scouts were sent out. The next farm was the plantation of Lt. Colonel W. D. Barnes of the 1st Florida Reserves, CSA. His plantation was located in the small community of Webbville. The Union forces next arrived at the Whitesville plantation belonging to Thomas M. White, then Mayor of Marianna. Here they raided and looted the farm, with many of White's enslaved population falling in behind the Army when it left. The last known stop was the Finlayson farm where the widow of a member of the original Jackson County Civil War militia operated a farm with her two sons. Much of her property was destroyed before the Army moved on.[53]

At this point the Army was less than 5 miles from Marianna. Colonel Montgomery decided to make a stand and chose Hopkins' Branch, a small stream three miles northwest of Marianna. He arrayed his men on the east bank and waited. Dale Cox estimates that Montgomery probably had about 100 men on the firing line, with another 60 holding the horses' reins to keep them from bolting during the fight.[54] It was here, at Hopkins' Branch, where the first shots of the Battle of Marianna were fired. It is uncertain how long

---

[52] Cox, Dale, *The Battle of Marianna, Florida*. (Ft. Smith, AR: Dale Cox, 2007), pp 49-62.
[53] Cox, Dale, *The Battle of Marianna, Florida*. (Ft. Smith, AR: Dale Cox, 2007), pp 49-53.
[54] Cox, Dale, *The Battle of Marianna, Florida*. (Ft. Smith, AR: Dale Cox, 2007), p 53.

Montgomery was able to hold his position and exchange a brisk fire with the Union cavalry. But Montgomery was outnumbered by a significant margin and did eventually pull back. He sent his men to Marianna via the northern bypass, a logging road that left the Campbellton Road west of town. He remained behind with his staff to continue to monitor the Union army. Asboth sent troops after them, as well as moved straight up the Campbellton road to town.[55]

Montgomery brought his forces up to Ely Corner, at the western edge of town, near the intersection of the St. Andrews Bay and Campbellton roads. Here he could bring his cavalry into a full line to fire upon the Union forces as they rounded a narrow bend of the Campbellton road.[56] Between Ely Corner and St. Luke's Episcopal Church, the men of the home guard erected a barricade of wagons and carts stretching across the street in the hopes of thwarting a cavalry charge. From the barricade to St. Luke's the home guard were deployed on both sides of the road. Most of the houses along the road and the church had board fences erected around them which provided some cover for the men.[57]

It would have been a good plan if Asboth had not divided his forces, advancing up both the Campbellton road and the logging road. Before Montgomery could adjust his men, the forward column of Asboth's men charged around Ely's Corner. The 2nd Maine Cavalry was in the advance and lost several men in the initial charge.[58] A second charge occurred very soon afterward, with Asboth in the lead, and this drove the Confederate forces back toward the river, creating casualties on both sides. The Union men coming around the bypass now entered the battle and

---

[55] Cox, Dale, *The Battle of Marianna, Florida.* (Ft. Smith, AR: Dale Cox, 2007), pp 53-54.
[56] Cox, Dale, The Battle of Marianna, Florida. (Ft. Smith, AR: Dale Cox, 2007), pp 55-56.
[57] Cox, Dale, *The Battle of Marianna, Florida.* (Ft. Smith, AR: Dale Cox, 2007), pp 55-58.
[58] *The War of the Rebellion: A Compilation of the Official Records of the Union and Confederate Armies,* 1997, [CD-ROM], Carmel, IN: Guild Press of Indiana, Series I, Vol XXXV/1 [S#65], pp 444-445 and Cox, Dale, *The Battle of Marianna, Florida,* (Ft. Smith, AR: Dale Cox, 2007), p 58.

close combat ensued through the streets of Marianna. Some of the Confederates managed to cross the bridge and take up the planks, restricting the Union to the west side of the river.[59]

Asboth was severely wounded during this early phase of the battle. Colonel Zulavsky assumed command and pressed the battle in the streets around St. Luke's Episcopal Church.[60] The Confederates were outnumbered and surrounded when some of the men who had approached town by the bypass came in behind the church. The Confederates did not give up easily but fought hard to defend their community. Zulavsky ordered the 82nd and 86th U.S. Colored Infantry to take the churchyard. Much controversy surrounds this part of the battle but the result was the church was burned with a number of Confederate men still in it. The battle was over.

Casualties were high on both sides. The original plan had been to turn south and disrupt the salt works at St. Andrews Bay but the casualties and the captured supplies and more than 600 freed enslaved persons forced a change in plans. The decision was made to leave Marianna in the early morning of 28 September. The march back home took them near Vernon, Florida where they engaged a company of Confederates on their way to Marianna. Leaving Vernon, the Union troops marched south toward Ebro, then to Point Washington on the Choctawhatchee Bay and home to Fort Barrancas.[61]

Expedition to Milton – 10/25-28/64

1864 Location: Blackwater Bay and the Towns of Milton and Bagdad

---

[59] Cox, Dale, *The Battle of Marianna, Florida*. (Ft. Smith, AR: Dale Cox, 2007), pp 58-62.
[60] *The War of the Rebellion: A Compilation of the Official Records of the Union and Confederate Armies*, 1997, [CD-ROM], Carmel, IN: Guild Press of Indiana, Series I, Vol XXXV/1 [S#65], pp 444-445.
[61] Cox, Dale, *The Battle of Marianna, Florida*. (Ft. Smith, AR: Dale Cox, 2007), pp 83-93.

Current Location: East side of Escambia Bay, west side of Blackwater Bay, south of the community of Bagdad and the town of Milton and north along Highway 87 approximately seven or eight miles.

Union Regiments Participating:

Lt. Colonel A. Spurling, commanding
        2nd Maine Veteran Cavalry
        19th Iowa Infantry
        1st FCUV
        25th U.S. Colored Infantry
        82nd U.S. Colored Infantry
        86th U.S. Colored Infantry

Confederate Regiments Participating:

        70 or 80 men of the 8th Mississippi Cavalry
        A small detachment of militia

Victor: Union

1st Florida Men Known to Participate:

Mentioned in each man's muster roll

James H. Armstrong, Co C, Private
Hugh Huston Barfield, Co F, Private
John H. Britt, Co C, Private
Henry W. Teel, Co B, Private
William Peter Ward, Co B, Private

Mentioned in Official Records

100 unnamed dismounted men

Summary of events:

Very early in 1864, the small town of Milton became an almost constant battleground between the Confederate troops positioned in the area and the Union troops stationed at Fort Barrancas.

Before the war, Milton had significant shipbuilding and lumbering infrastructure, a cotton mill, a building and sash-making shop and brickmaking facilities. The Union ventured into Milton repeatedly to take supplies, especially lumber, and to engage the Confederate Cavalry in the area. On 20 October 1864 Brevet Brigadier-General Joseph Bailey, then in command of the District of West Florida, wrote in a report that a detachment was sent on the 17th for logs and returned on the 19th for brick, doors and window sashes.[62] This engagement in late 1864 is the first mention of involvement of the men from the 1st FCUV in these skirmishes but likely wasn't the last.

Lt. Colonel Andrew Spurling of the 2nd Maine Cavalry commanded the men, including 100 men from the 2nd Maine Cavalry, 100 dismounted men from the 1st FCUV, 200 from the 19th Iowa Infantry and 300 men from the 25th, 82nd and 86th U.S. Colored Infantry. Spurling's plan was to attempt to catch the approximately 80 to 100 Confederates in the Milton area by creating a pincer movement to cut off the escape of the Confederates on the peninsula between Escambia Bay and Blackwater Bay and River.[63]

Captain Stearns of the 82nd Colored Infantry took 200 men aboard the Lizzie Davis and was supposed to land about thirteen miles below Milton and about eight below Pierce's Mill. The purpose was to raft logs and draw the Confederates down onto the peninsula. Spurling landed about 300 men under Major Mudgett at Mulat Bayou, directly across the peninsula from Pierce's Mill. They were instructed to move east once hearing the cannon to cut off any escape of the Confederates. He then went back around the peninsula to join with the men under Captain Stearns. He discovered that Stearns had not landed the men where he had directed but several miles further up the Blackwater Bay.

---

[62] *The War of the Rebellion: A Compilation of the Official Records of the Union and Confederate Armies*, 1997, [CD-ROM], Carmel, IN: Guild Press of Indiana, Series I, Vol XXXV/1 [S#65], pp 445-446.
[63] *The War of the Rebellion: A Compilation of the Official Records of the Union and Confederate Armies*, 1997, [CD-ROM], Carmel, IN: Guild Press of Indiana, Series I, Vol XXXV/1 [S#65], pp 448-45.

According to Spurling, this error kept the Confederates from coming far enough down the peninsula to cut them off with the pincer movement.[64]

The Confederates did engage the front of the Union movement above Pierce's Mill, where they were driven up through Bagdad and Milton about eight miles onto what was then called the Pollard Road. As the men moved north through Bagdad there was a sustained engagement at the bridge over Pond Creek and then a running engagement up through Milton. Nine Confederates were captured and 5 or 6 were killed. Approximately 85,000 feet of lumber was taken, as well as some corn, meal, ham and beef. Several horses were also taken with equipment.[65]

Expedition to Pine Barren Creek, FL – 11/17-18/64

1864 Location: Along Pine Barren Creek in north Escambia County, Florida.

Current Location: On the north side of Pine Barren Creek, near current Highway 29, south of the Florida/Alabama line.

Union Regiments Participating:

Lt. Colonel A. Spurling, commanding
       2nd Maine Veteran Cavalry, Maj Hutchinson
       1st FCUV, Major Ruttkay

Confederate Regiments Participating:

15th Confederate Cavalry, Captain Leigh's Company

Victor: Union

---

[64] *The War of the Rebellion: A Compilation of the Official Records of the Union and Confederate Armies*, 1997, [CD-ROM], Carmel, IN: Guild Press of Indiana, Series I, Vol XXXV/1 [S#65], pp 448-451.
[65] *The War of the Rebellion: A Compilation of the Official Records of the Union and Confederate Armies*, 1997, [CD-ROM], Carmel, IN: Guild Press of Indiana, Series I, Vol XXXV/1 [S#65], pp 448-451.

1st Florida Men known to Participate:

Seaborn S. Baggett, Co F, Corporal
Curtis G. H. Bagwell, Co F, Private
Daniel Monroe Dansby, Co F, Private
Emanuel George W. Dansby, Co F, Private
Hiram D. Dansby, Co F, Private
Leroy Davis, Co F, Private
Marion W. Franklin, Co A, Private
Albert Gill, Co A, Private
Lorenzo D. Gill, Co A, Bugler
Adam Cornelius Hollinger, Co E, Sergeant
Isaiah M. Morgan, Co C, Sergeant
Joseph Ganes Sanders, Co F, 2nd Lt.
James R. N. Woodham, Co F, Sergeant

Likely the rest of Co F enlisted in November 1864 also participated

Summary of events:

This expedition, led by Lt. Colonel Andrew B. Spurling of the 2nd Maine Veteran Cavalry, left Pensacola on 17 November with approximately 450 men. Records do not indicate the reason for the movement north from Pensacola but it was likely meant to harass and clean out some of the forward Confederate companies and to gather intelligence from the countryside and the Confederates. They camped that night about 4 miles from 15 Mile House at a point along the railroad and about eleven miles from Pensacola.[66]

At 3:00 a.m. the next morning they resumed the march north along the railroad with Lt. Joseph Sanders commanding Company F of the 1st FCUV in the advance guard. Twice during the march north, the advance guard came upon Confederate pickets that were captured. The second group captured indicated that they were to be relieved at 10 o'clock. The advance guard was sent forward to intercept the relief men. These men were also captured and the

---

[66] *The War of the Rebellion: A Compilation of the Official Records of the Union and Confederate Armies*, 1997, [CD-ROM], Carmel, IN: Guild Press of Indiana, Series I, Vol XLIV [S#92], pp 418-419.

column marched to the bridge at Pine Barren Creek. Here an additional picket was captured without firing a shot and alerting the Confederate camp nearby.[67]

Spurling moved the advance guard led by Lt. Sanders and several squadrons across the bridge and made a dash for the Confederate camp, succeeding in capturing 38 men, 47 horses, 3 mules and 75 stands of arms. Before leaving the camp, Spurling burned the barracks, stables and shelters along with the commissary and quartermaster stores. The march back to Fort Barrancas ended around midnight of the 18th, arriving back in the Fort with prisoners, mules and horses. In his after-action report, Spurling specifically mentioned and highly praised the leadership of Lt. Joseph G. Sanders who was in command of the forward squadrons during the entire engagement.[68]

Expedition to Mitchell & Pine Barren Creek – 12/13-19/64

1864 Location: The town of Pollard, Alabama just north of the Florida/Alabama line on the road running north from Pensacola, Florida.

Current Location: South of Brewton, Alabama in the community of Pollard. The community is located just off Highway 29/31.

Union Regiments Participating:

Colonel George D. Robinson, commanding
    2nd Maine Veteran Cavalry
    82nd U.S Colored Infantry
    86th U.S. Colored Infantry
    97th U.S. Colored Infantry

---

[67] *The War of the Rebellion: A Compilation of the Official Records of the Union and Confederate Armies*, 1997, [CD-ROM], Carmel, IN: Guild Press of Indiana, Series I, Vol XLIV [S#92], pp 418-419.
[68] *The War of the Rebellion: A Compilation of the Official Records of the Union and Confederate Armies*, 1997, [CD-ROM], Carmel, IN: Guild Press of Indiana, Series I, Vol XLIV [S#92], pp 418-419.

1ˢᵗ FCUV, mounted men

Confederate regiments participating:

General St. John R. Liddell, commanding
    Unidentified troops

Victor: Draw

1ˢᵗ Florida Cavalry men known to have participated

Eldred Benjamin Allen, Co E, Private
Zachariah R. Ard, Co E, Corporal
Seaborn S. Baggett, Co F, Corporal
Charles P. Bell, Co E, Private
Simeon Wilder Burleson, Co A, Corporal
William H. Buzbee, Co E, Corporal
Bethel Haines Callahan, Co E, Private
William Giles Caswell, Co E, Private
Henry H. Creamer, Co A, Corporal
William R. Crider, Co A, Private
Daniel Monroe Dansby, Co F, Private
Emanuel George W. Dansby, Co F, Private
Hiram D. Dansby, Co F, Private
Franklin J. Davis, Co E, Sergeant
Thomas Davis, Co E, Private
William S. Davis, Co E, Bugler
Henry H. Dixon, Co A, Sergeant
James D. Donaldson, Co A, Corporal
Charles Dumont, Co E, Private
James Dyson, Co A, Private
Marion W. Franklin, Co A, Private
Joseph Garrett, Co E, Private
Albert Gill, Co A, Private
Lorenzo D. Gill, Co A, Bugler
Emanuel R. Grubbs, Co E, Bugler
John Marcus L. Hathaway, Co E, Private
Joseph B. Hewett, Co A, Corporal
John Allen Hodge, Co D, Private
Godfrey Lee Holley, Co E, Corporal
Adam Cornelius Hollinger, Co E, Sergeant
John G. R. Hudson, Co A, Private

Andrew Jackson Johnson, Co A, Private
George H. Johnson, Co E, Private
John L. Kennedy, Co C, Private
Francis Lyons, Co E, Captain
Griffin Melvin, Co E, Corporal
Warren Mills, Co E, Private
Michael M. Moniac, Co E, Private
Isaac P. Mooney, Co E, Private
William A.C. Norton, Co C, Corporal
Jonathan Paulk, Co E, Private
Thomas Pullum, Co E, Sergeant
Soverign Frederick Ray, Co A, Sergeant
Samuel Benjamin Roberson, Co E, Corporal
Daniel L. Robinson, Co E, Private
Joseph Ganes Sanders, Co F, 2nd Lt.
Benjamin F. Stearns, Co A, Sergeant
George W. Stewart, Co E, Bugler
James H. Stewart, Co E, Sergeant
Reason Strickland, Co E, Private
Dawson T. Tramell, Co E, Sergeant
Jordan L. Waters, Co A, Bugler
Burton H. Watson, Co A, Corporal
John W. Watson, Co A, Private
Richard B. Wright, Co E, Corporal

Summary of events:

Pollard, Alabama was the location where the Confederates who remained in the area withdrew to when they left Pensacola in 1862. It was one of the larger communities along the Florida/Alabama boundary above Pensacola and during the war it was a major depot and junction on the railroad line between Montgomery and Mobile. Remaining in Pollard allowed the Confederates to protect the railroad from the Union and to scout and make forays into Florida.

This expedition was sent out to destroy the depot and other public buildings and infrastructure, and a significant amount of the public property including forage, clothing, camp and garrison equipment. The force under Colonel Robinson carried out their instructions; burning government and railroad buildings and taking baggage and supplies. On their return back along the road to Pensacola they encountered an enemy force up from Mobile commanded by General Liddell. Heavy fighting occurred from the Little Escambia Creek to Pine Barren Creek. At Pine Barren Creek the Confederates were finally repulsed and did not re-engage the Union. According to Confederate reports the Union was pursued for thirty miles, "losing a portion of their transportation, baggage and supplies" and leaving "many dead negro troops" on the road.[69] The Union troops returned to Fort Barrancas with about 30 prisoners and reported loss of 1 officer and 16 men killed and 3 officers and 61 men wounded.[70]

Expedition to Perdido Mills, AL – mid-February, 1865

1865 Location: Perdido Mills, Baldwin County, Alabama

Current Location: Crossing the Perdido would have likely taken place at Nueces' Ferry which was near where the river entered into the Bay. The mill was likely in the area between today's towns of Seminole and Lillian on the west side of the Perdido River.

Union regiments participating:

Lieutenant Cyrus P. Pickard, commanding
    1st FCUV

Confederate regiments participating:

    6th Alabama Cavalry

Victor: N/A

---

[69] *The War of the Rebellion: A Compilation of the Official Records of the Union and Confederate Armies*, 1997, [CD-ROM], Carmel, IN: Guild Press of Indiana, Series I, Vol XLIV [S#92], p 449.
[70] *The War of the Rebellion: A Compilation of the Official Records of the Union and Confederate Armies*, 1997, [CD-ROM], Carmel, IN: Guild Press of Indiana, Series I, Vol XLIV [S#92], p 449.

1st Florida Men Known to Participate:

>None mentioned specifically, but records indicate 50 men participated, possibility from Company D.

Summary of events:

Under the command of Lieutenant C. B. Pickard, fifty men from the 1st FCUV were sent to Baldwin County to capture the Confederate pickets at Perdido Mills. They crossed the Perdido River but found no Confederate pickets. On the return march to Pensacola the men came across tracks of three rebel scouts. They were successful in capturing two of the men belonging to the 6th Alabama Cavalry.[71]

Sander's Detachment to Alabama

1865 Location: Choctawhatchee Bay north to what was then Coffee and Dale Counties, AL.

Current Location(s): There are no current approximate routes from the northern portion of Choctawhatchee Bay to the towns of Geneva and Newton, AL. Geneva is northwest of Bonifay, just above the Florida/Alabama line and Newton is east of Enterprise, AL.

Union Men participating:[72]

2nd Lt. Joseph G. Sanders, commanding
>According to Sander's file there were 30 men:
>>4 privates from Co. A;
>>4 privates from Co. B;
>>2 privates and 2 sergeants from Co. C;
>>4 privates from Co. D;
>>3 privates and 1 sergeant from Co., E;

---

[71] *The War of the Rebellion: A Compilation of the Official Records of the Union and Confederate Armies*, 1997, [CD-ROM], Carmel, IN: Guild Press of Indiana, Series I, Vol XLIX/1 [S#103], pp 71-72.
[72] Joseph G. Sanders, compiled military record (Lt, Company F, 1st Florida Cavalry), *Compiled Service Records of Volunteer Union Soldiers Who Served in Organization from the State of Florida*, M400 (Washington, D.C.: The National Archives and Records Administration), Rolls 1-6 & 11.

9 privates and 1 sergeant from Co. F.

1st Florida Men Known to Participate:

Mentioned in each Man's or Sander's Muster Roll:

J. Elijah Adams, Co A, Private
Zachariah R. Ard, Co E, Private (made a statement during hearing)
Berry E. Bagwell, Co F, Private
William W. Barnes, Co A, Private – left in Skipperville, AL - broken leg
Constantine Butler, Co A, Private
Daniel Cato, Co F, Private
William B. Ellis, Co F, Private
James H. Evans, Co D, Corporal (made a statement during hearing)
Joseph D. Gatlin, Co E, Private (made a statement during hearing)
Joseph J. Graves, Co E, Private
Wiley F. Harrison, Co A, Sergeant (made a statement during hearing)
William F. Holley, Co D, Corporal
Edmond Jordan, Co F, Sergeant
James B. Kemp, Co F, Private
James E. Malloy, Co C, Private (made a statement during hearing)
Randal K. McDaniel, Co F, Private
Alfred C. McMillion, Co C, Sergeant
Thomas T. Murphy, Co B, Private (made a statement during hearing)
Daniel W. Paul, Co D, Private
John A. Paul, Co D, Private
William W. Pickron, Co B, Private
George M. Richardson, Co C, Sergeant
Samuel C. Settles, Co F, Sergeant
Sampson J. Shellhouse, Co F, Private
Joshua E. Wheeless, Co F, Private/Bugler

Mentioned in Testimony but no other records:

John Donelson (Murphy indicated he was killed)
Elias Stagner (Murphy indicated he was killed)

Mentioned in testimony but no other indication that he participated:

Celestine Josiah Ward, Co B, Sergeant

Summary of events:

This episode in the history of the war in South Alabama and Northwest Florida is certainly one of the most controversial. With more than its share of anger, assumptions and prevarication, it is not surprising that sorting through what has come down to the current day is problematic. And with most intense arguments between two sides of an issue, the truth likely lies somewhere in the middle.

Joseph G. Sanders and his family were in Dale County, Alabama in 1860 and in October 1861 he joined Captain Archer Griffeth's Company of the Mitchell Guards as a private for a period of 12 months. This company became Co. C of the 27th Regiment Georgia Infantry, which was subsequently changed to the 31st Regiment Georgia Infantry around April 1862. On 13 May 1862, he became a Captain in the 31st Georgia Infantry by election. Other than a period of recovery from a wound received at Sharpsburg/Antietam and a furlough, he appears to have served honorably and continuously with the Confederacy until he resigned on 29 January 1864 for unknown reasons. Val McGee in his article on Sanders references a letter by Isaac G. Bradwell, who served with Sanders in the 31st Georgia, which indicated an ongoing conflict between Clement Evans, Colonel of the regiment, and Sanders who was Captain of his company. Bradwell indicated in his letter than Evans had never accepted the men's election of Sanders as Captain but that Sanders had been an able Captain and courageous in battle.[73]

Regardless of the reason, he resigned and went home to Dale County. Though he had resigned, and was therefore not a deserter, he was still subject to the draft which by early 1864 was gathering up any able bodied white man between 17 and 50. As a millwright, Sanders could not claim an exemption so it would seem likely that weighting his options left him unable to remain at

---

[73] McGee, Val L, "The Confederate Who Switched Sides - The Saga of Captain Joseph G. Sanders." *The Alabama Review: A Quarterly Journal of Alabama History* (1994) 47: pp 20-28.

home and he made the decision to join the Union at Pensacola.[74] What is unknown with any specificity is how much time, if any, he spent with the gangs of deserters who were terrorizing the area before joining the Union.

Sanders joined the 1st FCUV on 5July1864 as a 2nd Lieutenant and led an advance guard of troops during the 17-18 November 1864 expedition to Pine Barren Creek. Lt. Colonel Spurling acknowledged his leadership in his reports on the expedition.[75] So it would seem reasonable that when someone was needed to lead a recruiting expedition into the interior that Lt. Sanders would be chosen. On 20 February 1865, he was ordered to take 30 men and bring in recruits from Santa Rosa, Walton and Holmes Counties and return within 14 days.

According to Sanders' statement in June 1865, he and his men took the steamer Matamoras to East Pass, Florida where they proceeded north for two days.[76] According to the statement of James Evans they were near Hewett's Bluff in Holmes County when Sanders disbanded them into three squads, each commanded by a non-commissioned officer, and kept a few men to travel with him. Sanders stated he did this because of the scarcity of rations and the men's "sore feet". He told them to procure horses and report to him at the campground on Big Creek in Dale County, Alabama.[77]

Lengthening their stay out beyond the 14 days is the first point of departure from his orders. According to Evans' account they

---

[74] McGee, Val L, "The Confederate Who Switched Sides - The Saga of Captain Joseph Sanders." *The Alabama Review: A Quarterly Journal of Alabama History* (1994) 47: pp 20-28.
[75] *The War of the Rebellion: A Compilation of the Official Records of the Union and Confederate Armies*, 1997, [CD-ROM], Carmel, IN: Guild Press of Indiana, Series I, Vol XLIV [S#92], pp 418-419.
[76] Joseph G. Sanders, compiled military record (Lt, Company F, 1st Florida Cavalry), *Compiled Service Records of Volunteer Union Soldiers Who Served in Organization from the State of Florida*, M400 (Washington, D.C.: The National Archives and Records Administration), Rolls 1-6 & 11.
[77] Joseph G. Sanders, compiled military record (Lt, Company F, 1st Florida Cavalry), *Compiled Service Records of Volunteer Union Soldiers Who Served in Organization from the State of Florida*, M400 (Washington, D.C.: The National Archives and Records Administration), Rolls 1-6 & 11.

disbanded into separate groups on 2 March to meet again on 14 March above Newton in Dale County, Alabama. This date of 14 March was well beyond the fourteen days of the order. If he was to collect recruits from the three Florida counties, why go north into Alabama at all if food was scarce and feet were sore? So, detouring north was his second point of departure from his orders. Interestingly, a large percentage of the men Sanders had with him were from South Alabama, specifically Dale County. And a number of those giving reports during the investigation indicated they went home and then returned to Fort Barrancas without Sanders.[78]

At the time for the rendezvous only fourteen men had arrived at the specified location. According to Sanders this was due to the heavy rains in the area that had swollen the creeks and streams and made them impassable. By this point he indicated in his report that he had rounded up 34 recruits, so with them and his few men who had arrived he started to Fort Barrancas. According to Sanders the subsequent first confrontation with Confederate cavalry was due to a "traitor" in his ranks. He makes no indication whether that was one of his own men or one of the recruits or what he based that on. According to his report, 130 cavalrymen "cut me off from the only passes by which I could reach my regiment".[79] He goes on to say that in less than a week there were 700 men in his front but that they didn't attack because of an exaggerated report of his strength (unclear how he knew this). According to Sanders these men were withdrawn when the Union forces began their march to Montgomery.[80]

---

[78] Joseph G. Sanders, compiled military record (Lt, Company F, 1st Florida Cavalry), *Compiled Service Records of Volunteer Union Soldiers Who Served in Organization from the State of Florida*, M400 (Washington, D.C.: The National Archives and Records Administration), Rolls 1-6 & 11.

[79] Joseph G. Sanders, compiled military record (Lt, Company F, 1st Florida Cavalry), *Compiled Service Records of Volunteer Union Soldiers Who Served in Organization from the State of Florida*, M400 (Washington, D.C.: The National Archives and Records Administration), Rolls 1-6 & 11.

[80] Joseph G. Sanders, compiled military record (Lt, Company F, 1st Florida Cavalry), *Compiled Service Records of Volunteer Union Soldiers Who Served in Organization from the State of Florida*, M400 (Washington, D.C.: The National Archives and Records Administration), Rolls 1-6 & 11.

He started again to Fort Barrancas, according to his written testimony, and after a day and a half found the river crossings were still blocked so he returned to his camp. The two sides did engage (location unknown) because according to Sanders he captured and paroled 28 men before returning to his swamp camp. He then learned that the 1st FCUV had arrived in Montgomery (this would have been after April 25th) so he started there but after two days he learned they had returned to Fort Barrancas so he again returned to his swamp camp. After a few preparations and an attempt to recover a man who had been wounded he left again for Fort Barrancas and finally arrived on 14 June 1865.[81]

What is missing from Sanders' account is the raid on Newton, Alabama. According to an account by Jesse M. Carmichael of the subsequent engagement between the Confederates and Sanders' few men and recruits he had collected, Sanders was well known to the people of Dale County as a bushwhacker (a guerrilla or ambusher, often a member of the deserter gangs in the area) who had made a number of incursions into the county. What is unclear is whether these incursions were before Sanders joined the 1st FCUV when he was likely a member of one of the deserter gangs infesting the area or after joining the Union. Jesse Carmichael indicates that it was he and another man who rode out and observed the Union forces moving up toward Newton and then rode back to town. He indicated in his account that Sanders lost three men and five were wounded. The fact that this entire encounter is missing from Sanders' report would seem to indicate the third point of departure from his orders and clearly a lie of omission.[82]

---

[81] Joseph G. Sanders, compiled military record (Lt, Company F, 1st Florida Cavalry), *Compiled Service Records of Volunteer Union Soldiers Who Served in Organization from the State of Florida*, M400 (Washington, D.C.: The National Archives and Records Administration), Rolls 1-6 & 11.
[82] [Unknown Author] "Their Raid on Newton and How They Were Put to Flight - A Few Brave and Determined Men Are Powerful in Any Good Cause." *The Southern Star*. 1899. Battle of Newton website. Accessed 2015. www.battleofnewton.org/battlehistory.html.

Once the Confederate Cavalry located him it is very likely they made every attempt to pin him down in the swamps and to capture or kill him and his men. But none of that would have happened if he had obeyed his orders and returned from the Florida counties within fourteen days. In total twenty-three of his men returned on their own according to the final report of Brigadier General Asboth, even while Lt. Sanders was hindered by heavy rains, high water, bad roads and Confederate Cavalry.[83]

This episode in the history of the 1st FCUV has come down through time with much anger attached. The folks in Newton, and this general area of south Alabama, still tell this story as an indication of the behavior of the Union in the Gulf area during the war and the meanness of the deserter gangs. The problem is it is impossible to determine if this series of events occurred because Lt. Sanders couldn't seem to follow written orders without using his own interests or agenda to adjust them or if this was an unwritten order to him to create destruction. We are likely to never know the whole truth. Sanders gave his initial report concerning his and his men's absence on 25 June 1865. On 20 July 1865, he tendered his resignation to attend to his "suffering family". The resignation was accepted for the good of the service.[84]

Mobile Campaign – March – April, 1865

(Author's Note: the men listed in the following four sections (the Mobile campaign and the Occupation of Montgomery) were all with Lt. Colonel Spurling on one continuous march from Pensacola to Andalusia; then to Evergreen, Brewton Station, Pollard, Canoe and finally Fort Blakeley. Lucas' Cavalry Division left Fort Blakeley and marched to Montgomery with Spurling's unit attached. The men are listed under the engagements noted in

---

[83] Joseph G. Sanders, compiled military record (Lt, Company F, 1st Florida Cavalry), *Compiled Service Records of Volunteer Union Soldiers Who Served in Organization from the State of Florida*, M400 (Washington, D.C.: The National Archives and Records Administration), Rolls 1-6 & 11.
[84] Joseph G. Sanders, compiled military record (Lt, Company F, 1st Florida Cavalry), *Compiled Service Records of Volunteer Union Soldiers Who Served in Organization from the State of Florida*, M400 (Washington, D.C.: The National Archives and Records Administration), Rolls 1-6 & 11.

their individual muster roll records. While these records are what we must work with, they are not always accurate or complete. It is likely that all of them were on all these engagements of the Mobile Campaign and the occupation of Montgomery unless they deserted along the way.)

Raid in South Alabama – 3/21-31/65

1865 Location: Pensacola to Crigler's Mill (by steamer) on the east side of the Blackwater River 4 miles south of Milton then northeast to Andalusia, AL (see Appendix, Map of Route)

Current Location(s): Pensacola along the coast to the east side of the river in East Milton. The route taken by the troops was likely on a road that no longer exists (see map insert at end of this section) but ran approximately north from the east side of the river to the vicinity of McClellan on Florida Highway 191/Alabama 19. Then the route followed northeast to Henley Roberts on AL CR4, Dixie on AL Highway 29 and then Andalusia, AL.

Union Regiments Participating:

Lt. Col. Andrew B. Spurling, commanding:
    2nd Illinois Cavalry, Maj. F. Moore, commanding
    2nd Maine Cavalry, Maj. Charles A. Miller, commanding
    1st FCUV

Confederate Regiments Participating:

None

Victor: Union

1st Florida Men Known to Participate:

John Anderson Allen, Co D, Private
Willis Anderson, Co A, Private
John Wesley Ard, Co D, Private
Curtis G. H. Bagwell, Co F, Private
Henry Bohannan, Co F, Private
Benjamin R. Braxton, Co A, Private

John Wesley Brown, Co A, Private
Daniel Nathaniel Carnley, Co D, Private
Joseph B. Carroll, Co C/D, 1st Lt.
John Richard Cauley, Co C, Sergeant
James Alexander Cockcroft, Co D, Private
Micajah Allen Cockcroft, Co D, Corporal
George W. Cox, Co D, Private
William R. Crider, Co A, Private
Jefferson H. Eddy, Co D, Private
Albert Gill, Co A, Private
Lorenzo D. Gill, Co A, Bugler
Joseph B. Hewett, Co A, Corporal
Green Norris, Co D, Private
Ephraim C. Parrish, Co D, Private
John Peacock, Co D, Private
Akis Franklin Register, Co D, Private
Thomas Sellers, Co D, Sergeant
Bennett G. Senterfitt, Co D, Private
Isaac Smith, Co D, Private
Josiah H. Snowden, Co D, Private
Abijah Lewis Sowell, Co D, Bugler
Joshua A. Yon, Co D, Private

Summary of events:

This expedition was intended to support the upcoming Mobile Campaign by distracting the Confederacy from the immediate Mobile area and to cut the Florida & Alabama Railroad at Evergreen. Led by Lt. Colonel Spurling of the 2nd Maine Cavalry, the force set out on March 21st on the steamer Matamoras and landed at Crigler's Mill on the east side of the Blackwater River about four miles south of Milton, Florida. Spurling had 847 men with him, 182 being officers and men from the 1st FCUV. Two days before, on the 19th, Capt. E. D. Johnson of the 2nd Maine had been sent to Milton with two companies of the 1st FCUV to push the Confederate pickets north toward Pollard, Alabama. He then held his position until Spurling and his men arrived. They remained in Milton after Spurling's troops left Crigler's Mill until noon on the 21st when they crossed the Blackwater River and caught up with Spurling's men moving toward Andalusia, Alabama.[85]

Per Spurling's report nothing much happened on the first day of the march. The constant rains that had preceded the march and the rain on the 21st had left the creeks swollen in the area but he reported that the roads were in fair condition. At 6:00 p.m. on the 21st they made camp about twenty-five miles from Milton. Leaving at 5:00 a.m. the following morning they continued their march northeast, passing through what was then Lewis Station across the line into Alabama. It was likely between here and the crossing of the Conecuh River where they took several Confederate prisoners and "quite a number" of horses and mules. They made camp the night of the 22nd about six miles out of Andalusia.[86]

During the night, the picket brought in two couriers bearing dispatches from the Captain stationed at McGowan's Bridge to the commanding officer at Andalusia indicating a force of 2000 was marching toward Andalusia, directing them to arm all able-bodied men and be prepared. It also stated that a force under the command of a Captain Keyser was retreating in front of the Union forces and would be in Andalusia to help repulse the Yankees. It closed by estimating that the force would arrive in Andalusia on the evening of the 23rd (they were six miles out on the evening of the 22nd).[87]

Spurling moved his men at 4:00 a.m. the next morning and arrived in Andalusia at 5:30 a.m., meeting no resistance. He destroyed all the arms and ammunition and the small amount of government property. Approximately two months later, Brig. General Asboth indicated that 656 (about 10% of the 1860 Covington County total

---

[85] *The War of the Rebellion: A Compilation of the Official Records of the Union and Confederate Armies*, 1997, [CD-ROM], Carmel, IN: Guild Press of Indiana, Series I, Vol XLIX/1 [S#103], pp 309-310.

[86] *The War of the Rebellion: A Compilation of the Official Records of the Union and Confederate Armies*, 1997, [CD-ROM], Carmel, IN: Guild Press of Indiana, Series I, Vol XLIX/1 [S#103], pp 309-310.

[87] *The War of the Rebellion: A Compilation of the Official Records of the Union and Confederate Armies*, 1997, [CD-ROM], Carmel, IN: Guild Press of Indiana, Series I, Vol XLIX/1 [S#103], pp 309-310.

population) citizens of Covington County had signed an oath of allegiance and applied for U.S. protection.[88] This county also provided a sizable portion of the men from Alabama who served with the 1st FCUV so it is not surprising that he met with no resistance from the townspeople in surrendering. Spurling and his troops left Andalusia around 8:00 a.m. on the 23rd, marching to Evergreen, Alabama for the next leg of his orders: cutting the railroad at Evergreen.[89]

FL/AL RR – Evergreen to Brewton Station – 3/23-26/65

1865 Location: Andalusia to Evergreen, Alabama then south, southwest to Sparta and southeast to Brooklyn, AL and back to the west to Pollard, AL.

Current Location(s): Andalusia along Highway 84/12 to Evergreen, CR 29, then 25 to Old Sparta, back to CR 29 to CR 6 and Brooklyn. CR 43 to Highway 29 then west to East Brewton. Turn right where Highway 29 joins Highway 31, go through Brewton and then south on 29/31 to Pollard (turn left at historical marker).

Union Regiments Participating:

Lt. Col. Andrew B. Spurling, commanding
    2nd Illinois Cavalry, Maj. F. Moore, commanding
    2nd Maine Cavalry, Maj. Charles A. Miller, commanding
    1st FCUV

Confederate Regiments Participating:

None

Victor: Union

---

[88] *The War of the Rebellion: A Compilation of the Official Records of the Union and Confederate Armies*, 1997, [CD-ROM], Carmel, IN: Guild Press of Indiana, Series I, Vol XLIX/2 [S#104], pp 826-827.
[89] *The War of the Rebellion: A Compilation of the Official Records of the Union and Confederate Armies*, 1997, [CD-ROM], Carmel, IN: Guild Press of Indiana, Series I, Vol XLIX/1 [S#103], pp 309-310.

1st Florida Men Known to Participate:

Curtis G. H. Bagwell, Co F, Private
Arthur Bailey, Co E, Private
Martin Braxton, Co A, Private
John Wesley Brown, Co A, Private
William Henry Carmichael, Co D, Private
William R. Crider, Co A, Private
Daniel Monroe Dansby, Co F, Corporal
Emanuel George W. Dansby, Co F, Private
Hiram D. Dansby, Co F, Private
Albert Gill, Co A, Private
Lorenzo D. Gill, Co A, Bugler
Joseph B. Hewett, Co A, Corporal
Noah Powell Kilpatrick, Co B, Private

Summary of events:

A primary reason for this part of the expedition into Alabama, as the Mobile Campaign got underway, was to cut the railroad between Montgomery and Mobile at Evergreen. After taking Andalusia without resistance, Lt. Colonel Spurling and his troops set out for the community of Evergreen, Alabama around 8:00 a.m. on the morning of March 23rd. Per his report, he met with no resistance on this part of his march until he was about six miles from Evergreen.[90] There he came upon three Confederates. They attempted to escape but two were wounded in the attempt and all were taken prisoner. One of the wounded was Lt. Watts, of General Clanton's staff, and the son of the Governor of Alabama.[91]

They continued marching and reached the railroad five miles above Evergreen around midnight. The telegraph lines were cut and the track was torn up. At 4:30 a.m. on the 24th a train arrived

---

[90] *The War of the Rebellion: A Compilation of the Official Records of the Union and Confederate Armies*, 1997, [CD-ROM], Carmel, IN: Guild Press of Indiana, Series I, Vol XLIX/1 [S#103], pp 309-310.
[91] *The War of the Rebellion: A Compilation of the Official Records of the Union and Confederate Armies*, 1997, [CD-ROM], Carmel, IN: Guild Press of Indiana, Series I, Vol XLIX/1 [S#103], pp 309-310 and Roberts, C. C., *General Andrew B. Spurling and Second Maine Cavalry*, 1904, p 68.

from Pollard. According to Spurling in his report it was "thrown from the track, set on fire and destroyed." It consisted of one locomotive, 1 baggage car, 2 passenger cars and 4 platform cars.[92] He does not indicate if any injuries or deaths occurred.

A few hours later the train from Montgomery arrived and was captured and destroyed resulting in the capture of 93 soldiers and 7 officers. This train was pulling a slightly larger load and consisted of 1 locomotive, 1 baggage car, 4 passenger cars and 2 freight cars. The load included corn and clothing, all of which was destroyed. After capturing both trains, the army continued to Evergreen where they obtained forage and rations and destroyed some military stores. Rolling stock at the station was burned. Spurling now turned the men toward the south, southeast and headed for Sparta about 2:00 p.m. on the 24th.[93]

Sparta was the county seat of Conecuh County, Alabama in 1865. It was a well-developed community and lay along the railroad track between Mobile and Montgomery.[94] Spurling and his men arrived around 4:00 p.m. and immediately set to destroying the six box cars they found there, as well as trestle-work and the stores and military material stored at the depot. The troops made camp at Sparta on the night of the 24th.[95]

The next morning the column moved out from Sparta at 5:00 a.m., heading toward Brooklyn, Alabama. They arrived in Brooklyn around 11:30 a.m. and continued on the road back to the southwest toward Brewton Station. At sundown, they stopped for the night about twelve miles outside Brewton Station. The following morning, they completed the march to Brewton Station,

---

[92] *The War of the Rebellion: A Compilation of the Official Records of the Union and Confederate Armies*, 1997, [CD-ROM], Carmel, IN: Guild Press of Indiana, Series I, Vol XLIX/1 [S#103], pp 309-310.
[93] *The War of the Rebellion: A Compilation of the Official Records of the Union and Confederate Armies*, 1997, [CD-ROM], Carmel, IN: Guild Press of Indiana, Series I, Vol XLIX/1 [S#103], pp 309-310.
[94] Riley, B. F. (Rev), "History of Conecuh County, Alabama." 1881, *Genealogy Trails*. http://genealogytrails.com/ala/conecuh/history_riley.html, Chapter VII
[95] *The War of the Rebellion: A Compilation of the Official Records of the Union and Confederate Armies*, 1997, [CD-ROM], Carmel, IN: Guild Press of Indiana, Series I, Vol XLIX/1 [S#103], pp 309-310.

arriving around 11:00 am to find the planks over the creek had been removed. Spurling had the men repair the bridge and sent a dismounted advance guard across to reconnoiter. According to Spurling's report, Confederates were located behind some breastworks and an exchange of fire occurred before the Confederates successfully retreated. Lt. Vose and two enlisted men from the 2nd Maine were wounded.[96]

After finishing the bridge repair the troops continued down to Pollard, Alabama, arriving there about 6:00 p.m. on Sunday, March 26th. There Spurling met up with the second column of the Army marching north from Pensacola. Spurling reported that his expedition had yielded 120 prisoners, 200 Negroes, and 250 horses and mules.[97]

The March to, and Siege of, Ft. Blakeley

1865 Location: Pollard to Canoe Station, west to Stockton and then to Fort Blakeley, Alabama.

Current Location(s): Pollard south on Highway 31 to Canoe (between Flomaton and Atmore), CR 47 to Rabun then south to CR 94, west on CR 94 to Highway 59, south to Stockton. Highway 225 south from Stockton to Fort Blakeley.

Union Regiments Participating:

(Author's Note: the column from Pensacola and Spurling's column became part of the much larger force around Mobile once they arrived at Fort Blakeley)

Maj. General Edward E. R. S. Canby commanding
    XIII Corps, Maj. Gen. Gordon Granger
        1st Division, Brig. Gen. James C. Veatch

---

[96] *The War of the Rebellion: A Compilation of the Official Records of the Union and Confederate Armies*, 1997, [CD-ROM], Carmel, IN: Guild Press of Indiana, Series I, Vol XLIX/1 [S#103], pp 309-310.
[97] *The War of the Rebellion: A Compilation of the Official Records of the Union and Confederate Armies*, 1997, [CD-ROM], Carmel, IN: Guild Press of Indiana, Series I, Vol XLIX/1 [S#103], pp 309-310.

        2nd Division, Brig. Gen. Christopher C. Andrews
        3rd Division, Brig. Gen. William P. Benton
XVI Corps, Maj. Gen. Andrew Jackson Smith
        1st Division, Brig. Gen. John McArthur
        2nd Division, Brig. Gen. Kenner Garrard
        3rd Division, Brig. Gen. Eugene A. Carr

Pensacola Column:

Maj. General Frederick Steele commanding
    First Division, Brig. Gen. John P. Hawkins
        First Brigade, Brig. Gen. William A. Pile
            73rd U.S. Colored Troops
            82nd U.S. Colored Troops
            86th U.S. Colored Troops
        Second Brigade, Col. Hiram Scofield
            47th U. S. Colored Troops
            50th U. S. Colored Troops
            51st U. S. Colored Troops
        Third Brigade, Col. Charles W. Drew
            48th U. S. Colored Troops
            68th U. S. Colored Troops
            76th U. S. Colored Troops
    Lucas' Cavalry Division, Brig. General Thomas J. Lucas
        First Brigade, Col. Morgan H. Chrysler
            1st Louisiana
            31st Massachusetts
            2nd New York Veteran
        Second Brigade, Lt. Col. Andrew B. Spurling
            1st Florida
            2nd Illinois
            2nd Maine
        Massachusetts Light Artillery, 2nd Battery

Confederate Regiments Participating:

Brig. General St. John R. Liddell commanding
    Liddell's Division, Brig Gen. St. John R. Liddell
        Gibson's Brigade, Brig Gen. Randall L. Gibson
        French's Division, Brig. Gen. Francis M. Cockrell
        Cockrell's Brigade, Col. James McCown
        Ector's Brigade, Col. David Coleman
        Sear's Brigade, Col. Thomas N. Adaire
        Clanton's Brigade, Brig. Gen. James H. Clanton
        Armistead's Cavalry Brigade
        Maury's Command, Col. Henry Maury
        Unassigned Brigades
            Thomas' Brigade
            Taylor's Command
            Holtzclaw's Brigade
            Sappers and Miners

Victor: Union

1st Florida Men Known to Participate:

Eldred Benjamin Allen, Co E, Private
Curtis G. H. Bagwell, Co F, Private
Charles P. Bell, Co E, Private
Henry Bohannan, Co F, Private
Bethel Haines Callahan, Co E, Private
William Giles Caswell, Co E, Private
Daniel Monroe Dansby, Co F, Corporal
Emanuel George W. Dansby, Co F, Private
Hiram D. Dansby, Co F, Private
Franklin J. Davis, Co E, Sergeant
William S. Davis, Co E, Bugler
Marion W. Franklin, Co A, Private
Joseph Garrett, Co E, Private
Emanuel R. Grubbs, Co E, Bugler
John Marcus Lafayette Hathaway, Co E, Private
Godfrey Lee Holley, Co E, Corporal/Sergeant
Adam Cornelius Hollinger, Co E, Sergeant
George H. Johnson, Co E, Private
Griffin Melvin, Co E, Corporal

Warren Mills, Co E, Private
Michael M. Moniac, Co E, Private
James I. Norris, Co A, Private
Jonathan Paulk, Co E, Private
Samuel Benjamin Roberson, Co E, Corporal
Daniel L. Robinson, Co E, Private
George W. Stewart, Co E, Bugler
James H. Stewart, Co E, Sergeant
Reason Strickland, Co E, Private/Corporal
John D. K. P. Thomas, Co E, Private
Richard B. Wright, Co E, Corporal

Summary of events:

At the start of the Federal final push to take Mobile two columns had been sent out from Pensacola. One commanded by Lt. Colonel Spurling and heading from Pensacola to Milton then north to Andalusia and over to cut the railroad at Evergreen; and one commanded by the overall commander of the forces out of Pensacola, Maj. General Frederick Steele, that marched straight up from Pensacola to Pollard. The two columns joined up in Pollard and moved out toward Mobile.

The column arrived at Canoe, Alabama in a heavy downpour that had left the roads nearly impassable. Canoe had been the headquarters of General Armistead's Brigade (6th and 8th Alabama Cavalry) but the location had been abandoned by the Confederate Army by the time the Federals arrived. The Federal Army was extremely short of supplies at this point. The depots at Pollard and Canoe did not provide much and Asboth had been unsuccessful at getting supplies up the Escambia River to re-supply the troops. In addition, the countryside was pretty much destitute of resources. Some teams of oxen driven to the depot at Canoe by the public for hauling away supplies were used as beef for the men.[98]

---

[98] *The War of the Rebellion: A Compilation of the Official Records of the Union and Confederate Armies*, 1997, [CD-ROM], Carmel, IN: Guild Press of Indiana, Series I, Vol XLIX/1 [S#103], pp 279-282.

The weather continued to hamper movement, requiring the men to corduroy the road as they moved forward but part of the command did reach Weatherford on the 29th. Here Steele sent two hundred handpicked men under Major Perry to Montgomery Landing for information and to capture a steamboat to bring back corn and beef to the troops. These men re-joined the command on the 30th with much needed beef. They had communicated with the command around Mobile and were instructed to march to Holyoke.[99] Unfortunately, the lack of forage and still limited rations forced them to Stockton, Alabama where they found enough for several days and a gristmill to process the corn.[100]

On April 1st, Lt. Colonel Spurling's command was sent ahead of the column to determine the best route from Stockton to Holyoke and to attempt to communicate with the command around Mobile concerning the column's movements. About four and a half miles out from Blakeley where the road forked toward Holyoke, the road was barricaded with an outpost of Confederate cavalry and infantry. Spurling charged and captured the battle flag of the 46th Mississippi and 74 prisoners. Spurling sent back word of the engagement bringing the rest of Lucas' Cavalry and Hawkins' Division up from Carpenter's Station to assist. The Confederates were driven back to Blakeley and also withdrew troops from Sibley's Mill. During Spurling's charge a horse was blown to pieces by a torpedo and the rider was badly wounded. Spurling's response was to require the Confederate prisoners to clear the road of the remaining torpedoes.[101]

General Canby, commanding the Federal forces around Mobile, sent word to Steele to attempt to make Holyoke the evening of the 1st. However, that wasn't possible. The Confederates sent a

---

[99] *The War of the Rebellion: A Compilation of the Official Records of the Union and Confederate Armies*, 1997, [CD-ROM], Carmel, IN: Guild Press of Indiana, Series I, Vol XLIX/1 [S#103], pp 279-282.
[100] Andrews, Christopher Columbus, *History of the Campaign of Mobile: Including the Cooperative Operations of Gen. Wilson's Cavalry in Alabama.* (Bedford, MA: Applewood Books, no date), pp 116-118.
[101] *The War of the Rebellion: A Compilation of the Official Records of the Union and Confederate Armies*, 1997, [CD-ROM], Carmel, IN: Guild Press of Indiana, Series I, Vol XLIX/1 [S#103], pp 279-282.

strong line of skirmishers against the Union line held by Hawkins. The Confederates were pushed back to their entrenchment lines and Steele decided to hold the ground gained by his men since the investment of Blakeley was in the near future. This would hold the bridge over Bayou Minette at Sibley's Mill and make it impossible for the Confederates to replant charges on the road.[102]

On arriving at Fort Blakeley, Major General Steele in his report in the Official Records described the Confederate works as follows:

> "The place was inclosed (sic) by a line of works about two miles in extent, composed of redoubts constructed of earth and timber, with ditches in front, which redoubts were connected by continuous rifle pits, with salients and stockade work, making a continuous line from the enemy's left, on Tensas River, to his right, which rested on an impassable swamp and thicket. The two principal avenues of approach were known as the Stockton and the Pensacola roads. The former entered the works to the left of the center, and the latter to the right of the center. The redoubts commanded the ground in their front, and had an enfilading fire on portions of the roads and a crossfire on almost every point of them within the range of their guns. Three marshy ravines, entering the works at different points, were obstructed by fallen timber and transverse by stockades which connected with the rifle pits on either side. The forts were mounted with both light and heavy guns, and Coehorn mortars were distributed along the faces. There were two continuous lines of abatis around the works, and at some points three. Outside of these were rifle pits for sharpshooters.... The timber was slashed in front of the works for about 1,000 yards, and the character of the ground such as to require the construction of approaches."[103]

Spurling's command was ordered to gather up all the flatboats on the river for the purpose of moving troops against the

---

[102] *The War of the Rebellion: A Compilation of the Official Records of the Union and Confederate Armies*, 1997, [CD-ROM], Carmel, IN: Guild Press of Indiana, Series I, Vol XLIX/1 [S#103], pp 279-282.

[103] *The War of the Rebellion: A Compilation of the Official Records of the Union and Confederate Armies*, 1997, [CD-ROM], Carmel, IN: Guild Press of Indiana, Series I, Vol XLIX/1 [S#103], pp 282-284.

Confederates. He indicated on 8 April that he had managed to collect 12, enough to carry two to three thousand men. He also indicated in the same report that his men were now collecting cattle. At about the same time General Canby, in charge of all Federal forces around Mobile requested six men from Steele's command that were best acquainted with the area between the Alabama River and the Choctawhatchee and north to Montgomery. There is no indication that the 1st FCUV, or the rest of the cavalry with Steele, were used in the taking of Fort Blakeley but were used in the capacities indicated above. Spanish Fort, adjacent to Fort Blakeley fell on 8 April and Fort Blakeley fell the following day.

Occupation of Montgomery, AL, April-May 1865

1865 Location: Montgomery, Alabama and surrounding countryside.

Current Location(s): Montgomery and Wetumpka, Alabama

Union Regiments Participating:

Lucas' Cavalry Division, Brig. General Thomas J. Lucas
    First Brigade, Col. Morgan H. Chrysler
        1st Louisiana
        31st Massachusetts
        2nd New York Veteran
    Second Brigade, Lt. Col. Andrew B. Spurling
        1st FCUV
        2nd Illinois
        2nd Maine
        Massachusetts Light Artillery, 2nd Battery

Confederate Troops Participating:

15th Confederate Cavalry

1st Florida Men Known to Participate:

Robert S. Abbott, Co A, Sergeant/Private

Eldred Benjamin Allen, Co E, Private
John Anderson Allen, Co D, Private
John Wesley Ard, Co D, Private
Robert T. Atkins, Co F, Private
Henry L. Baggett, Co F, Private
Elias L. Barnes, Co A, Private
William Lafayette Barrow, Co B, Private
Uriah Barton, Co F, Private
Charles P. Bell, Co E, Private
James M. Bishop, Co D, Private
Henry Bohannan, Co F, Private
John Askar Bolton, Co B, Private
Elijah Boon, Co F, Private
George M. D. Bottom, Co F, Private
Martin Braxton, Co A, Private
Daniel Eli Burdeshaw, Co F, Private
Simeon Wilder Burleson, Co A, Private
Bethel Haines Callahan, Co E, Private
William Henry Carmichael, Co D, Private
Frederick D. Carroll, Co C, Private
Joseph B. Carroll, Co C/D, 1st Lieutenant
William Cassida, Co E, Private
William Giles Caswell, Co E, Private
George Washington Caylor, Co B, Sergeant
James Alexander Cockcroft, Co D, Private
Micajah Allen Cockcroft, Co D, Corporal
George W. Cox, Co D, Private
John T. Coxwell, Co F, Private
William R. Crider, Co A, Private
James M. Crosby, Co C, Private
William T. Curry, Co E, Sergeant/Private
Jasper Cutherill, Co B, Private
Daniel Monroe Dansby, Co F, Corporal
Emanuel George W. Dansby, Co F, Private
Hiram D. Dansby, Co F, Private
Joshua Daughtry, Co B, Private
Franklin J. Davis, Co E, Sergeant
William S. Davis, Co E, Bugler
William C. Dockins, Co F, Private
James D. Donaldson, Co A, Corporal
Joseph William Donaldson, Co F, Private
Charles Dumont, Co E, Private

James Dyson, Co A, Private
Jefferson H. Eddy, Co D, Private
Asa Faulk, Co F, Private
Richard Fowler, Co A, Private
Marion W. Franklin, Co A, Private
Zinamon L. Garner, Co F, Private
Joseph Garrett, Co E, Private
Harvey H. Gatewood, Co E, Private
Albert Gill, Co A, Private
Lorenzo D. Gill, Co A, Bugler
John W. Givens, Co B, Private
Robert J. Givens, Co B, Corporal
John S. Godwin, Co C, Private
John Goodman, Co E, Private
Emanuel R. Grubbs, Co E, Bugler
Louis Marion Hall, Co C, Private
Robert Hardy, Co B, Bugler
James Wilburn Hathaway, Co E, Private
John Marcus Lafayette Hathaway, Co E, Private
John L. Henderson, Co F, Private
Joseph B. Hewett, Co A, Corporal
William Hicks, Co G, Private
Godfrey Lee Holley, Co E, Sergeant
Adam Cornelius Hollinger, Co E, Sergeant
William Wiliford Horton, Co E, Wagoner
Christopher C. Howard, Co B, Private
Francis Marion Hubbard, Co A, Private
Andrew J. Huckaby, Co A, Private
James T. Hudson, Co C, Corporal
John G. R. Hudson, Co A, Bugler
Andrew Jackson Johnson, Co A, Private
George H. Johnson, Co E, Private
Richard Jones, Co F, Undercook
Wright S. Jones, Co B, Private
Frederick C. Jost, Co B, 1st Lieutenant
Angus King, Co C, Private
Samuel P. Ludlam, Co A, Sergeant
William Thomas Manning, Co B, Private
John Thomas Martin, Co F, Private
Jonathan F. Martin, Co A, Wagoner
David McCuller, Co B, Corporal
Joseph McCurley, Co C, Private

Alexander C. McGee, Co F/E, Private
Robert Lewis Medlock, Co F, Teamster
Daniel V. Melvin, Co C, Private
Griffin Melvin, Co E, Corporal
James L. Miller, Co F, Private
Warren Mills, Co E, Private
Nathan K. Mims, Co F, Private
Michael M. Moniac, Co E, Private
Richard L. Moniac, Co F, Private
Hansel M. Murphy, Co F, Private
Silas D. Murphy, Co F, Private
Alexander (Adam) Wyrick Nettles, Co F, Farrier
Andrew J. Nobles, Co C, Private
Alvah Colby Norris, Co A, 1st Lieutenant
Green Norris, Co D, Private
Franklin Owens, Co A, Private
Ephraim C. Parrish, Co D, Private
Joel Pate, Co F, Private
Jonathan Paulk, Co E, Private
Thomas H. Pittman, Co F, 1st Sergeant
Andrew J. Potter, Co A, Undercook
James Jordan Prim, Co F, Quartermaster Sergeant
Akis Franklin Register, Co D, Private
Joseph M. Register, Co C, Private
Samuel Benjamin Roberson, Co E, Corporal
Daniel L. Robinson, Co E, Private
James W. Rogers, Co D, Private
Richard Wesley Scroggins, Co F, Private
Thomas Sellers, Co D, Quartermaster Sergeant
Bennett G. Senterfitt, Co D, Private
John W. Skinner, Co C, Corporal
William Smith, Co F, Corporal
Josiah H. Snowden, Co D, Private
Abijah Lewis Sowell, Co D, Bugler
Daniel W. Stagner, Co C, Sergeant
John M. Stagner, Co B, Private
Garrett S. Stanley, Co C, Corporal
Joseph S. Stanley, Co D, Private
Benjamin F. Stearns, Co A, 1st Sergeant
Reuben N. Stegall, Co B, Private
Benjamin F. Stephens, Co F, Private
George W. Stewart, Co E, Bugler

James H. Stewart, Co E, 1st Sergeant
James Pinckney Strickland, Co D, Private
John J. Strickland, Co D, Sergeant
Reason Strickland, Co E, Corporal
John D. K. P. Thomas, Co E, Private
Enoch Thompson, Co F, Private
Jesse Thompson, Co B, Private
Hezekiah Tolbert Jr., Co F, Bugler
Francis M. Vance, Co D, Private
Jordan L. Waters, Co A, Bugler
William H. Waters, Co A, Quartermaster Sergeant
John W. Watson, Co A, Private
Benjamin L. West, Co D, Private
Leonard Frank West, Co D, Corporal
William E. White, Co A, 1st Sergeant
William T. Fletcher Wilkinson, Co B, Private
James R. N. Woodham, Co F, Sergeant
Elias S. Worley, Co B, Private
Richard B. Wright, Co E, Corporal
Joshua A. Yon, Co D, Private

Summary of events:

On the morning of 5 April, Brigadier General Lucas moved out from just east of Fort Blakeley with all of his command, taking ten days of half rations and all the forage the men could carry. They went first to Claiborne where they engaged the 15th Confederate Cavalry. They then came back to Stockton and headed northeast to first Union Springs and then to Montgomery, Alabama. The column arrived in Montgomery around April 25th and remained there as part of the occupying force until May when they were ordered back to Fort Barrancas and became a part of the District of West Florida until they were mustered out on 17 November 1865 in Tallahassee. Florida.[104]

---

[104] Andrews, Christopher Columbus, *History of the Campaign of Mobile: Including the Cooperative Operations of Gen. Wilson's Cavalry in Alabama.* (Bedford, MA: Applewood Books, no date), 239-240.

Conclusions

What conclusions might be drawn from an assessment of this area of the United States prior to the War and how these men responded over time to the conflict? Does it tell us anything about "Unionists" in the Deep South during the War, or at least in the Florida panhandle and south Alabama, and what that might have meant at the time to their families, their communities and to themselves?

It might be appropriate to start with a discussion of what exactly was a Unionist during the War. It is a term that gets used pretty freely in discussions today about political sentiments before and during the conflict. It also gets confused with sentiments on race and slavery and on whether the Southern states should have seceded in cooperation with each other (co-operationist) and those who truly were opposed to secession at that time for the reasons put forth in at least some of the various secession conventions. Unionism in its purist sense might be defined as opposition to secession and creation of the Confederate States of America as a separate nation. Once the War started support of Unionism in its purist sense may have been a motivation for some, though most kept their feelings to themselves and a few trusted others, but more likely it was a response to the circumstances of the moment. This would indicate more a sentiment of pragmatism than Unionism. These sentiments included but may not have been confined to; 1) dissatisfaction with political decisions (draft, draft exemptions, confiscation), 2) dissatisfaction with military conditions (lack of food, clothing and adequate equipment), military command or military decisions (evacuations of large sections of Florida leaving the home front vulnerable, poor command or divisive command); 3) concern about circumstances at home with family (hunger, confiscation, and deserter gangs/security) and/or 4) what we might call now post-traumatic stress disorder (loss of friends and colleagues in battles and the horror of war in general).

There is little evidence that there was a sizable population of "Unionists" in its purist definition between Lincoln's inauguration and South Carolina's secession anywhere in the South, exceptions being some of the Border States and mountain areas of North Carolina, Virginia, Tennessee and Alabama. The Deep South was generally in favor of secession (immediately or through cooperation), or willing to go along with it, though there were pockets of Southerners who were opposed from the outset. Often these pockets can be correlated to areas that had been heavily supportive of the Whig party prior to its demise in 1856. Secessionists included those who held enslaved persons and those who were not slaveholders, as did cooperationists and Unionists. One reason for this might be the observation that slavery was not a moral issue for the vast majority of Southerners at the time; it was an economic and social issue. That can be a hard observation to hear today when most Americans see slavery as a moral issue.

In 1861, large amounts of Southern investment capital and household wealth were tied up in land to grow export crops (cotton and sugar) and the enslaved persons to plant and harvest in the most economical manner available for the time. Because this economic system was based on enslaved persons it meant a repressive slave society grew up around the economic system to control the interactions of the enslaved persons with the dominant white population. It would be difficult to sort out which came first: racism or race-based slavery but it is clear that it was easier to keep the capture, trading of, transporting and selling of enslaved persons as an economic system if there was an underlying sense of superiority of white people toward black people. And the social constructs of the slave society maintained and fueled those beliefs of superiority.

It must be remembered that racism was certainly not just a feature of Southern society but a belief system that pervaded American culture at the time. Abolitionists were never a large faction in Northern society and those that wanted to give slaves freedom and complete civil rights in America were an even smaller number prior to the War. Blacks did not have complete equal rights in many Northern states before the War. Some Northern states had laws on the books to restrict available employment and free black movements geographically; and sixteen restricted voting to whites. So, it would be fair to say that most men from Southern states who fought for the Union were neither abolitionist nor free of racism at some level. That can be seen by the few incidents at Fort Barrancas of black men stationed, working or living there being assaulted by some of the men of the 1st FCUV. It might be fair to say that at least some of the men were indifferent to slavery, did not see a reason to fight and die to maintain it for others after a certain point, and may not have felt either kinship or hatred toward the black men they served with during the War.

Unionist sentiments do not appear to have been present in any large numbers in Florida in the months leading up to the War. There were families in the area that were not in favor of secession over the issue of slavery, or were opposed to secession prior to an overt action on the part of the Federal government to substantially hamper slavery. They were not a large number but they were a bit more prevalent in the areas that had been settled the longest in Florida: Jacksonville and Pensacola. These were the urban areas that had attracted Northern businessmen prior to the War, and in the case of Pensacola brought men to the area through service in the U.S. Army and Navy. Many of these businessmen worried about the effects of war on their business interests, even if those interests included enslaved persons. As mentioned in the section on this area before the War, the area around Pensacola was not heavily populated by slaves and many who were there were skilled craftsmen and women working in industry and household workers in families with small numbers of enslaved persons. The rural areas around Pensacola and well up into south Alabama were populated mostly by yeomen farmers with no enslaved persons.

Alabama did have a large area in the northern, mountainous area that was quite Unionist in their sentiments, fought hard against secession at the convention and did talk about trying to secede from Alabama as West Virginia did from Virginia. The state of Alabama managed to quell the talk of secession but the area did contribute a significant number of men to the 1st Alabama Cavalry Union that fought in the area of northern Alabama and adjacent states during the War. The southern portion of the state was mostly yeoman farmers and therefore more motivated by a sense of need to protect the social structure of the slave society but not economically tangled in it to a great extent.

Early in the War, both south Alabama and the Florida panhandle produced several Confederate regiments and battalions. Like most areas of the South, many young men were eager to join and go off to war. It was going to be quick and decisive, according to the meme of the time, so many did not want to take the chance that they would miss the action. Or they were up for a change or an adventure. Then the fighting came, then the draft, then the hunger for both the men and their families back home. Families unable to sustain themselves without the adult male would have likely kept some of the older men from joining until the draft came. For those men, young and older, that did not join until forced by the draft, it is likely that a fair number of them had family commitments they placed before fighting for the Confederacy or they were not deeply motivated by the cause. Some did join then but some found ways to be discharged by the Army surgeon or to desert as soon as possible and some took to the woods to avoid the draft and the subsequent militia rounding up dodgers and deserters. Finally, some joined and fought bravely until an event happened to them or their families and they deserted to go home. The most significant event for many was the general hunger that overtook the home front as the war worn on. Limited food availability, with the Army taking precedent in distribution, quickly created severe hardship and many letters from home asking the men to come home before the family died of starvation.

Of the 704 men of the 1st FCUV, 256 of them have been identified that were enlisted or drafted with the Confederate army (36%) at some point before they joined the 1st FCUV. Three hundred and one (301) do not appear to have any record with the Confederacy

(43%). That leaves 147 (21%) that might have served but there are multiple records available that cannot be sorted out with existing information.

Of the 256 men who are known to have at least been enlisted/drafted into the Confederacy, 38 joined the military sometime in 1861. Only 6 of these 38 (16%) left the Confederate Army in 1861, while 9 (27%) left in 1862, 15 (39%) left in 1863 and 8 (21%) left in 1864. The end of their enlistment with the Confederacy ranged from desertion to disability discharges but it is clear that most of these men joined without threat of draft and stayed with the Confederacy for at least a year. 1862 saw 104 of the men who served in the Confederacy before enlisting in the 1st FCUV joining a Confederate regiment. This reflects the beginning of the draft in April 1862. Of these 105 men 34 (33%) had left the Confederacy by the end of 1862; another 52 (50%) left by the end of 1863 and 18 (17%) had deserted or been discharged by the end of 1864. And finally, of these 256 men who served on both sides, 114 of them joined or were drafted into a Confederate regiment in 1863. Only 10 of these 114 men served beyond the end of 1863. All of these men were likely drafted and therefore likely had the most opposition to serving with the Confederacy. As can be seen by these numbers, the year 1863 was the turning point for the Confederacy as far as desertion was concerned.

These numbers would tend to support a supposition that the men who fought with the 1st FCUV were likely not as emotionally and economically tied to the Confederate government or they became disillusioned by the draft controversy (exemptions for the rich through buying replacements and allowing a white male on a plantation for every 20 enslaved persons) or the impressment policies and failures of the government to ensure their families were fed. Of those who can be clearly shown to have joined the Confederacy, it is likely that the choice to leave the Confederate Army was one more of disillusionment with policies, concern for family or battle fatigue than a lack of support for succession or the Confederate government because most did join and serve, some for more than one enlistment before desertion. For those drafted in 1862 and 1863 it seems possible that their reasons were more mixed and may have included more of a sense that the South should not have seceded or the sense that the Confederate government was not protecting their homes and families as it should or was passing policies that were no better than what occurred in the United States and therefore did not deserve their support.

The 301 men who do not have any records with the Confederacy are an interesting mix. This group does include the small number of officers who were Northerners and transferred into the 1st FCUV. Of the Southerners, some were of draft age during 1862 and 1863 but do not appear to have enlisted or been drafted so they may have taken to the woods early to avoid being picked up. A good number of these men reached draft age in 1863 or 1864. Many of these young men were a younger brother of several men who were already in the Confederate Army. A preview of the section on families serving with the 1st FCUV shows an interesting pattern. A younger brother reaches draft age, or will soon reach draft age, and most or all of the male siblings and the younger brother wind up joining the 1st FCUV within a short period of time of each other.

The Confederacy struggled with desertion and the decimation of regiments that could not easily be replenished. By September 1864 Jefferson Davis openly admitted that approximately two-thirds (67%) of the Confederate Army was missing and the majority of those were absent without leave. Very early regiments began to be consolidated to try to field a full regiment, or at least a battalion. But it is clear when closely analyzing these records that many men were included in the muster rolls of a regiment but never actually served with that regiment. One example stands out very clearly. In reviewing the regiments that these men served with, there appears to have been 63 of these men who served with the 11th Florida Infantry. This regiment was formed in June 1864 by consolidating the 2nd and 4th Florida Battalions with new draftees primarily from Florida but some of the men were also from south Alabama. The regiment was sent to the Eastern Theatre and fought in the Florida Brigade with the 2nd, 5th, 8th, 9th, and 10th Florida Regiments. Only one of the 63 men listed in the 11th Florida Infantry's muster rolls who went on to serve with the 1st FCUV actually served with the 11th Florida Infantry. Everyone had deserted the 4th Florida Battalion prior to June 1864, including the one who did serve briefly with the 11th. He was returned after being captured and he promptly deserted again.

But to truly begin to grasp motivations for these men it is important to look at their behavior once enlisted with the 1st FCUV. There was a total of 704 men who enlisted, were appointed to the regiment, attempted to enlist or have at least one card in the miscellaneous records of the regiment. Four (4) men (0.6%) attempted to enlist but were rejected for one reason or another. There were 133 men (18.8%) who deserted the regiment and either did not return by voluntary action or by force. These men are scattered throughout the time period of the regiment and do not appear to have a pattern of when they decided to desert, though some did desert while on a mission near their homes. A few joined in the last few months of the war and deserted after the war was declared over. An additional 63 men (8.9%) joined early in the regiment's history, served with honor and deserted at or near the end of the war. These 63 men had their desertion charges dropped after the war and many filed for and received pensions. There were (8) men (1.1%) that were captured and killed by Confederates while on scouting duty or after going AWOL.

Death was an ever-present problem in the war, either from disease or from injuries, with 103 men (14.6%) of the 1st FCUV dying during their service. Most died of disease. Some have no indication in their records as to the cause of death. An additional 17 men (2.4%) were discharged due to disability or illness. Eleven (11) officers were honorably discharged (1.7%) and 2 enlisted men (0.3%) were dishonorably discharged. Two (2) men (0.3%) were killed in action and two (2) men (0.3%) were listed as missing in action. And finally, one (1) man decided to muster into the 14th NY Cavalry, Co M instead of the 1st FCUV after enlistment and one (1) transferred to the 7th Vermont Infantry (total of 0.3%). There is no known reason for the end of their service for 25 of the men (3.6%). That leaves the 332 men (47.2%) who served from their enlistment to the mustering out of the regiment on 17 November 1865 at Tallahassee, Florida.

If the men who resigned or were transferred, the men who deserted after the war ended and their desertion charges were dropped, the men who were discharged for illness or disability, the men who died during service, and the men who served until mustered out are added together a total of 539 men (76.6%) would appear to have been committed to serving with the 1st FCUV. This number does include a small number of men who were serving out a sentence at Fort Pickens for desertion or some other crime but were mustered out with the regiment in November 1865. This leaves out those rejected at enlistment, those who deserted and the record was never corrected or changed, those who were dishonorably discharged, those who were missing in action after an engagement and those who left the regiment at unknown times and for unknown reasons due to minimal records (23.4%). The few in this last category that may have served well likely offset the few who were imprisoned at Fort Pickens at the time the regiment was marched to Tallahassee to be mustered out.

This percentage of 23.4% is comparable or better than the estimates of men who were AWOL or deserted in the Confederacy during the last two years of the war. The regiment can then be presented as follows: 1) It was composed primarily of men from the Florida panhandle and south Alabama, 2) A good percentage of these men appear to have not wanted to serve the Confederacy and when forced to make a decision, chose the Union, 3) Desertion was a problem on both sides of the War, no worse in the 1st FCUV than in either the Confederacy or the Union and was a reflection of the struggle of some of these men to a change in the relationship of soldier to Army, 4) A large percentage of these men (31%) came from just 4 counties: Walton Co, FL; Santa Rosa Co, FL; Coffee Co, AL and Covington Co, AL, and 5) A good percentage of these men joined the Union in family groups, possibly reflecting family ties or Union sentiments in the family.

These men certainly did not have a major part to play in the war. The Florida panhandle and south Alabama played a minor role in terms of actual engagements and it seems clear that the Confederacy making the strategic decision to withdraw from this area of Florida except for a few outposts may have been a costly decision. It provided the Union with an excellent staging area for the New Orleans Campaign, the two Mobile Campaigns and the Gulf Blockade, all significant events in the unraveling of the Confederacy. And it created animosity among the population for the destruction by the Confederate Army and then a significant withdrawal from the area leaving families defenseless. Creating a Union presence at Pensacola also provided a magnet for men from the area that did not wish to fight for the Confederacy for whatever reason. The men in the 1st FCUV, unlike any of the other men stationed at Fort Barrancas, knew the area and that knowledge was critical in the movements by the Union into the countryside during the war and especially in the last campaign of the war in Mobile.

History is a look at the past through a wide lens, looking at the ebbs and flows and patterns of human cultures and societies. Genealogy is the study of individuals and families. Until recently these two seldom met. Hopefully, this effort will encourage others to take some aspect of history and attempt to draw some larger conclusions from the details of the individuals who experienced it.

The Men of the 1st Florida Cavalry Union

A

ABBOTT, Robert S.
AKA: Robert S. ABOTT
Birth: Mar1838; Thomas Co, GA
Death: 24Aug1911; Alabama
1860 Location: Vernon, Washington County, FL
Description: light complexion, blue eyes, sandy hair
CSA: 18Sept1861 - 12Dec1863; 4th FL Infantry, Co H, Private; re-enlisted then deserted.
Union Enlistment: 13Dec1863; Ft. Barrancas, FL; Co A, Private
Engagements: Montgomery, AL; Wetumpka, AL
Promotions: 01Apr1864; appointed Sergeant by Special Order
Demotion: 07May1865; Private
Desertion: 05May1865; Montgomery, AL
Military Finding: 04May1886; desertion charge dropped
Pension: 08Nov1886; App#588859; Cert#707619
Widow's Pension: 07Oct1911 in AL; App#973128, Cert#732869

ADAMS, Ellis W. O.
AKA: Ellis W. ADAMS
Birth: circa 1848; Stewart Co, GA
Death: 17Jun1880 – 1900; Alabama
1860 Location: Chipola, Henry County, AL
Description: light complexion, gray eyes, dark hair
Union Enlistment: 27Mar1865, East Pass, FL; Co. A, Private
Desertion: 07Aug1865; Ft. Barrancas, FL

ADAMS, J. Elijah
AKA: J. Eliger ADAMS; Eliger ADDAMS; Elisher ADAMS
Birth: circa 1820; Houston Co, GA
Death: after 1870
1860 Location: Dale County, AL
Description: light complexion, blue eyes, light hair
CSA: 12Oct1863 - 08Feb1864; 4th Battalion FL Infantry, Co F, Private, deserted; records transferred to 11th FL Infantry, Co L.

Union Enlistment: 15Feb1864, Barrancas, FL; Co A, Private
Desertion: 05May1865; Dale, AL; under Lt. Sanders
Military Confinement: 09Jun1865; Jacksonville, Duval, FL; arrested as a deserter
Military Finding: 25Apr1885; desertion charges dropped
Pension: 23May1881 in AL; App#422218, Cert#495987

ADAMS, John Quincy
AKA: John Q. ADAMS
Birth: circa 1818; Houston Co, GA
Death: after 30Sept1865
Description: fair complexion, blue eyes, light hair
Union Enlistment: 24Feb1864; Ft. Barrancas, FL; Co D, Private
Promotions: Jan1865; Wagoner/Teamster
Union Discharge: after Sept1865

ADAMS, Larkin A.
AKA: Larkin ADDAMS
Birth: circa 1830; Jones Co, GA
Death: after 30Jun1885; Florida
1860 Location: Auburn, Macon County, AL
Description: light complexion, blue eyes, brown hair
CSA: 10Feb1863 - 31Oct1863; 57th AL Infantry, Co G, 2nd Corporal, estimated desertion date.
Union Enlistment: 15Jan1864; Ft. Barrancas, FL; Co A, Private
Promotions: 01Jul1865; Corporal
Union Discharge: 17Nov1865; Tallahassee, FL; bounty due $120

ALEXANDER, Ezekiel
AKA: Eziekel ALEXANDER
Birth: circa 1820; Washington Co, NC
Burial: Apr 1864; Barrancas Cemetery, Escambia, FL; Sec 1, Site 958
1860 Location: Walker County, AL
Description: light complexion, blue eyes, brown hair
CSA: 21Mar - 17Jun1863; 57th AL Infantry, Co I, Private, discharged
Union Enlistment: 17Dec1863, Barrancas, FL; Co A, Private

Died: 07Apr1864; Ft. Barrancas, FL
Widow's Pension: 12Mar1880; App#261384, Cert#210148

ALLEN, Eldred Benjamin
AKA: Eldrid Benjamin ALLEN
Birth: 09Mar1846; Baldwin Co, AL
Death: 26Sept1914; Gateswood, Baldwin Co, AL
Burial: Sept1914, Gateswood, Baldwin Co, AL; New Hope Cemetery
1860 Location: Baldwin County, AL
Description: fair complexion, grey eyes, light hair
Union Enlistment: 28Mar1864; Ft. Barrancas, FL; Co E, Private
Engagements: Marianna, FL; Pollard, AL; Blakeley, AL; Montgomery, AL
Union Discharge: 17Nov1865; Tallahassee, FL; bounty due $275.00
Military Finding: 22Dec1903; soldier was discharged by reason of muster out with his company
Pension: 16Nov1903 in AL; App#1305714, Cert#1114402
Widow's Pension: 22Oct1914 in AL; App#1035805, Cert#817506

ALLEN, John Anderson
AKA: John ALLEN; John ALIN; John ALLIEN; John ALLIN
Birth: circa 1848; Baldwin Co, AL
Death: 15Apr1910 – 1920; Baldwin Co, AL
1860 Location: Escambia County, FL
Description: fair complexion, blue eyes, dark hair
Union Enlistment: 26Mar1864; Ft. Barrancas, FL; Co D, Private
Engagements: Raid in South Alabama; Montgomery, AL
Union Discharge: 17Nov1865, Tallahassee, FL; bounty due $120
Pension: 17Mar1910 in AL; App#1389315, Cert#1162293

ALLEN, Robert J.
Birth: circa 1838; Santa Rosa Co, FL
Death: after 17Nov1865
1850 Location: Santa Rosa County, FL
Description: light complexion, blue eyes, dark hair

CSA: 21Mar1862 - 27Jan1864; 1st FL Reorganized Infantry, Co F, Private, deserted from Dalton, GA
Union Enlistment: 27Jan1864; Ft. Barrancas, FL; Co A, Private
Union Discharge: 17Nov1865; Tallahassee, FL; bounty due $120

ALSOBROOK, Robert A.
AKA: Robert ALSOBROOK; Robert ALSOBROOKE
Birth: 08May1836; Baker Co, GA
Death: 15Dec1915; Harwood, Gonzales Co, TX
1860 Location: Almirante, Walton County, FL
Description: fair complexion, blue eyes, light hair
CSA: 01May - 31Oct1862; 1st FL Reorganized Infantry, Co D, Private, estimated desertion date
Union Enlistment: 01Feb1864, Ft. Barrancas, FL; Co B, Private
Engagements: Gonzales/Pollard
Promotions: 01Apr1864; Corporal
Military Charges: 13Apr1865; larceny for selling a Remington Revolver in Warrington or Woolsey, FL
Union Discharge: 17Nov1865; Tallahassee, FL; bounty due $120
Pension: 05Aug1882 in TX; App#456625, Cert#392293

ALSTON, John J.
Birth: circa 1831; Dooly Co, GA
Description: dark complexion, brown eyes, black hair
Union Enlistment: 28Apr1864; Ft. Barrancas, FL; unknown length of service

ANDERSON, Willis
Birth: Oct1836; Henry Co, AL
Death: 03May1910 – 1920; Washington Co, FL
1860 Location: Chipola, Henry County, AL
Description: dark complexion, dark eyes, dark hair
CSA: 27Mar1862 - 30Jun1862; 39th AL Infantry, Co D, Private, estimated desertion date
Union Enlistment: 16Sept1864; Ft. Barrancas, FL; Co A, Private
Engagements: Raid in South Alabama
Desertion: 22Mar1865; Andalusia, Covington, AL
Military Finding: 11Oct1889; removal of desertion charge denied

Pension: 09Oct 1888 in FL; App#675002

ARD, John Wesley
Birth: 12Jan1846; Milton, Santa Rosa Co, FL
Death: 04Apr1886; Lillian, Baldwin Co, AL
1860 Location: Milton, Santa Rosa County, FL
Description: fair complexion, dark eyes, dark hair
Union Enlistment: 13Feb1864; Ft. Barrancas, FL; Co D, Private
Engagements: Raid in South Alabama; Montgomery, AL
Union Discharge: 17Nov1865; Tallahassee, FL; bounty due $120
Widow's Pension: 26Jan1891 in AL; App#503040, Cert#322790

ARD, Zachariah R.
AKA: Zachariah P. ARD
Birth: May1828; Henry Co, AL
Death: 09Nov1909; Holmes Co, FL
Burial: Nov1909; Bonifay, Holmes, FL; Bethlehem Cemetery
1860 Location: Cerro Gordo, Holmes County, FL
Description: light complexion, blue/grey eyes, dark hair
CSA: 12Jun1862 - 28Jul1862; 2nd Battalion GA Sharpshooters, Co D, Private, disability discharge
Union Enlistment: 03Apr1864; East Pass, FL; Co. E, Private
Engagements: Little Escambia Bridge, FL; William's Creek, FL; Pine Barren Creek, FL
Promotions: 20Aug1864; Corporal
Union Discharge: 17Nov1865; Tallahassee, FL; bounty due $75
Pension: 09Jan1889 in FL; App#684512, Cert#867453
Widow's Pension: 15Feb1915 in AL; App#1042843

ARMSTRONG, James H.
Birth: circa Mar1843; Cherokee Co, GA
Death: 03Jul1902 – 1910; Washington Co, FL
1860 Location: Vernon, Washington County, FL
Description: light complexion, blue eyes, light hair
CSA: 08Mar1862 - 31Aug1863; 6th FL Infantry, Co K, Private, estimated desertion date
Union Enlistment: 01Jan1864; Ft. Barrancas, FL; Co C, Private
Desertion: 01Nov1864; Florida

Military Finding: 14Feb1889; request to have desertion charges dropped was denied

ARNOLD, John T.
Birth: circa 1846; Brunswick Co, NC
Death: 12Feb1926; Enterprise, LA
Burial: Feb1926; Glendale, Forrest Co, MS; Hickory Grove Cemetery
1860 Location: Marianna, Jackson County, FL
Description: fair complexion, blue eyes, light hair
Union Enlistment: 22Feb1865; Ft. Barrancas, FL; Co D, Private
Union Discharge: 17Nov1865; Tallahassee, FL; bounty due $100
Pension: 16Jun1910; App#1391087, Cert#1164371

ATKINS, Robert T.
AKA: Robert T. ADKINS
Birth: Mar1847; Barbour Co, AL
Death: 11Nov1910; Jackson Co, FL
1860 Location: Dale County, AL
Description: fair complexion, grey eyes, brown hair
Union Enlistment: 14Sep1864; Ft. Barrancas, FL; Co F, Private
Engagements: Montgomery, AL
Union Discharge: 17Nov1865; Tallahassee, FL
Pension: 25Aug1890 in FL; App#908703, Cert#934543
Widow's Pension: 11Jan1911 in FL; App#955852

B

BAGGETT, Henry Hilliard
AKA: Henry H. BAGGETT
Birth: Jan1845; Coffee Co, AL
Death: 30Jul1918; Monroeville, Monroe Co, AL
1860 Location: Coffee County, AL
Description: fair complexion, gray eyes, dark hair
Union Enlistment: 18Aug1864; East Pass, FL; Co F, Private
Union Discharge: 17Nov1865; Tallahassee, FL; bounty due $75
Pension: 15Feb1909 in AL; App#1381126, Cert#1156455
Widow's Pension: 29Aug1918 in AL; App#1126806, Cert#862519

BAGGETT, Henry L.
Birth: Oct1821; Escambia Co, FL
Death: 04Jun1900 - 01Nov1912; Santa Rosa Co, FL
1860 Location: Santa Rosa County, FL
Description: dark complexion, dark eyes, dark hair
Union Enlistment: 27Apr1864; Ft. Barrancas, FL; Co F, Private
Engagements: Montgomery, AL
Desertion: 07Aug1865; Ft. Barrancas, FL
Military Finding: 14Oct1884; charge of desertion dropped
Pension: 04Feb1884 in FL; App#687998, Cert#1010538
Widow's Pension: 01Nov1912 in FL; App#3772982, Cert#554311

BAGGETT, James
AKA: James Malcolm BAGGETT
Birth: circa 1827; Covington Co, AL
1860 Location: Almirante, Walton Co, FL
Description: light complexion, gray eyes, dark hair
Union Enlistment: 19Jan1864, Ft. Barrancas, FL; Co B, Private
Died: 27May1864; Ft. Barrancas, FL; bounty due $275
Widow's Pension: 20Dec1867; App#156424, Cert#150701

BAGGETT, Joel
Birth: circa 1840; Santa Rosa Co, FL
Death: 14Oct1873; Santa Rosa Co, FL
1860 Location: Santa Rosa County, FL
Description: light complexion, blue eyes, light hair
CSA: 14Oct1861 - 09Feb1863; 24th AL Infantry, Co F, Private, deserted
Union Enlistment: 12Jan1864; Ft. Barrancas, FL; Co B, Private
Desertion: 23May1865; East Pass, FL

BAGGETT, Lewis
Birth: circa 1838; Santa Rosa Co, FL
1860 Location: Milton, Santa Rosa Co, FL
Description: dark complexion, black eyes, black hair
CSA: 14Oct1861 - 10Dec1861; 24th AL Infantry, Co F, Private, disability discharge

Union Enlistment: 25Jan1864; Ft. Barrancas, FL; Co B, Private
Promotions: 01Apr1864; Quartermaster Sergeant
Died: 12Nov1864; Ft. Barrancas, FL

BAGGETT, Nicholas
Birth: 31Jul1840; Walton Co, FL
Death: 08Mar1928; Atmore, Escambia Co, AL
Burial: Mar1928; Bogia, Escambia Co, FL; Rays Chapel Cemetery, Row 3, Grave 349
1860 Location: Milton, Santa Rosa County, FL
Description: sandy complexion, blue eyes, brown hair
CSA: 13May1862 - 01Nov1863; 1st FL Reorganized Infantry, Co G, Private, deserted from hospital
Union Enlistment: 27Apr1864; Ft. Barrancas, FL; Co B, Private
Military Confinement: 23Aug - 15Sep1865; Ft. Pickens, FL; released due to insufficient witnesses, returned to company
Union Discharge: 17Nov1865; Tallahassee, FL
Military Finding: 14Feb1920; deserted July 1, 1865, returned 15July1865, confined 23August1865, released 15Sept1865
Pension: 26Aug1885; App#547962, Cert#350395

BAGGETT, Seaborn S.
AKA: Seaborn Serrell BAGGETT
Birth: Dec1836; Alabama
Death: 30Nov1908; Bay Minette, Baldwin Co, AL
Burial: Nov1908; Baldwin Co, AL; High Pine Cemetery
1860 Location: Santa Rosa County, FL
Description: medium complexion, hazel eyes, brown hair
CSA: 13Mar1862 - 31Dec1863; 33rd AL Infantry, Co K, Private, estimated end date
Union Enlistment: 26Apr1864; East Pass, FL; Co F, Private
Engagements: 15 Mile House, FL; Marianna, FL; Pine Barren, FL; Mitchell Creek, FL; Pine Barren, FL
Promotions: 10Jan1865; Sergeant
Union Discharge: 17Nov1865; Tallahassee, FL; bounty due $75
Pension: 23Mar1892 in AL; App#1100037, Cert#1112542
Widow's Pension: 18Dec1908 in AL; App#909983, Cert#707873

BAGWELL, Berry E.
Birth: circa 1824; South Carolina
Death: 20Oct1915; Hardee Co, FL
Burial: Oct1915; Zolfo, Hardee Co, FL; Friendship Cemetery
1850 Location: Forsyth County, GA
Description: fair complexion, blue eyes, light hair
Union Enlistment: 12Oct1864; Ft. Barrancas, FL; Co. F, Private
Promotions: 06Aug1865; 1st Sergeant
Union Discharge: 17Nov1865; Tallahassee, FL
Pension: 20Sep1890 in FL; App#912116, Cert#700590

BAGWELL, Curtis G. H.
Birth: 15Jun1845; Gwinnett Co, GA
Death: 24Sept1916; Dale Co, AL
Burial: Sept1916; Dale Co, AL; Woodham Cemetery
1860 Location: Newton, Dale County, AL
Description: fair complexion, blue eyes, light hair
CSA: 25Jun1863 - Dec1863; 4th Battalion FL Infantry, Co A, Private, deserted; records transferred to 11th FL Infantry, Co C.
Union Enlistment: 20May1864; East Pass, FL; Co. F, Private
Engagements: Marianna, FL; Pine Barren Creek; Raid in South Alabama; Capture of Railroad in Evergreen, AL; Blakeley, AL; Montgomery, AL
Union Discharge: 17Nov1865; Tallahassee, FL; bounty due $75

BAGWELL, Lewis

BAILEY, Arthur
AKA: Arter BAILY
Birth: 17Apr1835; Coffee Co, AL
Death: 15Mar1915; Chumuckla, Santa Rosa Co, FL
Burial: Mar1915; Chumuckla, Santa Rosa, FL; Bailey Cemetery
Description: light complexion, hazel eyes, light hair
CSA: 18Aug1862 - 30Dec1862; 53rd AL Partisan Rangers, Co H, Private, deserted
Union Enlistment: 24Mar1864; East Pass, FL; Co. E, Private
Union Discharge: 17Nov1865; Tallahassee, FL; bounty due $275
Pension: 11Sept1895 in FL; App#1170264, Cert#1053589

BAILEY, John
AKA: John BALEY; John BAILLY; John BAILY
Birth: circa 1825; Dooly Co, GA
Death: after 10Mar1881
1860 Location: Milton, Santa Rosa County, FL
Description: light complexion, grey eyes, light hair
CSA: 29Jan1863 - 14Dec1863; 4th Battalion FL Infantry, Co A, Private, deserted; records transferred to 11th FL Infantry, Co C.
Union Enlistment: 24Mar1864; East Pass, FL
Promotions: 01May1864; Corporal
Demotion: 30May1865; Private
Union Discharge: 17Nov1865; Tallahassee, FL; bounty due $160
Pension: 10Mar1881; App#416907, Cert #608794

BAKER, Murdock
Birth: circa 1831; Walton Co, FL
Death: after 1880
1860 Location: Almirante, Walton County, FL
Description: sandy complexion, blue eyes, brown hair
CSA: 04Oct1862 - Jun1864; 15th Confederate Cavalry, Co I, estimated desertion date; originally enlisted in 3rd Battalion Florida Cavalry, Co D, Private
Union Enlistment: 01Oct1864; Ft. Barrancas, FL; Co. B, Private
Desertion: 19Jan1865; Ft. Barrancas, FL

BANKS, Eli Ferguson
AKA: Eli F. BANKS
Birth: 1813 – 1817; Abbeville Co, SC
Death: after 29Dec1881 likely in FL
1860 Location: Santa Rosa County, FL
Description: fair complexion, blue eyes, grey hair
Union Enlistment: 24Feb1864; Ft. Barrancas, FL; Co. C, Private
Promotions: 23Mar1864; Corporal
Union Discharge: 17Nov1865; Tallahassee, FL
Pension: 10Aug1881; App#426549
Minor's Pension: App#511247

BAREFIELD, James J.
AKA: James J. BARFIELD
Birth: 08Jun1831; Darlington Co, SC
Death: 23Sep1897; Dale Co, AL
Burial: Sep1897; Clopton, Dale, AL; Old Salem Cemetery
1860 Location: Newton, Dale County, AL
Description: fair complexion, grey eyes, dark hair
CSA: 13May1862 - 11Dec1862; 39th AL Infantry, Co H, Private, War, deserted
Union Enlistment: 08Sept1864; Ft. Barrancas, FL; Co. E, Private
Union Discharge: 17Nov1865; Tallahassee, FL; bounty due $100
Pension: 21Mar1887 in AL; App#603020, Cert#444376

BARFIELD, Hugh Huston
AKA: Hughie BARFIELD
Birth: circa 1827; Robinson Co, SC
Death: 10Aug1870 - 02Sept1890; Florida
1860 Location: Albany, Dougherty County, GA
Description: fair complexion, gray eyes, brown hair
Union Enlistment: 21May1864; Ft. Barrancas, FL; Co. C, Private
Engagements: Detached service up Escambia Bay, FL in October1864
Union Discharge: 17Nov1865, Tallahassee, FL
Widow's Pension: 02Sept1890 in FL; App#476720, Cert#330635

BARKER, John
Birth: circa 1844; North Carolina
Death: after Jan1865
Description: black complexion, black eyes, black hair
Union Enlistment: 24Dec1864; Ft. Barrancas, FL; Co. D, Private
Desertion: 31Jan1865; New Orleans, LA
Additional Union Service: 18Jan1865; 86th US Colored Infantry, enlisted under a different name, arrested as a deserter

BARLOW, Lewis Alexander
AKA: Louis A. BARLOW
Birth: circa 1835; Conecuh Co, AL
Death: 19Apr1910 - 1920 in Conecuh Co, AL

1860 Location: Conecuh Co, AL
Description: fair complexion, blue eyes, light hair
Union Enlistment: 09Feb1864, Ft. Barrancas, FL; Co. B, Private
Promotions: 01Apr1864; Corporal
Desertion: 14Aug1865; Ft. Barrancas, FL
Pension: 16May1892; App#1111472

BARNES, Elias L.
AKA: Elijah BURNS
Birth: 14Dec1846; Dale Co, AL
Death: 18Nov1919; Holmes Co, FL
Burial: Nov1919; Holmes, FL; Cedar Grove Cemetery
1850 Location: Dale County, AL
Description: light complexion, blue eyes, light hair
Union Enlistment: 02Dec1864, Ft. Barrancas, FL; Co. A, Private
Engagements: Montgomery, AL
Desertion: 05May1865; Ft. Barrancas, FL
Pension: 07Sep1892 in FL; App#1129400

BARNES, William
AKA: William BARNS; William BURNS
Birth: circa 1837; Monroe Co, AL
1860 Location: Henry County, AL
Description: fair complexion, blue eyes, light hair
Union Enlistment: 26Mar1864, Ft. Barrancas, FL; Co. D, Private
Promotions: 09Aug1864; Sergeant
Military Injury: 17Dec1864; Coffee or Henry, AL; Wounded in leg, leg amputated
Died: 27Dec1864; Henry Co, AL

BARNES, William James
AKA: William J. BARNES
Birth: 19Jun1840; Talbot Co, GA
Death: 18Oct1912; Houston Co, AL
1850 Location: Talbot County, GA
Description: fair complexion, blue eyes, light hair
Union Enlistment: 24Jan1865; Ft. Barrancas, FL; Co. C, Private
Desertion: 12Aug1865

Pension: 12Jan1892 in AL; App#1083893

BARNES, William W.
Birth: 21Jan1833; Dale Co, AL
Death: 28May1910; Dale Co, AL
Burial: May1910; Andalusia, Covington Co, AL; Magnolia Cemetery
1860 Location: Newton, Dale County, AL
Description: fair complexion, blue eyes, dark hair
Union Enlistment: 15Mar1864; Ft. Barrancas, FL; Co. A, Private
Union Discharge: 17Nov1865; Tallahassee, FL; bounty due $120
Pension: 14Jul1892 in AL; App#1121151, Cert#1061296

BARROW, William Lafayette
Birth: 21Apr1845; Oak Grove, Walton Co, FL
Death: 19May1918; Millville, Escambia Co, FL
1860 Location: Santa Rosa County, FL
Description: sandy complexion, blue eyes, brown hair
Union Enlistment: 10Apr1864; Ft. Barrancas, FL; Co. B, Private
Engagements: Montgomery, AL
Union Discharge: 17Nov1865; Tallahassee, FL; bounty due $75
Pension: 17Dec1903 in FL; App#1306725, Cert#1125235

BARTON, Uriah
Birth: circa 1844; Darlington Co, SC
Death: after Aug1865
1860 Location: Almirante, Walton County, FL
Description: sandy complexion, blue eyes, light hair
CSA: 21Jul1861 - 31Mar1862; 1st FL Infantry, Co E, Private; 4Oct1862 - 13Aug1863, 3rd Battalion FL Cavalry, Co D; transferred to 15th Confederate Cavalry, Co I, July1863; deserted August 1863.
Union Enlistment: 07May1864; Ft. Barrancas, FL; Co. F, Private
Engagements: Montgomery, AL
Desertion: 08Aug1865; Ft. Barrancas, FL

BASFORD, Chesterfield
AKA: Chesterfield BASSFORD; Ches BASFORD
Birth: 26Oct1846; Brunswick Co, NC

Death: 25May1933; Grand Ridge, Jackson Co, FL
Burial: May1933; Jackson Co, FL; Cow Pen Pond Cemetery
1860 Location: Marianna, Jackson County, FL
Description: fair complexion, blue eyes, light hair
Union Enlistment: 27Nov1864; Ft. Barrancas, FL; Co. F, Private
Union Discharge: 17Nov1865; Tallahassee, FL
Military Finding: 08Nov1884; desertion charges dropped, changed to AWOL
Pension: 22Sep1880 in FL; App#410343, Cert#576685

BASS, Holland Middleton
AKA: Holland M. BASS; Holley BASS; Holley M. BASS
Birth: 21Dec1845; Covington Co, AL
Death: 31Jul1934; Covington Co, AL
Burial: Aug1934; Beda, Covington Co, AL; Zion Rock Cemetery
1860 Location: Andalusia, Covington County, AL
Description: light complexion, grey eyes, dark hair
Union Enlistment: 19Jan1864; Ft. Barrancas, FL; Co. B, Private
Union Discharge: 17Nov1865; Tallahassee, FL; bounty due $120
Pension: 15Oct1884; App#524405, Cert#954264

BASS, James W.
Birth: 25Mar - 30Sept1847; Covington Co, AL
1860 Location: Andalusia, Covington County, Alabama
Description: light complexion, blue eyes, light hair
Union Enlistment: 25Mar1864; East Pass, FL; Co. E, Private
Died: 25Nov1864; Ft. Barrancas, FL; bounty due $275

BASS, Willis T.
Birth: 24Feb1846; Barbour Co, AL
Death: 19Sept1904; Butler Co, AL
Burial: Sept1904; Georgiana, Butler Co, AL; Union Cemetery
1860 Location: Texasville, Barbour County, AL
Description: fair complexion, blue eyes, light hair
Union Enlistment: 15Feb1864; Ft. Barrancas, FL; Co. A, Private
Union Discharge: 17Nov1865; Tallahassee, FL; bounty due $120
Pension: 08Jan1895 in AL; App #1163153, Cert#1031568
Widow's Pension: 22Oct1904 in AL; App#815717, Cert#591434

BELL, Charles P.
AKA: Charlie P. BELL
Birth: 04Apr1846; Texas
Death: 28Apr1925; Pensacola, Escambia Co, FL
Burial: Apr1925; Pensacola, FL; St. John's Cemetery
Description: fair complexion, blue eyes, light hair
Union Enlistment: 05Apr1864, Ft. Barrancas, FL; Co. E, Private
Engagements: Marianna, FL; Pollard, AL; Blakely, AL; Montgomery, AL
Union Discharge: 17Nov1865; Tallahassee, FL; bounty due $75
Pension: 25Sept1890 in FL; App#919623, Cert#693750

BELL, Francis M.
AKA: Frank M. BELL
Birth: 26Aug1844; Dale Co, AL
Death: 02Feb1923; Argyle, Walton Co, FL
Burial: Feb1923; DeFuniak Springs, Walton, FL; Magnolia Cemetery
1860 Location: Shoal River, Walton County, FL
Description: fair complexion, blue eyes, light hair
Union Enlistment: 23Mar1864, Ft. Barrancas, FL; Co. D, Private
Promotions: 17Dec1864; Corporal
Union Discharge: 17Nov1865; Tallahassee, FL; bounty due $120
Pension: 20Nov1890 in FL; App#976023, Cert#702400
Widow's Pension: 17Feb1923 in FL; App#1201109, Cert#932158

BELL, Jacob H.
Birth: circa 1813; Duplin Co, NC
Death: after 1880
1860 Location: Shoal River, Walton County, FL
Description: fair complexion, blue eyes, gray hair
Union Enlistment: 26Mar1864, Ft. Barrancas, FL; Co. D, Private
Promotions: 01 Apr 1864; Sergeant
Disability Discharge: 14 Apr 1865; Tallahassee, FL

BELL, James
Birth: circa 1846; Holmes Co, FL

1860 Location: Shoal River, Walton County, FL
Description: fair complexion, gray eyes, dark hair
Union Enlistment: 29Sep1864, East Pass, FL; Private
Died: 23Oct1864; Ft. Barrancas, FL

BISHOP, James M.
Birth: circa 1843; Covington Co, AL
Death: 30Jul1915; Argyle, Walton Co, FL
Burial: Jul1915; Holmes Co, FL; Sandy Creek Cemetery
1860 Location: Walton County, FL
Description: fair complexion, hazel eyes, light hair
Union Enlistment: 15Mar1864; East Pass, FL; Co. D, Private
Engagements: Montgomery, AL
Union Discharge: 17Nov1865; Tallahassee, FL; bounty due $120
Pension: 21Jan1893 in FL; App#1143996, Cert#1045977

BLACK, James M.
AKA: James BLACK
Birth: circa 1846 in Pike Co, AL
Death: 12Sept1927 in Beaumont, Perry Co, MS
1860 Location: Santa Rosa County, FL
Description: fair complexion, hazel eyes, brown hair
Union Enlistment: 15Apr1864; Ft. Barrancas, FL; Co. C, Private
Military Confinement: Jul - Aug1864; Ft. Pickens, FL; temporarily attached to 1st FL Batty awaiting sentence
Union Discharge: 17Nov1865; Tallahassee, FL; bounty due $100
Pension: 20Jul1891 in MS; App #1039870, Cert #1038952
Widow's Pension: 10Oct1927 in MS; App #1593796, Cert #a6-18-28

BLACKMAN, John P.
AKA: John P. BLAKMON; John P. BLACKMON
Birth: May1837; Pike Co, AL
Death: 23Oct1907; Chattahoochee, Gadsden Co, FL
Burial: Oct1907; Chattahoochee, Gadsden Co, FL; Florida State Hospital Cemetery, div 4, cemetery 2, row 16, grave 24
1860 Location: Milton, Santa Rosa County, FL
Description: fair complexion, hazel eyes, dark hair

CSA: 21Mar - 20Oct1862; 1st FL Infantry, Co F, Private, deserted.
Union Enlistment: 20Apr1864; Ft. Barrancas, FL; Co. E, Private
Desertion: 06Aug1864; Ft. Barrancas, FL
Military Finding: 12Dec1892; removal of desertion charge denied
Pension: 25May1896 in FL; App #1025709

BLAKE, H.
Union Enlistment: Co. C, Private

BOHANNAN, Henry
AKA: Henry BOHANAN; Henry BOWHANAN
Birth: 20Aug1818; Jasper Co, GA
Death: 01Dec1905; Blount Co, AL
Burial: Dec 1905; Blount, AL; Sulphur Springs Cemetery
1860 Location: Milo, Pike County, AL
Description: fair complexion, blue eyes, sandy hair
Union Enlistment: 06Jul1864; East Pass, FL, Co. F, Private
Engagements: Raid in South Alabama; Blakeley, AL; Greenville, AL; Montgomery, AL
Union Discharge: 17Nov1865; Tallahassee, FL; bounty due $75
Pension: 19Sept1890 in AL; App#817275, Cert#578759
Widow's Pension: 13Jan1906 in AL; App #841097, Cert #624638

BOLTON, James Thomas
AKA: James T. BOLTON
Birth: 31Oct1844 in Pike Co, AL
Death: 13Jan1925 in Crestview, Okaloosa Co, FL
Burial: Jan1925, Dorcas, Okaloosa Co, FL; Dorcas Cemetery
1860 Location: Santa Rosa County, FL
Description: light complexion, gray eyes, light hair
Union Enlistment: 19Jan1864; Ft. Barrancas, FL; Co. B, Private
Union Discharge: 17Nov1865; Tallahassee, FL; bounty due $160
Pension: 03Feb1890 in FL; App #1010833, Cert #1075985
Widow's Pension: 05Feb1925 in FL; App#1228962, Cert#939619

BOLTON, John Askar
Birth: 16Nov1846; Pike Co, AL

Death: 22Feb1929; Niceville, Walton Co, FL
Burial: Feb1929; Niceville, Walton Co, FL; Padgett-Bolton Cemetery
1860 Location: Santa Rosa County, FL
Description: light complexion, blue eyes, light hair
Union Enlistment: 25Jan1864, Ft. Barrancas, FL; Co. B, Private
Engagements: Montgomery, AL
Union Discharge: 17Nov1865; Tallahassee, FL; bounty due $120
Pension: 27Sept1890 in FL; App#919638, Cert#754603

BOON, Elijah
AKA: Elijah BOONE
Birth: Jan1834; Baldwin Co, AL
Death: 24Dec1908; Escambia Co, AL
1860 Location: Baldwin County, AL
Description: fair complexion, gray eyes, dark hair
Union Enlistment: 30May1864; Ft. Barrancas, FL; Co. E, Private
Engagements: Montgomery, AL
Union Discharge: 17Nov1865; Tallahassee, FL; bounty due $100
Pension: 22Sep1890 in AL; App# 919641, Cert# 985302
Widow's Pension: 30Jan1909 in AL; App #912751, Cert #682684

BOTTOM, George M. D.
AKA: George M. D. BOTTOMS
Birth: circa 1846 in Lawrence Co, AR
Death: after 10 Oct 1865
Description: light complexion, blue eyes, sandy hair
Union Enlistment: 11Jul1864; Ft. Barrancas, FL; Co. F, Private
Engagements: Montgomery, AL
Desertion: 10Oct1865 in Monticello, FL

BOUTWELL, Bailey R.
AKA: Bailey R. BOWTWELL
Birth: circa 1844 in Pike Co, AL
Description: fair complexion, blue eyes, light hair
Union Enlistment: 10Mar1864; East Pass, FL; Co. D, Private
Died: 05Jun1864, Ft. Barrancas, FL

BOUTWELL, Elam D.
AKA: Elam D. BOWTWELL
Birth: circa 1843 in Pike Co, AL
1860 Location: Elba, Coffee Co, AL
Description: fair complexion, blue eyes, light hair
Union Enlistment: 16Mar1864; East Pass, FL; Co. D, Private
Died: 11Jun1864 at Ft. Barrancas, FL

BOUTWELL, William B.
AKA: William BOWTWELL
Birth: 31Dec1847; Pike Co, AL
Death: 17Jun1923 in Pike Co, AL
Burial: Jun1923, Brundidge, Pike Co, AL; Union Springs Primitive Baptist Church
1860 Location: Elba, Coffee County, AL
Description: fair complexion, blue eyes, light hair
CSA: 06Oct1863 - 31Oct1863; 61st AL Infantry, Co G, Private
Union Enlistment: 16Mar1864, East Pass, FL; Co D, Private
Union Discharge: 17Nov1865; Tallahassee, FL; bounty due $120
Pension: 10Aug1887; AL; App#618923, Cert#861115
Widow's Pension: 23Jul1923; AL; App #1208239, Cert #979324

BRAXTON, Benjamin R.
AKA: Benjamin BRAXSTON; Benjamin BRAXITON; Benjamin BRARITON; Ben R. BRAXTON
Birth: Apr1842; Henry Co, AL
Death: 20Nov1920; Rankin Co, MS
1860 Location: Cerro Gordo, Holmes County, FL
Description: dark complexion, blue eyes, dark hair
CSA: 20Apr1863 - 15May1863; Capt. Chaires' Independent Company (Hood's Guards), FL Infantry, Private, deserted; records transferred to 11th FL Infantry, Co I
Union Enlistment: 30Dec1863, Ft. Barrancas, FL; Co. A, Private
Engagements: Raid in South Alabama
Union Discharge: 17Nov1865; Tallahassee, FL; bounty due $275
Military Finding: 01Sept1888; desertion charges dropped
Pension: 23Jun1888 in AL; App#614716, Cert#1055000
Widow's Pension: 31Dec1920 in MS; App #1172572

BRAXTON, Isom
AKA: Isham BRAXTON
Birth: circa 1841 in Henry Co, AL
Death: 29Mar1920 in Conecuh Co, AL
1860 Location: Cerro Gordo, Holmes County, FL
Description: dark complexion, blue eyes, black hair
CSA: 25Mar - 03Jul1863; 4th FL Battalion Infantry, Co C, Private, deserted; records transferred to 11th FL Infantry, Co K
Union Enlistment: 30Dec1863; Ft. Barrancas, FL; Co. B, Private
Union Discharge: 17Nov1865; Tallahassee, FL; bounty due $120
Pension: 08May1889 in AL; App # 703496, Cert #916479
Widow's Pension: 11May1920 in AL; App#1157367, Cert#928633

BRAXTON, Jasper
AKA: Jasper BRAXITON
Birth: circa 1846; Henry Co, AL
Death: between 24Apr1877 - 1880 in Holmes Co, FL
1860 Location: Cerro Gordo, Holmes County, FL
Description: fair complexion, blue eyes, light hair
Union Enlistment: 20Jun1864; Ft. Barrancas, FL; Co. F, Private
Union Discharge: 17Nov1865; Tallahassee, FL; bounty due $75
Pension: 24Apr1877; App#234607, Cert#272137

BRAXTON, Martin
AKA: Martin BRARITON; Martin BRAXITON; Martin BRAXSTON
Birth: circa 1829; Barbour Co, AL
Death: Feb 1880; Grant Parish, LA
1860 Location: Burnt Corn, Monroe County, AL
Description: dark complexion, blue eyes, dark hair
Union Enlistment: 20Dec1863; Ft. Barrancas, FL; Co. A, Private
Engagements: Raid on the Florida and Alabama Railroad; Montgomery, AL
Union Discharge: 17Nov1865; Tallahassee, FL; bounty due $275

BRAXTON, Oliver O.
AKA: Oliver A. BRAXTON; Oliver BRAXITON
Birth: Sep1837; Barbour Co, AL

Death: after 23 Jun 1900
1860 Location: Holmes County, FL
Description: light complexion, blue eyes, black hair
CSA: 25Mar - 03Jul1863; 4th Battalion FL Infantry, Co. C,
Private, deserted; records transferred to 11th FL Infantry, Co K.
Union Enlistment: 18Sep1864; Ft. Barrancas, FL; Co. A, Private
Pension: 05Sept1892 in FL; App # 1128853
Union Discharge: 17Nov1865; Tallahassee, FL

BREWER, Henry O.
Birth: circa 1831; Kershaw County, SC
Burial: Jun1864 in Escambia, FL; Barrancas National Cemetery
1860 Location: Dale County, AL
Description: dark complexion, gray eyes, dark hair
CSA: 05Feb - 12Feb1863; 4th Battalion FL Infantry, Co A,
Private, deserted; records transferred to 11th FL Infantry, Co C.
Union Enlistment: 17Dec1863; Ft. Barrancas, FL; Co. A, Private
Died: 27 Jun 1864; Ft. Barrancas, FL

BRITT, John H.
Birth: circa 1822; Sampson Co, NC
Death: after 04 Jul 1870; Georgia
1860 Location: Coffee County, AL
Description: fair complexion, hazel eyes, brown hair
Union Enlistment: 28Feb1864; Ft. Barrancas, FL; Co. C, Private
Promotions: 23 Mar 1864; Blacksmith
Union Discharge: 17Nov1865; Tallahassee, FL; bounty due $120

BROWN, Allen
Birth: circa 1838; Stewart Co, Georgia
Death: 04Aug1883 - 05Jun1899; Florida
Description: dark complexion, dark eyes, dark hair
Union Enlistment: 24Feb1864; Ft. Barrancas, FL; Co. C, Private
Union Discharge: 17Nov1865, Tallahassee, FL; bounty due $120
Pension: 04Aug1880 in FL; App #409232, Cert # 443314
Widow's Pension: 05Jun1899 in FL; App#699569, Cert#548500

BROWN, F. M.
Union Enlistment: Jul1864; Co. C, Private

Desertion: Jul1864; absent without leave

BROWN, George Owen
AKA: Owen BROWN
Birth: Jul1845; Walton Co, FL
Death: 14Sept1907; Holmes Co, FL
Burial: Sept1907; Prosperity, Holmes Co, FL; Hudson Hill Church
1860 Location: Holmes County, FL
Description: fair complexion, blue eyes, light hair
Union Enlistment: 03Aug1864; East Pass, FL; Co. F, Private
Desertion: 10Jul1865
Military Finding: 16Feb1889; charge of desertion dropped
Pension: 20Dec1900 in FL; App # 1259271
Widow's Pension: 09May1915 in FL; App#893068, Cert#661341

BROWN, George W.
Birth: circa 1846; Conecuh Co, AL
Death: 07Jun1880 - 10Feb1893; Alabama
1860 Location: Sparta, Conecuh County, AL
Description: light complexion, blue eyes, brown hair
Union Enlistment: 23Mar1864; Ft. Barrancas, FL; Co. C, Private
Engagements: Fifteen Mile House, FL
Desertion: 24Jul1864 near Fifteen Mile House, FL
Widow's Pension: 10Feb1893 in AL; App #574179

BROWN, James
Birth: circa 1847; Walton Co, FL
Death: after 27Aug1865
1860 Location: Open Pond, Henry County, AL
Union Enlistment: 27Mar1865; East Pass, FL; Co. A, Private
Desertion: 27Aug1865; Camp Six Mile, Pensacola, FL
Military Finding: 18Jan1896; notation of the absence of records as evidence of service

BROWN, John
Birth: circa 1819; Stewart Co, GA
Death: 22Jun1880 - 10May1893; Walton Co, FL
1860 Location: Milton, Santa Rosa County, FL

Description: fair complexion, blue eyes, dark hair
Union Enlistment: 24Feb1864; Ft. Barrancas, FL; Co. C, Private
Union Discharge: 17Nov1865; Tallahassee, FL; bounty due $120
Pension: 22Jun1880; App #386400
Widow's Pension: 19May1893 in FL; App#576646, Cert#559460

BROWN, John Wesley
AKA: John W. BROWN
Birth: 30May1845; Walton Co, FL
Death: 17Apr1915; Hillsborough Co, FL
Burial: Apr1915; Brandon, Hillsborough Co, FL; New Hope Cemetery
1850 Location: Walton County, FL
Description: light complexion, blue eyes, light hair
Union Enlistment: 19Nov1864; Ft. Barrancas, FL; Co. A, Private
Engagements: Raid on the Florida & Alabama Railroad
Union Discharge: 17Nov1865; Tallahassee, FL
Military Finding: 14Sep1887; Certificate in lieu of lost discharge
Pension: 22Jul1890 in FL; App # 787253, Cert # 588833

BROWNING, John
Birth: circa 1845; Conecuh Co, AL
Death: 17Jul1905; Castleberry, Conecuh Co, AL
1860 Location: Conecuh County, AL
Description: fair complexion, dark eyes, light hair
Union Enlistment: 06Apr1864; Ft. Barrancas, FL; Co. E, Private
Union Discharge: 17Nov1865; Tallahassee, FL; bounty due $75
Military Finding: 04Jun1881; certificate in lieu of lost discharge
Pension: 08Nov1892 in AL; App#1137072
Widow's Pension: 22Sep1916 in AL; App#1076309, Cert#874907

BULLARD, James Wilburn
AKA: James W. BULLARD
Birth: circa 1839; Early Co, GA
Death: 12Dec1888-20Apr1891; Washington Co, FL
1860 Location: Washington County, FL
Description: light complexion, blue eyes, light hair

CSA: 28Feb1862 - 31Oct1863; 1st FL Reorganized Infantry, Co D, Private
Union Enlistment: 13Dec1863; Ft. Barrancas, FL; Co. C, Private
Union Discharge: 17Nov1865; Tallahassee, FL; bounty due $75
Military Finding: 18Mar1884; certificate in lieu of lost discharge
Pension: 12Dec1888 in FL; App#681404, Cert#499135
Widow's Pension: 20Apr1891 in FL; App#509916, Cert#231958

BURDESHAW, Daniel Eli
AKA: Daniel Eli BURDASHAW
Birth: 21Apr1845; Cotton Hill, Randolph Co, GA
Death: 22Feb1925; Dothan, Houston Co, AL
Burial: Feb1925; Houston, AL; Kinsey Baptist Church Cemetery
1860 Location: Henry County, AL
Description: fair complexion, blue eyes, light hair
CSA: 29Mar - 13Dec1862; 39th AL Infantry, Co D, Private, disability discharge
Union Enlistment: 14Sept1864, Ft. Barrancas, FL; Co F, Private
Engagements: Montgomery, AL
Promotions: 19Jul1865; Corporal
Union Discharge: 17Nov1865; Tallahassee, FL
Pension: 08Nov1892 in AL; App#1137076, Cert#1051123

BURK, Isaac
Birth: May - Sept1826 in Darlington Co, SC
Death: after 28Jun1880; Crenshaw Co, AL
1850 Location: Pike County, AL
Description: fair complexion, blue eyes, dark hair
CSA: 10Mar - 16Apr1863; 57th AL Infantry, Co F, Private, deserted.
Union Enlistment: 07 May 1864; East Pass, FL; Co F, Private
Desertion: 15 Nov 1864; Ft. Barrancas, FL
Pension: 28 Jun 1880; App #404518

BURK, Mark
AKA: Mark BURKE
Birth: circa 1840; Baker Co, GA
Death: after 07 Nov 1892

Description: fair complexion, blue eyes, brown hair
CSA: 01Apr1862 - 30Jun1864; 6th FL Infantry, Co H, Private, estimated desertion date
Union Enlistment: 06Oct1864; Ft. Barrancas, FL; Co. F, Private
Desertion: 08Aug1865; Ft. Barrancas, FL
Military Finding: 07Nov1892; charge of desertion dropped

BURLESON, Simeon Wilder
AKA: Simon BURLSON; Simeon BURLSON; Simon BURLISTON; Simeon BURLISON; Sim BURLESON
Birth: 15Sept1845; Pike Co, AL
Death: 05Feb1907; Boggy Bayou, Walton Co, FL
Burial: Feb1907; Niceville, Okaloosa Co, FL; Rocky Memorial Cemetery
1860 Location: Walton County, FL
Description: fair complexion, blue eyes, light hair
Union Enlistment: 13Dec1863, Ft. Barrancas, FL; Co. A, Private
Engagements: Marianna, FL; Fifteen Mile House, FL; Pollard, AL; Montgomery, AL
Promotions: 0 Jul1865; Corporal
Union Discharge: 17Nov1865; Tallahassee, FL; bounty due $75
Pension: 09Feb1891 in FL; App#998903, Cert#718268
Widow's Pension: 02Apr1907 in FL; App#866647, Cert#633525

BURNHAM, Francis M.
AKA: Frank M. BURNAM; Francis BURNHAM; Francis M. BURNHAN
Birth: circa 1841; Henry Co, GA
Death: 17Nov1865 - 07Oct1892
1860 Location: Holmes County, FL
Description: fair complexion, blue eyes, light hair
Union Enlistment: 26Jul1864, East Pass, FL; Co. F, Private
Union Discharge: 17Nov1865, Tallahassee, FL; bounty due $75
Widow's Pension: 07Oct1892; App#561369

BURNUM, Francis
AKA: Francis BURNAM
Birth: circa 1841; Barbour Co, AL

1850 Location: Barbour County, AL
Description: fair complexion, blue eyes, brown hair
Union Enlistment: 04May1864; Ft. Barrancas, FL; Co. F, Private
Died: 08Sep1864; Ft. Barrancas, FL

BUSBEE, William J.
AKA: William J. BUSHBEE; William J. BUZBEE; William BUSBEE; William J. BUSBY
Birth: circa 1844; Crawford Co, GA
Death: 18Jan1893 - 08Jan1906; Alabama
Description: fair complexion, gray eyes, dark hair
Union Enlistment: 05Mar1864; Ft. Barrancas, FL; Co. D, Private
Union Discharge: 17Nov1865; Tallahassee, FL; bounty due $120
Pension: 18Jan1893 in AL; App # 1143652, Cert # 961944
Widow's Pension: 08Jan1906 in AL; App#840853, Cert#611045

BUTLER, Constantine
AKA: Constantine BUTTLER
Birth: circa 1845; Henry Co, AL
Death: after 17Nov1865
1850 Location: Henry County, AL
Description: dark complexion, black eyes, black hair
CSA: 08Jul - 12Aug1863; Capt. Tanner's Co, FL Infantry, Private, deserted; records transferred to 11th FL Infantry, Co F
Union Enlistment: 06Jan1864; Ft. Barrancas, FL; Co A, Private
Engagements: Fifteen Mile House, FL
Union Discharge: 17Nov1865; Tallahassee, FL; bounty due $120

BUTLER, Evan Butler, Evan
AKA: Evan BUTTLER
Birth: circa 1840 in Henry Co, AL
Death: 08Jun1926; Cottonwood, Houston Co, AL
1860 Location: Henry County, AL
Description: dark complexion, dark eyes, dark hair
CSA: 26Apr-12Aug1863; Capt. Tanner's Co, FL Infantry, Private, deserted; records transferred to 11th FL Infantry, Co F
Union Enlistment: 02Jan1864; Ft. Barrancas, FL; Co A, Private
Union Discharge: 17Nov1865; Tallahassee, FL; bounty due $120

Pension: 13Nov1890 in AL; App#943865, Cert#695766
Widow's Pension: 03Jul1926 in AL; App#1545272, Cert#A121726

BUTLER, James D.
AKA: James BUTTLER
Birth: circa 1842; Henry Co, AL
Death: before 02 Dec 1902; Alabama
1860 Location: Henry County, AL
Description: light complexion, dark eyes, dark hair
CSA: 02May1862 - 10Jul1863; 37th AL Infantry, Co E, Private, paroled
Union Enlistment: 28Nov1864; Ft. Barrancas, FL; Co. A, Private
Desertion: 04Aug1865; Ft. Barrancas, FL
Widow's Pension: 02Dec1902 in AL; App #774249

BUZBEE, Elisha
AKA: Elisha BUSBEE
Birth: circa 1825; Houston Co, GA
Death: 16Sept1882 - 02Jun1888; Florida
1860 Location: Coffee County, AL
Description: dark complexion, dark eyes, dark hair
Union Enlistment: 28Jan1864; Ft. Barrancas, FL; Co E, Private
Discharge: 12May1865; liver disease and possible TB
Pension: 16Sept1882 in FL; App#460117
Widow's Pension: 02Jun1888 in FL; App#373765, Cert#343676

BUZBEE, William H.
Birth: circa 1833; Macon Co, GA
Death: 09Jun1886 - 23May1930
1860 Location: Baldwin County, AL
Description: dark complexion, gray eyes, dark hair
Union Enlistment: 26Apr1864; Ft. Barrancas, FL; Co. E, Private
Union Engagements: Pollard, AL; Williams Farm and Pine Barren Creek, FL
Promotions: 12Aug1864; Corporal
Union Discharge: 17Nov1865; Tallahassee, FL; bounty due $75
Pension: 09Jun1886; App#576188, Cert#1056717

Widow's Pension: 23May1930 in FL; App#719962, Cert#565542

BYRD, Seaborn J.
AKA: Severn J. BYRD; Saborrin J. BYRD; Sevone J. BYRD; Seabeorn J. BYRD; Seborin J. BIRD; S. J. BIRD
Birth: circa 1827 in Dale Co, AL
Death: 04Apr1899 in Jackson County, FL
Burial: Apr1899; Jackson Co, FL; Cow Pen Pond Cemetery
1860 Location: Walton County, FL
Description: light complexion, sandy eyes, light hair
CSA: 25Mar - 01Sept1863; 4th Battalion FL Infantry, Co. C, Sergeant; records transferred to the 11th FL Infantry, Co K
Union Enlistment: 06Dec1863, Ft. Barrancas, FL; Co A, Private
Desertion: 05Jun1865; East Pass, FL
Pension: 21Feb1890 in FL; App#757339, Cert#746116
Widow's Pension: 23May1900 in FL; App #719963
Minor's Pension: 12Sept1933 in FL; Mary L. Sutton, App #791221

BYRD, William
Birth: circa 1821 in Pike County, AL
Description: dark complexion, blue eyes, dark hair
CSA: 01May - 04Sept1863; 4th Battalion FL Infantry, Co. C, deserted; records transferred to the 11th FL Infantry, Co K
Union Enlistment: 30 Dec 1863, Ft. Barrancas, FL; Co A, Private
Died: 10Nov1864; Ft. Barrancas, FL
Military Finding: 30Mar1868; died 10 November 1864 in the regimental hospital

C

CAHANN, A. J.
AKA: A. J. CAHOUN; A. J. CAHOON; A. J. CALHOON
Birth: circa 1826 in Fayette Co, KY
Death: after 26May1865
Description: dark complexion, black eyes, black hair
Union Enlistment: 13Feb1865; Ft. Barrancas, FL; Co F, Private
Desertion: 12Apr1865; Ft. Barrancas, FL

CALLAHAN, Bethel Haines
AKA: Hans CALLAHAN; Hays CALAHAN; Haines CALLAGHAN; Bythel Haines CALLAHAN
Birth: 27Oct1829; North Carolina
Death: 16Nov1896; Westville, Holmes Co, FL
Burial: Nov1896; Holmes Co, FL; Westville Cemetery
1860 Location: Holmes County, FL
Description: dark complexion, blue eyes, black hair
CSA: 14Mar1862 - 30Nov1863; 6th FL Infantry, Co I, Private, deserted
Union Enlistment: 23Apr1864; Ft. Barrancas, FL; Co E, Private
Engagements: Marianna, FL; Pollard, AL; Blakeley, AL; Montgomery, AL
Union Discharge: 17Nov1865; Tallahassee, FL; bounty due $75
Pension: 15Feb1882 in FL; App#440044, Cert#599336
Widow's Pension: 24Nov1916 in FL; App#1087090, Cert#824057

CALLAWAY, Elijah Holcomb
AKA: Elisha H. CALLOWAY; Elisha H. CALLAWAY; Elijah H. CALLOWAY
Birth: 28Aug1835; Jackson Co, FL
Death: 06Dec1915; Nevilles Prairie, Houston Co, TX
Burial: Dec1915; Lovelady, Houston Co, TX; Antioch Cemetery
1860 Location: Henry County, AL
Description: dark complexion, blue eyes, dark hair
CSA: 30Aug1861 - 01Dec1863; 6th AL Infantry, Co K, Private, deserted
Union Enlistment: 09Feb1864; Ft. Barrancas, FL; Co D, Private
Desertion: 25Aug1864; Ft. Barrancas, FL

CAMPBELL, Allen
Birth: 05Apr1827; Escambia Co, FL
Death: 04Sept1911; Laurel Hill, Walton Co, FL
Burial: Sept1911; Okaloosa, FL; Magnolia (Clary) Cemetery
1860 Location: Walton County, FL
Description: light complexion, grey eyes, black hair

CSA: 04Feb1863 - 03Jul1863; 3rd Battalion FL Cavalry, Co D, Private, deserted.; records transferred to 15th Confederate Cavalry, Co I
Union Enlistment: 14Jan1864; Ft. Barrancas, FL; Co B, Private
Promotions: 01Apr1864; Corporal
Union Discharge: 17Nov1865; Tallahassee, FL; bounty due $120
Pension: 24Oct1890; App #986479, Cert #1054281

CAMPBELL, Charles D.
AKA: Charles CAMPBELL; Charles CAMPELL
Birth: Oct1844; Alabama
Death: 11Aug1924; Chancellor, Geneva Co, AL
1860 Location: Walton County, FL
Description: light complexion, blue eyes, light hair
CSA: 01May1862 - 24Sept1863; 3rd Battalion FL Cavalry, Co B, Private; transferred to 15th Confederate Cavalry, Co D, deserted.
Union Enlistment: 13Jan1864; Ft. Barrancas, FL; Co A, Private
Promotions: 01Apr1864; Corporal
Military Charges: 29May1865; with Burton Watson & Elisha Water assault and robbery ($30) of Abram McCloud
Military Confinement: 30May - 09Sept1865; Ft. Pickens, FL
Union Discharge: 17Nov1865; Tallahassee, FL; bounty due $275
Widow's Pension: 18Nov1929 in AL; App#1655194

CAMPBELL, Charles M.
Birth: 1820; Conecuh Co, AL
Death: 03May1889; Baldwin Co, AL
Burial: May1889; Baldwin, AL; High Pine Cemetery
1860 Location: Santa Rosa County, FL
Description: light complexion, gray eyes, dark hair
Union Enlistment: 25Jan1864; Ft. Barrancas, FL; Co B, Private
Union Discharge: 17Nov1865; Tallahassee, FL; bounty due $120
Pension: 18Sept1884 in AL; App#522472

CAMPBELL, David M.
Death: after 30Apr1865
Union Enlistment: 7Mar1864; Ft. Barrancas, FL; Private
Engagements: Montgomery, AL

Union Discharge: after 30 Apr 1865; no other recorded info

CAMPBELL, Malcolm
AKA: Malcom CAMPBELL
Birth: 13Dec1829; Walton Co, FL
Death: 27Dec1897; Milligan, Okaloosa Co, FL
Burial: Dec1897; Milligan, Okaloosa, FL; Wilkinson-Baggett Cemetery
1860 Location: Santa Rosa County, FL
Description: dark complexion, black eyes, dark hair
Union Enlistment: 25Feb1864; Ft. Barrancas, FL; Co B, Private
Promotions: 01Apr1864; 1st Sergeant (Orderly Sergeant)
Union Discharge: 17Nov1865; Tallahassee, FL; bounty due $160
Pension: 23Aug1890; App#908785, Cert#794534
Widow's Pension: 15Feb1898 in FL; App#670643, Cert#552853

CAMPBELL, Thomas
AKA: Thomas CAMBBELL; Thomas CAMMEL; Thomas CAMNELL
Birth: circa 1835; Twiggs Co, GA
Death: after 10Mar1865
Description: dark complexion, blue eyes, black hair
Union Enlistment: 12Jan1864; Ft. Barrancas, FL; Co A, Private
Desertion: 10Mar1865; East Pass, FL

CAMPBELL, William A.
Birth: circa 1835; Walton Co, FL
Death: 24Sept1885 - 23Aug1899; Escambia Co, FL
1850 Location: Santa Rosa County, FL
Description: dark complexion, dark eyes, dark hair
Union Enlistment: 25Jan1864, Ft. Barrancas, FL; Co B, Private
Promotions: 01Apr1864; Corporal
Promotions: 01July1864; Sergeant
Military Confinement: Jul1865; Ft. Pickens, FL
Union Discharge: 17Nov1865, Tallahassee, FL; bounty due $160
Pension: 24Sept1885; App#550349
Widow's Pension: 23Aug1899 in FL; App#704330, Cert#563062

CANTALINE, Henry
AKA: Henry CANTELINE; Henry CANTLIN; Henry CANTILINE
Birth: circa 1826; Monroe Co, AL
Burial: Jun 1864; Escambia Co, FL; Barrancas National Cemetery, Sec 1, Site 955
1860 Location: Coffee County, AL
Description: dark complexion, dark eyes, brown hair
CSA: 31Jan - 31Dec1863; 33rd AL Infantry, Co A, Private, estimated desertion date
Union Enlistment: 20May1864; East Pass, FL; Co F, Private
Died: 14Jun1864; Ft. Barrancas, FL
Widow's Pension: 06Jun1877; App#231730

CARLOVITZ, John
Birth: 1832; Prussia
Death: 1897; Milton, Santa Rosa Co, FL
Burial: 1897; Milton, Santa Rosa Co, FL; Milton Cemetery, Plot 25
Union Enlistment: 15Mar1864, Ft. Barrancas, FL; Field & Staff, 1st Lt.
Union Discharge: 17Nov1865; Tallahassee, FL
Pension: 15Jul1890 in FL; App#820098, Cert#908714
Widow's Pension: 18Dec1897 in FL; App#667651, Cert#478647

CARMICHAEL, James W.
AKA: James W. CARMICHAL; James W. CARMICHEL; James W. CARMICHIEL; James W. CARMIKIEL
Birth: 26Jul1844; Washington Co, FL
Death: 08Aug1928; Point Washington, Walton Co, FL
1850 Location: Washington County, FL
Description: dark complexion, black or blue eyes, dark hair
CSA: 23Aug1862 - 31Oct1863; 2nd FL Cavalry Regiment, Co G, Private, deserted
Union Enlistment: 14Dec1863, Ft. Barrancas, FL; Co C, Private
Engagements: Marianna, FL
Desertion: 09Oct1864; Florida
Military Finding: 10Apr1889; removal of desertion charge denied
Pension: 11Apr1889 in FL; App#698201

Widow's Pension: 25Feb1933 in FL; App#1731702

CARMICHAEL, William Henry
AKA: William H. CARMICHEAL
Birth: 24Jun1847; Washington Co, FL
Death: 17Jan1922; Washington Co, FL
Burial: Jan1922, Vernon, Washington, FL; New Hope Cemetery
1850 Location: Washington County, FL
Description: fair complexion, dark eyes, dark hair
Union Enlistment: 25Jan1864, Ft. Barrancas, FL; Co D, Private
Engagements: Raid on Florida & Alabama Railroad; Montgomery, AL
Desertion: 08May1865
Military Finding: 20Oct1884; charge of desertion removed
Pension: 19Jan1891 in FL; App#986483, Cert#973715

CARNLEY, Daniel Nathaniel
AKA: Daniel M. CARNELLY
Birth: 1844; Pike Co, AL
Death: 14Dec1931; Chipley, Washington Co, FL
Burial: Dec1931, Holmes, FL; East Mount Zion Methodist Church
1850 Location: Pike County, AL
Description: dark complexion, black eyes, black hair
Union Enlistment: 05Mar1864; Ft. Barrancas, FL; Co D, Private
Engagements: Raid in South Alabama
Union Discharge: 17Nov1865; Tallahassee, FL; bounty due $120
Pension: 15Aug1892 in FL; App#1125895, Cert#1126717

CARNLEY, William Eli
AKA: William E. CARNELLY
Birth: circa 1845; Pike County, AL
Death: 09Sept1870 - 21Mar1884; Holmes Co, FL
1850 Location: Pike County, AL
Description: dark complexion, dark eyes, dark hair
Union Enlistment: 05Mar1864; Ft. Barrancas, FL; Co D, Private
Union Discharge: 17Nov1865; Tallahassee, FL; bounty due $120
Pension: 21Mar1884 in FL; App#313965

CARR, W. Carr, W.
Desertion: 24Mar1865

CARROLL, Elijah Gibson
AKA: Elijah G. CARROLL
Birth: circa 1839; Twiggs Co, GA
1860 Location: Coffee County, AL
Description: light complexion, gray eyes, dark hair
Union Enlistment: 07Apr1864; East Pass, FL; Co E, Private
Military Confinement: 17Jan1865; Regimental guard house
Died: 11Nov1865; at home in AL, bounty due $75
Military Finding: 09Oct1886; AG's office indicated he died at his home on 11Nov1865 and canceled the muster out record
Widow's Pension: 15Oct1867 in FL; App#153642, Cert#228701

CARROLL, Frederick D.
Birth: circa 1846; Dale Co, AL
Death: after 17Aug1870
1860 Location: Barbour County, AL
Description: fair complexion, blue (gray) eyes, light hair
Union Enlistment: 20Jan1865; Ft. Barrancas, FL; Co C, Private
Engagements: Montgomery, AL
Desertion: 27May1865; AL; bounty paid $100

CARROLL, Joseph B.
Birth: circa 1841; Dale Co, AL
Death: 30Jun1885 - 15Dec1890; Jefferson Co, FL
1860 Location: Walton County, FL
Description: CSA & USA - fair complexion, grey eyes, light hair
CSA: 18Sept1861 - 31Mar1863; 4th FL Infantry, Co H, 2nd Lt, likely did not re-enlist. 30Jun - 31Dec1863; 4th Battalion FL Infantry, Co C, Private, deserted; records transferred to 11th FL Infantry, Co K.
Union Enlistment: 15Feb1864; Ft. Barrancas, FL; Co C, Private
Engagements: Raid in South Alabama; Montgomery, AL
Promotions: 29Mar1864; 2nd Lieutenant by order of Gen Banks
Promotions: 8Feb1865; 1st Lieutenant in Co D
Union Discharge: 17Nov1865; Tallahassee, FL

Pension: 28Oct1880; App#411279, Cert#257237
Widow's Pension: 15Dec1890 in FL; App #493293, Cert#290594

CARTER, Hardy H.
Birth: circa 1824; Fairfield Co, SC
1860 Location: Coffee County, AL
Description: light complexion, brown eyes, light hair
CSA: 16Mar1863 - 31Oct1863; 57th AL Infantry, Co K, Private, estimated desertion date
Union Enlistment: 24Mar1864, East Pass, FL; Co E, Private
Died: 19Oct1864; Ft. Barrancas, FL; bounty due $275
Widow's Pension: 07Mar1871; App#194348, Cert#169931

CARTER, Jasper J.
AKA: Jasper CARTER
Birth: circa 1844; Macon Co, GA
Death: 07Jun1880 – 1900; Florida
Burial: Wausau, Washington, FL; Barfield Cemetery
1860 Location: Lowndes County, GA
Description: dark complexion, brown eyes, brown hair
CSA: 07Sep1861 - 12Dec1863; 4th FL Infantry, Co H, Private, deserted
Union Enlistment: 19May1864, East Pass, FL; Co F, Private
Engagements: Marianna, FL
Desertion: 26Sep - 02Oct1864; Vernon, Washington, FL

CARTER, Lemuel
Birth: circa 1834; Dale Co, AL
Burial: May1864; Escambia, Florida; Barrancas National Cemetery, Sec 1, Site 954
1860 Location: Walton County, FL
Description: fair complexion, hazel eyes, brown hair
CSA: 16Mar - 01Jul1863; 57th AL Infantry, Co, K, Private, deserted
Union Enlistment: 11Mar1864; Ft. Barrancas, FL; Co D, Private
Promotions: 01Apr1864; 5th Sergeant
Died: 26May1864; Ft. Barrancas, FL
Widow's Pension: 18Jul1867; App #150067, Cert #106023

Minor's Pension: 17May1875; Grandson, Bartlett M. Tucker, App#221049, Cert#172133

CARTER, William Leonard
Birth: 22Oct1844; Dale Co, AL
Death: 16Jun1928; Laurel Hill, Okaloosa Co, FL
Burial: Almarante Cemetery, Okaloosa Co, FL
1860 Location: Walton County, FL
Description: light complexion, hazel eyes, brown hair
CSA: 21Oct - 31Oct1863; 57th AL Infantry, Co, K, Private, estimated desertion date
Union Enlistment: 11Mar1864; East Pass, FL; Co D, Private
Promotion: 11Mar1864; Corporal
Union Discharge: 17Nov1865; Tallahassee, FL; bounty due $160
Pension: 02Jan1891 in FL; App#987978, Cert#1071779
Widow's Pension: 28Feb1929 in FL; App #1636387

CASSIDA, William
AKA: William CARSIDA; William CAISDA; William CASIDA; William CASIDY; William CASSIDY
Birth: circa 1846; Holmes Co, FL
Death: Jun1885-24Jan1900; Freeport, Walton Co, FL
Description: light complexion, blue (gray) eyes, light (dark) hair
Union Enlistment: 27Mar1864, Ft. Barrancas, FL; Co E, Private
Engagements: Montgomery, AL
Union Discharge: 17Nov1865; Tallahassee, FL; bounty due $200
Pension: 11Jul1890 in FL; App#796983
Widow's Pension: 24Jan1900 in FL; App #712065, Cert #607316
Minor's Pension: 16Dec1903 in FL; Sarah J. Caswell; App#796389, Cert#607317

CASSIDY, Cornelius
AKA: Cornelius CASSADY; Cornelius CASADY; Cornelius CASSIDA
Birth: circa 1836; Alabama
Death: 25Aug1895; Walton Co, FL
Burial: Aug1895; Walton Co, FL; Hatcher Cemetery
1860 Location: Coffee County, AL

Description: light complexion, blue eyes, light hair
CSA: 03Apr - 31Dec1863; 6th AL Cavalry, Co K, Private, estimated end date
Union Enlistment: 25Mar1864; East Pass, FL; Co D, Private
Union Discharge: 17Nov1865; Tallahassee, FL; bounty due $120
Pension: 28May1888 in FL; App#656829, Cert#698493
Widow's Pension: 19Sept1895 in FL; App#620836, Cert#546012

CASWELL, William Giles
AKA: Gillis CASWELL
Birth: Jun 1835; Florida
Death: 01Jun1900 - 06Jul 1903; Walton Co, FL
1860 Location: Walton County, FL
Description: dark complexion, hazel eyes, dark hair
CSA: 01May - 01Aug1862; 1st FL Reorganized Infantry, Co D, Private
Union Enlistment: 12Apr1864; East Pass, FL; Co E, Private
Engagements: Marianna, FL; Pollard, AL; Blakeley, AL; Greenville, AL; Montgomery, AL
Desertion: 18Oct1865; Tallahassee, FL
Military Finding: 12Apr1890; desertion charges dropped
Pension: 14Aug1890 in FL; App#858127, Cert#726827
Widow's Pension: 06Jul1903 in TX; App#787560, Cert#563779

CATO, Daniel
Birth: 30Mar1825; Houston Co, GA
Death: 25May1904; Trafford, Jefferson Co, AL
Burial: May1904; Jefferson Co, AL; County Line Cemetery
1860 Location: Blount County, AL
Description: dark complexion, blue eyes, dark hair
CSA: 25Feb - 31Aug1863; 29th AL Infantry, Co I, Private, likely deserted
Union Enlistment: 06Jul1864; East Pass, FL; Co F, Private
Desertion: 04Aug1865; Ft. Barrancas, FL; bounty paid $25
Military Finding: 26May1904; desertion charges dropped
Widow's Pension: 18Jul1904; App #810288, Cert #587624

CAULEY, John Richard
AKA: John R. CAULEY; John R. CAWLEY
Birth: 08Mar1827; Covington Co, AL
Death: 19May1907; Coffee Co, AL
Burial: May1907; Opp, Covington, AL; Friendship United Methodist Church Cemetery
1860 Location: Coffee County, AL
Description: fair complexion, blue eyes, sandy hair
CSA: 22Jul1861 - 17Feb1863; 18th AL Infantry, Co A, Private, disability discharge
Union Enlistment: 24Feb1864; Ft. Barrancas, FL; Co C, Private
Engagements: Raid in South Alabama
Promotions: 06Sept1864; 5th Sergeant
Union Discharge: 17Nov1865; Tallahassee, FL; bounty due $275
Military Finding: 21Mar1887; charge of desertion dropped, absent without proper authority, reference to "prior desertion" removed as erroneous
Pension: 26Jun1882; App #1153119, Cert #417856

CAYLOR, George Washington
AKA: George W. TAYLOR
Birth: 1Sept1840; Houston Co, GA
Death: 09Feb1927; Galliver, Okaloosa Co, FL
Burial: Feb1927; Baker, Okaloosa Co, FL; Pilgrim's Rest Baptist Church Cemetery
Description: fair complexion, gray eyes, light hair
CSA: 13May1862 - 18Sept1863; 6th FL Infantry, Co I, Private, deserted
Union Enlistment: 28Jan1864; Ft. Barrancas, FL; Co D, Private
Engagements: Montgomery, AL
Promotions: 01Apr1864; Sergeant
Union Discharge: 17Nov1865; Tallahassee, FL; bounty due $120
Pension: 30Sept1902; App #1291318, Cert #1105711

CHANCEY, James Jackson
AKA: Jackson CHANCY; Jackson CHAUNCEY
Birth: circa 1846; Dale Co, AL
Death: after 10Aug1870

1860 Location: Coffee County, AL
Description: fair complexion, blue eyes, light hair
Union Enlistment: 27Aug1864; East Pass, FL; Co D, Private
Union Discharge: 17Nov1865; Tallahassee, FL

CHANCEY, John Wesley
AKA: John CHANCEY; John CHANCY; John CHAUNCY
Birth: Apr1818; Darlington Co, SC
Death: circa 1908; Lake Bird, Taylor Co, FL
1860 Location: Coffee County, AL
Description: fair complexion, blue eyes, light hair
Union Enlistment: 27Aug1864; East Pass, FL; Co D, Private
Union Discharge: 17Nov1865; Tallahassee, FL
Pension: 07Nov1883 in FL; App # 474705, Cert # 395690

CHESSER, Napoleon Bonaparte
AKA: Napoleon B. CHESSES
Birth: 30Jan1844; Pike Co, AL
Death: 06Dec1914; Caryville, Washington Co, FL
1860 Location: Covington County, AL
Description: fair complexion, gray eyes, light hair
Union Enlistment: 24Feb1864; Ft. Barrancas, FL; Co C, Private
Disability Discharge: 12May1865
Pension: 26Jul1883 in FL; App# 455913, Cert# 691673

CHESTNUT, Jasper
AKA: Jasper CHESNUT; Joseph CHESTNUT
Birth: Oct1837; Stewart Co, GA
Death: Jun1900 - 08Aug1907; Walton Co, FL
1860 Location: Walton County, FL
Description: dark complexion, dark eyes, dark hair
CSA: 07Feb - 10May1863; 3rd Battalion FL Cavalry, Co D, Private, deserted; records transferred to 15th Confederate Cavalry.
Union Enlistment: 19Jan1864; Ft. Barrancas, FL; Co B, Private
Desertion: 18Aug1865; Ft. Barrancas, FL
Military Finding: 12Jul1884; desertion charges dropped
Pension: 15Oct1892 in FL; App#1134602, Cert#1005192

Widow's Pension: 08Aug1907 in FL; App#874538, Cert#644417

CLARK, Hamilton
AKA: Clark HAMILTON
Birth: circa 1835; Tennessee
Death: 28Jun1880 - 18Feb1892; Crittenden Co, AR
Description: black complexion, black eyes, black hair
Union Enlistment: 14Jul1864; Ft. Barrancas, FL; Co C, Under cook
Union Discharge: 17Nov1865; Tallahassee, FL
Widow's Pension: 18Feb1892 in AR; App#544419, Cert#404666

CLARK, John H.
Birth: 5Jan1837; Pike Co, AL
Death: 17Nov1865 - 20Sep1882
Description: fair complexion, yellow eyes, light hair
CSA: 25Sep1863; Barbiere's AL Battalion Cavalry, Brown's Co, Private, discharged by Examining Board
Union Enlistment: 10Mar1864; Ft. Barrancas, FL; Co F
Union Discharge: 17Nov1865; Tallahassee, FL

CLARY, William P.
AKA: William B. CLARY
Birth: circa 1844; Walton Co, FL
Death: 1870 – 1880; Walton Co, FL
1860 Location: Walton County, FL
Description: sandy complexion, brown eyes, black hair
CSA: 02Apr1862 - 3 Jun1864; 6th FL Infantry, Co H, Private
Union Enlistment: 01Oct1864; Ft. Barrancas, FL; Co B, Private
Desertion: 19Jan1865; Ft. Barrancas, Florida

CLOUD, John
Birth: circa 1846; Jackson Co, FL
Death: after 22May1865
1860 Location: Jackson County, FL
Description: fair complexion, blue eyes, light hair
Union Enlistment: 27Nov1864; Ft. Barrancas, FL; Co F, Private
Desertion: 22May1865; Montgomery, AL

COBB, Ezekiel M.
Birth: circa 1830; Covington Co, AL
Death: after 17Nov1865
1850 Location: Covington County, AL
Description: light complexion, blue eyes, light hair
CSA: 01Aug - 31Aug1861; 12th AL Infantry, Co K, Private
Union Enlistment: 19Jan1864; Ft. Barrancas, FL; Co B, Private
Promotions: 09Nov1864; Corporal
Union Discharge: 17Nov1865; Tallahassee, FL; bounty due $120

COBB, James H.
Birth: circa 1822; Martin Co, NC
Death: after 20Jul1870; Baldwin Co, AL
1860 Location: Baldwin County, AL
Description: light complexion, blue eyes, light hair
Union Enlistment: 10Oct1864; Ft. Barrancas, FL; Co A, Private
Desertion: 11Aug1865; Ft. Barrancas, FL

COCKCROFT, James Alexander
AKA: James A. COCKCRAFT; James A. COCKROFT
Birth: circa 1844; Walton Co, FL
Death: after 14Jun1880; Taylor Co, FL
1860 Location: Walton County, FL
Description: fair complexion, blue eyes, light hair
Union Enlistment: 23Mar1864; Ft. Barrancas, FL; Co D, Private
Engagements: Raid in South Alabama; Montgomery, AL
Union Discharge: 17Nov1865; Tallahassee, FL; bounty due $120
Pension: 16Sep1879; App#309607, Cert#237977

COCKCROFT, Micajah Allen
AKA: McKager COCKCRAFT; McKager COCKCROFT; McKager COCKROFT; Mieayah Allen COCKCROFT
Birth: Jul1847; Walton Co, FL
Death: 25Aug1929; Carbur, Taylor Co, FL
Burial: Aug1929; Taylor, FL; Salem Cemetery
1860 Location: Walton County, FL
Description: fair complexion, gray eyes, light hair
Union Enlistment: 23Mar1864; Ft. Barrancas, FL; Co D, Private

Engagements: Raid in South Alabama; Montgomery, AL
Promotions: 17Dec1864; Corporal
Union Discharge: 17Nov1865; Tallahassee, FL; bounty due $120
Pension: 26Apr1892 in FL; App#1108107, Cert#976507
Widow's Pension: 11Oct1929; App#1652742, Cert#A3-13-30

COLEMAN, Allen V.
AKA: Allen V. COLMAN
Birth: circa 1839; Butler Co, AL
Death: after 28May1865
1860 Location: Baldwin County, AL
Description: light complexion, blue eyes, dark hair
CSA: 20Feb1862 - 28Aug1863; 32nd AL Infantry, Co B, Private, deserted
Union Enlistment: 19May1864; Ft. Barrancas, FL; Co F, Private
Desertion: 28May1865; Dale, AL

COLLINSWORTH, Abraham
AKA: Abraham COLLINGSWORTH; Abraham COLINGSWORTH Hammer COLLINSWORTH
Birth: 06Mar1841; Pike Co, AL
Death: 14Feb1917; Milton, Santa Rosa Co, FL
1850 Location: Coffee County, AL
Description: dark complexion, black eyes, dark hair
Union Enlistment: 08Sept1864; Ft. Barrancas, FL; Co D, Private
Desertion: 06Apr1865; Ft. Barrancas, FL
Pension: 04Sept1890 in FL; App# 928911

CONWAY, Charles W.
AKA: Charles W. CONAWAY
Birth: circa 1846; Gadsden Co, FL
Death: after 16Jun1880
1860 Location: Gadsden Co, FL
Description: light complexion, black eyes, dark hair
Union Enlistment: 07Jul1864; Ft. Barrancas, FL; Co A, Private
Military Charges: 03Aug1864; conduct prejudicial to good order and military discipline, refused to be mustered
Military Confinement: 04Aug1864 - Feb1865; Ft. Pickens, FL

Desertion: 11Aug1865; Ft. Barrancas, FL

COOK, Unknown
Desertion: 12Jun1865

COOLEY, Gillis
AKA: Achillis COOLEY
Birth: circa 1835; Florida
Death: 11Jul1897; Ponce de Leon, Holmes Co, FL
Description: light complexion, blue eyes, dark hair
Union Enlistment: 25Mar1864; East Pass, FL; Co D, Private
Union Discharge: 17Nov1865; Tallahassee, FL; bounty due $120
Pension: 24Oct1888; App#676728, Cert#875939
Widow's Pension: 17Aug1897 in FL; App#660229, Cert#616852

COON, James Jackson
Birth: 1812 – 1816; Twiggs Co, GA
1860 Location: Covington County, AL
Description: light complexion, blue eyes, gray hair
Union Enlistment: 24Feb1864, Ft. Barrancas, FL; Co C, Private
Promotions: 23Mar1864; Corporal
Promotions: July - Aug1864; Sergeant
Died: 06Sept1864; Ft. Barrancas, FL
Widow's Pension: 24Jul1868; App#163251, Cert#126161

COON, Joseph Jerold
Birth: Feb1846; Coffee Co, AL
Death: after 05Jun1900; Covington Co, AL
1860 Location: Covington County, AL
Description: fair complexion, gray eyes, brown hair
Union Enlistment: 24Feb1864; Ft. Barrancas, FL; Co C, Private
Desertion: 22Dec1864; Ft. Barrancas, FL
Military Finding: 14Nov1883; request for removal of desertion charge denied

COOPER, Thomas Jefferson
Birth: 31Mar1825; Laurens Co, GA
Death: 15Jun1880 - 19Apr1919; Swift, Baldwin Co, AL
1860 Location: Santa Rosa County, FL

Description: fair complexion, blue eyes, brown hair
Union Enlistment: 08Mar1864; East Pass, Co D, Private
Desertion: 07Aug1865; Ft. Barrancas, FL
Military Finding: 14May1919; desertion charges dropped
Widow's Pension: 19Apr1919 in FL; App#1139906

COPPAHANT, James H.

COX, George W.
Birth: circa 1846; Brunswick Co, NC
Death: 16Dec1924; Noma, Holmes Co, FL
1860 Location: Washington County, FL
Description: fair complexion, blue eyes, light hair
CSA: 2Mar 1863 - Jan1864; 4th Battalion FL Infantry, Co. C, Private, likely deserted; records transferred to 11th FL Infantry, Co K.
Union Enlistment: 02Feb1864, Ft. Barrancas, FL; Co D, Private
Engagements: Raid in South Alabama; Montgomery, AL
Union Discharge: 17Nov1865; Tallahassee, FL; bounty due $120
Pension: 14Oct1891; App#1063129, Cert#799078
Widow's Pension: 26Jan1925 in FL; App#1228615, Cert #A5326

COXWELL, John Thomas
AKA: John T. COXWELL
Birth: 31Jul1848; Henry Co, AL
Death: 08Feb1894; Clarke Co, AL
1860 Location: Covington County, AL
Description: fair complexion, blue eyes, dark hair
Union Enlistment: 16Nov1864; Ft. Barrancas, FL; Co F, Private
Engagements: Montgomery, AL
Union Discharge: 17Nov1865; Tallahassee, FL
Pension: 19Jan1885; App#530376, Cert#790685
Widow's Pension: 29Oct1903 in AL; App #793792, Cert #566043

CRAVEY, Jonas
Birth: circa 1844; Dale Co, AL
Burial: Jul1864; Escambia Co, Florida; Barrancas National Cemetery, Sec 1, Site 948
1860 Location: Washington County, FL

Description: light complexion, hazel eyes, light hair
CSA: 25Mar-Jul1863; Capt McLean's Independent Company, FL Infantry, Private, deserted; records transferred to 11th FL Infantry, Co K.
Union Enlistment: 02Apr1864, East Pass, FL; Co E, Private
Died: 13Jul1864; Ft. Barrancas, FL; bounty due $75

CREAMER, Henry H.
AKA: Henry CREAMER
Birth: circa 1820; Alabama
Death: after 16Oct1865
Description: fair complexion, blue eyes, light hair
Union Enlistment: 15Feb1864; Ft. Barrancas, FL; Co A, Private
Engagements: Raid on Fifteen Mile house, FL; Pollard, AL
Promotions: 01Apr1864; Corporal
Desertion: 16Oct1865; Monticello, FL

CRENSHAW, Aaron
AKA: Aaron GEONSHAW
Birth: circa 1839; Butler Co, AL
Death: after 14Aug1865
Description: black complexion, black eyes, black hair
Union Enlistment: 21Dec1864; Ft. Barrancas, FL; Co B, Under Cook
Desertion: 14Aug1865; Ft. Barrancas, FL

CREWS, John
Birth: circa 1831; Alabama
1860 Location: Coffee County, AL
Description: fair complexion, brown eyes, sandy hair
CSA: 17Feb - 17Nov1863; 11th FL Infantry, Co C, Private, deserted; records transferred from 4th Battalion FL Infantry, Co A to 11th FL Infantry
Union Enlistment: 27Apr1864; East Pass, FL; Co F, Private
Died: 28Aug1864; Ft. Barrancas, FL
Widow's Pension: 06Apr1867; App#145188, Cert#143488

CRIDER, William R.
AKA: William R. CRYDER

Birth: Oct1845; Pike Co, AL
Death: 15Au1922; Daleville, Dale Co, AL
1860 Location: Holmes County, FL
Description: dark complexion, black eyes, dark hair
CSA: 25Mar-Jul1863; 11th FL Infantry, Co K, Private, deserted
Union Enlistment: 13Dec1863; Ft. Barrancas, FL; Co A, Private
Engagements: "Has been on all raids and scouts with Regiment and Company"; Montgomery, AL
Union Discharge: 17Nov1865; Tallahassee, FL; bounty due $75
Pension: 12Jan1891 in AL; App#986518, Cert#701050

CROSBY, James M.
AKA: James M. CAUSBAY; James M. CRAUSBY; James M. CRAUSBAY; James M. CRANSBY; James M. CROUSBAY
Birth: circa 1828; Columbia Co, GA
Death: after 13Sept1881
1860 Location: Covington County, AL
Description: fair complexion, dark eyes, dark hair
Union Enlistment: 01Mar1864; Ft. Barrancas, FL; Co C, Private
Engagements: Montgomery, AL
Union Discharge: 17Nov1865; Tallahassee, FL; bounty due $120
Pension: 13Sept1881; App#428887, Cert#804101
Widow's Pension: App#637415

CUEY, William J.
AKA: William J. CAY; William J. COVEY
Birth: circa 1845; Holmes Co, FL
Death: 26Aug1870 - 01Sept1890
Description: fair complexion, brown eyes, brown hair
Union Enlistment: 14Apr1864; East Pass, FL; Co E, Private
Military Confinement: 24Jun - 31Aug1865; Ft. Pickens, FL
Union Discharge: 17Nov1865; Tallahassee, FL; bounty due $75
Widow's Pension: 01Sept1890 in FL; App #481323, Cert#286904

CULBRETH, Gilmore
AKA: Gilmore CULBRETT; Gilmore CULBERT; Gilmore CULBRITH

Birth: circa 1831; Randolph Co, GA
Death: 2 Jul1870 - 19Dec1887
1860 Location: Covington County, AL
Description: fair complexion, gray eyes, sandy hair
CSA: 07May1862 - 31Aug1863; 29th AL Infantry, Co I, Private, deserted
Union Enlistment: 01Mar1864; Ft. Barrancas, FL; Co C, Private
Union Discharge: 17Nov1865; Tallahassee, FL; bounty due $120
Widow's Pension: 19Dec1887 in MS; App#365024, Cert#380098

CUMBIA, Henry M.
AKA: Henry M. CAMBIA; Henry CUMBIE
Birth: circa 1845; Muscogee Co, GA
1860 Location: Coffee County, AL
Description: dark complexion, gray eyes, dark hair
Union Enlistment: 24Jan1864; Ft. Barrancas, FL; Co B, Private
Died: 18Oct1864; Ft. Barrancas, FL; bounty due $275

CURLEE, John
Birth: circa 1842; Henry Co, GA
Death: after 25Feb1865
1860 Location: Holmes County, FL
Description: fair complexion, dark eyes, light hair
CSA: 07Sept1861 - 31Jan1864; 4th FL Infantry, Co H, Private, deserted
Union Enlistment: 24Sept1864; East Pass, FL; Co E, Private
Desertion: 25Feb1865; Barrancas, FL

CURLEE, Richard
Birth: circa 1844; Stewart Co, GA
Death: after 25 Feb 1865; Holmes Co, FL
Burial: Holmes Co, FL; on private property
1860 Location: Holmes County, FL
Description: fair complexion, yellow eyes, light hair
CSA: 08May1862 - Jun1864; 6th FL Infantry, Co I, Private, deserted
Union Enlistment: 24Sept1864; East Pass, FL; Co E, Private
Desertion: 25Feb1865; Ft. Barrancas, FL

CURRY, William T.
Birth: circa 1829; Barbour Co, AL
Death: 01Sept1890 - 21Jan1902; Alabama
1860 Location: Walton County, FL
Description: fair complexion, blue eyes, sandy hair
CSA: 16Mar - 11Aug1863; 57th AL Infantry, Co K, Private
Union Enlistment: 12Apr1864; East Pass, FL; Co E, Private
Engagements: Montgomery, AL
Promotions: 12Aug1864; 5th Duty Sergeant
Union Discharge: 17Nov1865; Tallahassee, FL; bounty due $75
Pension: 01Sep1890 in AL; App#977706, Cert#789209
Widow's Pension: 21Jan1902 in AL; App #755235, Cert #663287

CUTHERILL, Jasper
AKA: Jasper CUTHRIELL; Jasper CUTHERELL; Jasper CUTHRULL
Birth: circa 1845; Houston Co, GA
Death: 17Aug1914; Wewahitchka, Gulf Co, FL
1860 Location: Holmes County, FL
Description: fair complexion, dark eyes, dark hair
CSA: 26Mar1863 - 25Nov1863; 6th FL Infantry, Co I, Private, deserted
Union Enlistment: 28Jan1864; Ft. Barrancas, FL; Co B, Private
Engagements: Montgomery, AL
Union Discharge: 17Nov1865; Ft. Barrancas, FL; bounty due $120
Pension: 27Jul1892 in AL; App#1044064, Cert#1145504

CUTTS, Zachariah
Birth: 21Feb1840; Thomas Co, GA
Death: 05Dec1914; Green Bay, Covington Co, AL
Burial: Dec1914; Bethel Cemetery, Babbie, Covington Co, AL
1860 Location: Walton County, FL
Description: fair complexion, blue eyes, light hair
CSA: 21Jul1861 - 30Mar1862; 1st FL Infantry, Co E, Private, did not re-enlist. 4Oct1862 – 1July1863; 3rd Battalion FL Cavalry, Co D, Private, deserted; records transferred to 15th Confederate Cavalry, Co I

Union Enlistment: 24Feb1864; Ft. Barrancas, FL; Co B, Private
Promotions: 18Jul1864; Bugler
Military Confinement: 14Jul1865 - Aug1865; Ft. Pickens, FL
Union Discharge: 17Nov1865; Ft. Barrancas, FL; bounty due $160
Pension: 07Feb1891 in FL; App#992767, Cert#1075875
Widow's Pension:28Jan1915 in FL; App #1040705, Cert#848305

D

DANIEL, Thomas J.
AKA: Thomas J. DANIELS
Birth: circa 1843; Washington Co, GA
Death: 13May1915; Troy, Pike Co, AL
1850 Location: Washington County, GA
Description: light complexion, blue eyes, light hair
Union Enlistment: 11Mar1865; East Pass, FL; Co E, Private
Union Discharge: 17Nov1865; Tallahassee, FL; bounty due $100
Pension: 08Aug1910 in AL; App#1391817
Widow's Pension:15May1928 in AL; App#1613250, Cert#091028

DANLEY, James H.
AKA: James H. DANNELLY; James H. DANNELLEY; James H. DONNELLY
Birth: 01Feb1829 in Covington Co, AL
Death: 04Sept1892; Alabama
Burial: Sep1892; River Falls Cemetery, Andalusia, Covington Co, AL
1860 Location: Covington County, AL
Description: dark complexion, dark eyes, dark hair
Union Enlistment: 24Feb1864; Ft. Barrancas, FL; Co D, Private
Disability Discharge: 12Jan1865; chronic rheumatism
Pension: 15Nov1878; App#262974, Cert#171399
Widow's Pension: 03Jan1894 in AL; App#587859, Cert#552226

DANSBY, Daniel Monroe
Birth: Oct1837; Barbour Co, AL
Death: 04Aug1918; Brundidge, Pike Co, AL
Burial: Aug1918; Barbour, AL; Dansby Cemetery

1860 Location: Barbour County, AL
Description: dark complexion, brown eyes, black hair
CSA: 10Mar1862 – 31Dec1862; 39th AL Infantry, Co C, Private, deserted
Union Enlistment: 20May1864; East Pass, FL; Co F, Private
Engagements: Marianna, FL; Pine Barren, FL; Mitchell's Creek & Pine Barren, FL; Evergreen, AL; Blakeley, AL; Montgomery, AL
Promotions: 10Jan1865; Corporal
Promotions: 18July1865; Sergeant
Union Discharge: 17Nov1865; Tallahassee, FL; bounty due $75
Military Finding: 07Oct1884; certificate in lieu of discharge
Pension: 23Apr1883 in AL; App#480934, Cert#483468
Widow's Pension:07Sep1918 in AL; App#1127409, Cert#885720

DANSBY, Emanuel George W.
AKA: Emanuel G. W. DANSBY
Birth: 26Feb1842; Barbour Co, AL
Death: 03Jan1901; Falls Co, TX
Burial: Jan1901; Lott, Falls, TX; Union Cemetery
1860 Location: Barbour County, AL
Description: dark complexion, brown eyes, dark hair
CSA: 12May1862 - 30Jun1862; 39th AL Infantry, Co C, Private, deserted
Union Enlistment: 2 May1864; East Pass, FL; Co F, Private
Engagements: Marianna, FL; Pine Barren, FL; Mitchell Creek & Pine Barren, FL; Evergreen, AL; Blakeley, AL; Montgomery, AL
Union Discharge: 17Nov1865; Tallahassee, FL; bounty due $75
Pension: 08Jan1891 in TX; App #977347
Widow's Pension: 21Sep1901 in TX; App#748896, Cert#557755

DANSBY, Hiram D.
AKA: Hyle DANSBY
Birth: 05Apr1832; Barbour Co, AL
Death: Jun1920; Cameron, Milam Co, TX
Burial: Jun1920; Cameron, Milam, TX; Salem Wilson Cemetery
1860 Location: Barbour County, AL
Description: fair complexion, gray eyes, light hair

CSA: 12May1862 - 27Jul1862; 39th AL Infantry, Co C, Private, disability discharge
Union Enlistment: 20May1864; East Pass, FL; Co F, Private
Engagements: Marianna, FL; Pine Barrens, FL; Mitchell's Creek and Pine Barrens, FL; Evergreen, AL; Blakeley, AL; Montgomery, AL
Union Discharge: 17Nov1865; Tallahassee, FL; bounty due $75
Pension: 09Apr1891 in TX; App#1009530, Cert#797626

DANSBY, John
Birth: circa 1839; Barbour Co, AL
1860 Location: Barbour County, AL
Description: dark complexion, brown eyes, dark hair
CSA: 10May1862 - 03Oct1863; 39th AL Infantry, Co C, Private, deserted
Union Enlistment: 20May1864; East Pass, FL; Co F, Private
Died: 14Dec1864; Ft. Barrancas, FL
Widow's Pension: 14Apr1868; App#159865, Cert#117951

DAUGHTERY, Drew
AKA: Drew DAUGHTRY; Drew DAUGHTREY; Drewry DAUGHTERY
Birth: circa 1825; Cumberland Co, NC
Death: 19Jun1880 - 02Aug1890; Mississippi
1860 Location: Santa Rosa County, FL
Description: dark complexion, black eyes, dark hair
Union Enlistment: 25Jan1864; Ft. Barrancas, FL; Co B, Private
Union Discharge: 17Nov1865; Tallahassee, FL; bounty due $120
Pension: 14Jun1879; App#292133
Widow's Pension: 02Aug1890 in MS; App#453000, Cert#302642

DAUGHTERY, Joshua S.
AKA: Joshua S. DAUGHTRY; Joshua S. DAUGHERTY
Birth: circa 1828; Washington Co, NC
1860 Location: Dale County, AL
Description: dark complexion, blue eyes, dark hair
CSA: 14Oct - 09Dec1863; 4th Battalion FL Infantry, Co A, Private, deserted; records transferred 11th FL Infantry, Co C/ F

Union Enlistment: 17Dec1863; Ft. Barrancas, FL; Co A, Private
Promotions: Apr1864; Corporal
Died: 29Oct1864; Ft. Barrancas, FL
Widow's Pension: 27Jun1868; App#162229, Cert#143623

DAUGHTRY, Joshua
AKA: Joshua DAUGHERTY; Josiah DAUGHTREY; Joshua DOUGHTREY; Joshua DAUGHTERY
Birth: circa 1839; Screven Co, GA
Death: 13Feb1910
1860 Location: Emanuel County, GA
Description: light complexion, gray eyes, sandy hair
Union Enlistment: 13Dec1863; Ft. Barrancas, FL; Co B, Private
Engagements: Montgomery, AL
Union Discharge: 17Nov1865; Tallahassee, FL; bounty due $75
Pension: 08Dec1890; App#958219, Cert#1051757
Widow's Pension: 04Jun1910; App#943592

DAVIS, Alexander T.
Birth: 01Sep1842; Conecuh Co, AL
Death: 21Nov1925; Pensacola, Escambia Co, FL
Burial: Nov1925; Pensacola, FL; Pfeiffer's Mill Cemetery
1860 Location: Monroe County, AL
Description: fair complexion, gray eyes, light hair
Union Enlistment: 15Mar1864; Ft. Barrancas, FL; Co D, Private
Promotions: 01Apr1864; Corporal
Promotions: 01May1864; Sergeant
Union Discharge: 17Nov1865; Tallahassee, FL; bounty due $120
Pension: 22Aug1902 in FL; App#1289770, Cert#1053699

DAVIS, Ashley J.
Birth: circa 1825; Georgia
1860 Location: Dale County, AL
Description: light complexion, blue eyes, brown hair
CSA: 06Oct1863 - 09Dec1863; 4th Battalion FL Infantry, Co A, Private, deserted; records transferred to 11th FL Infantry, Co C
Union Enlistment: 19Dec1863, Ft. Barrancas, FL; Co A, Private
Died: 29Sept1864; Ft. Barrancas, FL

DAVIS, Franklin J.
AKA: Francis J. DAVIS; Frank J. DAVIS
Birth: Apr1835; Wilkinson Co, GA
Death: 06Feb1917; Niceville, Walton Co, FL
1860 Location: Dale County, AL
Description: light complexion, grey eyes, dark hair
Union Enlistment: 02Apr1864; East Pass, FL; Co E, Private
Engagements: Marianna, FL; Pollard, AL; Blakeley, AL; Montgomery, AL
Promotions: 01May1864; Sergeant
Desertion: 22Jul1865
Military Finding: 26May1905; charges of desertion dropped
Pension: 07Jul1907; App#1337391, Cert#1119790

DAVIS, Harmon
Birth: circa 1831; Lowndes Co, AL
Description: light complexion, grey eyes, dark hair
Union Enlistment: 06Oct1864; Ft. Barrancas, FL; Co A, Private
Died: 01May1865; Ft. Barrancas, FL

DAVIS, Leroy
Birth: circa 1840; Rankin C, MS
Description: fair complexion, blue eyes, light hair
Union Enlistment: 03Aug1864; East Pass, FL; Co F, Private
Engagements: Pine Barren Creek, FL
Died: 17-29 Nov 1864; missing in action, Pine Barren Ridge, reported hanged by the Confederate cavalry after taken POW

DAVIS, Samuel
Birth: circa 1845; Washington Co, FL
Death: 09Dec1929; Bonifay, Holmes Co, FL
Description: fair complexion, gray eyes, light hair
CSA: 10Jun1863 - 18Dec1863; 4th Battalion FL Infantry, Co C, Private, deserted; records transferred to 11th FL Infantry, Co K
Union Enlistment: 05 Mar 1864; Ft. Barrancas, FL; Co D, Private
Union Discharge: 17Nov1865; Tallahassee, FL; bounty due $120
Pension: 21Oct1885; App#552426, Cert#1121028

DAVIS, Thomas
Birth: circa 1821; Montgomery Co, GA
Burial: 19Dec1864; Ft. Barrancas, Pensacola, Escambia Co, FL; Barrancas National Cemetery
1860 Location: Baldwin County, AL
Description: fair complexion, blue eyes, brown hair
Union Enlistment: 26Apr1864; Ft. Barrancas, FL; Co E, Private
Died: 19Dec1864; Nine Mile House, FL; bounty paid $75
Widow's Pension: 27Jul1868; App#163324, Cert#127279
Minor's Pension: App#215151, Cert#165318

DAVIS, Wade H.
Birth: circa 1834; Lawrence Co, AL
Death: after 18Feb1865
1850 Location: Lowndes County, AL
Description: fair complexion, blue eyes, dark hair
Union Enlistment: 15Sep1864; Ft. Barrancas, FL; Co D, Private
Desertion: 18Feb1865; Ft. Barrancas, FL

DAVIS, William A.
Birth: circa 1832; Moore Co, NC
Death: after 10May1876
1860 Location: Covington County, AL
Spouse name: Frances Unknown
Description: fair complexion, blue eyes, dark hair
Union Enlistment: 05Apr1864; Ft. Barrancas, FL; Co E, Private
Disability Discharge: 13Apr1865
Pension: 10May1876; App#218979, Cert#727780

DAVIS, William S.
Birth: 11Jan1839; Talbot Co, GA
Death: 16Jun1910; DeFuniak Springs, Walton Co, FL
Burial: Jun1910, DeFuniak Springs, Walton Co, FL; Cluster Springs Baptist Church
Description: light complexion, brown eyes, dark hair
Union Enlistment: 12Apr1864; East Pass, FL; Co E, Bugler
Engagements: Marianna, FL; Pollard, AL; Blakeley, AL; Montgomery, AL

Promotions: 20Apr - 30Apr1864; appointed trumpeter
Desertion: 22Jul1865; Ft. Barrancas, FL
Military Finding: 08Aug1887; charges of desertion dropped
Pension: 22Jul1887 in FL; App#616909, Cert#1060732
Widow's Pension: 01Jul1910, FL; App#945115, Cert#709901

DAVIS, Wilson
AKA: Willis SHACKLEFORD
Birth: circa 1827; Washington Co, FL
Death: 06Dec1911; Washington Co, FL
Description: black complexion, black eyes, black hair
Union Enlistment: 21Mar1864; Ft. Barrancas, FL; Co C, Under Cook
Desertion: 08Aug1865; Ft. Barrancas, FL
Military Finding: 02Nov1899; charge of desertion removed
Pension: 04Jan1899; App#1215721, Cert#1103680
Widow's Pension: 14Dec1911 in FL; App#976897, Cert#736142

DAVIS, Wilson A.
Birth: circa 1838l Conecuh Co, AL
1850 Location: Conecuh County, AL
Union Enlistment: 15Mar1864; Ft. Barrancas, FL

DIAMOND, Robert W.
Birth: circa 1838; Conecuh Co, AL
Death: 03May1890 - 20Jan1908
1860 Location: Escambia County, FL
Description: light complexion, blue eyes, dark hair
Union Enlistment: 19Jan1864; Ft. Barrancas, FL; Co A, Private
Union Discharge: 17Nov1865; Tallahassee, FL; bounty due $120
Pension: 03May1890 in FL; App#773032, Cert#812640
Widow's Pension: 20Jan1908 in MS; App#786755, Cert#581998

DIXON, Henry H.
AKA: Henry H. DIXSON
Birth: circa 1841; Conecuh Co, AL
Death: after 17Nov1865
1860 Location: Santa Rosa County, FL
Description: dark complexion, blue eyes, dark hair

CSA: 17Sep1861 - 6May1862; Capt. N. R. Leigh's Co, Independent Florida Cavalry, transferred. 5May1862 - 31Aug1863; 3rd Battalion FL Cavalry, Co C, Private, transferred. 1Sept1863 - 12Dec1863; 15th Confederate Cavalry, Co E, deserted.
Union Enlistment: 13 Jan 1864, Ft. Barrancas, FL; Co A, Private
Engagements: Raid on Fifteen Mile House, FL; Pollard, AL; Marianna, FL
Promotions: Jan - Feb1865; Sergeant
Union Discharge: 17Nov1865, Tallahassee, FL; bounty due $120

DIXON, Washington
Birth: circa 1846; Santa Rosa Co, FL
Death: after 17Nov1865
Description: dark complexion, gray eyes, light hair
Union Enlistment: 22Feb1865; Ft. Barrancas, FL; Co D, Private
Military Charges: 19Jun1865; desertion
Military Confinement: 19Jun - Aug1865; Ft. Pickens, FL
Union Discharge: 17Nov1865, Tallahassee, FL; bounty due $100

DOCKINS, George W.
AKA: George W. DOCKIN
Birth: circa 1842; Butler Co, AL
Death: after 17Nov1865
1860 Location: Covington County, AL
Description: fair complexion, blue eyes, dark hair
Union Enlistment: 06Oct1864; Ft. Barrancas, FL; Co F, Private
Union Discharge:17Nov1865; Tallahassee, FL

DOCKINS, William C.
AKA: William DOCKIN; William DORKIN; William DOCKINS; William F. DAUCKENS; William C. DAWKINS
Birth: circa 1844; Butler Co, AL
Death: 13Dec1925; Mossy Head, Walton Co, FL
Burial: Dec1925, Crestview, Okaloosa Co, FL; Garden of Memories
1860 Location: Covington County, AL
Description: dark complexion, gray eyes, light hair

Union Enlistment: 16Aug1864; East Pass, FL; Co F, Private
Engagements: Montgomery, AL
Union Discharge: 17Nov1865; Tallahassee, FL; bounty due $75
Pension: 26Sep1890 in FL; App #988042, Cert #895213

DOCKINS, William P.
Birth: circa 1820; Clarke Co, AL
1860 Location: Covington County, AL
Description: fair complexion, gray eyes, dark hair
Union Enlistment: 06Oct1864; Ft. Barrancas, FL; Co F, Private
Military Charges: 08Aug1865; charged with desertion after being sent home sick
Died: 20Aug1865; Covington Co, AL, at home
Military Finding: 14Nov1872; desertion charges dropped
Widow's Pension: 19Mar1868; App #158952, Cert #161200

DONALDSON, Benjamin F.
AKA: Benjamin F. DOLDALSON; Benjamin DONELSON; Benjamin DONOLDSON
Birth: 25Dec1825; Lowndes Co, AL
Death: Jan1892; Baldwin Co, AL
Burial: Jan1892, Lillian, Baldwin Co, AL; Donaldson Plantation Cemetery
1860 Location: Santa Rosa County, FL
Description: fair complexion, gray eyes, dark hair
CSA: 07Mar1862 - 30Aug1863; 1st FL Reorganized Infantry, Co E, Private/ Corporal, deserted
Union Enlistment: 12Sept1864; Ft. Barrancas, FL; Co E, Private
Desertion: 23Mar1865; Milton, Santa Rosa Co, FL
Military Finding: 02May1889; application for removal of desertion charge denied
Pension: 29Apr1891 in AL; App#1018760
Widow's Pension: 12Dec1892 in AL; App#565723

DONALDSON, James D.
AKA: James D. DONELDSON; James D. DONLDSON; James D. DOALSON
Birth: 22Feb1845; Coffee Co, AL

Death: 22Jul1919; Chickasha, Grady Co, OK
Burial: Jul1919; Chickasha, Grady Co, OK; Rose Hill Cemetery
1860 Location: Coffee County, AL
Description: light complexion, blue eyes, light hair
CSA: 16Mar1863 - 01Sept1863; 57th AL Infantry, Co K, Private, deserted
Union Enlistment: 19Jan1864; Ft. Barrancas, FL; Co A, Private
Engagements: Fifteen Mile House, FL; Pollard, AL; Marianna, FL; Montgomery, AL
Promotions: 01Jul1864; Corporal
Union Discharge: 17Nov1865; Tallahassee, FL; bounty due $120
Pension: 28Mar1891 in TX; App#1007743, Cert#1074537

DONALDSON, Joseph William
AKA: William Joseph DONALDSON; Billy DONALDSON
Birth: 16Apr1847; Coffee Co, AL
Death: 24Dec1889; Opp, Covington Co, AL
1860 Location: Coffee County, AL
Description: fair complexion, blue eyes, dark hair
Union Enlistment: 25Sep1864; East Pass, FL; Co F, Private
Engagements: Montgomery, AL
Union Discharge: 17Nov1865; Tallahassee, FL
Pension: 10Jul1889 in AL; App#716618
Widow's Pension: 14Feb1890 in AL; App#414782, Cert#576340

DONALDSON, Thomas H.
Birth: Oct1846; Coffee Co, AL
Death: 21Aug1928; Brewton, Escambia Co, AL
1850 Location: Coffee County, AL
Description: fair complexion, blue eyes, sandy hair
CSA: 07Sept1863 - 28May1864; 33rd AL Infantry, Co A, Private
Union Enlistment: 12Sept1864; East Pass, FL; Co D, Private
Desertion: 01Aug1865
Military Finding: 29Jul1903; desertion charge dropped
Pension: 14Jul1903 in AL; App#1301871, Cert#1067549

DOW, John H.
Birth: circa 1846; Conecuh Co, AL

Description: blue eyes, light hair, fair complexion
Union Enlistment: 25Oct1864; East Pass, FL
Union Discharge: no information

DUMONT, Charles
Birth: circa 1844; New Orleans, LA
Death: after 01May1865
Description: dark complexion, brown eyes, dark hair
Union Enlistment: 03Apr1864; East Pass, FL; Co E, Private
Engagements: Pollard, AL; Montgomery, AL
Promotions: 03Apr1864; 5th Sergeant
Desertion: 01May1865; Montgomery, AL

DUNCAN, James M.
Birth: circa 1841; Houston Co, GA
Death: after 10Jun1865
1850 Location: Jackson County, FL
Description: light complexion, blue eyes, sandy hair
Union Enlistment: 17Mar1865; Ft. Barrancas, FL; Co A, Private
Desertion: 10Jun1865; East Pass, FL

DYSON, James
AKA: James DISON; James DERVIN
Birth: circa 1829; North Carolina
Death: 21Jun1880 - 1885 in Holmes Co, FL
Burial: 1880 – 1885; Holmes Co, FL; Dyson Cemetery
1860 Location: Holmes County, FL
Description: dark complexion, gray eyes, black hair
CSA: 30Apr1863 - 15Jul1863; Capt Tanner's Co Independent Co, FL Infantry, Private, deserted; records transferred to 11th FL Infantry, Co F
Union Enlistment: 30Dec1863; Ft. Barrancas, FL; Co A, Private
Engagements: Raid on Fifteen Mile House, FL; Pollard, AL; Montgomery, AL
Union Discharge: 17Nov1865; Tallahassee, FL; bounty due $120

E

EARLY, Thomas J.
AKA: Thomas J. EARLEY
Birth: circa 1846; Georgia
1860 Location: Coffee County, AL
Description: fair complexion, blue eyes, light hair
Union Enlistment: 05Oct1864; Ft. Barrancas, FL; Co D, Private
Died: 20Jan1865; Ft. Barrancas, FL

EASTERS, John W.
Birth: circa 1824; Marengo Co, AL
Death: after 17Nov1865
1850 Location: Pike County, AL
Description: fair complexion, blue eyes, light hair
Union Enlistment: 07Feb1864; Ft. Barrancas, FL; Co D, Private
Promotions: 27Mar – 30Apr1864; Farrier
Union Discharge: 17Nov1865; Tallahassee, FL; bounty due $160

EATON, J. R.
Asst. Surgeon listed in the unassigned section of the muster rolls. He was in charge of the 1st FL Cavalry hospital. No other information available

EDDIN, William H.
AKA: William H. EDDINS; William H. EDDENS
Birth: circa 1837; Barbour Co, AL
Description: light complexion, blue eyes, light hair
Union Enlistment: 29Dec1863; Ft. Barrancas, FL; Co A, Private
Died: 05Oct1864; Ft. Barrancas, FL

EDDY, Jefferson H.
AKA: Jefferson H. EDEY; Jefferson H. EADY; Jefferson H. EADEY
Birth: circa 1846; Muscogee Co, GA
Death: after 17Nov1865
1860 Location: Covington County, AL
Description: fair complexion, blue eyes, light hair
Union Enlistment: 15Oct1864; Ft. Barrancas, FL; Co D, Private

Engagements: Raid in South Alabama; Montgomery, AL
Union Discharge: 17Nov1865; Tallahassee, FL

ELLIS, William B.
Birth: circa 1831; Upson Co, GA
Death: after 16Aug1870
1860 Location: Santa Rosa County, FL
Description: light complexion, blue eyes, dark hair
CSA: 25Mar1863 - 28Aug1863; 4th Battalion FL Infantry, Co. C, Private, deserted; records transferred to 11th FL Infantry, Co K.
Union Enlistment: 20Jun1864; Ft. Barrancas, FL; Co F, Private
Desertion: 28May1865; Newton, Dale, AL

ELLISON, John P.
AKA: John P. ELISON
Birth: circa 1826; Gwinnett Co, GA
1860 Location: Henry County, AL
Description: fair complexion, blue eyes, sandy hair
Union Enlistment: 15Feb1864; Ft. Barrancas, FL; Co A, Private
Died: 06Aug1864; Ft. Barrancas, FL
Widow's Pension: 22Feb1867; App #142733, Cert #125940

ELLISON, Samuel A.
Birth: circa 1835; Stewart Co, GA
Death: 04Jun1880 - 07Jan1889; Florida
1860 Location: Henry County, AL
Description: light complexion, blue eyes, light hair
CSA: Nov1863 - 09Dec1863; 4th Battalion FL Infantry, Co A, Private, deserted; records transferred to 11th FL Infantry, Co C.
Union Enlistment: 17Dec1863; Ft. Barrancas, FL; Co A, Private
Promotions: May - June1864; Blacksmith
Military Charges: 15Apr1865; Woolsey, FL; attempted desertion
Military Confinement: 15Apr - Aug1865; Ft. Pickens, FL
Union Discharge: 17Nov1865; Tallahassee, FL; bounty due $75
Military Finding: 16Sept1890; removal of desertion denied
Widow's Pension: 07Jan1889 in FL; App# 386714

ELLISON, Young R.
Birth: circa 1828; Walton Co, GA

1860 Location: Henry County, AL
Description: light complexion, blue eyes, dark hair
CSA: 29Jan1863 - 09Dec1863; 4th Battalion FL Infantry, Co A, Private, deserted; records transferred to 11th FL Infantry, Co C.
Union Enlistment: 17Dec1863; Ft. Barrancas, FL; Co A, Private
Died: 19May1864; Ft. Barrancas, FL

ELMORE, James H.
AKA: James H. ELLMORE
Birth: 29Jan1833; Darlington Co, SC
Death: 27Feb1907; Alabama
Burial: Feb1907; Covington Co, AL; Good Hope Cemetery
1860 Location: Dale County, AL
Description: fair complexion, blue eyes, light hair
CSA: 05Feb - 28Apr1863; Capt Curry's Independent Company, FL Infantry, Private, deserted; records transferred to 11th FL Infantry, Co C
Union Enlistment: 20May1864; East Pass, FL; Co F, Private
Desertion: 25Jul1865; Ft. Barrancas, FL
Military Finding: 18Oct1884; charges of desertion dropped
Pension: 25Aug1890 in AL; App#800126, Cert#822384
Widow's Pension: 10Apr1907 in AL; App#867388, Cert#633973

ERICKSON, John
AKA: Johan ERICKSON
Birth: circa 1832; Sweden
Death: 29May1889 - 08Aug1890; Arkansas
Description: fair complexion, blue eyes, red hair
Union Enlistment: 14Sept1864; Ft. Barrancas, FL; Co F, Private
Desertion: 02May1865; Ft. Barrancas, FL
Military Finding: 08Dec1884; charges of desertion dropped
Pension: 29May1889 in AR; App#707410
Widow's Pension: 08Aug1890 in AR; App#421984, Cert#325711

EVANS, James H.
AKA: James H. EVINS
Birth: circa 1837 in Pike County, AL
Death: between 17Nov1865 - 10Aug1897

1860 Location: Walton County, FL
Description: light complexion, gray eyes, dark hair
Union Enlistment: 26Mar1864, East Pass, FL; Co D, Private
Promotions: 17Dec1864; Corporal
Union Discharge: 17Nov1865; Tallahassee, FL; bounty due $120
Widow's Pension: 10 Aug 1897 in Florida; App #660340

EVANS, John T.
AKA: John T. EVVINS; John T. EVENS
Birth: Sept1844; Henry Co, AL
Death: 02Jan1904; Sexton, FL
1860 Location: Santa Rosa County, FL
Description: dark complexion, black eyes, dark hair
Union Enlistment: 19Jan1864; Ft. Barrancas, FL; Co C, Private
Union Discharge: 17Nov1865; Tallahassee, FL; bounty due $120
Pension: 07May1883 in FL; App#482529, Cert#914978
Widow's Pension: 19Jan1904 in FL; App#798251, Cert#585838

F

FAULK, Alfred J.
Birth: circa 1830; Marion Co, SC
Death: after 09Nov1894
1850 Location: Washington County, FL
Description: fair complexion, blue eyes, light hair
Union Enlistment: 15Jan1864; Ft. Barrancas, FL; Co A, Private
Union Discharge: 17Nov1865; Tallahassee, FL; bounty due $120
Pension: 09Nov1894; App #1161951, Cert #940410

FAULK, Asa
Birth: May1836; Houston Co, GA
Death: 1903; Santa Rosa Co, FL
Burial: 1903; Santa Rosa Co, FL; Hickory Hammock Cemetery
1860 Location: Santa Rosa County, FL
Description: dark complexion, black eyes, dark hair
CSA: 21Mar1862 - 01Sep1863; 1st FL Reorganized Infantry, Co F, Private, deserted.
Union Enlistment: 06Jun1864; Ft. Barrancas, FL; Co F, Private
Engagements: Montgomery, AL

Military Discharge: 17Nov1865; Tallahassee, FL; bounty due $75
Pension: 06Mar1882; App#441906, Cert#665038

FAULK, Phillip
Birth: 01Nov1847; Troy, Pike Co, AL
Death: 25Jan1923; Holt, Okaloosa Co, FL
Burial: Jan1923; Okaloosa Co, FL; Faulk Cemetery
1860 Location: Santa Rosa County, FL
Description: fair complexion, gray eyes, dark hair
Union Enlistment: 30May1864; Ft. Barrancas, FL; Co F, Private
Desertion: 01Aug1865; Ft. Barrancas, FL
Military Finding: 13Jul1869; desertion charge dropped
Pension: 02Aug1880 in FL; App#409250, Cert#611846

FAULKNER, Chesley
Birth: circa 1820; Edgefield Co, SC
Death: after 12Aug1870
Description: fair complexion, blue eyes, light hair
Union Enlistment: 05Mar1864; Ft. Barrancas, FL; Co E, Private
Union Discharge: 17Nov1865; Tallahassee, FL; bounty due $160

FLINN, James M.
AKA: James M. FLYNN
Death: 18Nov1898
Union Enlistment: 15Aug1864; Co A, Private
Union Discharge: 17Nov1865; Tallahassee, FL
Pension: 02Aug1890 in FL; App#917294, Cert#779530
Widow's Pension: 16Jan1899 in FL; App#690203

FLOWERS, Benjamin
Birth: circa 1844; Darlington Co, SC
Death: after 15Feb1865
1860 Location: Dale County, AL
Description: dark complexion, blue eyes, dark hair
Union Enlistment: 05Mar1864; Ft. Barrancas, FL; Co C, Private
Desertion: 15Feb1865; Ft. Barrancas, FL

FLOWERS, Thomas
Birth: circa 1840; Darlington Co, SC

Death: after 18Sept1864
Description: fair complexion, yellow eyes, dark hair
CSA: 29Jan1863 - 10Aug1863; 4th Battalion FL Infantry, Co A, Private, deserted; records transferred to 11th FL Infantry, Co C.
Union Enlistment: 05Mar1864; Ft. Barrancas, FL; Co C, Private
Desertion: 18Sept1864

FLOYD, Charles J.
AKA: Charles J. FLOYED
Birth: circa 1830; Dallas Co, AL
1860 Location: Santa Rosa County, FL
Description: light complexion, blue eyes, light hair
Union Enlistment: 24Mar1864; East Pass, FL; Co E, Private
Died: 25Dec1864; Elba, Coffee, AL; bounty due $275
Military Finding: 31Jul1878; notation dated Aug 19, 1874 canceled. Found he was killed while he and comrades were trying to burn and possibly rob Elba
Widow's Pension: 23Jun1874; App#216111

FOREHAND, James
Birth: circa 1827; Dooly Co, GA
Death: after 15Nov1864
1860 Location: Washington County, FL
Description: fair complexion, gray eyes, light hair
Union Enlistment: 06Oct1864; Ft. Barrancas, FL; Co F, Private
Desertion: 15Nov1864; near Pensacola, FL

FOWLER, John Franklin
AKA: John FOWLLER; John FOULLER
Birth: Jan1837; Henry Co, AL
Death: after 17Aug1908; Henry Co, AL
1860 Location: Henry County, AL
Description: fair complexion, blue eyes, dark hair
CSA: 09Jul1863 - 12Aug1863; Capt Tanner's Co, FL Infantry, Private, deserted; records transferred to 11th FL Infantry, Co F.
Union Enlistment: 15Feb1864; Ft. Barrancas, FL; Co A, Private
Desertion: 12Jan1865; while on furlough
Military Finding: 18Dec1888; removal of desertion charge denied

Pension: 17Aug1908; App#1376632

FOWLER, Richard
AKA: Richard FOULER; Richardson FOULER; Richardson FAULLY; Richard FOULLER; Richardson FOWLER; Richard FOWLEY
Birth: May1828; Henry Co, AL
Death: 05Apr1888 – 1900; Henry Co, AL
1860 Location: Henry County, AL
Description: fair complexion, grey eyes, brown hair
CSA: 01Jul1863 - 12Aug1863; Capt Tanner's Company, FL Infantry, Private, deserted; records transferred to 11th FL Infantry, Co F
Union Enlistment: 05Jan1864; Ft. Barrancas, FL; Co A, Private
Engagements: Montgomery, AL
Desertion: 05May1865
Military Finding: 10Oct1884; desertion charges dropped
Pension: 05Apr1888 in AL; App#648745

FRANKLIN, Marion W.
Birth: Aug1845; Baldwin Co, AL
Death: 07Dec1918; Pensacola, Escambia Co, FL
Burial: Dec1918, Bluff Springs, Escambia Co, FL; Crary Memorial Cemetery
1850 Location: Escambia County, FL
Description: fair complexion, grey eyes, black hair
CSA: 01Apr1862 - 01Sep1863; 1st FL Reorganized Infantry, Co I, Private, deserted
Union Enlistment: 04Jan1864; Ft. Barrancas, FL; Co A, Private
Engagements: All Expeditions w/Co; Marianna, FL; Pine Barren Creek, FL; Pollard, AL; Mobile, AL; Montgomery, AL
Desertion: 16Aug1865
Military Finding: 03Aug1886; desertion charge dropped
Pension: 24May1883 in FL; App#484444, Cert#610519

FRANKLIN, William H.
AKA: William FRANKLIN
Birth: Jun1845; Santa Rosa Co, FL

Death: 15Jun1925; Blackman, Okaloosa Co, FL
1860 Location: Santa Rosa County, FL
Description: fair complexion, hazel eyes, dark hair
Union Enlistment: 01Mar1864; Ft. Barrancas, FL; Co C, Private
Union Discharge: 17Nov1865; Tallahassee, FL; bounty due $120
Pension: 19Jan1897 in FL; App#1185356, Cert#1091956
Widow's Pension: 03Jul1925 in FL; App#1234737, Cert#969454

FREEMAN, Hardy
AKA: Hary FREMAN; Freeman HARDY
Birth: circa 1834; Georgia
Death: after 30Oct1864
Description: fair complexion, gray eyes, brown hair
Union Enlistment: 28Dec1863; Ft. Barrancas, FL; Co A, Private
Desertion: 30Oct1864

FRENCH, Robert
Birth: Mar1837; Dooly Co, GA
Death: 08Dec1912; Cerro Gordo, Holmes Co, FL
Burial: Dec1912; Westville, Holmes Co, Florida; Campground Church Cemetery
1860 Location: Holmes County, Florida
Description: dark complexion, dark eyes, dark hair
CSA: 09Sep1862 - 30Jun1863; 2nd FL Cavalry, Co G, Private, estimated desertion date.
Union Enlistment: 30Dec1863; Ft. Barrancas, FL; Co B, Private
Union Discharge: 17Nov1865; Tallahassee, FL; bounty due $275
Pension: 15Jul1890 in FL; App#809092 Cert#1065011
Widow's Pension: 08Jan1913 in FL; App#999344, Cert#756456

G

GAAL, Alexander G.
AKA: Alexander GAAL
Birth: circa 1832; Hungary
Death: 29Feb1912; New Orleans, Orleans Parish, LA
Burial: Feb1912; Chalmette, St Bernard Parish, LA; Chalmette National Cemetery, Section 136, Grave 12596
Union Enlistment: 10Oct1864, Ft. Barrancas, FL; Co F, Captain

Promotions: 05Jul1864; Captain
Honorable Discharge: 27Nov1864; resigned
Pension: 12Sep1890 in LA; App #952404, Cert #825919
Widow's Pension: 15Apr1912 in LA; App #984563, Cert#749117

GAINEY, Silas Jackson
AKA: Silas GANNEY, Jr.; Silas GANEY, Jr.
Birth: Apr1849; Walton Co, FL
Death: 09Jun1915; Lottie, Baldwin Co, AL
1860 Location: Walton County, FL
Description: dark complexion, black eyes, dark hair
Union Enlistment: 25Sept1864; East Pass, FL; Co C, Private
Union Discharge: 17Nov1865; Tallahassee, FL
Pension: 29Mar1904 in AL; App#1310849, Cert#1097866
Widow's Pension: 01Jul1915 in AL; App #1049827, Cert#803567

GAINEY, Silas
AKA: Silas GANNEY; Silas GANEY
Birth: circa 1815; Burke Co, GA
Death: 29Jul1887 - 05May1893; Florida
1860 Location: Walton County, FL
Description: dark complexion, black eyes, black hair
Union Enlistment: 25Sept1864; East Pass, FL; Co C, Private
Union Discharge: 17Nov1865[Tallahassee, FL
Pension: 29Jul1887 in FL; App#617616, Cert#680375
Widow's Pension: 05May1893 in FL; App#575804

GALLOWAY, James Levi
AKA: James L. GALLAWAY
Death: 17Nov1865 - 21Oct1874
Union Enlistment: 28Jan1864; Co A and E, Captain
Union Discharge: 17Nov1865; Tallahassee, FL; pay due from enlistment
Widow's Pension: 21Oct1874; App#217926, Cert#409266

GARDNER, William D.
Birth: circa 1841; Darlington Co, SC
Description: blue eyes, dark hair, dark complexion
Union Enlistment: 27Aug1864; East Pass, Florida; Private

Union Discharge: not recorded

GARNER, Zinamon L.
Birth: circa 1845; Dale Co, AL
Death: 10Jun1880 – 1900; Dale Co, AL
1860 Location: Dale County, AL
Description: fair complexion, blue eyes, light hair
CSA: 15Aug1862 - 11Feb1864; 15th AL Infantry, Co K, Private, deserted
Union Enlistment: 20May1864; East Pass, FL; Co F, Private
Engagements: Montgomery, AL
Promotions: 06Aug1865; Sergeant
Union Discharge: 17Nov1865; Tallahassee, FL; bounty due $75

GARRETT, George W.
Birth: circa 1830; Dale Co, AL
1860 Location: Covington County, AL
Description: dark complexion, dark eyes, dark hair
Union Enlistment: 09Feb1864; Ft. Barrancas, FL; Co B, Private
Died: 31Jul1864; 1st Florida Battery camp; bounty due $275
Minor's Pension: 10Jan1871; App#192963, Cert#167158

GARRETT, Joseph
AKA: Joseph GARRET; Joseph GARROTT
Birth: circa 1836; Barbour Co, AL
Death: after 17Nov1865
1860 Location: Walton County, FL
Description: fair complexion, dark eyes, dark hair
CSA: 02Apr1862 - 12Feb1864; 6th FL Infantry, Co H, Private, deserted.
Union Enlistment: 31Mar1864; Ft. Barrancas, FL; Co E, Private
Engagements: Marianna, FL; Pollard, AL; Blakeley, AL; Montgomery, AL
Military Confinement: Jul - Aug1865; Ft. Pickens, FL; under sentence
Union Discharge: 17Nov1865; Tallahassee, FL; bounty due $275

GARRETT, Overstreet William
AKA: Street GARRETT

Birth: 25May1847; Coffee Co, AL
Death: 27Oct1919; Castleberry, Conecuh Co, AL
Burial: Oct1919; Castleberry, Conecuh Co, AL; Buffington Cemetery
1860 Location: Coffee County, AL
Description: fair complexion, gray eyes, light hair
Union Enlistment: 05Oct1864; Ft. Barrancas, FL; Co D, Private
Desertion: 06Apr1865; East Pass, FL

GARRETT, Robert
AKA: Robert GARROTT
Birth: circa 1844; Coffee Co, AL
Death: after 06Aug1864
Description: dark complexion, dark eyes, dark hair
1860 Location: Walton County, FL
Union Enlistment: 20Apr1864; Ft. Barrancas, FL; Co E, Private
Desertion: 06Aug1864; Ft. Barrancas, FL

GARRETT, William Robert
Birth: 21Jan1846; Coffee Co, AL
Death: 13Mar1926; Milligan, Okaloosa Co, FL
Burial: Mar1926; Okaloosa Co, FL; Griffith Cemetery
1860 Location: Coffee County, AL
Description: light complexion, brown eyes, brown hair
Union Enlistment: 11Mar1864; East Pass, FL; Co D, Private
Military Charges: Jun - Sept1865; court martial, sentence disapproved, Gen Order No 7
Military Confinement: 25Jun - 10Sept1865, Ft. Pickens, FL
Union Discharge: 17Nov1865; Tallahassee, FL
Pension: 02Jan1891 in FL; App#988081, Cert#840835
Minor's Pension: 07Apr1916 in FL; granddaughter App#1244110, Cert# A52726

GASKIN, James Millard
AKA: James Millard GASKINS; James M. GASKINS
Birth: circa 1829; Rock Creek, Walton Co, FL
Burial: May1865; Escambia Co, FL; Barrancas National Cemetery, Sec 1, Site 933

1860 Location: Santa Rosa County, FL
Description: light complexion, gray eyes, dark hair
CSA: 23Apr - 09Jun1862; 5th FL Infantry, Co I, Private, discharged
Union Enlistment: 25Jan1864; Ft. Barrancas, FL; Co B, Private
Promotions: Nov - Dec1864; 2nd Master Sergeant
Died: 14May1865; Ft. Barrancas, FL; bounty due $160
Widow's Pension: 20Apr1866; App#125405, Cert#122051

GASKIN, Seth J.
AKA: Seth J. GASKINS
Birth: 14Nov1836 in Walton Co, FL
Burial: Sep1864; East Pass, FL; grave was washed away in the 1950s, headstone at Almarante Cemetery, Okaloosa Co, FL
1860 Location: Santa Rosa County, FL
Description: light complexion, blue eyes, brown hair
CSA: 04Oct1862 - 12Aug1863; 3rd FL Battalion Cavalry, Co D, Private, deserted; records transferred to 15th Confederate Cavalry, Co I.
Union Enlistment: 25Jan1864; Ft. Barrancas, FL; Co B, Private
Promotions: 01Apr1864; Commissary Sergeant
Died: 26Sep1864; East Pass, FL, bounty due $275
Widow's Pension: 27Feb1866; App#122512, Cert#120188

GATEWOOD, Harvey H.
Birth: 16Jun1848; Conecuh Co, AL
Death: after 08Apr1930; Alabama
1850 Location: Conecuh County, AL
Description: fair complexion, blue eyes, dark hair
Union Enlistment: 31Mar1864; Ft. Barrancas, FL; Co E, Private
Engagements: Montgomery, AL
Union Discharge: 17Nov1865; Tallahassee, FL
Pension: 12Apr1895 in AL; App#1165971, Cert#1147728

GATHER, Charles
Birth: circa 1840; Hancock County, GA
Death: after 14Aug1865
Description: black complexion, black eyes, black hair

Union Enlistment: 21Dec1864; Ft. Barrancas, FL; Co B, Under cook
Desertion: 14Aug1865; Ft. Barrancas, FL

GATLIN, Harmon S.
AKA: Harmon S. GATLEN
Birth: Jun1839; Butler Co, AL
Death: 15Aug1928; Opp, Covington Co, AL
Burial: Aug1928; Opp, Covington, AL; Bethel Cemetery
1850 Location: Lowndes County, AL
Description: fair complexion, blue eyes, light hair
CSA: 22Jul - 16Nov1861; 1st FL Infantry, Co A, Private, disability discharge
Union Enlistment: 07Apr1864; Ft. Barrancas, FL; Co E, Private
Promotions: 30Apr1864; Saddler
Desertion: 01May1865; bounty due $75
Military Finding: 02Jun1883; desertion charge dropped
Pension: 26Jul1882 in AL; App#490892, Cert#678747
Widow's Pension: 17Dec1928 in AL; App#1630383, Cert#A41529

GATLIN, Joseph D.
Birth: circa 1834; Butler Co, AL
Death: 07Nov1893; Opp, Covington Co, AL
Burial: Nov1893; Opp, Covington, AL; Cool Springs Cemetery
1860 Location: Covington County, AL
Description: light complexion, blue eyes, light hair
CSA: 16Mar - 01Jul1863; 57th AL Infantry, Co K, Private, deserted
Union Enlistment: 03Apr1864; East Pass, FL; Co E, Private
Engagements: Skirmish in Milton, FL
Union Discharge: 17Nov1865; Tallahassee, FL; bounty due $75
Pension: 23Sept1892 in AL; App #928997
Widow's Pension: 25Aug1894 in AL; App#600611, Cert#568109

GAVIN, Charles W.
AKA: Charles GAVIN; Charles GAVINS
Birth: Oct1822; Walterboro, Colleton Co, SC

Death: Jun1900 - 1910 in Walton Co, FL
1860 Location: Coffee County, AL
Description: light complexion, blue eyes, light hair
Union Enlistment: 11Mar1864; East Pass, FL; Co D, Private
Promotions: 01Apr1864; Corporal
Demotion: Jun1865; Private
Military Charges: 1865; convicted of desertion by a General Court Martial
Military Confinement: 28Jun1865; Ft. Pickens, FL
Union Discharge: 17Nov1865; Tallahassee, FL
Military Finding: 31Jan1887; desertion charges dropped
Pension: 16Aug1890 in FL; App#976155, Cert#760476

GEORGE, Moses Andrew
Birth: 03Oct1835; Clayton, Barbour Co, AL
Death: 29Mar1918; Florala, Covington Co, AL
Burial: Apr1918 in Florala, Covington Co, AL; Greenwood Cemetery
1860 Location: Santa Rosa County, FL
Description: dark complexion, gray eyes, dark hair
CSA: 13May - 31Jul1862; 1st FL Reorganized Infantry, Co G, Private, deserted
Union Enlistment: 06May1864; Ft. Barrancas, FL; Co B, Private
Military Confinement: 03Aug1864 - Feb1865; 6 months' hard labor, refused to be mustered in
Desertion: 16Aug1865; Ft. Barrancas, FL
Widow's Pension: 24Feb1921 in AL; App#1170440

GIBSON, John F.
AKA: John F. GIPSON
Birth: circa 1838; Henry Co, AL
Death: after 29Sept1890
Description: dark complexion, grey eyes, dark hair
Union Enlistment: 04Jan1864; Ft. Barrancas, FL; Co A, Private
Promotions: 01Apr1864; Corporal
Union Discharge: 17Nov1865; Tallahassee, FL
Military Finding: 22Jan1869; desertion charges dropped
Pension: 29Sept1890; App#919801, Cert#917802

Widow's Pension: App#680473, Cert#486146

GIBSON, Jordan J.
Birth: circa 1839; Henry Co, AL
1860 Location: Henry County, AL
Description: dark complexion, brown eyes, dark hair
CSA: 26Apr - 10Aug1863; Capt Tanner's Co, Florida Infantry,
Private, deserted; records transferred to 11th FL Infantry, Co F
Union Enlistment: 10Jun1864; Ft. Barrancas, FL; Co F, Private
Died: 18Oct1864; Ft. Barrancas, Florida

GIBSON, Sidney
Birth: circa 1848; Henry Co, AL
1860 Location: Henry County, AL
Description: dark complexion, dark eyes, dark hair
Union Enlistment: 29Dec1863; Ft. Barrancas, FL; Co A, Private
Died: 29Sept1864; Ft. Barrancas, FL

GIBSON, Stephen D.
Birth: circa 1828; Henry Co, AL
1860 Location: Baldwin County, AL
Description: dark complexion, gray eyes, dark hair
CSA: 23May - 15Jun1863; Capt Tanner's Co, FL Infantry,
Private, deserted; records transferred to 11th FL Infantry, Co F
Union Enlistment: 03Jan1864; Ft. Barrancas, FL; Co C, Private
Promotions: Jan - Mar 1864; Sergeant
Died: 04Oct1864; Ft. Barrancas, FL
Widow's Pension: 19Jun1867; App#148787, Cert#222520
Minor's Pension: 23Dec1884 in TX; granddaughter, Louisiana M.
Kelly App#322234, Cert#222521

GILL, Albert
AKA: Albert RICHERSON
Birth: circa 1840; Marion Co, GA
1850 Location: Dale County, AL
Description: fair complexion, gray eyes, light hair
CSA: 04Oct1863 - 09Dec1863; 4th Battalion FL Infantry, Co A,
Private, deserted; records transferred to 11th FL Infantry, Co C
Union Enlistment: 17Dec1863; Ft. Barrancas, FL; Co A, Private

Engagements: all raids & scouts with regiment & company, Montgomery, AL
Died: 27Aug1865; Ft. Barrancas, FL
Widow's Pension: 23Aug1869; App#178886, Cert#152491

GILL, Lorenzo Dow
AKA: Lorenzo Dow RICHERSON
Birth: Jul1843; Georgia
Death: 08Feb1925; Eufaula, Barbour Co, AL
1850 Location: Dale County, AL
Description: fair complexion, blue eyes, dark hair
CSA: 29Jan1863 - 09Dec1863; 4th Battalion FL Infantry, Co A, Private, deserted; records transferred to 11th FL Infantry, Co C.
Union Enlistment: 17Dec1863; Ft. Barrancas, FL; Co A, Private
Engagements: all expeditions since enlistment, Montgomery, AL
Promotions: 01Sept1864; Bugler
Union Discharge: 17Nov1865; Tallahassee, FL; bounty due $75
Pension: 16Apr1878; App#261629, Cert#705942

GILMORE, Thomas
Union Enlistment: Sept1864; Ft. Barrancas, FL; Co E, Private
Union Discharge: not listed in records

GIVENS, John Daniel
AKA: John D. GIVINS; John D. GIVENS
Birth: circa 1846; Coffee Co, AL
1860 Location: Baldwin County, AL
Description: dark complexion, gray eyes, sandy hair
Union Enlistment: 07Feb1864; Ft. Barrancas, FL; Co D, Private
Promotions: 27Mar1864 - 30Apr1864; Bugler
Died: 02Jun1864; Ft. Barrancas, FL

GIVENS, John H.
AKA: John H. GIVINS
Birth: 01Sept1825; Barnwell Co, SC
Death: 10Mar1916; Ocean Springs, Jackson Co, MS
Burial: Mar1916; Ocean Springs, MS; Antioch Cemetery
1860 Location: Baldwin County, AL
Description: fair complexion, blue eyes, light hair

Union Enlistment: 07Feb186; Ft. Barrancas, FL; Co D, Private
Desertion: 08Aug1865; Ft. Barrancas, FL
Military Finding: 05May1885; desertion charges dropped
Pension: 03Dec1884; App#527222, Cert#477449

GIVENS, John W.
AKA: John W. GIVINS
Birth: 17Feb1836; Mecklenburg Co, NC
Death: 06Aug1908; Okaloosa Co, FL
Burial: Aug1908; Laurel Hill, Okaloosa Co, FL; Almarante Cemetery
1860 Location: Baldwin County, AL
Description: dark complexion, gray eyes, dark hair
CSA: 07Oct1862 - 31Oct1863; 2nd AL Cavalry, Co B, Private, deserted
Union Enlistment: 01Feb1864; Ft. Barrancas, FL; Co B, Private
Engagements: Montgomery, AL
Union Discharge: 17Nov1865; Tallahassee, FL; bounty due $120
Pension: 22Mar1893; App#1148256, Cert#1000707
Widow's Pension: App#903753

GIVENS, Robert J.
AKA: Robert J. GIVINS
Birth: circa 1840; Coffee Co, AL
Death: after 17Nov1865
1860 Location: Baldwin County, AL
Description: dark complexion, gray eyes, dark hair
Union Enlistment: 01Feb1864; Ft. Barrancas, FL; Co B, Private
Engagements: Montgomery, AL
Promotions: 01Jul1864; Corporal
Military Confinement: Jul - Sept1865; Ft. Pickens, FL; arrested and confined for desertion
Union Discharge: 17Nov1865; Tallahassee, FL; bounty due $120

GLASS, James C.
Birth: May 1847; Early Co, GA
Death: after 19Oct1916; Florida
1860 Location: Henry County, AL

Description: dark complexion, black eyes, black hair
Union Enlistment: 23Mar1865; East Pass, FL; Co A, Private
Desertion: 07Aug1865; East Pass, FL
Pension: 19Oct1916 in FL; App#1425398

GLISSON, Henry
AKA: Henry GLEASON
Birth: circa 1838; Early Co, GA
Death: after 26Dec1864
1860 Location: Jackson County, FL
Description: dark complexion, blue eyes, dark hair
CSA: 30Apr1863 - 05Sept1864; 11th FL Infantry, Co F, Private, deserted. Transferred from 4th Battalion FL Infantry, Co D.
Union Enlistment: 10Oct1864; Ft. Barrancas, FL; Co F, Private
Desertion: 26Dec1864; Ft. Barrancas, FL

GLOVER, Burrell
Birth: circa 1821; Richland Co, SC
1860 Location: Washington County, FL
Description: fair complexion, blue eyes, light hair
Union Enlistment: 23Apr1864; Ft. Barrancas, FL; Co E, Private
Died: 26Sept1864; bounty due $75
Widow's Pension: 03May1873; App#209283, Cert#164229
Minor's Pension: 12Jun1877; App#231847, Cert#188540

GODWIN, John S.
AKA: John S. GOODWIN; John S. GORDWIN
Birth: circa 1844; Thomas Co, GA
Burial: Jul1865; Escambia, Florida; Barrancas National Cemetery, Sec 1, Site 939
1860 Location: Washington County, FL
Description: light complexion, gray eyes, light hair
CSA: 11Aug1862 - 31Dec1863; 4th Battalion FL Infantry, Co C, Private, estimated desertion date; records transferred to 11th FL Infantry, Co K.
Union Enlistment: 05Jan1864, Ft. Barrancas, FL; Co C, Private
Engagements: Montgomery, AL
Died: 17Jul1865; Ft. Barrancas, FL

Widow's Pension: 22May1868; App#161143, Cert#117777
Minor's Pension: 01Mar1872; Granddaughter E. Haddock; App#202096, Cert#159430

GOODMAN, John
Birth: circa 1844; Baldwin Co, AL
Burial: 18Sep1865; Pensacola, FL; Presbyterian Cemetery (City Cemetery?)
1860 Location: Baldwin County, AL
Description: dark complexion, dark eyes, black hair
Union Enlistment: 20Aug1864; Ft. Barrancas, FL; Co E, Private
Engagements: Montgomery, AL
Died: 17Sept1865; bounty due $100

GOSS, William S.
Birth: circa 1837; Henry Co, AL
Burial: Sept1864; Escambia Co, FL; Barrancas National Cemetery
1860 Location: Walton County, FL
Description: light complexion, blue eyes, dark hair
CSA Service: 26Oct1863 - 13Feb1864; 4th Battalion FL Infantry, Co. C, Private, deserted; records transferred to 11th FL Infantry, Co K
Union Enlistment: 03Apr1864; East Pass, FL; Co E, Private
Died: 26Sept1864; Ft. Barrancas, FL, bounty due $75

GRANT, John B.
Birth: circa 1847; Jackson Co, FL
Death: 30Jun1885 - 12Apr1897; Jackson Co, FL
1860 Location: Jackson County, FL
Description: dark complexion, gray eyes, dark hair
Union Enlistment: 31Mar1865; Ft. Barrancas, FL; Co D, Private
Desertion: 04Aug1865
Widow's Pension: 12Apr1897 in FL; App#652627

GRAVES, Joseph J.
Birth: circa 1821; Marion Co, SC
Death: 31Mar1888
1860 Location: Pike County, AL

Description: light complexion, blue eyes, light hair
CSA: 01Nov1863 - 25Feb1864; 4th Battalion FL Infantry, Co C, Corporal, deserted; records transferred to 11th FL Infantry, Co K
Union Enlistment: 06Apr1864; East Pass, FL; Co E, Private
Union Discharge: 17Nov1865; Tallahassee, FL; bounty due $75
Pension: 11Jul1885; App#544245
Widow's Pension: 15Jul1891 in TX; App#520302, Cert#685231

GREENWOOD, Zebedee
Birth: circa 1833; Marion Co, SC
Death: 19Mar1891 - 29Aug1895; Florida
1850 Location: Marion County, SC
Description: dark complexion, gray eyes, brown hair
Union Enlistment: 20Dec1863; Ft. Barrancas, FL; Co C, Private
Union Discharge: 17Nov1865; Tallahassee, FL; bounty due $120
Pension: 13Mar1891 in FL; App#1007785
Widow's Pension: 29Aug1895 in FL; App#619898, Cert#544486

GRIMES, Felix Kenan
AKA: Felix K. GRIMES; Felix R. GRIMES; Phelix K. GRIMES
Birth: circa 1824; Duplin Co, NC
Death: 26Jun1880 - 06Dec1890; Coffee Co, AL
1860 Location: Coffee County, AL
Description: dark complexion, blue eyes, brown hair
CSA Service: 02Oct - 31Oct1863; 57th AL Infantry, Co K, Private, estimated desertion date
Union Enlistment: 26Apr1864; East Pass, FL; Co F, Private
Union Discharge: 17Nov1865; Tallahassee, FL; bounty due $75
Widow's Pension: 06Dec1890 in AL; App#489456, Cert#481701

GRIMES, Jesse F.
Birth: circa 1825; Wilcox Co, AL
1860 Location: Santa Rosa County, FL
Description: light complexion, gray eyes, light hair
CSA Service: 22Mar1862 - 01Jun1863; 1st FL Reorganized Infantry, Co E, Private, deserted
Union Enlistment: 21Jan1864; Ft. Barrancas, FL; Co C, Private
Died: 06Aug1864; Ft. Barrancas, FL

Widow's Pension: 20Apr1866; App#125399, Cert#138652

GRUBBS, Emanuel R.
AKA: Manuel R. GRUBBS; Emanuel R. GRUBS
Birth: 15Apr1844; Escambia Co, FL
Death: 18Jun1919; Summerdale, Baldwin Co, AL
Burial: Jun1919; Gateswood, Baldwin Co, AL; Pittman Cemetery
1850 Location: Escambia County, FL
Description: light complexion, blue eyes, brown hair
CSA: 01Sept1863 - 23Dec1863; 15th Confederate Cavalry, Co D, Private, deserted. Transferred from 3rd Battalion FL Cavalry, Co B.
Union Enlistment: 07Jan1864; Ft. Barrancas, FL; Co E, Private
Engagements: Marianna, FL; Pollard, AL; Blakely, AL; Greenville, AL; Montgomery, AL
Promotions: 26Apr1864; Bugler
Military Confinement: May1865 - Aug1865; Ft. Pickens, FL
Union Discharge: 17Nov1865; Tallahassee, FL; bounty due $275
Pension: 12Jul1882; App#489683, Cert#782631
Widow's Pension: 21Jul1919; App#1144190, Cert#884967

GUNTER, Francis Marion
AKA: Francis M. GUNTHER
Birth: 1834; Marion Co, GA
Death: circa 1912; Montgomery Co, TX
Burial: 1912; Willis, Montgomery Co, TX; Willis Cemetery
1860 Location: Coffee County, AL
Description: dark complexion, gray eyes, dark hair
CSA: 01Sept1862 - 31Oct1862; 18th AL Infantry, Co A, Private, deserted
Union Enlistment: 27Aug1864; East Pass, FL; Co D, Private
Desertion: 21Nov1864; Ft. Barrancas, FL

H

HALL, Henry J.
AKA: Henry J. HALE
Birth: circa 1824; Darlington Co, SC
Death: before 20Dec1889

1860 Location: Washington County, FL
Description: light complexion, blue eyes, light hair
Union Enlistment: 25Jan1864; Ft. Barrancas, FL; Co A, Private
Union Discharge: 17Nov1865; Tallahassee, FL; bounty due $275
Military Finding: 09Jan1888; the desertion charge dropped
Widow's Pension: 20Dec1889 in FL; App#411122

HALL, John F.
Birth: 28Nov1838; Marion Co, GA
Death: 22Mar1896; Washington Co, FL
Burial: Aug 1897 in Washington Co, FL; Vernon Cemetery
1860 Location: Holmes County, FL
Description: fair complexion, gray eyes, light hair
Union Enlistment: 08Mar1864; Ft. Barrancas, FL; Co C, Private
Union Discharge: 17Nov1865; Tallahassee, FL; bounty due $120
Pension: 14Feb1883 in FL; App#472431
Widow's Pension: 23Aug1897 in FL; App#661093, Cert#482516

HALL, Louis Marion
AKA: Lewis Marion HALL
Birth: 19Jan1842; Marion Co, GA
Death: 20Sept1920; Mayo, Vernon Parish, LA
Burial: Sept1920; Slagle, Vernon, LA; Glass Window Cemetery
1860 Location: Holmes County, FA
Description: fair complexion, gray eyes, light hair
CSA: 06May - 29May1863; 61st AL Infantry, Co H, Private, deserted
Union Enlistment: 21Feb1864; Ft. Barrancas, FL; Co C, Private
Engagements: Montgomery, AL
Desertion: 19May1865; Montgomery, AL
Military Finding: 26Jan 904; desertion charge dropped
Pension: 11Mar1904 in LA; App#1309910, Cert#1116686

HALL, Thomas
Birth: circa 1830; Appling Co, GA
Death: 05Jun1900 - 03Jul1906; Newton Co, TX
1850 Location: Covington County, AL
Description: dark complexion, gray eyes, dark hair

Union Enlistment: 21Feb1864; Ft. Barrancas, FL; Co C, Private
Union Discharge: 17Nov1865; Tallahassee, FL; bounty due $160
Pension: 09Oct1889; App#733222, Cert#791655
Widow's Pension: 03Jul1906 in TX; App#851632

HARDY, Patrick
Birth: circa 1827; Barnwell Co, SC
Death: 03Nov1882 - 05Nov1885; Florida
1860 Location: Coffee County, AL
Description: dark complexion, gray eyes, dark hair
CSA: 16Mar - 12Sept1863; 57th AL Infantry, Co K, Private, deserted
Union Enlistment: 11Feb1864; Ft. Barrancas, FL; Co B, Private
Union Discharge: 17Nov1865; Tallahassee, FL; bounty due $120
Pension: 03Nov1882 in FL; App#464076, Cert#415145
Widow's Pension: 05Nov1885 in FL; App#332336, Cert#255942

HARDY, Robert
Birth: circa 1847; Santa Rosa Co, FL
Death: after 12Sept1865
1860 Location: Santa Rosa County, FL
Description: fair complexion, gray eyes, light hair
Union Enlistment: 26Feb1864; Ft. Barrancas, FL; Co B, Private
Engagements: Montgomery, AL
Promotions: 01Apr1864; Bugler
Military Charges: 13Feb1865; Larceny 2 counts
Military Court Martial: 23Jul1865; found guilty of stealing and robbery, sentenced 2 years in prison, forfeit pay and allowances
Military Confinement: 23Aug - 12Sept1865; Ft Pickens, FL; escaped
Dishonorable Discharge: 23Aug1865
Military Finding: 20Jun1895; overturned 1870 decision and dishonorably discharged him

HARDY, William Franklin
Birth: 19Mar1819; Montgomery Co, GA
Death: 24Jun1884; Winn Parish, LA
Burial: Jun1884; Winnfield, LA; New Hope Cemetery

1860 Location: Henry County, Al
Description: fair complexion, brown eyes, dark hair
Union Enlistment: 06Apr1864; Ft. Barrancas, FL; Co E, Private
Union Discharge: 17Nov1865; Tallahassee, FL; bounty due $75
Pension: 14Mar1877; App#232457

HARDY, William Spencer
Birth: 16Oct1845; Shelby Co, TN
Burial: Jun1864; Barrancas National Cemetery, Pensacola, FL; Sec 1, Site 953
1860 Location: Henry County, AL
Description: dark complexion, black (blue on inventory of effects) eyes, black hair
Union Enlistment: 30Mar1864; East Pass, FL; Co E, Private
Died: 09 Jun 1864; Ft. Barrancas, FL; bounty due $275

HARRIS, John W.
Birth: circa 1833; Pike County, AL
Death: 02Jun1880 – 1900; Alabama
Description: fair complexion, gray eyes, dark hair
Union Enlistment: 26Feb1864; Ft. Barrancas, FL; Co B, Private
Union Discharge: 17Nov1865; Tallahassee, FL; bounty due $160

HARRISON, John A.
Birth: circa 1828; Coffee Co, AL
Death: 05Oct1891-20Feb1893; Alabama
Description: light complexion, gray eyes, dark hair
Union Enlistment: 25Jan1864; Ft. Barrancas, FL; Co B, Private
Union Discharge: 17Nov1865; Tallahassee, FL; bounty due $120
Pension: 05Oct1891; App#1061871, Cert#1104279
Widow's Pension: 20Feb1893 in AL; App#570940, Cert#587430

HARRISON, Jonathan D.
Birth: 08 Oct 1847; Henry Co, AL
Death: 23Dec1913; Houston Co, AL
Burial: Dec1913, Ashford, AL; Rocky Creek Methodist Cemetery
1860 Location: Henry County, AL
Description: light complexion, grey eyes, dark hair
Union Enlistment: 27Mar1865; East Pass, FL; Co A, Private

Union Discharge: 17Nov1865; Tallahassee, FL; bounty due $100
Pension: 13Sept1897 in AL; App#1235533, Cert#1170492
Widow's Pension: 28Feb1914 in AL; App#1022876

HARRISON, Wiley F.
Birth: 21Apr1821; Jones Co, GA
Death: 06Jun1900 - 22Jun1907; Alabama
1860 Location: Henry County, AL
Description: dark complexion, blue eyes, light hair
Union Enlistment: 19Jan1864; Ft. Barrancas, FL; Co A, Private
Engagements: Marianna, FL
Promotions: 01Apr1864; 6th Sergeant
Union Discharge: 17Nov1865; Tallahassee, FL; bounty due $120
Pension: 23Apr1881 in AL; App#420606, Cert#329065
Widow's Pension: 22Jun1907 in AL; App#872033

HART, David Allen
AKA: Daniel A. HART; David HART; David H. HART
Birth: 16Apr1832; Walton Co, FL
Death: 20Feb1910; Wing, Covington Co, AL
Burial: Feb1910; Wing, Covington Co, AL; Beda Cemetery
1860 Location: Covington County, AL
Description: dark complexion, dark eyes, dark hair
Union Enlistment: 06May1864; Ft. Barrancas, FL; Co B, Private
Military Charges: Aug1864; mutinous conduct, conduct prejudicial to good order and military discipline
Military Confinement: Aug1864 - Oct1864; Ft. Pickens, FL; under sentence of court martial for six months at hard labor without forfeiture of pay
Desertion: 16Aug1865
Military Finding: 17Jan1891; desertion charge dropped
Pension: 17Jun1892 in AL; App#1118048, Cert#877868
Widow's Pension: 25Mar1910 in FL; App#938806, Cert#710664

HATCHER, Phillip G.
Birth: circa 1837; Crawford Co, GA
Death: 09Nov1898; Gadsden Co, FL

Burial: Nov 1898; Gadsden, Florida; FL State Hospital Cemetery, Div. 2, Cemetery 2, Row 2, Grave 20
1860 Location: Decatur County, GA
Description: dark complexion, brown eyes, dark hair
Union Enlistment: 29Jun1864; East Pass, FL; Co F, Private
Desertion: 15Nov1864 near Pensacola, FL

HATCHER, William J.
Birth: circa 1845; Lee Co, GA
Death: 15Jun1900 – 1910; Florida
1860 Location: Decatur County, GA
Description: light complexion, brown eyes, dark hair
Union Enlistment: 29Jun1864; East Pass, FL; Co F, Private
Desertion: 15Nov1864 near Pensacola, FL

HATHAWAY, James Wilburn
Birth: 22Jun1847; Dale Co, AL
Death: 11Apr1916; Caryville, Holmes Co, FL
Burial: Apr1916; New Effort Church, Holmes, FL
1860 Location: Dale County, AL
Description: fair complexion, blue eyes, auburn hair
Union Enlistment: 25Sept1864; East Pass, FL; Co E, Private
Engagements: Montgomery, AL
Union Discharge: 17Nov1865; Tallahassee, FL; bounty due $200
Pension: 14Jul1890 in FL; App#787054, Cert#954168

HATHAWAY, John Marcus Lafayette
AKA: John Marion Lafayette HATHAWAY; John M. L. HATHAWAY; John Mc. L. HATHAWAY
Birth: 10Mar1844; Dale Co, AL
Death: 11Aug1925; Esto, Holmes Co, FL
Burial: Aug1925; Holmes, FL; Bethlehem Church Cemetery
1860 Location: Dale County, AL
Description: light complexion, blue eyes, light hair
Union Enlistment: 03Apr1864; East Pass, FL; Co E, Private
Engagements: Marianna, FL; Pollard, AL; Blakeley, AL; Greenville, AL; Montgomery, AL
Union Discharge: 17Nov1865; Tallahassee, FL; bounty due $75

Pension: 17Nov1888 in FL; App#679090, Cert#893330
Widow's Pension: 24Sept1924 in FL; App#1237276, Cert#968257

HATHCOCK, James T.
AKA: James F. HATHCOCK; James H. HATHCOCK; James F. HEATHCOCK
Birth: circa 1834; Alabama
Death: after 25Aug1902
1850 Location: Covington County, AL
Description: dark complexion, blue eyes, dark hair
Union Enlistment: 29Sept1864; East Pass, FL; Co B, Private
Desertion: 19Jan1865; Ft. Barrancas, FL
Pension: 25Aug1902; App#1289891

HATHCOCK, Thomas O.
Birth: Oct1839; Alabama
Death: 01Jun1900 – 1910; Alabama
1860 Location: Covington County, AL
Description: dark complexion, blue eyes, dark hair
Union Enlistment: 29Sept1864; East Pass, FL; Co B, Private
Desertion: 19Jan1865; Ft. Barrancas, FL
Pension: 19Apr1907; App#1363140

HAYS, Needham R.
Birth: circa 1834; Newberry Co, SC
Death: 13Dec1908; Alabama
1860 Location: Henry County, AL
Description: dark complexion, black eyes, dark hair
CSA: 13Jul - 08Aug1863; Capt Tanner's Co, FL Infantry, Private, deserted; records transferred to 11th FL Infantry, Co F
Union Enlistment: 20Feb1864; Ft. Barrancas, FL; Co E, Private
Promotions: 01May1864; Commissary Sergeant
Union Discharge:17Nov1865; Tallahassee, FL; bounty due $160.
Pension: 27Jun1881 in AL; App#414700, Cert#267950
Widow's Pension: Jan1909 in AL; App#911981

HEAD, John F.
Birth: circa 1833; Houston Co, GA

Death: after 21Nov1864
1860 Location: Conecuh County, AL
Description: fair complexion, gray eyes, light hair
CSA: 18Aug1862 - 31Dec1862; 53rd AL Partisan Rangers, Co G
& H, Private, estimated desertion date
Union Enlistment: 05Mar1864; Ft. Barrancas, FL; Co D, Private
Desertion: 21Nov1864; Ft. Barrancas, FL

HEAD, Thomas W.
Birth: circa 1825; Butts Co, GA
Death: before 05Jun1883
1860 Location: Coffee County, AL
Description: fair complexion, gray eyes, light hair
Union Enlistment: 05Mar1864; Ft. Barrancas, FL; Co D, Private
Promotions: 01Apr1864; Corporal
Demotion: 09Aug1864; Private
Desertion: 21Nov1864; Ft. Barrancas, FL
Minor's Pension: 05Jun1883 in AL; Grandson App #305178

HEATH, William T.
Birth: circa 1817; Warren Co, GA
Death: after 17Nov1865
1860 Location: Covington County, AL
Description: fair complexion, gray eyes, gray hair
Union Enlistment: 21Feb1864; Ft. Barrancas, FL; Co C, Private
Union Discharge: 17Nov1865; Tallahassee, FL; bounty due $120

HELF, William
Birth: circa 1835 in Germany (Prussia)
Death: 20Sept1902; Luzerne Co, PA
Burial: Sept1902; Lackawanna, PA; Ransom Valley Cemetery
Union Enlistment: 05Dec1864; New Orleans, LA; Co B, 2nd Lt.
Engagements: Montgomery, AL
Union Discharge: 17Nov1865; Tallahassee, Leon Co, FL

HENDERSON, John G.
Birth: 19Mar1840; Dale Co, AL
Death: 21Apr1910 – 1920; Bonifay, Holmes Co, FL
1860 Location: Santa Rosa County, FL

Description: light complexion, hazel eyes, dark hair
CSA: 17Sep1861 - 06Oct1862; 3rd Battalion FL Cavalry, Co C, Private, disability discharge.
Union Enlistment: 03Apr1864[East Pass, FL; Co E, Private
Military Appointment: 30Jun1865; Acting Veterinary Surgeon
Union Discharge: 17Nov1865; Tallahassee, FL; bounty due $75
Pension: 19Jul1889 in FL; App#717223, Cert#1061403

HENDERSON, John L.
Birth: 21Sept1839; Conecuh Co, AL
Death: 05Sept1922; Repton, Conecuh Co, AL
Burial: Sept1922, Repton, AL; Repton Methodist Church
1860 Location: Conecuh County, AL
Description: fair complexion, gray eyes, dark hair
Union Enlistment: 09May1864; Ft. Barrancas, FL; Co F, Private
Engagements: Montgomery, AL
Desertion: 05Aug1865; Ft. Barrancas, FL
Military Finding: 31Aug1887; desertion charges dropped
Pension: 20Jul1888 in AL; App#665141, Cert#732990

HEWETT, John L.
AKA: John L. HEWITT
Birth: circa 1829; Jackson Co, FL
Death: after 17Nov1865
1860 Location: Holmes County, AL
Description: fair complexion, blue eyes, dark hair
Union Enlistment:16Feb1864; Ft. Barrancas, FL; Co D/F, Private
Promotions: 01Apr1864; Farrier
Demotion: 20Oct1864; Private
Military Confinement: 04Jul - 10Sept1865, Ft. Pickens, FL; court martial, confined for 6 months with $10/mo. in lost pay
Union Discharge: 17Nov1865; Tallahassee, FL; bounty due $275

HEWETT, Joseph B.
Birth: Oct1844; Tennessee
Death: 19Nov1922; Vernon, Washington Co, FL
Burial: Nov1922; Vernon, Washington, FL; Vernon Cemetery
1860 Location: Washington County, FL

Description: light complexion, black eyes, dark hair
CSA: 25Mar - 15Nov1863; 4th Battalion FL Infantry, Co C, Private, deserted; records transferred to 11th FL Infantry, Co K
Union Enlistment: 13Dec1863; Ft. Barrancas, FL; Co A, Private
Engagements: "been on all scouts and raids with Regiment & Company", Montgomery, AL
Promotions: 01Jul1864; Corporal
Union Discharge: 17Nov1865; Tallahassee, FL; bounty due $75
Pension: 23Aug1892 in FL; App#968956, Cert#1057997
Widow's Pension: 09Jun1930; App#1669496, Cert#A63030

HICKS, George
Birth: circa 1833; New York
Burial: 18Jan1865; Hilton Head, Beaufort, SC; Hilton Head Military Cemetery, #493
Union Enlistment: before 17Jan1865, Hilton Head, Beaufort Co, SC; unassigned, Private
Died: 17Jan1865; Hilton Head Island, Beaufort, SC

HICKS, James J.
Birth: circa 1839; Dale Co, AL
Death: after 02Jul1865
Description: light complexion, blue eyes, light hair
Union Enlistment: 20Apr1865; East Pass, FL; Co E, Private
Desertion: 02Jul1865

HICKS, William
Birth: circa 1845; Randolph Co, GA
Death: 16Dec1890 - 30 Apr 1898; Santa Rosa Co, FL
1850 Location: Covington County, AL
Description: dark complexion, brown eyes, dark hair
Union Enlistment: 25Mar1864; Ft. Barrancas, FL; Co C, Private
Engagements: Montgomery, AL
Desertion: 22May1865; Alabama
Military Finding: 06Feb1891; desertion charges dropped
Pension: 16Dec1890 in FL; App#969481, Cert#718548
Widow's Pension: 30Apr1898 in FL; App#674978, Cert#475897

HINOTE, John Wesley
AKA: John HYNOTE; John HIGHNOTE
Birth: 19Jan1843; Henry Co, AL
Death: 11Feb1925; Santa Rosa Co, FL
Burial: Feb1925; Santa Rosa, FL; Spring Hill (Bass) Cemetery
1860 Location: Santa Rosa County, FL
Description: light complexion, blue eyes, light hair
CSA: 29Oct - 31Oct1863; 6th AL Cavalry, Co I, Private, estimated desertion date.
Union Enlistment: 28Apr1864; Ft. Barrancas, FL; Co D, Private
Union Discharge: 17Nov1865; Tallahassee, FL; bounty due $100
Pension: 28Dec1891 in FL; App#1080908, Cert#1130832

HINOTE, William P.
AKA: William HIGHNOTE; William HYNOTE; William M. HINOTE; William H. HINOTE
Birth: 24Mar1844; Henry Co, AL
Death: Aug1934; Baldwin Co, AL
1860 Location: Santa Rosa County, FL
Description: light complexion, blue eyes, light hair
Union Enlistment: 28Apr1864; Barrancas, FL; Co D, Private
Union Discharge: 17Nov1865; Tallahassee, FL; bounty due $100
Pension: 25Sept1891; App#1060650, Cert#1162280

HOBBS, Benjamin Franklin
Birth: circa 1844; Santa Rosa Co, FL
Death: 03Jan1909; Mississippi
1860 Location: Escambia County, FL
Description: fair complexion, gray eyes, dark hair
CSA: 24Apr1862 - 24 Sept1863; 3rd Battalion FL Cavalry, Co B, Private, transferred.   25Sept1863 – 19Jan1864; 15th Confederate Cavalry, Co D, deserted.
Union Enlistment: 25Feb1864; Ft. Barrancas, FL; Co A, Private
Promotions: 01Jan1865; Sergeant
Union Discharge: 17Nov1865; Tallahassee, FL; bounty due $120
Military Finding: 29Sept1887; certificate in lieu of lost discharge
Pension: 16Aug1890; App#976220, Cert#699799
Widow's Pension: 30Jan1909; App#912767, Cert#684002

HODGE, John Allen
Birth: circa 1846; Dooly Co, GA
Death: 28May1920; Mortimer, AL
Description: fair complexion, dark eyes, dark hair
Union Enlistment: 05Mar1864; Ft. Barrancas, FL; Co D, Private
Engagements: Dec1864; Pine Barrens, FL
Promotions: 01Apr1864; Bugler
Military Injury: 17Dec1864; Pine Barren Creek, FL; wounded in action
Union Discharge: 17Nov1865; Tallahassee, FL; bounty due $120
Pension: 28Jan1885; App#530997, Cert#344051

HODGE, McFadden
AKA: Mac HODGE
Birth: circa 1844; Conecuh Co, AL
1860 Location: Holmes County, FL
Description: dark complexion, gray eyes, dark hair
Union Enlistment: 21Feb1864; Ft. Barrancas, FL; Co C, Private
Died: 07Jul1865; Ft. Barrancas, FL

HOLLAND, Elias
AKA: Elias HOLLAN; Elias HALLAND
Birth: circa 1829; Darlington Co, SC
Death: before 28May1895; Florida
1860 Location: Covington County, AL
Description: sandy complexion, blue eyes, black hair
Union Enlistment: 29Apr1864; Ft. Barrancas, FL; Co F, Private
Desertion: 01Aug1865; Barrancas, FL
Military Finding: 27Jun1895; desertion charge dropped
Widow's Pension: 28May1895 in FL; App#614899

HOLLEY, Godfrey Lee
AKA: Godfrey L. HOLLY; Godfrey Lee HOLLY
Birth: 02Aug1835; Wilcox Co, AL
Death: 22Feb1905; Coffee Co, AL
Burial: Feb1905; Coffee, AL; Weeks Assembly of God Church
1850 Location: Wayne County, MS
Description: fair complexion, blue eyes, light hair

Union Enlistment: 27Mar1864; Ft. Barrancas, FL; Co E, Private
Engagements: Marianna, FL; Pollard, AL; Blakeley, AL; Greenville, AL; Montgomery, AL
Promotions: 01May1864; Corporal
Promotions: 01Apr1865; Sergeant
Military Confinement: Jul - Aug 1865; Ft. Pickens, FL
Union Discharge: 17Nov1865; Tallahassee, FL; bounty due $275
Military Finding: 24Dec1881; certificate in lieu of lost discharge
Pension: 24Sept1881 in AL; App#430450, Cert#819100

HOLLEY, William F.
AKA: William F. HOLLY
Birth: 06Sept1846 in Coffee Co, AL
Death: 21Jun1900 – 1910; Walton Co, FL
1860 Location: Coffee County, AL
Description: fair complexion, blue eyes, light hair
Union Enlistment: 15Mar1864; East Pass, FL; Co D, Private
Promotions: 01Apr1864; Corporal
Union Discharge: 17Nov1865; Tallahassee, FL; bounty due $120
Pension: 22Jul1891 in FL; App#1044146, Cert#774802

HOLLINGER, Adam Cornelius
Birth: Apr1837; Baldwin Co, AL
Death: 22Jun1902; Santa Rosa Co, FL
1860 Location: Mobile County, AL
Description: dark complexion, dark eyes, dark hair
CSA: 20Dec1861 - 30Apr1862; 2nd Battalion AL Light Artillery, Co C, Private
Union Enlistment: 27Mar1864; Ft. Barrancas, FL; Co E, Private
Engagements: Marianna, FL; Pine Barren Creek; Pollard, AL; Blakeley, AL; Montgomery, AL
Promotions: 01May1864; Corporal
Promotions: 12Aug1864; Sergeant
Union Discharge: 17Nov1865; Tallahassee, FL; bounty due $160
Pension: 10Sept1891 in FL; App#1054677
Widow's Pension: 20Sept1913; FL; App#1014554, Cert#895146

HOLLIS, William
Birth: circa 1824; Morgan Co, GA
Death: before 16 Oct 1890; Alabama
Description: fair complexion, blue eyes, light hair
Additional Union Service: 01Jan1863 - 08Jan1864; In the Navy, Landsman, USS Potomac, blockade of Pensacola
Union Enlistment: 16May1864; Ft. Barrancas, FL; Co E, 2nd Lt
Honorable Discharge: 17Feb1865; resigned
Widow's Pension: 16Oct1890 in AL; App#470618, Cert#615222

HOLLY, Calvin H.
Birth: Aug 1846; Covington Co, AL
Death: 08Jan1918; Alabama
1860 Location: Covington County, AL
Description: light complexion, hazel eyes, brown hair
Union Enlistment: 12Mar1864; East Pass, FL; Co E, Private
Promotions: 01May1864; Corporal
Military Confinement: 10Sept1864 - 30Jun1865; Ft. Pickens, FL
Union Discharge: 17Nov1865; Tallahassee, FL; bounty due $275
Military Finding: 18Aug1888; desertion charge dropped
Pension: 12Mar1884; App#507993, Cert#1163000
Widow's Pension: 15Jan1918; App#1113326

HOLMAN, Andrew Lewis Jr.
AKA: Andrew L. HOLLMAN; Andrew L. HOLMAN
Birth: circa 1843; Baldwin Co, AL
Burial: Oct1864; Escambia Co, FL; Barrancas National Cemetery
1860 Location: Baldwin County, AL
Description: dark complexion, dark eyes, dark hair
Union Enlistment: 09Jan1864; Barrancas, FL; Co A, Private
Died: 28Oct1864; Ft. Barrancas, FL

HOLMAN, Henry A.
Birth: circa 1846; Baldwin Co, AL
Burial: Oct1864; Escambia Co, FL; Barrancas National Cemetery
1860 Location: Baldwin County, AL
Description: dark complexion, dark eyes, dark hair
Union Enlistment: 26Jul1864; Ft. Barrancas, FL; Co F, Private

Died: 16Oct1864; Ft. Barrancas, FL; never paid

HOLMAN, John D.
AKA: John D. HOLLMAN; John D. HALLMAN; John D. HALLMON
Birth: 07Feb1840; Baldwin Co, AL
Death: 22Nov1897; Roberts, Escambia Co, FL
Burial: Nov1897; Gateswood, Baldwin Co, AL; Clear Springs UMC Church
1860 Location: Baldwin County, AL
Description: light complexion, gray eyes, brown hair
CSA: 24Apr1862 – 24Sept1863; 3rd Battalion FL Cavalry, Co B, Private, transferred. 25Sept1863 – 23Dec1863; 15th Confederate Cavalry, Co D, Private, deserted.
Union Enlistment: 12Jan1864; Ft. Barrancas, FL; Co C, Private
Union Discharge: 17Nov1865; Tallahassee, FL; bounty due $120
Widow's Pension: 27Apr1901 in FL; App#740144, Cert#557761

HOLMAN, Lewis
AKA: Lewis HOLMES
Birth: circa 1838; Jackson Co, FL
Death: after 01Aug1865
Description: light complexion, dark eyes, dark hair
Union Enlistment: 17Apr1865; East Pass, FL; Co F, Private
Desertion: 01Aug1865; Ft. Barrancas, FL

HOOKS, John Franklin
Birth: circa 1840; Putnam Co, GA
Death: after 17Nov1865
1850 Location: Pike County, AL
Description: light complexion, blue eyes, dark hair
Union Enlistment: 11Mar1865; East Pass, FL; Co E, Private
Union Discharge: 17Nov1865; Tallahassee, FL; bounty due $100

HORTON, Hubbard H.
AKA: Hubbard R. HORTON; Hubber H. HORTON
Birth: circa 1827; Wilkinson Co, GA
Death: after 05Mar1887; Florida
1860 Location: Henry County, AL

Description: light complexion, blue eyes, light hair
CSA: 09Jun1863 - 07Oct1863; 4th Battalion FL Infantry, Co. C, Private, deserted; records transferred to 11th FL Infantry, Co K
Union Enlistment: 03Apr1864; East Pass, FL; Co E, Private
Union Discharge: 17Nov1865; Tallahassee, FL; bounty due $75
Pension: 05Mar1887 in FL; App#600673, Cert#456568

HORTON, William Wiliford
AKA: Wiliford W. HORTON; W. W. HORTON
Birth: circa 1837; Wilkinson Co, GA
Death: 30Jul1890 – 1901; Alabama
1860 Location: Jefferson County, FL
Description: dark complexion, dark eyes, dark hair
Union Enlistment: 25Sept1864; East Pass, FL; Co E, Private
Engagements: Montgomery, AL
Promotions: 20Oct1864; Wagoner
Union Discharge: 17Nov1865; Tallahassee, FL; bounty due $200
Pension: 30Jul1890 in AL; App#889544, Cert#1042255
Widow's Pension: 09Mar1901(?), in AL; App#737146, Cert#532901

HOWARD, Christopher C.
Birth: 12Oct1844; Pike Co, AL
Death: Jun1900 – 1910; Walton Co, FL
1860 Location: Walton County, FL
Description: light complexion, gray eyes, brown hair
Union Enlistment: 19Jan1864; Ft. Barrancas, FL; Co B, Private
Engagements: Montgomery, AL
Union Discharge: 17Nov1865; Tallahassee, FL; bounty due $120
Pension: 13Oct1890; App#919855, Cert#1031914
Widow's Pension: App#857059, Cert#626377

HOWARD, Jefferson H.
AKA: Jefferson J. HOWARD
Birth: circa 1846; Pike Co, AL
Description: fair complexion, blue eyes, light hair
Union Enlistment: 08Sept1864; Ft. Barrancas, FL; Co D, Private
Died: 09Nov1864; Ft. Barrancas, FL

HOWELL, Francis
Birth: circa 1845; Barbour Co, AL
1860 Location: Walton County, FL
Description: light complexion, grey eyes, sandy hair
CSA: 13Sept - 09Dec1863; 4th Battalion FL Infantry, Co A, Private, deserted; records transferred to 11th FL Infantry, Co C
Union Enlistment: 30Dec1863; Ft. Barrancas, FL; Co B, Private
Died: 29Jul1864; Ft. Barrancas, FL

HOWELL, Thomas
Birth: circa 1828; Edgefield Co, SC
1850 Location: Walton County, FL
Description: light complexion, blue eyes, light hair
CSA: 27Apr - 09Dec1863; 4th Battalion FL Infantry, Co A, Private, deserted; records transferred to 11th FL Infantry, Co C
Union Enlistment: 30Dec1863; Ft. Barrancas, FL; Co A, Private
Died: 09May1864; Ft. Barrancas, FL, never paid

HUBBARD, Francis Marion
AKA: Francis M. HUBERT; Francis M. HUBBERD; Francis M. HUBBERT; Francis M. HUBBIRD
Birth: Jan1844; Escambia Co, FL
Death: 12Mar1925; Gonzales, Escambia Co, FL
1860 Location: Baldwin County, AL
Description: fair complexion, dark eyes, dark hair
Union Enlistment: 01Feb1864; Ft. Barrancas, FL; Co A, Private
Engagements: Montgomery, AL
Desertion: 05May1865 between Montgomery & Andalusia, AL
Military Finding: 11Jul1901; desertion charges dropped
Pension: 07Apr1906; App#1347517, Cert#1124078
Widow's Pension: 18Apr1925; App#1231989, Cert#962662

HUCKABY, Andrew J.
AKA: A. J. HUCKABAY; Andrew J. HUCKABYE; Andrew J. HUCKBY; Andrew J. HUCKEBY
Birth: circa 1837; Lee Co, GA
1860 Location: Washington County, FL
Description: light complexion, blue eyes, brown hair

Union Enlistment: 07Jan1864; Ft. Barrancas, FL; Co A, Private
Engagements: Montgomery, AL
Military Injury: 12 - 14May1865; admitted to St. Mary's Hospital in Montgomery with gunshot wound
Died: 14May1865; Montgomery, AL; from wounds received while foraging
Military Finding: 01May1885; He is considered as having been wounded while foraging, exact date not known and recorded as wounded in line of duty

HUDGENS, James J.
AKA: James J. HUDGINS
Birth: 16Apr1834; Montgomery Co, AL
Death: 17Apr1908; Yellowpine, Sabine Co, TX
Burial: Apr1908; Sabine, TX; Pleasant Hill Cemetery
1860 Location: Pike County, AL
Description: fair complexion, gray eyes, light hair
CSA: 08Oct1863 - 16Jan1864; 4th Battalion AL Cavalry, Co A, Private, deserted
Union Enlistment: 28Jan1864; Ft. Barrancas, FL; Co B, Private
Promotions: 01Apr1864; Sergeant
Disability Discharge: 31May1865; bounty due $160
Pension: 10Jul1893 in TX; App#1152274, Cert#1086249
Widow's Pension: 08May1908 in TX; App#892680

HUDSON, George F.
Birth: 28Nov1834; Harris Co, GA
Death: 28Oct1925; Covington Co, AL
Burial: Oct1925; Covington Co, AL; Good Hope Primitive Baptist Church
1850 Location: Marion County, GA
Description: fair complexion, gray eyes, light hair
Union Enlistment: 24Feb1864; Ft. Barrancas, FL; Co C, Private
Desertion: 22Dec1864; Ft. Barrancas, FL

HUDSON, James T.
AKA: James G. HUDSON; James F. HUDSON
Birth: May1844; Washington Co, FL

Death: 10Nov1914; Vernon, Washington Co, FL
Burial: Nov1914, Chipley, Washington Co. FL; Hard Labor Cemetery
1860 Location: Washington County, Florida
Description: fair complexion, blue eyes, light hair
CSA: 07Sept1861 - 17Dec1862; 4th FL Infantry, Co H, Private, discharged
Union Enlistment: 02Feb1864; Ft. Barrancas, FL; Co C, Private
Engagements: Montgomery, AL
Promotions: 23Mar1864; Corporal
Union Discharge: 17Nov1865; Tallahassee, FL; bounty due $160
Pension: 07Jun1892 in FL; App#782224, Cert#672831

HUDSON, John G. R.
AKA: John G. R. HUDTSON
Birth: circa 1847; Washington Co, FL
Death: after 02Mar1897
1860 Location: Washington County, FL
Description: dark complexion, gray eyes, dark hair
CSA: 25Mar - 31Dec1863; 4th Battalion FL Infantry, Co C, Corporal, deserted; records transferred to 11th FL Infantry, Co K.
Union Enlistment: 02Feb1864; Ft. Barrancas, FL; Co A, Private
Military Appointment: 01Sept1864; Bugler
Engagements: Marianna, FL; 15 Mile House, FL; Pollard, AL; Montgomery, AL
Union Discharge: 17Nov1865; Tallahassee, FL; bounty due $120
Pension: 02Mar1897; App#1187331

HUDSON, Thomas J.
Birth: circa 1831; Harris Co, GA
Burial: Jun1864; Escambia Co, Florida; Ft. Barrancas National Cemetery, Section 1, Site 951
1850 Location: Marion County, GA
Description: fair complexion, blue eyes, light hair
Union Enlistment: 24Feb1864; Ft. Barrancas, FL; Co C, Private
Died: 20Jun1864; Ft. Barrancas, FL
Minor's Pension: 03Dec1883; App#321685

HUGGINS, John
Birth: 22May1821; Darlington Co, SC
Death: 12Jun1906; Excel, Monroe County, AL
Burial: Jun1906; Frisco City, Monroe Co, AL; Coleman Cemetery
1860 Location: Dale County, AL
Description: dark complexion, dark eyes, black hair
Union Enlistment: 17Dec1863; Ft. Barrancas, FL; Co A, Private
Promotions: 01Apr1864; 2nd Sergeant
Union Discharge: 17Nov1865; Tallahassee, FL; bounty due $75
Pension: 27Jan1881; App#414737, Cert#308852
Widow's Pension: after 12Jun1906; App#862512, Cert#747853
Minor's Pension: 19Jul1932; App#1721873, Cert#A-2-23-33

HUGHES, John
AKA: John HEWES
Birth: circa 1824; Dale Co, AL
Description: fair complexion, blue eyes, light hair
Union Enlistment: 01Nov1864; East Pass, FL; Co D, Private
Union Discharge: Unknown length of service
Pension: 01Aug1882; App # 456296

HUTTO, John W.
Birth: circa 1820; Henry Co, AL
Death: 03Feb1910; Walton Co, FL
Description: fair complexion, grey eyes, light hair
CSA: 06Aug1863 - 08Mar1864; 4th Battalion FL Infantry, Co. C, Private, deserted; records transferred to 11th FL Infantry, Co C.
Union Enlistment: 13Apr1864, Ft. Barrancas, FL; Co E, Private
Engagements: Skirmish in Milton, FL
Desertion: 09Aug1865; Ft. Barrancas, FL
Military Finding: 05Nov1886; desertion charge dropped
Widow's Pension: 26Apr1916 in FL; App#1065215

I

INFINGER, Absalom
Birth: Feb1826; Dale Co, AL
Death: 23Jun1900 – 1910; Washington Co, FL
Description: fair complexion, gray eyes, sandy hair

CSA: 25Mar1863 - 25Jan1864; 4th Battalion FL Infantry, Co. C, 1st Sergeant, deserted; records transferred to 11th FL Infantry, Co K.
Union Enlistment: 05Mar1864; Ft. Barrancas, FL; Co C/E, Private
Union Discharge: 17Nov1865; Tallahassee, FL; bounty due $275
Pension: 30Dec1885; App #557813, Cert #387303

J

JAY, James J.
AKA: James JACEY; James JAY
Birth: circa 1845; Santa Rosa Co, FL
Description: light complexion, grey eyes, light hair
Union Enlistment: 25Jan1864; Ft. Barrancas, FL; Co B, Private
Died: 16Aug1864; Ft. Barrancas, FL, bounty due $275

JERDAVIL, Unknown
Union Discharge: Sept1865; Unknown cause

JERNIGAN, McKay
AKA: McKay JERIGAN; McKEY JERNAGAN
Birth: circa 1830; Sampson Co, NC
Death: after 16Jun1894
1860 Location: Dale County, AL
Description: light complexion, gray eyes, black hair
CSA: 29Jan1863 - 22Dec1863; 4th Battalion FL Infantry, Co A, Private, deserted, records transferred to 11th FL Infantry, Co C
Union Enlistment: 05Jan1864; Ft. Barrancas, FL; Co D, Private
Desertion: 06Jun1864; on special service beyond Federal lines
Pension: 13Feb1894; App#1156031

JOHNSON, Andrew Jackson
Birth: Nov1841; Alabama
Death: 25Jul1911; Milam Co, TX
1860 Location: Escambia County, FL
Description: dark complexion, gray eyes, dark hair
Union Enlistment: 09Jan1864; Ft. Barrancas, FL; Co A, Private

Engagements: Marianna, FL; 15 Mile House, FL; Pollard, AL; Montgomery, AL
Union Discharge: 17Nov1865; Tallahassee, FL; bounty due $120
Pension: 17Sept1883 in TX; App#495433, Cert#634231
Widow's Pension: 22Aug1911 in TX; App#970642, Cert#762716

JOHNSON, Bryant
AKA: Bryant JOHNSTON
Birth: circa 1820; Washington Co, GA
Burial: Jul1864; Escambia, FL; Barrancas National Cemetery, Sec 1, Site 943
1860 Location: Covington County, AL
Description: dark complexion, brown eyes, dark hair
Union Enlistment: 03Apr1864; East Pass, FL; Co E, Private
Died: 10Jul1864; Ft. Barrancas, FL; bounty due $75
Widow's Pension: 05May1866; App #126273, Cert #139811

JOHNSON, Edmund J.
Birth: circa 1826; Alabama
Death: after 18Aug1870; Alabama
Description: light complexion, brown eyes, black hair
Union Enlistment: 10Mar1864; East Pass, FL; Co D, Private
Promotions: 09Aug1864; Corporal
Desertion: 08Dec1864; Ft. Barrancas, FL

JOHNSON, George H.
AKA: George H. JOHNSTON; George W. JOHNSON
Birth: circa 1843; Baker Co, GA
Death: 11Nov1892 - 19Jan1896; Florida
1860 Location: Covington County, AL
Description: light complexion, gray eyes, dark hair
Union Enlistment: 03Apr1864; East Pass, FL; Co E, Private
Engagements: Marianna, FL; Pollard, AL; Blakeley, AL; Greenville, AL; Montgomery, AL
Union Discharge: 17Nov1865; Tallahassee, FL; bounty due $75
Pension: 11Nov1892 in FL; App#1137458, Cert#978545
Widow's Pension: 19Jan1896 in FL; App#669146, Cert#475987

JOHNSON, Jackson
Birth: circa 1845 in Conecuh Co, AL
1850 Location: Conecuh County, AL
Description: Blue eyes, brown hair, fair complexion
Union Enlistment: 27Jul1864; Ft. Barrancas, FL; unknown company and rank
Union Discharge: Unknown length of service

JOHNSON, Jonathan M.
AKA: Jonathan M. JOHNSTON
Birth: circa 1846; Randolph Co, GA
Burial: Jun1864; Escambia, FL; Barrancas National Cemetery, Sec 1, Site 940
Description: dark complexion, brown eyes, dark hair
Union Enlistment: 03Apr1864; East Pass, FL; Co E, Private
Died: 26Jun1864; Ft. Barrancas, FL, bounty due $75

JOHNSON, William
Birth: circa 1818; Twiggs Co, GA
1860 Location: Gadsden County, FL
Description: fair complexion, blue eyes, sandy hair
Union Enlistment: 24Jan1864; Ft. Barrancas, FL; Co D, Private
Died: 22Sept1864; Ft. Barrancas, FL
Widow's Pension: 16May1867; App#147186, Cert#138257

JONES, Alexander W.
Birth: circa 1833; Lowndes Co, AL
Death: after 12Jan1865
1850 Location: Lowndes County, AL
Description: fair complexion, blue eyes, dark hair
Union Enlistment: 18Aug1864; East Pass, FL; Co F, Private
Desertion: 12Jan1865; East Pass, FL

JONES, Dixon
AKA: Dixon JONAS
Birth: 06Apr1850; Walton Co, FL
Death: 20May1927; Portland, Walton Co, FL
Burial: May1927; Freeport, Walton Co, FL; Hatcher Cemetery
1860 Location: Washington County, FL

Description: light complexion, blue eyes, light hair
Union Enlistment: 19Mar1864; East Pass, FL; Co E, Private
Disability Discharge: 13Apr1865
Pension: 18Sept1880 in FL; App#729958, Cert#1057442
Widow's Pension: 20Jul1927 in FL; App#1587033, Cert#A12627

JONES, Henry
Birth: circa 1828; Jackson Co, FL
Death: 1876 - Apr1880 in Holmes Co, FL
1860 Location: Holmes County, FL
Description: dark complexion, gray eyes, dark hair
CSA: 13May1862 - 10Jan1863; 6th FL Infantry, Co I, Private, deserted.
Union Enlistment: 28Jan1864; Ft. Barrancas, FL; Co D, Private
Disability Discharge: 29Dec1864
Widow's Pension: 13May1880; App#265060, Cert#326449

JONES, James M.
Birth: 12Nov1842; Covington Co, AL
Death: 18Mar1933; Andalusia, Covington Co, AL
Burial: Mar1933; Covington, AL; Carter Cemetery
1860 Location: Covington County, AL
Description: fair complexion, blue eyes, light hair
Union Enlistment: 01Mar1865; Ft. Barrancas, FL; Co B, Private
Union Discharge: 17Nov1865; Tallahassee, FL; bounty due $100
Pension: 10Aug1894 in AL; App#1159917, Cert#1278967

JONES, Lionel
AKA: Leonard JONES
Birth: circa 1844; Dale Co, AL
Death: 22Feb1929; Newton, Dale Co, AL
Description: fair complexion, blue eyes, red hair
Union Enlistment: 17Sept1864; Ft. Barrancas, FL; Co F, Private
Union Discharge: 17Nov1865; Tallahassee, FL
Pension: 29Jun1876; App#221724, Cert#552840
Widow's Pension: 22Mar1929; App#1638286, Cert#A9929

JONES, Mathew
Birth: circa 1842; Washington Co, FL

Death: 29Jun1880 - 04 Aug 1890; Escambia Co, FL
Description: black complexion, black eyes, black hair
Union Enlistment: 28Mar1864; Ft. Barrancas, FL; Co E, Under Cook
Desertion: 10Sept1865; Tallahassee, FL
Military Finding: 22Aug1887; desertion charges dropped
Widow's Pension: 04Aug1890 in FL; App#458481, Cert#342885

JONES, Richard
Birth: circa 1839; Barbour Co, AL
Death: after 18Aug1865
Description: black complexion, black eyes, black hair
Union Enlistment: 05Aug1864; East Pass, FL; Co F, Under Cook
Engagements: Montgomery, AL
Desertion: 18Aug1865; Ft. Barrancas, FL

JONES, Samuel T.
Birth: circa 1828; Covington Co, AL
1860 Location: Covington County, AL
Description: dark complexion, brown eyes, dark hair
CSA: 09Apr - 31Dec1863; 6th AL Cavalry, Co I, Sergeant, estimated end date
Union Enlistment: 24Feb1864; Ft. Barrancas, FL; Co B, Private
Promotions: 01Apr1864; Corporal
Died: 17Jul1864; Ft. Barrancas, FL; bounty due $75
Widow's Pension: 09Mar1866; App#123047, Cert#75367
Minor's Pension: App#229440, Cert#182383

JONES, Thomas J.
Birth: circa 1842; Covington Co, AL
Description: light complexion, blue eyes, light hair
CSA: 31Mar - 31Dec1862; 42nd AL Infantry, Co E, Private, estimated desertion date
Union Enlistment: 09Feb1864; Ft. Barrancas, FL; Co B, Private
Died: 01Aug1864; Ft. Barrancas, FL; bounty due $275

JONES, Wright S.
AKA: Wright J. JONES
Birth: 15Apr1845; Williams Mills, Covington Co, AL

Death: 20Jul1909; Rose Hill, Covington Co, AL
Burial: Jul1909; Covington Co, AL; Mt Zion United Methodist Church Cemetery
1860 Location: Covington County, AL
Description: light complexion, black eyes, light hair
Union Enlistment: 25Jan1864; Ft. Barrancas, FL; Co B, Private
Engagements: Montgomery, AL
Union Discharge: 17Nov1865; Tallahassee, FL; bounty due $120
Widow's Pension: 08Oct1909 in AL; App#728469, Cert#697651

JORDAN, Edmond
Birth: circa 1842; Henry Co, AL
Death: after 17Nov1865
Description: fair complexion, blue eyes, light hair
Union Enlistment: 07May1864; Ft. Barrancas, FL; Co F, Private
Promotions: 02Oct1864; Sergeant
Military Charges: Jul1866; two letters in file concerning larceny charges while he was with the Army, in jail at Marianna
Union Discharge: 17Nov1865; Tallahassee, FL

JORDAN, James Monroe
AKA: James M. JORDAN
Birth: circa 1837; Marion Co, GA
Death: 25Dec1884; Elmore Co, AL
1860 Location: Pike County, AL
Description: dark complexion, gray eyes, dark hair
Union Enlistment: 07May1864; Ft. Barrancas, FL; Co F, Private
Promotions: 03Aug1864; 2nd Master Sergeant
Military Charges: 19May1865; sold a bale of hay to a "colored man" in Warrington for ten dollars
Military Confinement: 10Apr1865 - 05Jun1865; Ft. Pickens, FL
Desertion: 02Aug1865; Ft. Barrancas, FL
Military Finding: 24Mar1896; desertion charges dropped
Widow's Pension: 01Dec1890 in AL; App#446905

JORDAN, William M.
AKA: William M. JERDON; William M. JORDEN; William M. JORDIN

Birth: circa 1822; Monroe Co, AL
Death: 26Oct1893; Portland, Walton Co, FL
1860 Location: Walton County, FL
Description: dark complexion, dark eyes, dark hair
Union Enlistment: 29Mar1864; Ft. Barrancas, FL; Co E/A, Private
Union Discharge: 17Nov1865; Tallahassee, FL; bounty due $120
Pension: 07Dec1889; App#742036, Cert#925777
Widow's Pension: 01Dec1893; App#586468, Cert#438499

JOST, Frederick C.
Birth: circa 1839; Holstein, Germany
Death: before 30Dec1891; Alabama
Additional Union Service: 25Mar1863 - 12May1864; 14th NY Cavalry, Co M, 1st Sergeant (19Apr1863)
Union Enlistment: 29Mar1864; Ft. Barrancas, FL; Co B/F, 2Lt/1Lt
Engagements: Montgomery, AL
Promotions: 13Aug1864; 1st Lt
Union Discharge: 17Nov1865; Tallahassee, FL
Widow's Pension: 30Dec1891 in AL; App#536577, Cert#504300

K

KELLEY, William A.
AKA: William A. KELLY
Birth: Jan1843; Upson Co, GA
Death: 15May1915; Covington Co, AL
1860 Location: Covington County, AL
Description: light complexion, blue eyes, light hair
Union Enlistment: 10Mar1864; East Pass, FL; Co D, Private
Military Appointment: 01May1864; Bugler
Union Discharge: 17Nov1865; Tallahassee, FL; bounty due $120
Military Finding: 21Jul1886; certificate in lieu of lost discharge
Pension: 09May1893 in FL; App#1150696, Cert#1053626
Widow's Pension: 18Sept1916 in FL; App#1074379

KEMP, James B.
Birth: circa 1832; Georgia
1860 Location: Walton County, FL

Description: dark complexion, blue eyes, light hair
Union Enlistment: 20Apr1864; Ft. Barrancas, FL; Co G/F, Private
Died: 26Jul1865; Ft. Barrancas, FL
Widow's Pension: 01Feb1869; App#171176, Cert#164831

KEMP, William T.
Birth: circa 1847; Marion Co, GA
Death: after 25Jul1865
1860 Location: Henry County, AL
Description: light complexion, gray eyes, dark hair
Union Enlistment: 27Mar1865; East Pass, FL; Co A, Private
Desertion: 25Jul1865; Ft. Barrancas, FL

KENNEDY, John L.
Birth: 29 Jul 1829; Duplin Co, NC
Death: 20Sept1909; Dale Co, AL
Burial: Sept1909; Midland City, Dale Co, AL; Kennedy Cemetery
1860 Location: Newton County, AL
Description: fair complexion, black eyes, dark hair
Union Enlistment: 03Oct1864; Ft. Barrancas, FL; Co C, Private
Engagements: Pollard, AL
Missing in Action: 17Dec1864; Michael's Creek, FL

KENNEDY, Samuel
AKA: Samuel KENEDY
Birth: circa 1844; Barbour Co, AL
Death: 17Dec1864 - 31Dec1864 in Dale Co, AL
Burial: Dec1864 in Dale Co, AL; Kennedy Cemetery
1860 Location: Newton, Dale County, AL
Description: fair complexion, dark eyes, dark hair
Union Enlistment: 05Mar1864; Ft. Barrancas, FL; Co C, Private
Promotions: Apr1864; Corporal
Missing in Action: 17Dec1864; Michael's Creek, FL

KIELMANSEGGE, Eugene
AKA: Eugene von KIELMANSEGGE
Death: 03Sep1868; St. Andrews Bay, Washington Co, FL
Additional Union Service: 1st MD Cavalry, disability discharge
Military Appointment: 26Jun1864; Ft. Barrancas, FL; Lt. Colonel

Disability Discharge: 17Apr1865
Widow's Pension: 17Nov1890; Austria; App#452091, Cert#332683

KILPATRICK, Noah Powell
Birth: circa 1821; Kershaw Co, SC
Death: after 13Aug1889; Covington Co, AL
Description: fair complexion, blue eyes, grey hair
Union Enlistment: 01Apr1864; Ft. Barrancas, FL; Co B, Private
Engagements: Raid on the Florida & Alabama Railroad
Desertion: 24Mar1865; Evergreen, AL

KIMMONS, John
AKA: John KIMMONES
Birth: circa 1831; Putnam Co, GA
Death: 25Dec1910; Walton Co, FL
Burial: Dec1910; Walton, FL; Children's Home Cemetery
Description: fair complexion, blue eyes, light hair
Union Enlistment: 28Sept1864; East Pass, FL; Co C, Private
Desertion: 08Aug1865
Military Finding: 06Sept1893; desertion charge dropped
Pension: 17Jul1893 in FL; App#1152524, Cert#1059357
Widow's Pension: 30Mar1911 in AL; App#761740, Cert#737323

KING, Angus
AKA: Angers KING
Birth: 20Sept1831; Henry Co, AL
Death: 20Feb1914; Gateswood, Baldwin Co, AL
Burial: Feb1914; Gateswood, Baldwin Co, AL; Pittman Cemetery
1860 Location: Vernon, Washington County, FL
Description: fair complexion, gray eyes, dark hair
CSA: 13May1862 - 27Feb1863; 8th FL Infantry, Co. E, Private, disability discharge
Union Enlistment: 28Sept1864; East Pass, FL; Co C, Private
Engagements: Montgomery, AL
Union Discharge: 17Nov1865; Tallahassee, FL
Pension: 30Jun1880; App#899205, Cert#589013
Widow's Pension: 30Sept1915 in AL; App#1053664

KING, Benjamin
Birth: circa 1818; Georgia
1860 Location: Walton County, FL
Description: light complexion, blue eyes, light hair
Union Enlistment: 19Jan1864; Ft. Barrancas, FL; Co B, Private
Died: 05Apr1865; Ft. Barrancas, FL; bounty due $275
Widow's Pension: 04Nov1869; App#181215, Cert#192610

KING, William
AKA: Williamson KING
Birth: circa 1826; Conecuh Co, AL
Description: fair complexion, hazel eyes, brown hair
Union Enlistment: 26Apr1864; East Pass, FL; Co F, Private
Died: 14Jul1864; East Pass, FL
Widow's Pension: 19Aug1867; App#178754, Cert#164913

KING, William Johnson
AKA: William KING
Birth: circa 1845; Clay Co, GA
Death: 05Jul1919; Perdido, Baldwin Co, AL
Burial: Jul1919; Perdido, AL; Baptist Church Cemetery
1860 Location: Walton County, FL
Description: light complexion, blue eyes, light hair
Union Enlistment: 19Jan1864; Ft. Barrancas, FL; Co D, Private
Military Confinement: 21Jun1865; Ft Pickens, FL
Union Discharge: 17Nov1865; Tallahassee, FL; bounty due $275
Pension: 11Jan1895; App#1163300, Cert#1139804

KIRKLAND, Emanuel
Birth: circa 1845; Barbour Co, AL
Death: after 21Sept1871
Description: fair complexion, blue eyes, light hair
Union Enlistment: 23Feb1864; Ft. Barrancas, FL; Co C, Private
Disability Discharge: 12Sep1864; chronic rheumatism

KITTRELL, Zenith Andrew
AKA: Zeawath A. KITTRELL, Zenith A. KITTRELL, Zenith A. KITREL
Birth: circa 1845; Walton Co, FL

1860 Location: Holmes County, FL
Description: fair complexion, dark eyes, dark hair
Union Enlistment: 24Feb1864; Ft. Barrancas, FL; Co D, Private
Mustered in: 27Mar1864; mustered into 14th NY Cavalry, Co M

KNOWLES, James H.
Birth: circa 1841; Jackson Co, FL
Death: after 08Sept1865
Description: dark complexion, brown eyes, black hair
Union Enlistment: 07May1864; Ft. Barrancas, FL; Co B, Private
Military Confinement: Oct1864 - 26Apr1865; Ft. Pickens, FL; refused to be mustered in, lame finger & couldn't hold a sword; encouraged others not to take the oath
Union Discharge: 08Sep1865 - 17Nov1865; released from confinement, no record after that

KRIMMINGER, John N.
AKA: John N. KRIMENGER, John N. KRIMINGER
Birth: 16Dec1818; Cabarrus Co, NC
Death: 05Oct1872; Branford, Suwannee Co, FL
Burial: Oct1872; Branford, Suwannee Co, FL; Maypop Cemetery
1860 Location: Darlington County, SC
Description: dark complexion, dark eyes, dark hair
CSA: 20May1862 - 01Jul1863; 18th SC Infantry, Co G, Private, deserted
Union Enlistment: 15Feb1864; Ft. Barrancas, FL; Co D, Private
Promotions: 01Apr1864; Sergeant
Union Discharge: 17Nov1865; Tallahassee, FL; bounty due $120

L

LANGFORD, Jesse
AKA: Jesse LANKFORD
Birth: circa 1820; Bulloch Co, GA
Death: after 08Jul1870
1850 Location: Clinch County, GA
Description: light complexion, blue eyes, light hair
Union Enlistment: 02Apr1864; East Pass, FL; Co E, Private
Desertion: 23Mar1865; Milton, Santa Rosa Co, FL

LANGLEY, Levi
AKA: Levy LANGLEY, Levi LONGLEY
Birth: 01Jan1829; Gwinnett Co, GA
Death: 02Jun1900 - 22Jun1906; Thomas Co, GA
1860 Location: Coffee County, AL
Description: light complexion, blue eyes, brown hair
Union Enlistment: 18Feb1864; Ft. Barrancas, FL; Co A, Private
Military Charges: 26Mar1865; attempted desertion
Military Confinement: May - Sept1865; Ft. Pickens, FL
Union Discharge: 17Nov1865; Tallahassee, FL; bounty due $275
Pension: 29May1896 in GA; App#1178106, Cert#968041
Widow's Pension: 22Jun1906 in FL; App#851107, Cert#636269

LEE, George W.
Birth: circa 1836; Columbia Co, GA
Description: fair complexion, dark (blue) eyes, dark hair
Union Enlistment: 01Mar1864; Ft. Barrancas, FL; Co C, Private
Promotions: 07Jun1864; Corporal
Died: 11Dec1864; Ft. Barrancas, FL
Widow's Pension: 21Mar1866; App#121563, Cert#78661
Minor's Pension: 17Dec1892 in AL; Georgianna App#566561, Cert#973203

LEE, Johnson
Birth: circa 1819; Burke Co, GA
Description: dark complexion, dark eyes, dark hair
Union Enlistment: 26Jan1864; Ft. Barrancas, FL; Co B, Private
Died: 30Sep1864; Ft. Barrancas, FL, bounty due $275

LEVINS, Alexander C.
AKA: Alexander C. LEVIENS
Birth: circa 1844; Jackson Co, FL
Death: after 30Sept1864
1860 Location: Washington County, FL
Description: dark complexion, dark eyes, auburn hair
CSA:08Mar - 14Jun1862; 6th FL Infantry, Co K, Private, deserted.
Union Enlistment: 03Jan1864; Ft. Barrancas, FL; Co D, Private

Desertion: 30Sept1864 near Vernon, FL

LEVINS, John
AKA: John LEAVENS, John LEAVEANS, John LEAVINAS; John LEVANS
Birth: circa 1837; Baker Co, GA
1860 Location: Walton County, FL
Description: fair complexion, blue eyes, light hair
CSA: 25Mar1863-20Nov1863; 4th Battalion FL Infantry, Co C, Private, deserted, records transferred to 11th FL Infantry, Co K.
Union Enlistment: 28Jan1864; Ft. Barrancas, FL; Co B, Private
Died: 29Jul1864; Ft. Barrancas, FL; bounty due $275
Widow's Pension: 06Nov1877; App#136832, Cert#153209
Minor's Pension: App#230500, Cert#178615

LEVINS, Richard
AKA: Richard LARONS, Richards LEVANS, Richard LEVEN
Birth: circa 1829; Baker Co, GA
1860 Location: Euchee Anna, Walton County, FL
Description: light complexion, blue eyes, light hair
CSA: 02Apr1862 - 14Jun1862; 6th FL Infantry, Co H, Private, deserted
Union Enlistment: 03Jan1864; Ft. Barrancas, FL; Co A, Private
Died: 08Jul1864; Ft. Barrancas, FL
Widow's Pension: 22Apr1867; App#146060, Cert#119748

LEVINS, William Jackson
AKA: William J. LEVINS, William J. LEVANS, William J. LEVENS, William J. LEAVENS
Birth: circa 1842; Jackson Co, FL
Death: 27Apr1923; Bonifay, Holmes Co, FL
1860 Location: Washington County, FL
Description: dark complexion, dark eyes, auburn hair
CSA: 08Mar1862 - 14Jun1862; 6th FL Infantry, Co K, Private, deserted.
Union Enlistment: 03Jan1864; Ft. Barrancas, FL; Co C, Private
Union Discharge: 17Nov1865; Tallahassee, FL; bounty due $160
Pension: 26Jun1888 in FL; App#661825, Cert#1064123

Widow's Pension: 26May1923 in FL; App#1206103, Cert#937534

LEWIS, Alia
Birth: circa 1827; Telfair Co, GA
Death: 09Jun1880 - 06Feb1904; Georgia
Description: light complexion, hazel eyes, brown hair
Union Enlistment: 26Apr1864; East Pass, FL; Co F, Private
Desertion: 12Jan1865; East Pass, FL
Widow's Pension: 06Feb1904 in GA; App#799344

LEWIS, James M.
Birth: 13Nov1833; Telfair Co, GA
Death: 17Feb1919; Earnestville, Escambia Co, FL
Burial: Feb1919, Escambia Co, FL; Enon Baptist Church
1860 Location: Covington County, AL
Description: fair complexion, brown eyes, brown hair
CSA: 31Mar1862 - 31Oct1862; 42nd AL Infantry, Co E, Private, estimated desertion date
Union Enlistment: 03May1864; Ft. Barrancas, FL; Co F, Private
Union Discharge: 17Nov1865; Tallahassee, FL; bounty due $75
Pension: 02Dec1890 in AL; App#976273, Cert#1062466
Widow's Pension: 19Mar1919 in FL; App#1137976

LISENBY, William
AKA: William LESENBER, William LESEMBEE, William LISEMBER
Birth: circa 1828; Decatur Co, GA
Death: 17Jun1880 - 1900
1860 Location: Dale County, AL
Description: dark complexion, brown eyes, dark hair
CSA: 16Mar1863 - Dec1863; 57th AL Infantry, Co K, Private, estimated desertion date
Union Enlistment: 07Apr1864; East Pass, FL; Co E, Private
Desertion: 06Aug1864; on detached service

LITTLE, James P.
AKA: James P. SITTLES
Birth: circa 1820; Edgefield Co, SC

Death: after 17Nov1865
Description: light complexion, blue eyes, dark hair
Union Enlistment: 15Feb1864; Ft. Barrancas, FL; Co A, Private
Union Discharge: 17Nov1865; Tallahassee, FL; bounty due $275

LOCKLIN, Erastus Martin
Birth: 28Nov1836; Lyndon Co, VT
Death: 31Jul1909; Montpelier, Washington Co, VT
1860 Location: Washington County, VT
Description: light complexion, blue eyes, light hair
Union Appointment: 01Jul1864; Staff, Hospital Steward
Union Discharge: 17Nov1865; Tallahassee, FL
Pension: 15May1890 in VT; App#1023476, Cert#777131
Widow's Pension: 23Sep1909 in FL; App#927545

LOVE, James
Death: Jul1865; Ft. Barrancas, Escambia Co, FL
Union Enlistment: no info

LOVE, James Samuel
AKA: James LOVE
Birth: Jun1845; Lee Co, GA
Death: 12Jan1932; Point Washington, Walton Co, FL
Burial: Jan1932; Walton Co, FL; Community Cemetery
1860 Location: Santa Rosa County, FL
Description: fair complexion, blue eyes, brown hair
Union Enlistment: 24Feb1864; Ft. Barrancas, FL; Co C, Private
Union Discharge: 17Nov1865; Tallahassee, FL
Military Finding: 28Aug1884; certificate in lieu of lost discharge
Pension: 01Sept1890; App#905638, Cert#1163447

LOVE, William H.
Birth: circa 1846; Calhoun Co, GA
Description: light complexion, gray eyes, dark hair
Union Enlistment: 27Mar1865; East Pass, FL; Co A, Private
Died: 27Aug1865; Ft. Barrancas, FL

LOWERY, Joel H.
AKA: Joel LOWRIE

Birth: circa 1822; Darlington Co, SC
1860 Location: Geneva, Coffee County, AL
Description: fair complexion, gray eyes, dark hair
CSA: 20Mar1863 - 30Jun1863; Capt Curry's Independent Co, FL Infantry, Private, deserted, records transferred to 11th FL Infantry, Co C
Union Enlistment: 05Mar1864; Ft. Barrancas, FL; Co C, Private
Promotions: 05Mar1864; Blacksmith
Died: 01Aug1864; Ft. Barrancas, FL
Widow's Pension: 06Aug1866; App#131334, Cert#130370
Minor's Pension: 11Oct1890 in FL; Francis W; App#496494

LOWERY, William D.
AKA: William D. LOWREY, William D. LOWRY, William C. LOWERY, William LEARY
Birth: 15Aug1849; Coffee Co, AL
Death: 26Jan1926; Lowery, Geneva Co, AL
Burial: Jan1926, Lowery, Geneva Co, AL; Weeks Chapel Cemetery
1850 Location: Coffee County, AL
Description: dark complexion, black eyes, dark hair
Union Enlistment: 14Oct1864; East Pass, FL; Co F, Private
Union Discharge: 17Nov1865; Tallahassee, FL
Pension: 19Jul1923; App#1384758, Cert#1158373
Widow's Pension: 18Feb1926; App#1242294, Cert#971916

LUDLAM, Samuel P.
AKA: Samuel P. LUDMAN, S. P. LUDLMAN, Samuel P. LUDLUM, S. P. LUDLAM
Birth: circa 1837; Pike Co, AL
Death: Jun1880 - 02Jul1892; Alabama
Burial: before 02Jul1892; Georgiana, Butler Co, AL; Oakwood Cemetery
1850 Location: Pike County, AL
Description: light (fair) complexion, dark eyes, brown (gray) hair
CSA: 10Mar1862; 31st AL Infantry, Co I, Private, deserted
Union Enlistment: 28Jan1864, Ft. Barrancas, FL; Co A, Private
Engagements: Montgomery, AL

Promotions: 01Apr1864; Sergeant
Demotion: 01May1864; estimated date, to Private
Union Discharge: 17Nov1865; Tallahassee, FL; bounty due $120
Widow's Pension: 02Jul1892 in AL; App#554164, Cert#456457

LYONS, Francis
Birth: 22Jan1832; Philadelphia, PA
Death: after 13Aug1865
Additional Union Service: 18Aug1863 - 12Dec1863; 86th USCT Infantry, Co C
Union Appointment: 27Apr1864; Co E, Captain
Engagements: Gonzales, FL; Marianna, FL; Big Escambia River, FL; Mitchell's Creek, FL; Pine Barren Creek, FL
Union Discharge: 13Aug1865

M

MAIN, Travis
Birth: circa 1814; North Carolina
1850 Location: Covington County, Alabama
Description: light complexion, blue eyes, light hair
Union Enlistment: 11Mar1864; Ft. Barrancas, FL; Co D, Private
Died: 14Jul1864; Ft. Barrancas, FL

MALLOY, James E.
AKA: James E. MALOY, James E. MELOY
Birth: circa 1845; Baker Co, GA
Death: after 20Aug1917; Florida
Description: fair complexion, gray eyes, red hair
CSA: 10Mar1862 - 29Jun1862; Capt Dunham's Company (A), Milton Light Artillery, Private, discharge due to age & size.
7Nov1863 – 10Dec1863; 4th Battalion FL Infantry, Co C, Private, deserted, records transferred to 11th FL Infantry, Co K
Union Enlistment: 17Dec1863; Ft. Barrancas, FL; Co C, Private
Desertion: 12Oct1865; Monticello, FL
Military Finding: 31Jul1917; desertion charges dropped
Pension: 20Aug1917 in FL; App#1428659

MALOY, John E.
AKA: John E. MELOY, John E. MILLOY
Birth: 05Dec1843; Gadsden Co, FL
Death: 06Sept1922; Haskell, Polk Co, FL
Burial: Sept1922; Malloy Cemetery, Lakeland, Polk Co, FL
Description: dark complexion, gray eyes, black hair
CSA: 13May1862 - 16July1862; 8th FL Infantry, Co E, Private, deserted. 25Mar1863 - 10Dec1863; 4th Battalion FL Infantry, Co C, Private, deserted, records transferred to 11th FL Infantry, Co K
Union Enlistment: 17Dec1863; Ft. Barrancas, FL; Co C, Private
Union Discharge: 17Nov1865; Tallahassee, FL; bounty due $75
Pension: 18Dec1890 in FL; App#969584, Cert#698208
Widow's Pension: 27Sept1922 in FL; App#1194392, Cert#932653

MALOY, William H.
AKA: William H. MELOY, William MALLOY, William P. MALLOY
Birth: circa 1841; Washington Co, FL
Death: 17Nov1865 - 27Jul1891; Florida
Description: dark complexion, dark eyes, dark hair
CSA: 08Mar1862 - 10Dec1863; 6th FL Infantry, Co K, Private
Military Enlistment: 17Dec1863; Ft. Barrancas, FL; Co C, Private
Union Discharge: 17Nov1865; Tallahassee, FL; bounty due $75
Widow's Pension: 27Jul1891 in FL; App#518292

MANN, John T.
Birth: circa 1844; Henry Co, AL
Description: gray eyes, dark hair, fair complexion
Union Enlistment: 15Feb1864; Ft. Barrancas, FL; Private
Union Transfer: 01Mar1864 to 7th VT Infantry, Co B

MANNING, William Thomas
AKA: William T. MANNING
Birth: 10Feb1844; Andalusia, Covington Co, AL
Death: 27Oct1911; Fairhope, Baldwin Co, AL
Burial: Oct1911; Foley, Baldwin Co, AL; Foley Cemetery
1860 Location: Santa Rosa County, FL
Description: fair complexion, gray eyes, light hair

Union Enlistment: 06Apr1864; Ft. Barrancas, FL; Co B, Private
Engagements: Montgomery, AL
Union Discharge: 17Nov1865; Tallahassee, FL; bounty due $75
Pension: 14Mar1906; App#1346592, Cert#1120708
Widow's Pension: 04Dec1911; App#976066, Cert#736709

MARSHALL, John Thomas
Birth: Aug1834; Decatur Co, GA
Death: 12Jun1900 - 22Mar1906; Washington Co, FL
Burial: Jun1900 - Mar1906, Bay Co, FL; West Bay Cemetery
1850 Location: Decatur County, GA
Description: light complexion, gray eyes, dark hair
Union Enlistment: 13Dec1863; Ft. Barrancas, FL; Co A, Private
Disability Discharge: 13Jul1865
Pension: 05Jul1877; App#238723, Cert#153586
Widow's Pension: 22Mar1906 in FL; App#845598, Cert#621646

MARTIN, Burrell
Birth: circa 1845; Pike Co, AL
Death: 19Apr1909; Santa Rosa Co, FL
1860 Location: Walton County, FL
Description: fair complexion, hazel eyes, dark hair
Union Enlistment: 20Apr1864; Ft. Barrancas, FL; Co E, Private
Union Discharge: 17Nov1865; Tallahassee, FL; bounty due $75
Military Finding: 01Oct1885; removal of desertion charge denied
Pension: 04Nov1882; App#464146, Cert#1122616
Widow's Pension: 06May1909; App#919338, Cert#686825

MARTIN, John Thomas
AKA: John T. MARTEN, John T. MORTIN
Birth: Nov1845; Heard Co, GA
Death: 14Apr1930; Milligan, Okaloosa Co, FL
Burial: Apr1930, Crestview, Okaloosa Co, FL; Old Bethel Cemetery
1860 Location: Coffee County, AL
Description: dark complexion, black eyes, dark hair
CSA: 01Oct1863 - 30May1864; 57th AL Infantry, Co G, Private
Union Enlistment: 18Aug1864; East Pass, Florida; Co F, Private

Engagements: Montgomery, AL
Desertion: 24May1865; Camp Montgomery, AL
Military Finding: 31Oct1890; desertion charge dropped
Pension: 30Oct1900 in FL; App#1256762, Cert#1124523
Widow's Pension: 14May1930 in FL; App#1667575, Cert#A72630

MARTIN, Jonathan F.
Birth: Nov 1833; Georgia
Death: 07Jun1900 - 01 Nov 1906; Choctaw County, MS
Description: light complexion, gray eyes, dark hair
Union Enlistment: 01Mar1864; Ft. Barrancas, FL; Co A, Private
Engagements: Montgomery, AL
Promotions: between Mar - Apr 1865; Wagoner
Union Discharge: 17Nov1865; Tallahassee, FL; bounty due $120
Pension: 06Dec1893 in MS; App#1154671
Widow's Pension: 01Nov1906 in MS; App#857790

MATHEWS, Benjamin C.
Birth: circa 1835; Crawford Co, GA
1860 Location: Coffee County, AL
Union Enlistment: 29Apr1864; East Pass, FL; Co F, Private
Died: 01Aug1864; Ft. Barrancas, Escambia, FL
Military Finding: 20Feb1868; died in hospital
Widow's Pension: 17Dec1879; App#256256, Cert#194271
Minor's Pension: 13Mar1878; Grandson James H. Bunsvant; App#202321, Cert#166442

MATHEWS, James H.
Birth: circa 1823; Twiggs Co, GA
Death: after 01Sept1870
1860 Location: Henry County, AL
Description: fair complexion, grey eyes, light hair
Union Enlistment: 26Feb1864; Ft. Barrancas, FL; Co C, Private
Union Appointment: 23Mar1864; Bugler
Union Discharge: 17Nov1865; Tallahassee, FL; bounty due $160

MATHEWS, James Madison
AKA: James Madison MATTHEWS

Birth: circa 1834; Crawford Co, GA
Death: 17Nov1865 - 13Sept1890
1850 Location: Coffee County, AL
Description: light complexion, gray eyes, sandy hair
Union Enlistment: 16Jan1864; Ft. Barrancas, FL; Co C, Private
Promotions: 23Mar1864; 1st Sergeant
Union Discharge: 17Nov1865; Tallahassee, FL; bounty due $120
Widow's Pension: 13Sep1890; App#443837, Cert#363951

MATHIS, Samuel Wesley
AKA: Wesley MATHEWS, Wesley, MATHAS, Wesley MATTHEWS
Birth: Feb1844; Macon Co, AL
Death: after 12Oct1914; Florida
1860 Location: Covington County, AL
Description: fair complexion, gray eyes, dark hair
Union Enlistment: 18Aug1864; East Pass, FL; Co F, Private
Desertion: 20May1865; East Bay, FL
Pension: 12Oct1914 in FL; App#1416601

MAUND, Joseph P.
Birth: circa 1827; Georgia
Death: after Jun1864
1860 Location: Dale County, AL
Union Enlistment: 29Jun1864; East Pass, FL
Union Discharge: not recorded

MAUND, Samuel J.
Birth: 19Dec1828; Barbour Co, AL
Death: 02Jun1915; Dale Co, AL
Burial: Jun1915, Dale Co, AL; Chalkhead Baptist Church Cemetery
1850 Location: Dale County, AL
Description: dark complexion, blue eyes, black hair
CSA: 06May1862 - 30Jun1862; 39th AL Infantry, Co G, Private, estimated end date
Union Enlistment: 22Dec1863; Ft. Barrancas, FL; Co A, Private
Military Confinement: 16Apr1865 - 30Jul1865; Ft. Pickens, FL

Desertion: 30Jul1865
Military Finding: 13Mar1901; dishonorable discharge voided, listed as deserter
Pension: 24Feb1898 in AL; App#1204894

McARTHUR, Charles Columbus
AKA: Charles M. McARTHUR
Birth: circa 1824; Walton Co, FL
Death: before 23Jun1887
1860 Location: Santa Rosa County, FL
Description: sandy complexion, gray eyes, sandy hair
Union Enlistment: 27Apr1864; Ft. Barrancas, FL; Co B, Private
Military Charges: approximately Sept1864; mutinous conduct (refused to be mustered in due to ill health), conduct prejudicial to good order & military discipline
Military Court Martial: Sept - Oct1864; sentenced to 6 months of hard labor without forfeiture of pay
Military Confinement: Oct1864 - Apr1865; Ft. Pickens
Desertion: 16Aug1865; Ft. Barrancas, FL
Military Finding: 10Aug1891; charge of desertion dropped
Widow's Pension: 23Jun1887 in FL; App#356389, Cert#342589

McCULLER, David
AKA: David McCULLAR, David McCULER
Birth: Jan1828; Wilkinson Co, GA
Death: 28Feb1911; Houston, Harris Co, TX
1850 Location: Wilkinson County, GA
Description: dark complexion, blue eyes, dark hair
CSA: 05May1863 - 26Jun1863; 12th GA Battalion Light Artillery, Co A, Private, deserted from hospital. He was a substitute for Montgomery L. Thomas.
Union Enlistment: 25Jan1864; Ft. Barrancas, FL; Co B, Private
Engagements: Montgomery, AL
Promotions: 18Jul1864; Corporal, replaced Sam Jones, deceased
Union Discharge: 17Nov1865; Tallahassee, FL; bounty due $120
Pension: 27Aug1890 in TX; App#909064, Cert#710287
Widow's Pension: 31May1911 in TX; App#965818, Cert#914121

McCURLEY, Joseph
AKA: Joseph E. McCARTHY, Joseph McCURLY, Joseph McCARTHY
Birth: circa 1845; Georgia
Death: after 27May1865
Description: fair complexion, grey eyes, light hair
Union Enlistment: 20Jan1865; East Pass, FL; Co C, Private
Engagements: Montgomery, AL
Desertion: 27May1865; Alabama

McDANIEL, Randal K.
AKA: Randolph McDANIEL, Randolph McDONALD, Randal McDONALD
Birth: circa 1834; Franklin, GA
Death: 22Jun1908; Darlington, Walton Co, FL
Burial: Jun1908; Darlington, Walton, FL; Limestone Community Cemetery
1860 Location: Dale County, AL
Description: dark complexion, brown eyes, brown hair
Union Enlistment: 20May1864; East Pass, FL; Co F, Private
Union Discharge: 17Nov1865; Tallahassee, FL; bounty due $75
Military Finding: 05Jul1884; desertion charges dropped
Pension: 10Aug1881 in AL; App#427115, Cert#398308
Widow's Pension: 24Sept1908 in FL; App#904896

McGEE, Alexander C.
AKA: Alexander MAGEE, Alexander McGHEE
Birth: circa 1842; Baldwin Co, AL
Death: 22Jun1900 - 1910 in Escambia Co, AL
1860 Location: Baldwin County, AL
Description: dark complexion, black eyes, dark hair
Union Enlistment: 03Jun1864; Ft. Barrancas, FL; Co F/E, Private
Engagements: Montgomery, AL
Union Discharge: 17Nov1865; Tallahassee, FL; bounty due $100

McGEE, Richard
AKA: Richard MAGEE, Richard McGHEE
Birth: Jan1845; Baldwin Co, AL

Death: 30Apr1910 - 1920 in Escambia Co, AL
Description: dark complexion, gray eyes, black hair
1860 Location: Baldwin County, AL
Union Enlistment: 01Apr1865; Blakeley, Baldwin Co, AL; Co E, Private
Union Discharge: 01Apr1865 in Blakeley, Baldwin Co, AL

McKINEY, John R.
AKA: John R. McKENEY, John R. KINNEY
Birth: circa 1843; DeKalb Co, AL
Death: after 15Jun1864
Description: light complexion, blue eyes, light hair
Union Enlistment: 23Mar1864; East Pass, FL; Co D, Private
Desertion: 15Jun1864

McLEAN, William F.
AKA: William F. McCLEAN
Birth: circa 1846; Covington Co, AL
Death: after 20Dec1864
Description: fair complexion, blue eyes, dark hair
CSA: 02Apr - 25Jun1862; 4th AL Volunteer Militia, Gantt's Co, Private, 90 days
Union Enlistment: 05Sept1864; Ft. Barrancas, FL; Co E, Private
Desertion: 20Dec1864; Ft. Barrancas, FL

McLELLAN, Alexander
AKA: Alexander McCLELLAN
Birth: circa 1819; Cumberland Co, NC
Death: after 25Sept1890
1860 Location: Santa Rosa County, FL
Description: light complexion, blue eyes, dark hair
Union Enlistment: 25Jan1864; Ft. Barrancas, FL; Co B, Private
Promotions: 01Apr1864; Sergeant
Union Discharge: 17Nov1865; bounty due $120
Pension: 25Sept1890 in AL; App#919949

McLELLAN, Angus
AKA: August McLELLAN; Angers McLELLAN
Birth: 01Jan1838; Cumberland Co, NC

Death: 26Mar1920; Heidelberg, Jasper Co, MS
Burial: Mar1920; Jasper, MS; Philadelphia Cemetery
1860 Location: Santa Rosa County, FL
Description: light complexion, blue eyes, dark hair
Union Enlistment: 25Jan1864; Ft. Barrancas, FL; Co B, Private
Union Discharge: 17Nov1865; Tallahassee, FL; bounty due $160
Pension: 09Jul1892 in MS; App#1121394, Cert#1051361

McLELLAN, Duncan
AKA: Duncan McLELLAND
Birth: circa 1842; Cumberland Co, NC
Death: after 25Sept1890
Burial: Santa Rosa, FL; Butler Cemetery
1860 Location: Santa Rosa County, FL
Description: light complexion, gray eyes, black hair
CSA: 21Mar1862 - 01Sept1863; 1st FL Infantry, Co F, Private, deserted
Union Enlistment: 25Jan1864; Ft. Barrancas, FL; Co B, Private
Union Discharge: 17Nov1865; Tallahassee, FL; bounty due $160
Pension: 25Sept1890 in AL; App#919948

McLELLAN, William M.
AKA: William McLELLAN
Birth: circa 1829; Cumberland Co, NC
Death: 17Nov1865 - 07Jul1880
1860 Location: Covington County, AL
Description: light complexion, blue eyes, dark hair
CSA: 01Jun1863 - 11Aug1863; 3rd FL Battalion Cavalry, Co D, Private, deserted, records transferred to 15th Confederate Cavalry, Co I.
Union Enlistment: 25Jan1864; Ft. Barrancas, FL; Co B, Private
Union Discharge: 17Nov1865; Tallahassee, FL; bounty due $160
Widow's Pension: 07Jul1880; App#276347, Cert#331655
Minor's Pension: 07Jul1880; Amanda Livingston App#276348

McLENDON, John A.
AKA: John A. McLENDAN
Birth: circa 1825; Wilkinson, GA

1860 Location: Holmes County, FL
Description: fair complexion, brown eyes, light hair
CSA: 10Mar1862 - 01Mar1864; 2nd FL Cavalry, Co A,
Private/Corporal, deserted
Union Enlistment: 14Mar1864; Ft. Barrancas, FL; Co C, Private
Died: 21Aug1864; Ft. Barrancas, FL

McMILLAN, Jackson
AKA: Jackson McMILLEN
Birth: circa 1828; Twiggs Co, GA
Death: after 2Sept1882
Description: light complexion, gray eyes, dark hair
Union Enlistment: 19Jan1864; Ft. Barrancas, FL; Co B, Private
Promotions: 1Apr1864; Wagoner
Disability Discharge: 16Apr1865; Ft. Barrancas, FL
Pension: 2Sept1882; App#458889

McMILLAN, Thomas B.
AKA: Thomas B. McMILLEN
Birth: circa 1832; Conecuh Co, AL
Death: 13Mar1920; Toro, Sabine Co, LA
1860 Location: Monroe County, AL
Description: fair complexion, blue eyes, light hair
Union Enlistment: 19May1864; Ft. Barrancas, FL; Co F, Private
Promotions: 06Aug1865; Sergeant
Union Discharge: 17Nov1865; Tallahassee, FL; bounty due $75
Pension: 24Aug1889 in AL; App#724093, Cert#382115
Widow's Pension: 09Jun1920 in LA; App#1158826, Cert#901376

McMILLION, Alfred C.
AKA: Alfred C. McMILLIEN; A. McMILLAN; Alfred C. McMILLEN;
Alfred C. McMELLEN
Birth: circa 1823; Spartanburg Co, SC
Death: after 17Nov1865
1860 Location: Dale County, AL
Description: light complexion, gray eyes, dark hair
Union Enlistment: 19Dec1863; Ft. Barrancas, FL; Co A, Private
Promotions: 01Apr1864; Sergeant (3rd)

Reduction in Rank: Jun1865; demoted to Private
Union Discharge: 17Nov1865; Tallahassee, FL; bounty due $75

MEADOWS, William H.
AKA: William J. MEADOWS
Birth: circa 1844; Henry Co, AL
Death: after 26Jan1891
Description: light complexion, gray eyes, dark hair
Union Enlistment: 27Mar1865; East Pass, FL; Co A, Private
Union Discharge: 17Nov1865; Tallahassee, FL; bounty due $100
Pension: 26Jan1891; App#999266

MEDLOCK, Robert Lewis
AKA: Robert L. MADLOCK, Robert L. MEDDOCK
Birth: Mar1840; Talladega Co, AL
Death: 29Jun1900 - 11Jun1902; Jackson Co, FL
Description: fair complexion, blue eyes, brown hair
CSA: 15Aug1862 - 31Dec1863; 15th AL Infantry, Co G, Private
Union Enlistment: 20May1864; East Pass, FL; Co F, Private
Engagements: Montgomery, AL
Promotions: 22Aug1864; Teamster
Union Discharge: 17Nov1865; Tallahassee, FL; bounty due $75
Pension: 17Jun1892 in FL; App#1117668, Cert#834507
Widow's Pension: 11Jun1902 in FL; App#764834, Cert#554767

MELVIN, Daniel V.
AKA: Daniel D. MELVIN
Birth: 11Apr1838; Pike Co, AL
Death: 10Jul1911; Kynesville, Jackson Co, FL
Burial: Jul1911; Kynesville, Jackson Co, FL; Salem Freewill Baptist Church
1860 Location: Washington County, FL
Description: dark complexion, blue eyes, light hair
CSA: 07Sep1861 - 03Sept1863; 4th FL Infantry, Co H, Private, deserted
Union Enlistment: 02Feb1864; Ft. Barrancas, FL; Co C, Private
Engagements: Montgomery, AL
Union Discharge: 17Nov1865; Tallahassee, FL; bounty due $275

Military Finding: 26Jul1886; charge of desertion dropped
Pension: 29Jan1879; App#265826, Cert#601167
Widow's Pension: 20Jul1911 in FL; App#968905, Cert#918364
Minor's Pension: 12Feb1912 in FL; Granddaughter, Addie;
App#982365, Cert#738157

MELVIN, Griffin
Birth: circa 1832; Houston Co, GA
Death: 07Jun1880 – 1900; Washington Co, FL
1860 Location: Washington County, FL
Description: fair complexion, blue eyes, brown hair
CSA: 07Sept1861 - 05Oct1863; 4th FL Infantry, Co H, Private, deserted
Union Enlistment: 20Apr1864; East Pass, FL; Co E, Private
Engagements: Marianna, FL; Pollard, AL; Blakeley, AL; Greenville, AL; Montgomery, AL
Promotions: 01May1864; Corporal
Union Discharge: 17Nov1865; Tallahassee, FL

MERRITT, Henry
Birth: circa 1830; Sampson Co, NC
1860 Location: Calhoun County, GA
Description: dark complexion, gray eyes, black hair
CSA: 05Oct1863 - 09Dec1863; 4th Battalion FL Infantry, Co A, Private, deserted, records transferred to 11th FL Infantry, Co C
Union Enlistment: 30Dec1863; Ft. Barrancas, FL; Co D, Private
Died: 16Aug1864; Ft. Barrancas, FL
Widow's Pension: 24Jun1874; App#216151

MERRITT, Leroy R.
Birth: Jun 1837; Houston Co, GA
Death: 19Aug1914; Cottonwood, Houston Co, AL
Description: dark complexion, brown eyes, dark hair
Union Enlistment: 06Jul1864; East Pass, FL; Co F, Private
Desertion: 04Aug1865
Military Finding: 03Apr1886; desertion charge removed
Pension: 18Mar1889 in AL; App#694640, Cert#893262

Widow's Pension: 25Sept1914 in AL; App#1034543, Cert#880089

MERRITT, William
AKA: William MERRIT
Birth: circa 1840; Georgia
Death: after 14May1892; Florida
1860 Location: Gadsden County, FL
Description: dark complexion, dark eyes, dark hair
Union Enlistment: 26May1864; Ft. Barrancas, FL; Co F/C, Private
Promotion: 03Aug1864; Corporal
Promotion: 18July1865; Sergeant
Desertion: 04Aug1865; Ft. Barrancas, FL
Pension: 14May1892 in FL; App#1111266

MESZAROS, Emeric
Birth: circa 1830; Poland
Death: after 09Oct1890; Florida
Union Appointment: 27Jun1864 - 17Nov1865; Ft. Barrancas, FL; Co C, Captain
Union Discharge: 17Nov1865; Tallahassee, FL
Pension: 09Oct1890 in FL; App#978507

MILLER, Abraham L.
AKA: Abraham MILLER
Birth: circa 1841; Dale Co, AL
Death: 1917; Hickory Hill, Holmes Co, FL
Burial: 1917; Ponce de Leon, Holmes Co, FL; Sandy Creek Baptist Church
1850 Location: Barbour County, AL
Description: fair complexion, gray eyes, light hair
Union Enlistment: 12Sept1864; East Pass, FL; Co D, Private
Desertion: 02Aug1865; Ft. Pickens, FL
Military Finding: 27Nov1883; removal of charge of desertion and request for an honorable discharge was denied
Pension: 28Nov1912 in AL; App#1402372

MILLER, Elias B.
Birth: circa 1827; Washington Co, FL
Death: after 12Jan1865
1860 Location: Washington County, FL
Description: light complexion blue eyes, light hair
CSA: 28Feb1862 - 28Feb1864; 1st FL Reorganized Infantry, Co D, Private, estimated desertion date
Union Enlistment: 15Mar1864; Ft. Barrancas, FL; Co A, Private
Desertion: 12Jan1865; Live Oak Point

MILLER, Henry J.
Birth: May1846; Jackson Co, FL
Death: after 06May1910; Jackson Co, FL
1860 Location: Santa Rosa County, FL
Description: dark complexion, black eyes, dark hair
Union Enlistment: 06Oct1864; Ft. Barrancas, FL; Co F, Private
Desertion: 15Dec1864; Holmes Valley, FL; scouting duty

MILLER, James L.
AKA: James MILLER
Birth: circa 1845; Barbour Co, AL
Death: after 21Oct1901
1860 Location: Dale County, AL
Description: dark complexion, black eyes, dark hair
Union Enlistment: 05Aug1864; East Pass, FL; Co F, Private
Engagements: Montgomery, AL
Desertion: 20May1865; Montgomery, AL
Military Finding: 21Oct1901; dishonorable discharge canceled, final record officially recorded as a deserter

MILLER, James W.
Birth: circa 1826; Coffee Co, AL
Death: 07Jan1886; Escambia Co, FL
1860 Location: Santa Rosa County, FL
Description: fair complexion, blue eyes, light hair
Union Enlistment: 24Feb1864; Ft. Barrancas, FL; Co C, Private
Promotions: 04Oct1864; Sergeant
Union Discharge: 17Nov1865; Tallahassee, FL; bounty due $160

Widow's Pension: 31Jul1909 in FL; App#924772

MILLER, John
Birth: 17Oct1830; Dale Co, AL
Death: after 05Sept1864
Description: fair complexion, gray eyes, brown hair
CSA: 13May1862-30Apr1863; 1st FL Reorganized Infantry, Co H, Private
Union Enlistment: 04May1864; Ft. Barrancas, FL; Co F, Private
Desertion: 05Sept1864 near Pensacola, Florida; picket duty
Military Finding: 27Jan1887; removal of desertion charge denied

MILLER, John B.
AKA: John MILLER
Birth: Aug1833; Washington Co, FL
Death: 06Jun1900-1910; Washington Co, FL
1860 Location: Washington County, FL
Description: light complexion, blue eyes, light hair
CSA: 04Oct1862 - 25Dec1862; 3rd Battalion FL Cavalry, Co D, Private, deserted while POW, records transferred to 15th Confederate Cavalry, Co D
Union Enlistment: 15Mar1864; Ft. Barrancas, FL; Co A, Private
Desertion: 26Jul1864; East Pass, FL
Military Finding: 21May1889; removal of desertion charge denied
Pension: 16Oct1895 in FL; App#1171098

MILLER, John M.
Birth: circa 1839; Washington Co, FL
Death: after 25Jul1870; Washington Co, FL
1860 Location: Washington County, FL
Description: light complexion, blue eyes, sandy hair
CSA: 07Sept1861 - 29Feb1864; 4th FL Infantry, Co H, Sergeant, deserted
Union Enlistment: 06Oct1864; Ft. Barrancas, FL; Co A, Private
Promotions: 06Oct1864; Sergeant
Union Discharge: 17Nov1865; Tallahassee, FL

MILLER, William
Birth: Mar1843 in Henry Co, AL

Death: 01Jun1900 - 27Feb1907
Description: dark complexion, dark eyes, brown hair
Union Enlistment: 28Feb1864; Ft. Barrancas, FL; Co D, Private
Union Discharge: 17Nov1865; Tallahassee, FL; bounty due $120
Pension: 07Oct1889 in FL; App#734000, Cert#674328
Widow's Pension: 27Feb1907 in AL; App#877073, Cert#670486

MILLS, Warren
Birth: circa 1846; Pike Co, AL
Death: after 22Nov1880
Description: light complexion, blue eyes, light hair
Union Enlistment: 01Apr1864; East Pass, FL; Co E, Private
Engagements: Marianna, FL; Pollard, AL; Blakeley, AL; Greenville, AL; Montgomery, AL
Union Discharge: 17Nov1865; Tallahassee, FL; bounty due $75
Pension: 22Nov1880; App#412591
Widow's Pension: after 22Nov1880; App#411715, Cert#395569
Minor's Pension: after 22Nov1880; App#625670

MILLS, William
Birth: circa 1826; Early Co, GA
Death: 17Nov1865 - 27May1882
Description: fair complexion, blue eyes, light hair
Union Enlistment: 09Jan1865; Ft. Barrancas, FL; Co F, Private
Union Discharge: 17Nov1865; Tallahassee, FL
Minor's Pension: 27May1882; App#297490

MILTON, Andrew H.
Birth: circa 1840; Lawrence, AL
Death: after 31May1865
Description: sandy complexion, blue eyes, sandy hair
CSA: 21Jul1861 - 28Aug1863; 1st FL Infantry, Co E (New D), Private, deserted
Union Enlistment: 19Apr1864; Ft. Barrancas, FL; Co B, Private
Disability Discharge: 31May1865

MIMS, Columbus C.
AKA: Cader C. MIMS; Cato C. MIMS
Birth: circa 1835; Dale Co, AL

Death: 23Oct1881; Cypress, Jackson Co, FL
1860 Location: Dale County, AL
Description: dark complexion, dark eyes, dark hair
Union Enlistment: 22Dec1863; Ft. Barrancas, FL; Co D, Private
Desertion: 26Jul1865; Ft. Barrancas, FL
Military Finding: 21Dec1911; desertion charges dropped
Widow's Pension: 12Jul1911; App#968600

MIMS, Nathan K.
AKA: Nathan K. MINNS
Birth: Nov1846; Dale Co, AL
Death: 11May1923; Skipperville, Dale Co, AL
1850 Location: Dale County, AL
Description: dark complexion, brown eyes, dark hair
CSA: 13May1862 - 14Apr1864; 37th AL Infantry, Co A, Private, estimated desertion date
Union Enlistment: 29Jun1864; East Pass, FL; Co F, Private
Engagements: Montgomery, AL
Desertion: 24May1865; Montgomery, AL
Military Finding: 19Dec1889; desertion charges dropped
Pension: 16Jul1890 in AL; App#819661, Cert#584051

MITCHEM, Joseph
AKA: Joseph MITCHEAN; Joseph MITCHUM; Joseph MITCHEN
Birth: circa 1826; South Carolina
Death: before 25Mar1891; Florida
1860 Location: Walton County, FL
Description: dark complexion, brown eyes, dark hair
CSA: 02May1863 - 01Aug1863; 6th AL Cavalry, Co K, Private, deserted
Union Enlistment: 03Apr1864; East Pass, FL; Co E, Private
Desertion: 22Mar1865; Ft. Barrancas, FL
Military Finding: 26Mar1891; desertion charges dropped
Widow's Pension: 25Mar1891 in FL; App#519442, Cert#331567

MONIAC, James R.
AKA: James P. MONIAC
Birth: circa 1842; Baldwin Co, AL

Death: 09Jun1880 - 1900; Alabama
1860 Location: Baldwin County, AL
Description: dark complexion, yellow eyes, black hair
CSA: 24Sept1863 - 30Jun1864; 15th Confederate Cavalry, Co C, Private, estimated desertion date. 9Apr1862 – 24Sept1863; Capt Barlow's Co, AL Cavalry, Private, transferred.
Union Enlistment: 01Apr1865; Blakeley, Baldwin Co, AL; rejected
Union Discharge: 01Apr1865; Blakeley, Baldwin Co, AL

MONIAC, Michael M.
AKA: Michael MONICK
Birth: circa 1840; Baldwin Co, AL
Death: after 20Aug1865
1860 Location: Baldwin County, AL
Description: dark complexion, dark eyes, dark hair
CSA: 24Sept1863 - 01Mar1864; 15th Confederate Cavalry, Co C, Private, estimated desertion date. 9Apr1862 – 24Sep1863; Capt Barlow's Co, AL Cavalry, transferred
Union Enlistment: 27Mar1864; Ft. Barrancas, FL; Co E, Private
Engagements: Marianna, FL; Pollard, AL; Blakely, AL; Greenville, AL; Montgomery, AL
Promotions: 01May1864; Corporal
Desertion: 20Aug1865; Ft. Barrancas, FL

MONIAC, Richard L.
AKA: Richard L. MONIACK; Richard L. MONIAK; Richard L. MORIAC
Birth: circa 1844; Baldwin Co, AL
Death: before 24Feb1892; Alabama
1860 Location: Baldwin County, AL
Description: dark complexion, dark eyes, dark hair
CSA: 17Oct1861 - 06Jul1863; 23rd AL Infantry, Co I, Private
Union Enlistment: 12May1864; Ft. Barrancas, FL; Co F/E, Private
Engagements: Montgomery, AL
Union Discharge: 17Nov1865; Tallahassee, FL; bounty due $100

MONTEN, Christian
Birth: circa 1828
Death: after 15 May 1865
Additional Union Service: 29 Oct 1861 - 03 Oct 1862; 52 NY Infantry, Co K transferred to Co B, enlisted as a Private
Union Appointment: 29 Mar 1864, Ft. Barrancas, FL; 1st Lt
Union Discharge: 15 May 1865; honorably discharged

MOONEY, Isaac P.
Birth: circa 1822; North Carolina
Death: 03Dec1892 - 1900 in Wood Co, TX
1860 Location: Coffee County, AL
Description: light complexion, gray eyes, dark hair
Union Enlistment: 24Mar1864, Walton Co, FL; Co E, Private
Engagements: Pollard, AL; Escambia Bridge, FL
Union Discharge: 17Nov1865; Tallahassee, FL; bounty due $275
Pension: 03Dec1892 in TX; App#1140169, Cert#1050904
Widow's Pension: 18Dec1905 in TX; App#839814, Cert#634447

MORGAN, Isaiah M.
AKA: Isiah MORGAN
Birth: circa 1837; Henry Co, GA
Death: before 13May1897; Alabama
Description: fair complexion, dark eyes, brown hair
1850 Location: Randolph County, GA
CSA: 05May1862 - 25Jul1862; 2nd GA Cavalry, Co A, Private, deserted
Union Enlistment: 21Feb1864; Ft. Barrancas, FL; Co C/F, Private
Engagements: Pine Barren Creek, FL
Promotions: Apr1864; Sergeant
Desertion: 12Oct1865; Monticello, FL
Minor's Pension: 13May1897 in AL; John R; App#654090

MORRIS, Eli
Birth: Sept1827; Coffee Co, AL
Death: Jun1900 - 1910 in Calhoun Co, FL
Burial: Jun1900 - 1910 in Jackson Co, FL; Grant Cemetery

1860 Location: Coffee County, AL
Description: fair complexion, blue eyes, dark hair
CSA: 16Mar1863 - 29Aug1863; 57th AL Infantry, Co K, Private, deserted
Union Enlistment: 11Feb1864; Ft. Barrancas, FL; Co B, Private
Union Discharge: 17Nov1865; Tallahassee, FL; bounty due $160
Pension: 09Apr1889; App#698340, Cert#821215

MORRISON, Alexander
AKA: Alex MORRISON
Birth: circa 1847; Walton Co, FL
Death: 12Dec1897 - 30Jan1907; Florida
1860 Location: Walton County, FL
Description: light complexion, dark eyes, brown hair
Union Enlistment: 01Oct1864; Ft. Barrancas, FL; Co B, Private
Desertion: 18Aug1865; Ft. Barrancas, FL
Military Finding: 30Nov1897; desertion charge dropped
Pension: 12Dec1897 in FL; App#1202685, Cert#1006163
Minor's Pension: 30Jan1907 in FL; Pinkney; App#862593, Cert#733860

MORRISON, Henry
Birth: circa 1845; Walton Co, FL
Death: 16Nov1899; Holmes Co, FL
Burial: Nov1899 in Holmes Co, FL; Westville Cemetery
1860 Location: Walton County, FL
Description: fair complexion, blue eyes, light hair
Union Enlistment: 16Feb1864; Ft. Barrancas, FL; Co B, Private
Union Discharge: 17Nov1865; Tallahassee, FL; bounty due $120
Pension: 29Jan1879; App#965886, Cert#1026990
Widow's Pension: 12Dec1899 in FL; App#709973, Cert#515392

MORRISON, John
Birth: circa 1827; Walton Co, FL
1860 Location: Bibb County, AL
Description: fair complexion, blue eyes, light hair
Union Enlistment: 28Jan1864; Ft. Barrancas, FL; Co B, Private
Died: 17Jun1864; Ft. Barrancas, FL; bounty due $275

Minor's Pension: 27Feb1897 in AL; App#692640

MORRISON, Robert
Birth: circa 1826; Walton Co, FL
Death: after 1870
1860 Location: Santa Rosa County, FL
Description: dark complexion, blue eyes, dark hair
CSA: 21Mar1862 - 30Apr1863; 1st FL Reorganized Infantry, Co F, Private, deserted
Union Enlistment: 25Jan1864; Ft. Barrancas, FL; Co B, Private
Desertion: 22Mar1865; Ft. Barrancas, FL

MOSES, Dennis F.
Birth: circa 1842; Mobile Co, AL
Death: after 21Jun1870
Description: dark eyes, dark hair, dark complexion
CSA: 19Feb1861 - 15Aug1864; 1st Battalion AL Artillery, Private, deserted
Union Enlistment: 12Nov1864; Ft. Barrancas, FL; Private
Union Discharge: no details in record

MURPHY, Hansel M.
AKA: Hondrel MURPHY; Handsel M. MURPHY; Handrel MURPHY
Birth: circa 1842; Georgia
Death: 1870 - 04Apr1883
1860 Location: Walton County, FL
Description: fair complexion, gray eyes, dark hair
CSA: 16Mar1863 - 31Dec1863; 57th AL Infantry, Co K, Private, deserted
Union Enlistment: 16Aug1864; East Pass, FL; Co F, Private
Engagements: Montgomery, AL
Union Discharge: 17Nov1865; Tallahassee, FL; bounty due $75
Military Finding: 01Oct1883; mustered out with the company
Widow's Pension: 04Apr1883; App#302869, Cert#349780

MURPHY, Silas D.
AKA: Silas MURPHY
Birth: 1845; Dale Co, AL

Death: 16Apr1926; Holmes Co, FL
Burial: Apr1926; Walton, FL; Gum Creek Cemetery
1860 Location: Walton County, FL
Description: fair complexion, grey eyes, dark hair
Union Enlistment: 18Aug1864; East Pass, FL; Co F, Private
Engagements: Montgomery, AL
Union Discharge: 17Nov1865; Tallahassee, FL; bounty due $75
Military Finding: 19Jan1891; mustered out with the company
Pension: 20May1890 in FL; App#775871, Cert#835853
Widow's Pension: 07May1926 in FL; App#1537823, Cert#A7126

MURPHY, Thomas T.
AKA: Thomas T. MURFREY
Birth: circa 1814; Charleston, South Carolina
Death: 01Sept1865, Walton Co, FL
1860 Location: Walton County, FL
Description: fair complexion, blue eyes, grey hair
Union Enlistment: 24Feb1864; Ft. Barrancas, FL; Co B, Private
Desertion: 01Aug1865; Ft. Barrancas, FL
Military Finding: 01Mar1886; desertion charge dropped
Widow's Pension: 04Apr1883; App#302870, Cert#487077

N

NEAL, Hugh William
AKA: Hugh NEIL; William H. NEEL
Birth: circa 1846; Jackson Co, FL
Death: 18Jun1880 - 18Aug1904; Jackson Co, FL
1860 Location: Jackson County, FL
Description: light complexion, blue eyes, light hair
Union Enlistment: 31Mar1865; Ft. Barrancas, FL; Co D., Private
Desertion: 04Aug1865; Ft. Barrancas, FL
Widow's Pension: 18Aug1904; App#812180

NELSON, Jonah
AKA: Jonas NELSON; Jona NELSON
Birth: circa 1846; Alabama
Death: 02Feb1915; Westville, Holmes Co, FL
Burial: Feb1915; Leonia, Holmes Co, FL; Leonia Cemetery

1860 Location: Walton County, FL
Description: fair complexion, dark eyes, dark hair
CSA: Mar1863 - Jun1863; 57th AL Infantry, Co K, Private, deserted
Union Enlistment: 05Mar1864; Ft. Barrancas, FL; Co C, Private
Desertion: 01Aug1865; Ft. Barrancas, FL
Military Finding: 12Nov1892; desertion charge dropped
Pension: 05May1894 in FL; App#1109518, Cert#1147098
Widow's Pension: 20Mar1915 in FL; App#1043891, Cert#821555

NETTLES, Adam Wyrick
AKA: Alexander W. NETTLES; A. W. NETTLES
Birth: circa 1830; Escambia Co, FL
Death: 30Jun1880 – 1900; Escambia Co, AL
1850 Location: Escambia County, FL
Description: fair complexion, dark eyes, dark hair
Union Enlistment: 26May1864; Ft. Barrancas, FL; Co F, Farrier
Union Appointment: 27Aug1864; Blacksmith (date also listed as 1Dec1864)
Engagements: Montgomery, AL
Union Discharge: 17Nov1865; Tallahassee, FL; bounty due $75
Pension: 02Feb1880; App#344041, Cert#452283

NEWBERRY, Nathaniel
AKA: Nathaniel NEWBERY; Nathaniel NEWBEARY
Birth: circa 1845; Alabama
1860 Location: Holmes County, FL
Description: light complexion, blue eyes, dark hair
Union Enlistment: 30Dec1863; Ft. Barrancas, FL; Co C, Private
Died: 11Jul1864; Ft. Barrancas, FL

NEWSOM, James M.
AKA: James M. NEWSOME; James M. NEWSON
Birth: circa 1837; Wilson Co, TN
Death: after 01Jul1870; Tennessee
1850 Location: Wilson County, TN
Description: fair complexion, dark eyes, dark hair

Union Enlistment: 28Jan1864; Ft. Barrancas, FL; Co D, Private
Promotions: 01Apr1864; 7th Sergeant
Union Appointment: 02May1864; 2nd Lt
Military Charges: Aug - Sept1864; disobedience of orders, drunkenness, conduct unbecoming an officer and a gentleman
Disability Discharge: 29Dec1864

NICHOLS, Elias
AKA: Elias NICKELS; Elias NICKOLS
Birth: Feb1847; Holmes Co, FL
Death: 01Jun1919; Panacea, Wakulla Co, FL
Burial: Jun1919, Panacea, Wakulla Co, Florida; Old Field Cemetery
1860 Location: Baldwin County, AL
Description: dark complexion, black eyes, light hair
Union Enlistment: 05Aug1864; East Pass, FL; Co F, Private
Union Discharge: 17Nov1865, Tallahassee, FL
Pension: 09Nov1892 in FL; App#1137525, Cert#969586

NOBLES, Andrew J.
Birth: circa 1840; Lee Co, GA
Death: 27May1865 - 05Feb1867
Description: fair complexion, blue eyes, dark hair
CSA: 16Mar1863 - Nov1863; 57th AL Infantry, Co K, Private, deserted
Union Enlistment: 05Mar1864; Ft. Barrancas, FL; Co C, Private
Engagements: Gonzalez/15 Mile House; Montgomery, AL
Desertion: 27May1865; Montgomery, AL
Widow's Pension: 05Feb1867; App#141735

NORRIS, Alvah Colby
AKA: Alvah J. COLBY
Birth: 11Mar1840; New Hampshire
Death: 07Jul1893; Las Animas Co, CO
1860 Location: Middlesex County, MA
Additional Union Service: 31Aug1861 - 1863; 26th MA Volunteers, Co D, Private/Sergeant
Union Appointment: 29Mar1864; Ft. Barrancas, FL; Co A, 1st Lt

Engagements: Montgomery, AL
Union Discharge: 17Nov1865; Tallahassee, FL
Pension: 05Aug1890 in CO; App#862109

NORRIS, Green
AKA: Green NORIS
Birth: Mar1836; Barbour Co, AL
Death: 20May1901; Escambia Co, FL
1860 Location: Santa Rosa County, FL
Description: light complexion, blue eyes, light hair
CSA: 01May1862 - Aug1862; 1st FL Infantry, Co D, Private, estimated desertion date.
Union Enlistment: 11Mar1864; East Pass, FL; Co D, Private
Engagements: Raid in South Alabama; Montgomery, AL
Union Discharge: 17Nov1865; Tallahassee, FL; bounty due $120
Pension: 10Apr1882; App#445819, Cert#666523
Widow's Pension: after 20May1901; App#780438
Minor's Pension: 21May1912; App#987014

NORRIS, James I.
AKA: James NORIS
Birth: circa 1820; Pike Co, AL
Death: 27May1865 - 11Nov 889
Description: light complexion, gray eyes, brown hair
CSA: 14Mar1862 - 01Oct1862; 6th FL Infantry, Co I, Private, deserted
Union Enlistment: 30Dec1863; Ft. Barrancas, FL; Co A, Private
Engagements: Blakeley, AL
Desertion: 27Mar1865l Blakeley, Baldwin Co, AL
Widow's Pension: 11Nov1889; App#408441

NORRIS, Joel B.
AKA: Joel B. NORIS
Birth: circa 1835; Washington Co, AL
Description: light complexion, blue eyes, dark hair
Union Enlistment: 30Dec1863; Ft. Barrancas, FL; Co A, Private
Died: 20Aug1864; Ft. Barrancas, FL
Widow's Pension: 06Apr1880; App#262836

Minor's Pension: App#323241, Cert#233106

NORTON, William A. C.
AKA: William NORWOOD
Birth: circa 1834; Covington Co, AL
1860 Location: Covington County, AL
Description: fair complexion, grey eyes, light hair
Union Enlistment: 24Feb1864; Ft. Barrancas, FL; Co C, Private
Promotions: Sept - Oct1864; Corporal
Engagements: Pollard, AL
Killed in Action: 17Dec1864; Michael's Creek, Escambia Co, FL
Minor's Pension: 12Feb1883; App#301039, Cert#369049

NOWLAND, Henry
AKA: Henry NOWLEN; Henry NAWLAN; Henry NOWLAN
Birth: circa 1820; Montevallo, Shelby Co, AL
Death: after 08Dec1864
Description: light complexion, blue eyes, brown hair
Union Enlistment: 10Mar1864; East Pass, FL; Co D, Private
Desertion: 08Dec1864; Ft. Barrancas, FL
Pension: 12Jun1882; App#452079

O

OGLESBEE, Benjamin
AKA: Benjamin OGLESBA; Benjamin OGLESBIA; Benjamin OGLESBY
Birth: circa 1827; Twiggs Co, GA
Death: after 17Nov1865
1860 Location: Holmes County, FL
Description: fair complexion, blue eyes, light hair
Union Enlistment: 05Mar1864; Ft. Barrancas, FL; Co C, Private
Military Charges: 05Aug1865; desertion and theft of a mule
Military Confinement: Sept1865; Ft Pickens, FL; sick in confinement
Union Discharge: 17Nov1865; Tallahassee, FL; bounty due $120

OGLESBEE, George W.
AKA: George W. OGLESBA; George W. OGLESBIA

Birth: circa 1835; Twiggs Co, GA
Death: 24Jan1890 – 1900; East Pass, FL
1860 Location: Holmes County, FL
Description: fair complexion, blue eyes, gray hair
Union Enlistment: 25Feb1864; Ft. Barrancas, FL; Co C, Private
Military Charges: 2 Apr1864; Marine Hospital Yard; shot and killed Samuel Graves, 1st FCUV.
Military Confinement: 25Apr1864; Ft. Pickens; in irons
Dishonorable Discharge: 15Oct1864; for killing a recruit
Pension: 24Jan1890 in FL; App#751101

OMOSRO, David
No information other than name on card

OVERSTREET, Henry
Birth: circa 1824; Conecuh Co, AL
Death: 22Sept1886 - 16Sept1890; Alabama
1860 Location: Coffee County, AL
Description: fair complexion, yellow eyes, dark hair
CSA: 10Mar1863 - 10May1863; 57th AL Infantry, Co K, Private, deserted
Union Enlistment: 05Mar1864; Ft. Barrancas, FL; Co C, Private
Union Discharge: 17Nov1865; Tallahassee, FL; bounty due $120
Pension: 22Sept1886; App#585688, Cert#617883
Widow's Pension: 16Sept1890 in AL; App#443875, Cert#321679

OWENS, Franklin
Birth: circa 1821; Georgia
Death: after 22Jun1888
1860 Location: Dale County, AL
Description: light complexion, blue eyes, dark hair
Union Enlistment: 01Mar1864; Ft. Barrancas, FL; Co A, Private
Engagements: Montgomery, AL
Desertion: 05May1865; Montgomery, AL
Military Finding: 22Jun1888; desertion charge dropped

OWENS, William Daniel
AKA: William D. OWENS
Birth: 27Jun1844; Washington Co, FL

Death: 27Oct1914; Wausau, Washington Co, FL
Burial: Oct1914; Washington Co, FL; Glenwood Cemetery
1860 Location: Washington County, FL
Description: light complexion, gray eyes, brown hair
CSA: 07Sept1861 - Mar1864; 4th FL Infantry, Co H, Private/Sergeant, estimated desertion date.
Union Enlistment: 20Apr1864; East Pass, FL; Co E, Private
Promotions: 30Jun1864; Corporal
Promotions: 20Aug1864; Sergeant
Demotion: 17Jun1865; Private
Union Discharge: 17Nov1865; Tallahassee, FL; bounty due $75
Pension: 04May1881 in FL; App#1363520, Cert#1143421
Widow's Pension: 23Jan1915 in FL; App#1040389, Cert#773677

OWENS, Willis W.
Birth: Mar1848; Washington Co, FL
Death: 12Dec1923; Wausau, Washington Co, FL
Burial: Dec1923; Wausau, Washington Co, FL; Ferguson Cemetery
1860 Location: Washington County, Florida
Description: dark complexion, blue eyes, dark hair
Union Enlistment: 19May1864; East Pass, FL; Co F/E, Private
Military Confinement: 23Aug1865 - 15Sept1865; Ft. Pickens, FL
Union Discharge: 17Nov1865; Tallahassee, FL; bounty due $100
Military Finding: 18Sept1889; desertion charge dropped
Pension: 12Jun1889 in FL; App#709675, Cert#805348

P

PARKER, George W.
Birth: circa 1846; Covington Co, AL
Death: 26Apr1882 - 01Jul1882; Alabama
1860 Location: Coffee County, AL
Description: fair complexion, gray eyes, dark hair
Union Enlistment: 05Mar1864; Ft. Barrancas, FL; Co C, Private
Engagements: 15 Mile House, FL
Union Discharge: 17Nov1865; Tallahassee, FL; bounty due $120
Pension: 26Apr1882 in AL; App#447511, Cert#278060

Widow's Pension: 01Jul1882; App#294693, Cert#238513
Minor's Pension: 10Jul1890 in FL; grandson James M. Seigler; App#429158, Cert#460530

PARKER, Greenberry G.
AKA: Greenberg G. PARKER
Birth: circa 1834; Butler Co, AL
Death: 27Jan1918; Atmore, Escambia Co, AL
1860 Location: Baldwin County, AL
Description: fair complexion, blue eyes, light hair
Union Enlistment: 26Mar1864; Ft. Barrancas, FL; Co D, Private
Union Discharge: 17Nov1865; Tallahassee, FL; bounty due $120
Pension: 14Oct1890 in AL; App#912529, Cert#764703
Widow's Pension: 25Mar1918 in AL; App#1117557, Cert#861757

PARKER, John
Birth: circa 1846; Butler Co, AL
Death: 21Oct1890 - 14Jun1898; Baldwin Co, AL
1860 Location: Baldwin County, AL
Description: fair complexion, blue eyes, light hair
Union Enlistment: 05Feb1864; Ft. Barrancas, FL; Co B, Private
Union Discharge: 17Nov1865; Tallahassee, FL; bounty due $120
Pension: 21Oct1890 in AL; App#973972, Cert#9907470
Widow's Pension: 14Jun1898 in AL; App#397350, Cert#488074

PARKER, Richard P.
AKA: Richard PARKER
Birth: circa 1839; Baker Co, GA
Description: fair complexion, black eyes, dark hair
1860 Location: Coffee County, AL
CSA: 16Mar1863 - 11Aug1863; 57th AL Infantry, Co K, Private, deserted
Union Enlistment: 05Mar1864; Ft. Barrancas, FL; Co C, Private
Engagements: Gonzalez/15 Mile House
Promotions: 20Oct1864; Corporal
Died: 12Sept1865; Ft. Barrancas, FL

Military Finding: 10Jun1891; "Language of the order restoring this man to duty that the charge of desertion...is erroneous"

PARKER, William
Birth: circa 1835; Butler Co, AL
Death: after 17Nov1865
1860 Location: Butler County, AL
Description: light complexion, blue eyes, dark hair
Union Enlistment: 19May1864; Ft. Barrancas, FL; Co F, Private
Promotions: 18Jul1865; Corporal
Union Discharge: 17Nov1865; Tallahassee, FL; bounty due $75

PARRISH, Charles Wesley
AKA: Charles W. PARRISH; Charles W. PARISH
Birth: Oct1846; Holmes Co, FL
Death: 03Mar1911; Lowndes Co, AL
1860 Location: Holmes County, FL
Description: fair complexion, grey eyes, light hair
Union Enlistment: 26Feb1864; Ft. Barrancas, FL; Co C, Private
Union Discharge: 17Nov1865; Tallahassee, FL; bounty due $120
Pension: 17Jul1892 in AL; App#1127139, Cert#1115132
Widow's Pension: 27Mar1911 in AL; App#961512, Cert#721879

PARRISH, Christopher Columbus
AKA: Columbus C. PARRISH
Birth: May1842; Alabama
Death: 01Jan1907 - 27Apr1907; Wise Co, TX
Burial: Jan1907 - Apr1907; Decatur, Wise Co, TX; Oaklawn Cemetery
1860 Location: Holmes County, FL
Description: dark complexion, dark eyes, dark hair
Union Enlistment: 28Jan1864; Ft. Barrancas, FL; Co C, Private
Union Discharge: 17Nov1865; Tallahassee, FL; bounty due $120
Pension: 02Sept1889 in TX; App#726488, Cert#877219
Widow's Pension: 27Apr1907 in TX; App#868056, Cert#637516

PARRISH, Ephraim C.
AKA: Ephram C. PARRISH; Ephram C. PERRISH; Ephragm PARISH

Birth: Feb1848; Holmes Co, FL
Death: May1918; Decatur, Wise Co, TX
1860 Location: Holmes County, FL
Description: fair complexion, brown eyes, dark hair
Union Enlistment: 23Mar1864; Ft. Barrancas, FL; Co D, Private
Engagements: Raid in South Alabama; Montgomery, AL
Union Discharge: 17Nov1865; Tallahassee, FL; bounty due $160
Pension: 07Jul1904; Oklahoma Territory; App#1320330, Cert#1093893

PARRISH, George W.
AKA: George W. PARISH
Birth: 30Sept1844; Henry Co, AL
Death: 27Nov1918; Niceville, Okaloosa Co, FL
Burial: Nov1918; Niceville, Okaloosa Co, FL; Rocky Memorial Cemetery
1860 Location: Holmes County, FL
Description: fair complexion, gray eyes, light hair
Union Enlistment: 15Apr1864; Ft. Barrancas, FL; Co E/C, Private
Promotions: 22Jan1865; Corporal
Union Discharge: 17Nov1865; Tallahassee, FL; bounty due $75
Pension: 05Dec1890 in FL; App#970769, Cert#1146507
Widow's Pension: 30Dec1918 in FL; App#1133475, Cert#880010

PARRISH, Owen T.
Birth: 16Oct1841; Henry Co, AL
Death: 20Jan1879; Holmes Co, FL
Burial: Jan1879; Holmes Co, FL; Sandy Creek Baptist Church Cemetery
1860 Location: Holmes County, FL
Description: fair complexion, gray eyes, light hair
Union Enlistment: 28Jan1864; Ft. Barrancas, FL; Co C, Private
Union Discharge: 23Dec1864; discharged due to epilepsy (episodes on an average once a week)

PARRISH, Robert J.
Birth: circa 1846; Henry Co, AL

Description: fair complexion, gray eyes, light hair
1860 Location: Holmes County, FL
Union Enlistment: 28Jan1864; Ft. Barrancas, FL; Co C, Private
Died: 12Sept1864; Ft. Barrancas, FL

PATE, David
Birth: circa 1837; Thomas Co, GA
Death: 17Jun1880 – 1900; Walton Co, FL
1860 Location: Calhoun County, FL
Description: fair complexion, gray eyes, light hair
CSA: 08Mar1862 - 30Apr1862; 6th FL Infantry, Co K, Private, deserted
Union Enlistment: 15Feb1864; Ft. Barrancas, FL; Co C, Private
Desertion: 23Jul1864; East Pass, FL

PATE, Joel
Birth: Apr1847; Coffee Co, AL
Death: 05Jan1910; Holmes Co, FL
Burial: Jan1910; Caryville, Washington Co, FL; Bethel Cemetery
1860 Location: Calhoun County, FL
Description: fair complexion, blue eyes, light hair
Union Enlistment: 08Jun1864; Ft. Barrancas, FL; Co F/C, Private
Engagements: Montgomery, AL
Union Discharge: 17Nov1865; Tallahassee, FL; bounty due $75
Pension: 03Sept1890 in FL; App#963801, Cert#1126407
Widow's Pension: 17Feb1910 in FL; App#936190, Cert#705566

PATE, Mathew
Birth: circa 1842; Dale Co, AL
Death: 22Nov1921; Baker, Okaloosa Co, FL
Description: fair complexion, dark eyes, dark hair
CSA: 21Jul1861 - 31Mar1862; 1st FL Infantry, Co E, Private
Union Enlistment: 05Mar1864; Ft. Barrancas, FL; Co C, Private
Union Discharge: 17Nov1865; Tallahassee, FL; bounty due $120
Pension: 05Nov1896 in FL; App#1182483, Cert#1088886

PATE, Rudolph F.
Birth: circa 1846; Alabama

Burial: Jun1864 in Escambia Co, FL; Barrancas National Cemetery, Sec 1, Site 945
1860 Location: Calhoun County, FL
Description: fair complexion, blue eyes, light hair
Union Enlistment: 15Feb1864; Ft. Barrancas, FL; Co C, Private
Died: 28Jun1864; Ft. Barrancas, FL

PAUL, Daniel William
Birth: 06Dec1841; Dale Co, AL
Death: 20Feb1914; Waynesboro, Wayne Co, MS
Burial: Feb1914; Wayne Co, MS; Arrington Cemetery
1860 Location: Coffee County, AL
Description: fair complexion, gray eyes, dark hair
CSA: 22Feb1862 - Sept1863; 33rd AL Infantry, Co A, Private, estimated end date
Union Enlistment: 10Oct1864; East Pass, FL; Co D, Private
Desertion: 01Aug1865; Ft. Barrancas, FL
Military Finding: 04Aug1886; desertion charges dropped
Pension: 02Nov1881 in AL; App#482678, Cert#554601

PAUL, David Enoch
AKA: David E. PAUL; Enoch David PAUL
Birth: circa 1846; Alabama
Death: 1884; Henry Co, AL
1860 Location: Coffee County, AL
Description: fair complexion, brown eyes, brown hair
Union Enlistment: 11Mar1864; East Pass, FL; Co D, Private
Desertion: 01Aug1865; Ft. Barrancas, FL
Military Finding: 01May1909; desertion charge dropped
Widow's Pension: 26Jul1909; App#924541

PAUL, John A.
AKA: John H. PAUL
Birth: circa 1831; Barbour Co, AL
Death: May1881 – 1900; Alabama
1860 Location: Coffee County, AL
Description: dark complexion, gray eyes, dark hair

CSA: 16Mar1863 - 31Oct1863; 57th AL Infantry, Co K, Private, deserted
Union Enlistment: 10Oct1864; East Pass, FL; Co D, Private
Union Discharge: 17Nov1865: Tallahassee, FL
Pension: 05May1881; App#421772, Cert#664676
Widow's Pension: App#705415, Cert#555410

PAULK, Jonathan
AKA: Yallaton POLK; Johnathan POLK
Birth: circa 1832; Stewart Co, GA
Death: before 15Feb1876
1850 Location: Decatur County, Georgia
Description: fair complexion, blue eyes, black hair
CSA: 30Mar1861 - 12Dec1861; 1st FL Infantry, Co E, Private, discharged
Union Enlistment: 23Apr1864; Ft. Barrancas, FL; Co E, Private
Engagements: Marianna, FL; Pollard, AL; Blakeley, AL; Greenville, AL; Montgomery, AL
Desertion: 01May1865; attempted desertion
Military Confinement: 01May1865 - 17Nov1865; Montgomery, AL; confined for attempting to desert
Military Finding: 15Apr1887; desertion charges dropped
Widow's Pension: 15Feb1876; App#224747, Cert#552952

PEACOCK, John
AKA: John P. PEACOCK; John PECOCK
Birth: circa 1846; Santa Rosa Co, FL
Death: 04May1865; Wetumpka, Elmore Co, AL
Description: light complexion, blue eyes, dark hair
1860 Location: Santa Rosa County, FL
CSA: 21Mar1862 - 30Oct1863; 1st FL Reorganized Infantry, Co F, Private, discharged due to health
Union Enlistment: 28Apr1864; Ft. Barrancas, FL; Co D, Private
Engagements: Raid in South Alabama; Montgomery, AL
Killed in Action: 04May1865; Wetumpka, Elmore Co, AL; while on scouting duty

PENTON, John T.
Birth: circa 1829; Montgomery, AL
Death: 1867 – 1880; Alabama
1860 Location: Covington County, AL
Description: fair complexion, blue eyes, grey hair
CSA: 09Apr1863 - Nov1863; 6th AL Cavalry, Co I, Private, estimated desertion date
Union Enlistment: 01May1864; Ft. Barrancas, FL; Co F, Private
Promotions: 03Aug1864; Sergeant
Desertion: 01Aug1865; Ft. Barrancas, FL
Military Finding: 16Oct1884; desertion charges dropped

PETERSON, William J.
AKA: William J. PETTERSON; William J. PEATERSON
Birth: circa 1824; Sampson Co, NC
Death: after 17Nov1865
1860 Location: Barbour County, AL
Description: fair complexion, blue eyes, dark hair
Union Enlistment: 05Mar1864; Ft. Barrancas, FL; Co D, Private
Union Discharge: 17Nov1865; Tallahassee, FL; bounty due $120

PHILLIPS, William
Birth: circa 1845; Georgia
Death: after 17Nov1865
Description: fair complexion, blue eyes, dark hair
Union Enlistment: 18Mar1865; Ft. Barrancas, FL; Co A, Private
Union Discharge: 17Nov1865; Tallahassee, FL; bounty due $100

PHILMON, Jesse
AKA: Jesse FILLMON
Birth: circa 1846; Early Co, GA
Death: after 08Aug1865
1860 Location: Henry County, AL
Description: fair complexion, dark eyes, dark hair
Union Enlistment: 24Jan1865; Ft. Barrancas, FL; Co C, Private
Desertion: 08Aug1865

PICKARD, Cyrus P.
Birth: Mar 1842; New Hampshire

Death: 09Jan1921; Acton, Middlesex Co, MA
1860 Location: Middlesex County, MA
Additional Union Service: US CT 86th Infantry, Co B
Union Appointment: 02May1864; Ft. Barrancas, FL; Co C/D/E, 1st Lt
Union Discharge: 17Nov1865; Tallahassee, FL
Pension: 12May1898 in MA; App#1207336, Cert#1026333

PICKRON, William W.
AKA: William W. PICKERON; William H. PICKRON; William W. PICKEROW
Birth: circa 1839; Decatur Co, GA
Death: before 11Apr1904
1860 Location: Holmes County, FL
Description: light complexion, blue eyes, brown hair
CSA: 14Mar1862 - 11Feb1864; 6th FL Infantry, Co I, Private, deserted
Union Enlistment: 11Mar1864; East Pass, FL; Co B, Private
Desertion: 14Aug1865; Ft. Barrancas, FL
Military Finding: 11Dec1903; desertion charges removed
Widow's Pension: 11Apr1904; App#803940, Cert#592941

PIPPIN, Griffin Lambert
AKA: Griffin PIPPIN
Birth: 20Nov1833; Georgia
Death: 02Mar1889; Walton Co, FL
Burial: Mar1889; Freeport, Walton Co, FL; Hatcher Cemetery
1860 Location: Walton County, FL
Description: light complexion, gray eyes, dark hair
Union Enlistment: 19Jan1864; Ft. Barrancas, FL; Co B, Private
Promotions: 01Apr1864; Blacksmith
Union Discharge: 17Nov1865; Tallahassee, FL; bounty due $160
Widow's Pension: 27Sept1890; App#476521, Cert#295582
Minor's Pension: App#714116; Cert#494008

PITMAN, George Washington
AKA: George Washington PITTMAN
Birth: circa 1834; Walton Co, FL

Death: 30Apr1923; Darlington, Walton Co, FL
1860 Location: Holmes County, FL
Description: fair complexion, blue eyes, dark hair
Union Enlistment: 05Oct1864; Ft. Barrancas, FL; Co F, Private
Union Discharge: 17Nov1865; Tallahassee, FL
Military Finding: 19Feb1885; desertion charge dropped
Pension: 03Sept1890; App#963807, Cert#1055185

PITTMAN, Thomas H.
AKA: Thomas H. PITMAN
Birth: 12Dec1830l Dale Co, AL
Death: 21Jun1897; Holmes Co, FL
Burial: Jun1897; Westville, Holmes Co, FL; Campground Church Cemetery
1850 Location: Holmes County, FL
Description: fair complexion, blue eyes, light hair
CSA: 14Mar1862 – 18May1864; 6th FL Infantry, Co I, Sergeant/2nd Lt/1st Lt
Union Enlistment: 29Apr1864; East Pass, FL; Co F, Private
Engagements: Montgomery, AL
Promotions: 03Aug1864; 1st Sergeant
Union Discharge: 17Nov1865; Tallahassee, FL; bounty due $75
Pension: 24Feb1890; App#757450, Cert#760324
Widow's Pension: after 21Jun1897; App#657856, Cert#552416

PITTS, Isaac Porter
Birth: 13Feb1841; Jackson Co, FL
Death: 1907; Holmes Co, FL
Burial: 1907; Holmes Co, FL; Bethlehem Methodist Church
1860 Location: Walton County, FL
Description: light complexion, blue eyes, dark hair
CSA: 01Mar1862 - 31Dec1863; 1st FL Reorganized Infantry, Co E, Bugler
Union Enlistment: 03Jan1864; Ft. Barrancas, FL; Co C, Private
Military Confinement: 14Jan1865; no evidence can be found against him and he was released
Desertion: 20May1865; East Pass, FL
Military Finding: 11Jul1888; desertion charges dropped

Pension: 16Jan1888 in FL; App#636019

PITTS, Lewis
AKA: Louis PITTS
Birth: circa 1833; Henry Co, AL
1860 Location: Washington County, FL
Description: dark complexion, gray eyes, dark hair
CSA: 02Apr1862 - 01Jun1862; 6th FL Infantry, Co K, Private, estimated desertion date
Union Enlistment: 20Dec1863; Ft. Barrancas, FL; Co C, Private
Promotions: 01Apr1864; Corporal
Died: 13Oct1864; Ft. Barrancas, FL
Minor's Pension: 21Nov1895; Benjamin P.; App#624579, Cert#586668

PITTS, William Henry
Birth: 20Jan1835; Jackson Co, FL
Death: 15Dec1919; Duncan Community, Washington Co, FL
Burial: Dec1919; Chipley, Washington Co, FL; Piney Grove Cemetery
1860 Location: Holmes County, FL
Description: dark complexion, blue eyes, dark hair
Union Enlistment: 03Jan1864; Ft. Barrancas, FL; Co C, Private
Desertion: 15Jan1865; East Pass, FL
Pension: 17Sept1888; App#672594
Widow's Pension: 30Oct1922; App#1196186

POE, Aaron
Birth: circa 1819; Lincoln Co, NC
Death: after 10Jun1865
Description: black complexion, black eyes, black hair
Union Enlistment: 25Mar1864; Ft. Barrancas, FL; Co F, Under Cook
Desertion: 10Jun1865; Ft. Barrancas, FL

POLATTA, John M.
AKA: John N. John M. PALATTO; John N. POLATHA
Birth: circa 1843; Chambers Co, AL
Death: after 30Jun1885

1860 Location: Covington County, AL
Description: fair complexion, gray eyes, light hair
Union Enlistment: 01May1864; Ft. Barrancas, FL; Co F, Private
Union Discharge: 17Nov1865; Tallahassee, FL; bounty due $75

POLATTA, William
AKA: William POLATO; William POLATTO: Wilson PALLOTTY
Birth: circa 1825; South Carolina
Death: before 19Dec1879; Madison Co, FL
1860 Location: Covington County, AL
Description: fair complexion, blue eyes, dark hair
Union Enlistment: 01May1864; Ft. Barrancas, FL; Co F, Private
Union Discharge: 17Nov1865; Tallahassee, FL; bounty due $75
Widow's Pension: 19Dec1879; App#256455

POMPEY, Jackson
AKA: Jackson WILSON
Birth: May1824; Dooley Co, GA
Death: 11Nov1908; Jackson Co, FL
Description: mulatto complexion, gray eyes, dark hair
Union Enlistment: 13Mar1864; Ft. Barrancas, FL; Co C/D, Under Cook
Desertion: 01Sept1865; Ft. Barrancas, FL
Military Finding: 21Sept1891; desertion charge dropped
Pension: 09Jan1893 in FL; App#1147224, Cert#939937
Widow's Pension: 09Dec1908 in FL; App#909333, Cert#676372

POTTER, Andrew J.
Birth: circa 1834; Washington Co, FL
Death: after 07Aug1865
Description: black complexion, black eyes, black hair
Union Enlistment: 23Mar1864; Ft. Barrancas, FL; Co A, Under Cook
Engagements: Montgomery, AL
Desertion: 07Aug1865; Ft. Barrancas, FL

POTTER, George
AKA: George BROWN
Birth: circa 1838; Washington Co, FL

Death: before 22Jul1896; Florida
Description: black complexion, black eyes, black hair
Union Enlistment: 25Mar1864; Ft. Barrancas, FL; Co E, Under Cook
Desertion: 04Sept1865; Tallahassee, FL
Widow's Pension: 22Jul1896 in FL; App#637835

POTTS, Alexander Dunbar
AKA: Dunbar POTTS
Birth: 06Jun1843; New York
Death: after 09Sept1865
1860 Location: New York, NY
Additional Union Service: 02Jul1863 - 14Jul1864; 1st NY Mounted Rifles, Private
Union Appointment: 15Jul1864; Ft. Barrancas, FL; Co D, 2nd Lt
Honorable Discharge: 09Sept1865

POWELL, John W.
Birth: circa 1834; Lawrence Co, GA
Death: 18Mar1897 – 1900; Florida
1860 Location: Coffee County, AL
Description: fair complexion, brown eyes, dark hair
Union Enlistment: 11Mar1864; East Pass, FL; Co D, Private
Promotions: 01Apr1864; 1st Sergeant
Union Discharge: 17Nov1865; Tallahassee, FL; bounty due $120
Pension: 16Mar1887 in FL; App#602260, Cert#429476

POWELL, Joseph
Birth: circa 1830; Kershaw Co, SC
Death: 31Oct1874 – 1880; Alabama
1860 Location: Barbour County, AL
Description: dark complexion, brown eyes, black hair
CSA: 10Mar1862 - 30Apr1863; 39th AL Infantry, Co C, Private
Union Enlistment: 20May1864; East Pass, FL; Co F, Private
Union Discharge: 17Nov1865; Tallahassee, FL; bounty due $75
Pension: 31Oct1874; App#197006, Cert#343292

PRICE, Andrew J.
Birth: Jan1840; Macon Co, AL

Death: after 15Apr1910; Coffee Co, AL
1860 Location: Coffee County, AL
Description: fair complexion, gray eyes, light hair
Union Enlistment: 01May1865; Montgomery, AL; Co E, Private
Union Discharge: 17Nov1865; Tallahassee, FL; bounty due $100
Pension: 31Jan1882 in AL; App#438565

PRIM, Benjamin Franklin
Birth: circa 1841; Stewart Co, GA
Death: 05Dec1864; Dale Co, AL
Description: fair complexion, blue eyes, brown hair
1860 Location: Barbour County, AL
CSA: 03Mar1862 - 12Jun1863; 15th AL Infantry, Co E, Private, deserted during furlough
Union Enlistment: 20May1864; East Pass, FL; Co E, Private
Union Discharge: 05Dec1864; Dale Co, AL; killed by Confederates

PRIM, D. J.
Union Enlistment: about May1865; unknown place or length of service
Union Discharge: unknown place or length of service

PRIM, James Jordan
AKA: James J. PRIME; James J. PRINN
Birth: 29Jan1838; Stewart Co, GA
Death: 22Apr1933; Jackson, Clarke Co, AL
1860 Location: Barbour County, AL
Description: fair complexion, blue eyes, red hair
CSA: 13Mar1861 - 12Mar1864; 1st AL Battalion Light Artillery, Co F, Corporal, discharged
Union Enlistment: 20May1864; East Pass, FL; Co F, Private
Engagements: Montgomery, AL
Promotions: 03Aug1864; Quartermaster Sergeant
Union Discharge: 17Nov1865; Tallahassee, FL; bounty due $75
Pension: 04Dec1891 in AL; App#1076475, Cert#1074174

PROVOST, Richard V.
Birth: circa 1839; Montgomery, AL

Death: after 07Jun1880; Alabama
1860 Location: Washington County, FL
Description: dark complexion, brown eyes, brown hair
CSA: 18Sep1861 - 28Feb1864; 4th FL Infantry, Co H, Private, estimated desertion date
Union Enlistment: 09Jul1864; East Pass, FL; Co F, Private
Desertion: 12May1865; Blakeley, AL

PULLUM, Thomas
Birth: 16Nov1822; Georgia
Death: 26Mar1886; Houston Co, AL
Burial: Mar1886; Houston Co, AL; Clark Cemetery
1860 Location: Dale County, AL
Description: fair complexion, blue eyes, light hair
CSA: 09Oct1861 - 10Jun1863; 31st GA Infantry, Co C, Private/1st Lt, resigned
Union Enlistment: 15Feb1864; Ft. Barrancas, FL; Co E, Private
Engagements: Marianna, FL; Pollard, AL
Promotions: 01May1864; Sergeant
Union Discharge: 17Nov1865; Tallahassee, FL; bounty due $160
Pension: 03Jun1872; App#1118478

R

RAMER, Elias J.
AKA: Elias RAIMER
Birth: Jun1832; Covington Co, AL
Death: 20Oct1915; Perdido, Baldwin Co, AL
1860 Location: Covington County, AL
Description: light complexion, blue eyes, light hair
Union Enlistment: 19Jan1864; Ft. Barrancas, FL; Co B, Private
Promotions: 01Apr1864; Saddler
Desertion: 17Aug1865; Ft. Barrancas, FL
Military Finding: 07Oct1889; desertion charge dropped
Pension: 16Jul1890; App#884981, Cert#1093350
Widow's Pension: 17Dec1915 in OK; App#1057483

RAY, Jesse
Birth: 05Apr1825 in Lowndes Co, AL

Death: 09Ju1894; Escambia Co, FL
Burial: Jun1894; Beulah, FL; Beulah Baptist Church Cemetery
1860 Location: Baldwin County, AL
Description: dark complexion, blue eyes, dark hair
Union Enlistment: 16Mar1864; Ft. Barrancas, FL; Co A, Private
Desertion: 11Aug1865; Ft. Barrancas, FL
Military Finding: 16Apr1886; desertion charge dropped
Pension: 11Aug1890 in FL; App#864635, Cert#980085
Widow's Pension: after 09Jun1894; App#598184, Cert#407081

RAY, Soverign Frederick
AKA: Soverign F. RAY
Birth: 06May1830; Lowndes Co, AL
Death: 08May1899; Baldwin Co, AL
Burial: May1899; Gateswood, AL; Clear Springs Cemetery
Description: light complexion, blue eyes, black hair
Union Enlistment: 07Jan1864; Ft. Barrancas, FL; Co A, Private
Engagements: Marianna, FL; Fifteen Mile House; Pollard, FL
Promotions: 01Apr1864; Sergeant
Union Discharge: 17Nov1865; Tallahassee, FL; bounty due $120
Pension: 30Oct1891 in AL; App#1069773
Widow's Pension: 23Sept1899 in AL; App#706135, Cert#563312

RAYBURN, Ira W.
AKA: Ira J. RAYBURN; Ira W. RABORN; Ira W. RAYBORN
Birth: circa 1820; Darlington Co, SC
Death: 25Jul1870 – 1880; Alabama
1850 Location: Pike County, AL
Description: fair complexion, blue eyes, dark hair
Union Enlistment: 01Apr1864; Ft. Barrancas, FL; Co B, Private
Military Confinement: Jul1865 - Sept1865; Ft. Pickens, FL
Union Discharge: after Sept1865
Military Finding: 11Dec1883; removal of desertion charge denied

REGISTER, Akis Franklin
AKA: Achis F. REGISTER; Akis F. REGISTER
Birth: 20Oct1848; Washington Co, FL
Death: 28Jan1900; Vernon, Washington Co, FL

Burial: Jan1900; Washington Co, Florida; Vernon Cemetery
1860 Location: Washington County, FL
Description: fair complexion, blue eyes, dark hair
Union Enlistment: 25Jan1864; Ft. Barrancas, FL; Co D, Private
Engagements: Raid in South Alabama; Montgomery, AL
Union Discharge: 17Nov1865; Tallahassee, FL; bounty due $160
Pension: 19Apr1887 in FL; App#606942, Cert#412352
Widow's Pension: 16Sep1916 in FL; App#1073225, Cert#819815

REGISTER, Joseph M.
AKA: Joseph M. REGERSTER
Birth: circa 1846; Washington Co, FL
Death: Feb1873
1860 Location: Washington County, FL
Description: dark complexion, black eyes, black hair
CSA: 25Mar1863 - 30Nov1863; 4th Battalion FL Infantry, Co. C, Private, deserted, records transferred to 11th FL Infantry, Co K.
Union Enlistment: 13Dec1863; Ft. Barrancas, FL; Co C, Private
Engagements: Montgomery, AL
Union Discharge: 17Nov1865; Tallahassee, FL; bounty due $75
Widow's Pension: 20Feb1922 in FL; App#1185345

RHODES, John M.
AKA: John M. RHOADES
Birth: circa 1835; Screven Co, GA
Death: 25Jun1865 - 17Nov1865; Coffee Co, AL
1860 Location: Coffee County, AL
Description: fair complexion, blue eyes, brown hair
Union Enlistment: 12Apr1864; East Pass, FL; Co E, Private
Desertion: 25Jun1864; Ft. Barrancas, FL
Widow's Pension: 16Jun1889; App#300856

RICHARDS, John S.
AKA: John J. RICHARDS
Birth: circa 1828; Burke Co, GA
Death: 03May1892; Charlotte Harbor, DeSoto Co, FL
1850 Location: Dale County, AL

Description: light complexion, brown eyes, brown hair
Union Enlistment: 01Jan1864; Ft. Barrancas, FL; Co A, Private
Union Discharge: 17Nov1865; Tallahassee, FL; bounty due $120
Pension: 19May1886; App#574007, Cert#514688
Widow's Pension: 21Jun1893; App#578897

RICHARDSON, Francis M.
Birth: circa 1844; Decatur, Morgan Co, AL
Death: before 08Dec1890
1860 Location: Santa Rosa County, FL
Description: light complexion, blue eyes, light hair
Union Enlistment: 01Apr1864; East Pass, FL; Co E, Private
Union Discharge: 17Nov1865; Tallahassee, FL; bounty due $75

RICHARDSON, George M.
AKA: George M. RICHERSON
Birth: circa 1844; Coffee Co, AL
Death: between 17Nov1865 - 12Feb1895
1860 Location: Coffee County, AL
Description: fair complexion, black eyes, black hair
Union Enlistment: 29Feb1864; Ft. Barrancas, FL; Co C, Private
Promotions: 23Mar1864; Corporal
Promotions: 22Jan1865; Sergeant
Union Discharge: 17Nov1865; Tallahassee, FL

RICHARDSON, Wade H.
Birth: Dec1846; Troup Co, GA
Death: 21Jan1923; Whitefish Bay, Milwaukee Co, WI
1860 Location: Macon County, AL
Description: light complexion, blue eyes, light hair
Union Enlistment: 03Jan1864; Ft. Barrancas, FL; Co A, Private
Promotions: 01Apr1864; Corporal
Promotions: 01July1865; Sergeant
Union Discharge: 17Nov1865; Tallahassee, FL; bounty due $120
Pension: 01Sep1897 in WI; App#1198110, Cert#1152440
Widow's Pension: 02Feb1923 in WI; App#1200556,
Cert#938792

RICHBOURG, William L.
AKA: William L. RICHBOURGH; William L. RICHBURG
Birth: circa 1825; Sumter Co, SC
Death: after 09May1885; Walton Co, FL
1860 Location: Santa Rosa County, FL
Description: fair complexion, blue eyes, sandy hair
Union Enlistment: 18Apr1864; Ft. Barrancas, FL; Co B, Private
Promotions: 01Dec1864; Sergeant
Desertion: 13Aug1865
Military Finding: 09May1885; desertion charges dropped

RILEY, Daniel
AKA: Daniel REILEY
Birth: Aug1836; Henry Co, AL
Death: 09Jun1900 - 09Jun1905; Dale Co, AL
1860 Location: Dale County, AL
Description: light complexion, brown eyes, brown hair
Union Enlistment: 29Jun1864; East Pass, FL; Co F, Private
Desertion: 25Jul1865; Ft. Barrancas, FL
Military Finding: 23Oct1884; desertion charges dropped
Pension: 04Jun1891 in AL; App#1029543, Cert#791208
Widow's Pension: 09Jun1905 in AL; App#819895, Cert#859784

ROBERSON, Samuel Benjamin
AKA: Benjamin ROBERSON; Benjamin ROBERTSON; Benjamin ROBINSON; Samuel B. ROBERSON; D. B. ROBINSON
Birth: circa 1836; Conecuh Co, AL
Death: 30Dec1911; Flomaton, Escambia Co, AL
1850 Location: Conecuh County, AL
Description: fair complexion, blue eyes, light hair
Union Enlistment: 26Apr1864; Ft. Barrancas, FL; Co E, Private
Engagements: Marianna, FL; Pollard, AL; Blakely, AL; Greenville, AL; Montgomery, AL
Promotions: 11Aug1864; Corporal
Promotions: 17Jun1865; Sergeant
Union Discharge: 17Nov1865; Tallahassee, FL; bounty due $75
Pension: 23Jun1905; App#1337372, Cert#1114330
Widow's Pension: 05Mar1912; App#981974, Cert#779275

Minor's Pension: 24Jan1916; App#1059577

ROBERTS, Daniel D.
Birth: 01Jan1848; Coffee Co, AL
Death: 18Jun1894; Geneva Co, AL
Burial: Jun1894; Hacoda, Geneva Co, AL; Corner Creek Upper Cemetery
1860 Location: Coffee County, AL
Description: fair complexion, gray eyes, dark hair
Union Enlistment: 18Aug1864; East Pass, FL; Co F, Private
Promotions: 19Jul1865; Corporal
Union Discharge: 17Nov1865; Tallahassee, FL; bounty due $75
Pension: 23Oct1882 in AL; App#463124
Widow's Pension: 14Jun1895 in AL; App#616044

ROBERTS, Francis M.
AKA: Francis M. ROBERT
Birth: circa 1838; Troup Co, GA
1860 Location: Santa Rosa County, FL
Description: dark complexion, black eyes, dark hair
CSA: 25Mar1863 - Dec1863; 4th Battalion FL Infantry, Co. C, Private, deserted, records transferred to 11th FL Infantry, Co K
Union Enlistment: 05Jan1864; Ft. Barrancas, FL; Co D, Private
Promotions: 30Apr1864; appointed Wagoner by SO #24
Died: 15Oct1864; Ft. Barrancas, FL

ROBERTS, Gray S.
Birth: circa 1847; Coffee Co, AL
Death: after 20Aug1908
1860 Location: Coffee County, AL
Description: fair complexion, hazel eyes, brown hair
Union Enlistment: 15Mar1864; East Pass, FL; Co D, Private
Disability Discharge: 29Dec1864
Pension: 20Aug1908 in AL; App#1376769, Cert#1151785

ROBINSON, Daniel L.
AKA: Daniel L. ROBERSON; Daniel L. ROBERTSON
Birth: circa 1832; Conecuh Co, AL
Death: 11Sept1890 - 18Aug1909; Conecuh Co, AL

1860 Location: Baldwin County, AL
Description: dark complexion, dark eyes, dark hair
Union Enlistment: 26Apr1864; Ft. Barrancas, FL; Co E, Private
Engagements: Marianna, FL; Pollard, AL; Blakeley, AL; Greenville, AL; Montgomery, AL
Promotions: 17Jun1865; Corporal
Union Discharge: 17Nov1865; Tallahassee, FL; bounty due $75
Pension: 11Sept1890; App#968348, Cert#937521
Widow's Pension: App#607885, Cert#1148640
Minor's Pension: 18Aug1909; App#925766, Cert#709013

ROGERS, James W.
AKA: James W. RODGERS
Birth: circa 1841; Covington Co, AL
Death: after 26Jun1890
1860 Location: Covington County, AL
Description: fair complexion, yellow eyes, light hair
CSA: 29Aug1861 - 28Sept1863; 25th AL Infantry, Co A, Private
Union Enlistment: 22Mar1864; Ft. Barrancas, FL; Co D, Private
Engagements: Montgomery, AL
Promotions: 01Apr1864; Corporal
Desertion: 08May1865; Montgomery, Montgomery Co, AL
Military Finding: 26Jun1890; desertion charges dropped
Pension: 02Jun1890 in TN; App#779464, Cert#674943

ROLAND, John
Birth: circa 1846; Baldwin Co, AL
Death: after 19Aug1865
Description: dark complexion, black eyes, dark hair
Union Enlistment: 25Mar1865; Blakeley, AL; Co E, Private
Desertion: 19Aug1865

ROMBAUER, Roland T.
AKA: Roland F. ROMBAUER; Roderish ROMBAUER; Roland ROMBAUR
Birth: circa 1833; Hungary
Death: after 24Jun1880; Missouri

Additional Union Service: 1862 - 1863; 1st MO Infantry, Co B; 1st MO Light Artillery, Co B; 1st MO Infantry, Co A
Union Appointment: 27Aug1864; appointed Captain by General Banks from civil life
Union Discharge: 17Nov1865; Tallahassee, FL
Pension: 24Jun1880; App#391831, Cert#305508

ROOKS, George Daniel
Birth: 02Sept1844; Walton Co, FL
Death: 10Apr1895; Washington Co, FL
Burial: Apr1895; Vernon, Washington Co, FL; Vernon Cemetery
1860 Location: Walton County, FL
Description: fair complexion, gray eyes, sandy hair
CSA: 03Apr1863 - 31Oct1863; 6th AL Cavalry, Co K, Corporal, estimated desertion date
Union Enlistment: 21Dec1863; Ft. Barrancas, FL; Co D, Private
Promotions: 01Apr1864; Corporal
Military Confinement: 11Jul1865 - 10Sept1865; Ft. Pickens, FL; returned to duty without trial
Union Discharge: 17Nov1865; Tallahassee, FL
Military Finding: 27Sept1886; desertion charges dropped
Pension: 18Feb1889; App#689296
Widow's Pension: 07May1895; App#613884

ROOKS, Isaac
Birth: circa 1823; Jefferson Co, GA
Burial: Apr1864; Ft. Barrancas, FL; Ft. Barrancas National Cemetery
1860 Location: Worth County, GA
Description: light complexion, blue eyes, light hair
Union Enlistment: 20Dec1863; Ft. Barrancas, FL; Co C, Blacksmith
Died: 10Apr1864; Ft. Barrancas, Florida

ROOKS, James Franklin
AKA: James F. ROOKS
Birth: Feb1834; Lowndes Co, GA
Death: 20Dec1910; Walton Co, FL

1860 Location: Walton County, Florida
Description: fair complexion, blue eyes, light hair
Union Enlistment: 14Nov1864; Ft. Barrancas, FL; Co A, Private
Union Discharge: 17Nov1865; Tallahassee, FL
Pension: 29Jul1890 in FL; App#873449, Cert#951805
Widow's Pension: 23Jul1911; App#956800, Cert#420662

ROOKS, Thomas F.
Birth: circa 1837; Lowndes Co, GA
Death: 20Dec1864; Walton Co, FL
1860 Location: Walton County, FL
Description: light complexion, blue eyes, light hair
CSA: 20Jul1861 – 28Feb1862; 1st FL Infantry, Co D, Private, deserted
Union Enlistment: 21Dec1863; Ft. Barrancas, FL; Co C, Private
Military Assignment: Sept1864; Commissary Sergeant
Died: 20Dec1864; Walton Co, FL

ROSSVALLEY, Max L.
AKA: Max L. ROSSVALLY
Birth: circa 1827; Pennsylvania
Death: after 31Dec1864
1860 Location: Caddo Parish, LA
Union Appointment: 29Jan1864; Ft. Barrancas, FL; Staff Officer, 1st Surgeon
Dishonorable Discharge: 31Dec1864; for refusing to appear before a Medical Board of Examiners

ROUSE, Charles A.
Birth: circa 1838; Lenoir Co, NC
Death: 12Jul1880 - 1900 in Escambia Co, FL
Description: black complexion, black eyes, dark hair
Union Enlistment: 17Mar1864; Ft. Barrancas, FL; Co A, Under Cook
Desertion: 12Aug1865; Ft. Barrancas, FL

ROWLEY, Lyman W.
Birth: circa 1826; Rutland, Rutland Co, VT
Death: 05Apr1899; Pensacola, Escambia Co, FL

Burial: Apr1899; Pensacola, FL; St. Johns Cemetery, Section 1
1860 Location: Santa Rosa County, FL
Miscellaneous: Arrested by Confederate Vigilance Committee in 1861. A prisoner in Montgomery, Tuscaloosa, Macon and Libby Prison before escaping and returning to the Pensacola area.
Description: light complexion, gray hair, blue eyes
Union Appointment: 29Mar1864; 1st Lt from civil life by Gen. Asboth
Promotions: 15Mar1865; Captain
Military Injury: 27Sep1864; gunshot wound to the left side of head, fracturing skull
Union Discharge: 17Nov1865; Tallahassee, FL
Pension: 18Apr1879; App#282748, Cert#236067

RUSS, Robert S.
Birth: 14May1840; Washington Co, FL
Death: 20Jun1912; Millville, Washington Co, FL
Burial: Jun1912; Millville, FL; Millville Cemetery, Sec D17
1860 Location: Washington County, FL
Description: light complexion, gray eyes, light hair
CSA: 08Mar1862 - 04Feb1864; 6th FL Infantry, Co K, 1st Lt, discharged
Union Enlistment: 09Feb1864; Ft. Barrancas, FL; Co A, Private
Union Appointment: 29Mar1864; 2nd Lt
Union Discharge: 17Nov1865; Tallahassee, FL
Pension: 23Apr1888 in FL; App#652051, Cert#625696
Widow's Pension: 11Jul1912 in FL; App#989982, Cert#748237

RUSSELL, Henry
AKA: Henry RUSCELL; Henry RUSELL
Birth: circa 1830; Screven Co, GA
Death: after 21Sept1889
1860 Location: Franklin County, FL
Description: fair complexion, gray eyes, light hair
CSA: 10Mar1862 - 15Sept1863; 2nd FL Cavalry, Co A, Private, transferred. 15Sept1863 – 31Dec1863; 5th FL Battalion Cavalry, Co E, deserted
Union Enlistment: 21Feb1864; Ft. Barrancas, FL; Co C, Private

Union Discharge: 17Nov1865; Tallahassee, FL; bounty due $120
Pension: 21Sept1889 in FL; App#730074, Cert#968800

RUTTKAY, Albert
Birth: circa 1842; Hungary
Death: before 15Jan1884; New York
1860 Location: Orange County, NY
Additional Union Service: 1863; 4th US CT Heavy Artillery, Co D
Union Appointment: 29Mar1864; Ft. Barrancas, FL; Field & Staff, Major
Honorable Discharge: 31May1865; resigned
Widow's Pension: 15Jan1884 in NY; App#588502, Cert#608900

S

SANDERS, Joseph Ganes
Birth: circa 1827; South Carolina
Death: 19Feb1867; Decatur Co, GA
1860 Location: Dale County, AL
CSA: 05Oct1861 - 29Jan1864; 31st GA Infantry, Co C, Private/Captain, resigned
Union Enlistment: 05Jul1864; Ft. Barrancas, FL; Co F, 2nd Lt
Engagements: Pine Barren Creek, FL
Resignation: 13Sept1865; discharged for "good of service" (no criminality but gross negligence and incompetency)
Widow's Pension: 10Nov1890 in FL; App#470861, Cert#343512

SANDERS, William
AKA: William SANDRES
Birth: circa 1844; Russell Co, AL
Death: after 08Aug1865
Description: fair complexion, blue eyes, light hair
Union Enlistment: 25Sep1864; East Pass, FL; Co C, Private
Desertion: 08Aug1865

SARRIS, William V.
Union Enlistment: 18Jan1865; Hilton Head, SC; Private
Union Discharge: 17Jul1865; New York City, NY

SCAMMELL, William
AKA: William SCAMELL
Birth: circa 1847; Dale Co, AL
Death: after 27Aug1865
1860 Location: Dale County, AL
Description: light complexion, gray eyes, light hair
Union Enlistment: 27Mar1865; East Pass, FL; Co A, Private
Desertion: 27Aug1865; Six Mile Pond

SCROGGINS, Richard Wesley
AKA: Wesley SCOGGINS
Birth: circa 1845; Oglethorpe Co, GA
Death: 22Aug1870 - 18Nov1921; Alabama
1860 Location: Barbour County, AL
Description: dark complexion, blue eyes, black hair
CSA: 28Apr1862 - 07Feb1863; 39th AL Infantry, Co C, Private, estimated desertion date, likely didn't return from furlough
Union Enlistment: 21Jan1865; Ft. Barrancas, FL; Co F, Private
Engagements: Montgomery, AL
Military Injury: 12May1865 in Montgomery, AL; wounded through the carelessness of the sentinel Lewis Hall, Co C when on camp guard, left leg amputated after gunshot wound
Union Discharge: 05Dec1865 in post hospital in Mobile, AL
Pension: 14Apr1868; App#132728, Cert#91973
Widow's Pension: 18Nov1921 in AL; App#1181593, Cert#920952

SEAGERS, William
AKA: William SEGERS; William SEGARS; William SEGER
Birth: circa 1834; Gwinnett Co, GA
Death: after 24Jan1891
1860 Location: Dale County, AL
Description: light complexion, brown eyes, dark hair
CSA: 29May - 16Jul1863; 61st AL Infantry, Co I, Private, deserted
Union Enlistment: 30Mar1864; East Pass, FL; Co E, Private
Promotions: 01May1864; Blacksmith
Military Confinement: 16Apr1865 - 30Jul1865; Ft. Pickens

Desertion: 30Jul1865; Ft. Pickens, FL; escaped while confined at hard labor for attempted desertion
Military Finding: 13Mar1877; tried by court martial for AWOL, hard labor at Ft. Pickens for 6 months and forfeit of $10 mo. pay
Pension: 24Jan1891 in FL; App#999407

SEGARS, Southerd P.
AKA: Southward P. SEGARS; South P. SEGGARS; Southford P. SEGGERS
Birth: circa 1830; Marion Co, GA
1860 Location: Henry County, AL
Description: dark complexion, blue eyes, dark hair
CSA: 01Aug1863 - 09Dec1863; 4th Battalion FL Infantry, Co C, Private, deserted
Union Enlistment: 17Dec1863; Ft. Barrancas, FL; Co A, Blacksmith
Died: 26Jul1865; Ft. Barrancas, Florida
Widow's Pension: 22Feb1867; App#142633, Cert#118795
Minor's Pension: 07Feb1911; App#958042, Cert#766325

SEGERS, William R.
Birth: circa 1826; Gwinnett Co, GA
Death: before 19Dec1864; Newton, Dale Co, AL
1850 Location: Early County, GA
Description: fair complexion, blue eyes, dark hair
CSA: 1863; Alabama McWhorter's Light Artillery
Union Enlistment: 15Feb1864; Ft. Barrancas, FL; Co E, Private
Promotions: Apr1864; Blacksmith
Desertion: 19Dec1864; Newton, Dale Co, AL
Widow's Pension: 22Feb1867; App#142632

SELLERS, Henry T.
Birth: circa 1831; Columbia Co, GA
Death: before 22May1891
1850 Location: Jackson County, FL
Description: fair complexion, blue eyes, light hair
Union Enlistment: 12Sept1864; East Pass, FL; Co D, Blacksmith
Desertion: 06Apr1865; Ft. Barrancas, FL

Widow's Pension: 22May1891 in FL; App#514231, Cert#325580

SELLERS, John
Birth: circa 1829; Brunswick Co, NC
Death: 09Jul1890 - 11Sept1890; Florida
1860 Location: Jackson County, FL
Description: light complexion, blue eyes, brown hair
CSA: 25Mar1863 - 13Feb1864; 4th Battalion FL Infantry, Co C, Private, deserted. Records transferred to 11th FL Infantry, Co K.
Union Enlistment: 11Mar1864; East Pass, FL; Co D, Private
Union Discharge: 17Nov1865; Tallahassee, FL; bounty due $160
Pension: 09Jul1890 in FL; App#819790
Widow's Pension: 11Sept1890 in FL; App#620678, Cert#548102

SELLERS, John F.
Birth: circa 1845; Brunswick Co, NC
1860 Location: Jackson County, FL
Description: dark complexion, black eyes, black hair
CSA: 11Sept1863 - 29Dec1863; 5th Battalion FL Cavalry, Co A, Private, estimated desertion date
Union Enlistment: 11Mar1864; East Pass, FL; Co D, Private
Died: 09Jul1865; Ft. Barrancas, FL

SELLERS, Julius
AKA: Julius SELLES
Birth: circa 1846; Jackson Co, FL
Death: 20Nov1865; Ft. Barrancas, FL
Burial: 21Nov1865; Escambia, FL; Presbyterian Cemetery
1860 Location: Jackson County, FL
Description: light complexion, blue eyes, dark hair
Union Enlistment: 31Mar1865; Ft. Barrancas, FL; Co A, Private
Union Discharge: 17Nov1865; Tallahassee, FL; bounty due $100

SELLERS, Norman L.
AKA: Norman L. SELLARS
Birth: Jul1847; Henry Co, AL
Death: 02Aug1919; Ashford, Houston Co, AL
1860 Location: Henry County, AL
Description: light complexion, dark eyes, dark hair

Union Enlistment: 27Mar1865; East Pass, FL; Co A, Private
Union Discharge: 17Nov1865; Tallahassee, FL; bounty due $100
Pension: 08Oct1895 in FL; App#1210272, Cert#1174096

SELLERS, Thomas
Birth: circa 1841; Brunswick Co, NC
Death: 16Jan1901; Whittier, Osceola Co, FL
1850 Location: Jackson County, FL
Description: light complexion, blue eyes, brown hair
Union Enlistment: 11Mar1864; East Pass, FL; Co D, Private
Engagements: Raid in South Alabama; Montgomery, AL
Promotions: 01Apr1864; 3rd Sergeant
Union Discharge: 17Nov1865; Tallahassee, FL; bounty due $160
Pension: 02Sep1889 in FL; App#726546, Cert#932979
Widow's Pension: 25Feb1905; Edith App#823376

SELLERS, Thomas L.
Birth: 17Nov1832; Henry Co, AL
Death: 13Jan1913; Red Level, Covington Co, AL
Burial: 15Jan1913; Red Level, AL; Fairmount Cemetery
1860 Location: Holmes County, FL
Description: fair complexion, blue eyes, brown hair
CSA: 13May1862 - 15Jul1862; 6th FL Infantry, Co I, Private, deserted
Union Enlistment: 25Sept1864; East Pass, FL; Co E, Private
Military Charges: 26Jun1865; desertion, voluntarily gave himself up at the Marine Hospital
Union Discharge: 17Nov1865; Tallahassee, FL; bounty due $100
Pension: 17Oct1890 in AL; App#968387, Cert#1066020

SENTERFITT, Bennett G.
AKA: Bennett G. SENTERFEIT; Bennett G. SENTERFEITT; Bennett G. SENTERFIET
Birth: 02Dec1825; Pulaski Co, GA
Death: 17Mar1870; Walton Co, FL
Burial: Mar1870; Laurel Hill, Okaloosa Co, FL; Magnolia Cemetery
1860 Location: Walton County, FL

Description: fair complexion, gray eyes, light hair
Union Enlistment: 26Mar1864; Ft. Barrancas, FL; Co D, Private
Engagements: Raid in South Alabama; Montgomery, AL
Union Discharge: 17Nov1865; Tallahassee, FL; bounty due $160

SESSIONS, James A.
AKA: James A. SESSIONNS; James A. SESSONS
Birth: circa 1828; South Carolina
Death: 04Jun1900 – 1910; Conecuh Co, AL
1860 Location: Conecuh County, AL
Description: fair complexion, blue eyes, light hair
Union Enlistment: 19May1864; Ft. Barrancas, FL; Co F, Private
Desertion: 26Dec1864; Ft. Barrancas, FL
Pension: 13Oct1890 in AL; App#1015236

SETTLES, Samuel C.
Birth: circa 1846; Coffee Co, AL
1860 Location: Coffee County, AL
Description: fair complexion, hazel eyes, light hair
Union Enlistment: 06Jul1864; East Pass, FL; Co F, Private
Promotions: 03Aug1864; Corporal
Promotions: July1865; Sergeant
Died: 31Jul1865; Ft. Barrancas, FL

SHEFFIELD, Joseph
Birth: circa 1824; Marion Co, GA
Description: Black complexion, black eyes, black hair
Union Enlistment: 27Mar1864; Ft. Barrancas, FL; Under Cook
Union Discharge: Unknown

SHELLHOUSE, Sampson J.
AKA: Samson SHELLHOUSE; Sampson SHELLHOUSE
Birth: circa 1846; Georgia
Death: 08Jun1880 – 1900; Taylor Co, FL
1860 Location: Randolph County, GA
Description: fair complexion, blue eyes, light hair
Union Enlistment: 20May1864; East Pass, FL; Co F, Private
Desertion: 05Jun1865; Dale Co, AL

SIKES, James E.
Birth: Mar 1844; Coffee Co, AL
Death: 28Jun1923; Noma, Holmes Co, FL
1860 Location: Holmes County, FL
Description: fair complexion, blue eyes, light hair
Union Enlistment: 28Jan1864; Ft. Barrancas, FL; Co D, Private
Union Discharge: 17Nov1865; Tallahassee, FL; bounty due $160
Pension: 15Jan1873; App#180515, Cert#405570
Widow's Pension: 01Aug1923 in FL; App#1208435, Cert#945349

SIMMONS, James A.
Birth: circa 1824; Henry Co, AL
Death: Jun1880 – 1900; Dale Co, AL
1860 Location: Dale County, AL
Description: dark complexion, brown eyes, black hair
No other recorded information

SINGLETARY, Elijah
Birth: circa 1842; Pulaski Co, GA
1850 Location: Pulaski County, GA
Description: dark complexion, blue eyes, dark hair
Union Enlistment: 24May1864; East Pass, FL; Unassigned
No discharge information

SINGLETARY, William L.
AKA: W. L. SINGLETARY, William L. SINGLETARRY, William L. SINGLETERY
Birth: circa 1838; Sumter Co, GA
Death: after 29Dec1892
1860 Location: Walton County, FL
Description: dark complexion, dark eyes, dark hair
CSA: 25Mar1863 - 25Nov1863; 4th Battalion FL Infantry, Co. C, Private, deserted. Records transferred to 11th FL Infantry, Co K.
Union Enlistment: 13Dec1863; Ft. Barrancas, FL; Co A, Private
Union Discharge: 17Nov1865; Tallahassee, FL; bounty due $75
Pension: 29Dec1892 in FL; App#986866, Cert#699633

SKINNER, John W.
Birth: circa 1838; Darlington Co, SC
Description: fair complexion, black eyes, dark hair
CSA: 16Nov1863 - 31Dec1863; 4th FL Infantry, Co A, Private, estimated desertion date, records transferred to 11th FL Infantry, Co C
Union Enlistment: 15Mar1864: Ft. Barrancas, FL; Co C, Private
Engagements: Montgomery, AL
Promotions: 01Jan1865; Corporal
Killed in Action: 19May1865; Hobby's Bridge, AL
Military Finding: 07Jan1892; charged with desertion 20May1865, removed 7Jan1892 (notation 11580.C.1883)
Widow's Pension: 16Apr1869; App#174860, Cert#570206

SMITH, Archibald
Birth: 16Aug1829; Richland Co, SC
Death: 30Oct1909; Santa Rosa Co, FL
Burial: Oct1909; Okaloosa Co, Florida; Stewart Cemetery
1860 Location: Santa Rosa County, FL
Description: light complexion, blue eyes, dark hair
CSA: 13May1862 - 29Aug1863; 1st FL Reorganized Infantry, Co G, deserted
Union Enlistment: 25Jan1864; Ft. Barrancas, FL; Co B, Private
Promotions: 01Apr1864; Corporal
Union Discharge: 17Nov1865; Tallahassee, FL; bounty due $160
Pension: 16Oct1889 in FL; App#734058, Cert#1052811

SMITH, Derrell Malcolm
AKA: Derrell M. SMITH
Birth: Apr1845; Pike Co, AL
Death: 14May1922; Falco, Covington Co, AL
1860 Location: Santa Rosa County, Florida
Description: light complexion, blue eyes, light hair
Union Enlistment: 25Jan1864; Ft. Barrancas, FL; Co B, Private
Union Discharge: 17Nov1865; Tallahassee, FL; bounty due $120
Pension: 01Nov1881 in AL; App#432715, Cert#1119738
Minor's Pension: 29Jun1922 in AL; Mattie Smith, App#1191273, Cert#934742

SMITH, Dred H.
Birth: circa 1846; Conecuh Co, AL
Death: 12Jun1880 – 1900
1860 Location: Conecuh County, AL
Description: fair complexion, blue eyes, black hair
Union Enlistment: 21May1864; Ft. Barrancas, FL; Co F, Private
Desertion: 5Sept1864 near Pensacola, Florida; on picket duty

SMITH, Isaac
Birth: circa 1827; Guernsey Co, OH
Death: before 14Aug1895; Alabama
Description: light complexion, blue eyes, light hair
Union Enlistment: 23Mar1864; East Pass, FL; 1st Co D, Private
Engagements: Raid in South Alabama
Desertion: 11May1865; Montgomery, AL
Military Finding: 13Feb1895; desertion charges dropped
Widow's Pension: 14Aug1893 in AL; App#581425, Cert#412339

SMITH, Jacob
Birth: circa 1846; Conecuh Co, AL
Death: after 11May1910
1860 Location: Conecuh County, AL
Description: light complexion, blue eyes, light hair
CSA: 04Mar1863 - 25Aug1863; 3rd FL Battalion Cavalry, Co D, Private, deserted
Union Enlistment: 03Jan1864; Ft. Barrancas, FL; Co C, Private
Desertion: 24Jul1864; during the expedition to 15 Mile House

SMITH, Thomas
Birth: circa 1820; Pitt Co, NC
Death: after 1870
1860 Location: Covington County, AL
Description: fair complexion, blue eyes, brown hair
Union Enlistment: 08May1864; East Pass, FL; Co F, Private
Desertion: 14Oct1865; Monticello, FL

SMITH, William
Birth: circa 1842; Henry Co, AL
Death: 03Nov1922; Midland City, Dale Co, AL

Burial: Nov1922; Echo, Dale Co, AL; Mt. Carmel Methodist Church
1860 Location: Henry County, AL
Description: fair complexion, brown eyes, sandy hair
CSA: 03Jul1861 - 28Feb1864; 15th AL Infantry, Co G, Private, deserted
Union Enlistment: 20May1864; East Pass, FL; Co F, Private
Engagements: Montgomery, AL
Promotions: 10Jan1865; Corporal
Military Injury: 10May1865 - 30Aug1865; St. Mary's Hospital, Montgomery, Alabama; wounded
Union Discharge: 17Nov1865; mustered out late due to hospitalization, bounty due $75
Pension: 17Aug1877; App#240707, Cert#526557
Widow's Pension: 01Dec1922 in AL; App#1197516, Cert#928546

SMITH, William J.
Birth: circa 1841; Pike Co, AL
Death: 07Apr1915; Glendale, Walton Co, FL
1860 Location: Dale County, AL
Description: dark complexion, black eyes, black hair
Union Enlistment: 25Jan1864; Ft. Barrancas, FL; Co B, Private
Union Discharge: 17Nov1865; Tallahassee, FL; bounty due $120
Pension: 13Sept1881; App#429494, Cert#1094407
Widow's Pension: 29Apr1915; App#1046347, Cert#799644

SNELL, James Barnett
AKA: Barnett SNELL
Birth: circa 1824; Dale Co, AL
1860 Location: Dale County, AL
Description: fair complexion, blue eyes, dark hair
Union Enlistment: 08Sept1864; Ft. Barrancas, FL; Co E, Private
Died: 22Dec1864; Ft. Barrancas, FL; bounty due $100
Widow's Pension: 22Feb1867; App#142636, Cert#127390

SNOWDEN, James M.
AKA: James M. SNODEN

Birth: circa 1822; Conecuh Co, AL
1860 Location: Covington County, AL
Description: dark complexion, hazel eyes, gray hair
Union Enlistment: 01Mar1864; Ft. Barrancas, FL; Co C, Private
Died: 02Sept1864; Ft. Barrancas, FL
Widow's Pension: 31May1866; App#127516, Cert#170179
Minor's Pension: 08Aug1872; Grandson Milton Pate, App#204893, Cert #170180

SNOWDEN, Josiah H.
AKA: Josiah SNOWDEN; Josiah SNODEN
Birth: May1846; Covington Co, AL
Death: after 14Jan1902; Andalusia, Covington Co, AL
1860 Location: Covington County, AL
Description: light complexion, blue eyes, light hair
Union Enlistment: 23Mar1864; East Pass, FL; Co D, Private
Engagements: Raid in South Alabama; Montgomery, AL
Union Discharge: 17Nov1865; Tallahassee, FL; bounty due $120
Pension: 14Jan1902; App#1279597, Cert#1090603

SOWELL, Abijah Lewis
AKA: Abijah SOWELL; Abijah L. SOWELL
Birth: 17Jun1848; Dale Co, AL
Death: 1944; Washington Co, FL
Burial: 1944; Chipley, Washington Co, FL; Glenwood Cemetery
1860 Location: Covington County, AL
Description: dark complexion, blue eyes, light hair
Union Enlistment: 15Feb1864; Ft. Barrancas, FL; Co D, Private
Engagements: Raid in South Alabama; Montgomery, AL
Promotions: 20Oct1864; Bugler
Desertion: 11May1865; Montgomery, AL
Military Finding: 27Apr1888; desertion charges removed
Pension: 30Jul1889 in AL; App#719384, Cert#1093351

SOWELL, John W.
AKA: John W. SAWELL; John W. SEWELL; John W. LOWELL; John W. SOWEL
Birth: Feb1847; Henry Co, AL

Death: 02Jun1928; River Falls, Covington Co, AL
1860 Location: Henry County, AL
Description: dark complexion, blue eyes, dark hair
Union Enlistment: 15Feb1864; Ft. Barrancas, FL; Co B, Private
Union Discharge: 17Nov1865; Tallahassee, FL; bounty due $120
Pension: 01Sept1890 in AL; App#963871, Cert#1051461
Widow's Pension: 13Jul1928 in AL; App#1618725, Cert#A111328

SPEARS, John
Birth: 20Feb1832; Alabama
Death: 23Oct1908 Alabama
Burial: Oct1908; Samson, Geneva Co, AL; Piney Grove Baptist Church
1860 Location: Coffee County, AL
Description: fair complexion, blue eyes, brown hair
CSA: 09May1863 - 20Jun1863; 4th Battalion FL Infantry, Co A, Private, deserted, records transferred to 11th FL Infantry, Co C
Union Enlistment: 29Apr1864; East Pass, FL; Co F, Private
Military Confinement: 02Jul1865 - 14Se 1865; Ft. Pickens, FL; returned to duty without trial
Union Discharge: 17Nov1865; Tallahassee, FL; bounty due $75
Military Finding: 03Sept1891; desertion charges dropped
Pension: 10Jul1891 in AL; App#1040062, Cert#1051731
Widow's Pension: 05Apr1909 in AL; App#917330, Cert#680813

SPENCE, Joshua
AKA: Joshua SPENCER
Birth: circa 1839; Thomas Co, GA
Death: before 01Jul1891
Description: light complexion, blue eyes, light hair
CSA: 25Mar1863 - 25 Nov 1863; 4th Battalion FL Infantry, Co. C, Private, deserted, records transferred to 11th FL Infantry, Co K
Union Enlistment: 13Dec1863; Ft. Barrancas, FL; Co A, Private
Military Charges: 14Apr1892; desertion charges dropped
Desertion: 23Mar1865; Ft. Barrancas, FL; bounty due $120

SPURLOCK, Samuel H.
Birth: Nov1846; Butler Co, AL
Death: 10Jan1916; Dellwood, Jackson Co, FL
Burial: Jan1916; Grand Ridge, Jackson Co, FL; Cow Pen Pond Cemetery
1860 Location: Henry County, AL
Description: light complexion, dark eyes, dark hair
Union Enlistment: 27Mar1865; East Pass, FL; Co A, Private
Union Discharge: 17Nov1865; Tallahassee, FL
Pension: 21Jul1915 in FL; App#1420418
Widow's Pension: 21Feb1916 in FL; App#1061276

STAGNER, Daniel W.
Birth: circa 1840; Pike Co, AL
Death: before 14Jun1880; Smith Co, TX
1860 Location: Walton County, FL
Description: dark complexion, black eyes, black hair
CSA: 21Jul1861 - 13May1862; 1st FL Infantry, Co E, Private, mustered out. 13May1862 – 24May1862; 8th FL Infantry, Co E, Private, deserted.
Union Enlistment: 30Jan1864; Ft. Barrancas, FL; Co C, Private
Engagements: Montgomery, AL
Promotions: 23Mar1864; Sergeant
Union Discharge: 17Nov1865; Tallahassee, FL; bounty due $120
Widow's Pension: 21Apr1881; App#282119, Cert#292199

STAGNER, George W.
Birth: circa 1846; Pike Co, AL
Burial: Aug1864; Escambia Co, Florida; Barrancas National Cemetery, Plot 1, 0, 956
1860 Location: Walton County, FL
Description: light complexion, light eyes, red hair
Union Enlistment: 13Jan1864; Ft. Barrancas, FL; Co B, Private
Died: 12Aug1864; Ft. Barrancas, FL; bounty due $275

STAGNER, John M.
Birth: 25Sep1843; Pike Co, AL
Death: 20Sep1919; Hawkins, Wood Co, TX

Burial: Sep1919; Pine Mills, Wood Co, TX; Mt. Pisgah Cemetery
1860 Location: Walton County, FL
Description: dark complexion, black eyes, black hair
CSA: 04Oct1862 - 05Jul1863; 3rd Battalion FL Cavalry, Co D, Private, deserted, records transferred to 15th Confederate Cavalry, Co I
Union Enlistment: 27Jan1864; Ft. Barrancas, FL; Co B, Private
Engagements: Montgomery, AL
Union Discharge: 17Nov1865; Tallahassee, FL; bounty due $120
Pension: 07Dec1906 in TX; App#1354636, Cert#1135486

STANLEY, Garrett S.
AKA: Garret S. STANLEY; Garreth S. STANLEY
Birth: 01Oct1827; Montgomery, AL
Death: 30Dec1913; Opp, Covington Co, AL
Burial: Dec1913; Andalusia, Covington, AL; Enon Baptist Church
1860 Location: Coffee County, AL
Description: fair complexion, blue eyes, brown hair
CSA: 22Jul1861 - 07Jan1862; 18th AL Infantry, Co A, Private, disability discharge
Union Enlistment: 24Feb1864; Ft. Barrancas, FL; Co C, Private
Promotions: July - Aug 1864; Corporal
Engagements: Montgomery, AL
Union Discharge: 17Nov1865; Tallahassee, FL
Military Finding: 30Aug1869; desertion charges unfounded, given an honorable discharge to 17Nov1865
Pension: 14Jun1882 in KY; App#452525, Cert#736487
Widow's Pension: 31Jan1914 in AL; App#102581, Cert#775584

STANLEY, Joseph S.
AKA: Joseph STANDLY
Birth: Jan1845; Barbour Co, AL
Death: 26Apr1918; Norum, Washington Co, Florida
1850 Location: Holmes County, FL
Description: light complexion, blue eyes, light hair
Union Enlistment: 28Dec1863; Ft. Barrancas, FL; Co D, Private
Engagements: Montgomery, AL
Union Discharge: 17Nov1865; Tallahassee, FL; bounty due $120

Pension: 09Jan1892 in FL; App#1384293, Cert#1016611
Widow's Pension: 27May1918; App#1121006, Cert#873833

STANLEY, Kinion
AKA: Kinion STANDLY
Birth: circa 1823; Sampson Co, NC
Death: after 17Nov1865
1850 Location: Holmes County, FL
Description: dark complexion, blue eyes, dark hair
Union Enlistment: 29Dec1863; Ft. Barrancas, FL; Co D, Private
Promotions: 01Apr1864; Saddler
Union Discharge: 17Nov1865; Tallahassee, FL; bounty due $275

STEARNS, Benjamin F.
AKA: Benjamin F. STARNES; Benjamin F. STERN
Birth: Nov1842; Escambia Co, FL
Death: 31Oct1915; Pensacola, Escambia Co, FL
1860 Location: Escambia County, FL
Description: dark complexion, gray eyes, dark hair
CSA: 13Feb1862 - 13Oct1862; 1st Battalion Confederate Infantry, Co B, Private, POW at Corinth, MS and paroled.
Union Enlistment: 07Jan1864; Ft. Barrancas, FL; Co A, Private
Engagements: Marianna, FL; Fifteen Mile House, FL; Pollard, AL; Montgomery, AL
Promotions: 01Sept1864; 1st Sergeant
Union Discharge: 17Nov1865; Tallahassee, FL; bounty due $275
Pension: 15Nov1900 in FL; App#1244293, Cert#1055682

STEEL, William C.
AKA: William C. STEELE
Birth: Apr1822; Covington Co, AL
Death: 03Jul1900 – 1910; Baldwin Co, AL
1860 Location: Baldwin County, AL
Description: fair complexion, gray eyes, light hair
CSA: 18Feb1863 - 04Jul1863; Mobile City Troops, Arrington's Co A, Private, deserted while driving cattle
Union Enlistment: 26Mar1864; Ft. Barrancas, FL; Co D, Private
Union Discharge: 17Nov1865; Tallahassee, FL; bounty due $120

Pension: 23Jun1880; App#389438, Cert#708408

STEELE, Henry William
AKA: Henry STEELE; Henry W. STEELE; Henry TEEL
Birth: 13Dec1818; Covington Co, AL
Death: 04Jul1892; Walton Co, FL
1860 Location: Santa Rosa County, FL
Description: light complexion, blue eyes, sandy hair
Union Enlistment: 30Dec1863; Ft. Barrancas, FL; Co B, Private
Promotions: 18Jul1864; Blacksmith
Union Discharge: 17Nov1865; Tallahassee, FL; bounty due $120
Pension: 08Oct1890; App#920102

STEGALL, Reuben N.
AKA: Reuben N. STAGAL; Reubin M. STEGALL; Reubin M. STAGAL
Birth: circa 1842; Walton Co, FL
Death: 04Nov1882 - 18Jul1890; Copiah Co, MS
1860 Location: Mobile County, AL
Description: fair complexion, gray eyes, light brown hair
Union Enlistment: 27Apr1864; Ft. Barrancas, FL; Co B, Private
Engagements: Montgomery, AL
Union Discharge: 17Nov1865; Tallahassee, FL; bounty due $75
Pension: 04Nov1882 in MS; App#464155
Widow's Pension: 18Jul1890 in MS; App#441045

STEPHENS, Benjamin F.
AKA: Benjamin S. STEPHENS
Birth: circa 1840; Dale Co, AL
Death: after 17Nov1865
1860 Location: Conecuh County, AL
Description: dark complexion, blue eyes, dark hair
Union Enlistment: 20Sept1864; Ft. Barrancas, FL; Co F, Private
Engagements: Montgomery, AL
Union Discharge: 17Nov1865; Tallahassee, FL

STEWART, George W.
Birth: May1844; Baldwin Co, AL
Death: 25Aug1932; Pensacola, Escambia Co, FL

1860 Location: Baldwin County, AL
Description: dark complexion, dark eyes, dark hair
Union Enlistment: 27Mar1864; Ft. Barrancas, FL; Co E, Private
Engagements: Marianna, FL; Pollard, AL; Blakeley, AL; Greenville, AL; Montgomery, AL
Promotions: 01Dec1864; Bugler
Union Discharge: 17Nov1865; Tallahassee, FL; bounty due $160
Pension: 24Jul1896 in AL; App#1179789, Cert#1139192
Widow's Pension: 19Sept1932 in FL; App#1725220, Cert# A3753

STEWART, James H.
AKA: James H. STEWARD
Birth: circa 1838; Baltimore, Baltimore Co, MD
Death: after 17Nov1865
Description: light complexion, blue eyes, light hair
Union Enlistment: 03Apr1864; East Pass, FL; Co E, Private
Engagements: Marianna, FL; Pollard, AL; Blakeley, AL; Greenville, AL; Montgomery, AL
Promotions: 01May1864; 1st Sergeant
Union Discharge: 17Nov1865; Tallahassee, FL; bounty due $75

STOKES, John O.
AKA: John O. STOAKES
Birth: circa 1821; South Carolina
1860 Location: Dale County, AL
Description: light complexion, grey eyes, light hair
Union Enlistment: 15Dec1863; Ft. Barrancas, FL; Co D, Private
Died: 25Jul1864; Ft. Barrancas, FL
Widow's Pension: 19Apr1915 in AL; App#1048503

STREETS, Hugh
AKA: Hughey STREETS; Hugh STREET
Birth: circa 1817; Duplin Co, NC
Description: fair complexion, gray eyes, gray hair
Union Enlistment: 24Feb1864; Ft. Barrancas, FL; Co D, Private
Died: 24Sept1864; Ft. Barrancas, FL
Minor's Pension: 05May1898; App#675056

STRICKLAND, Eli J.
AKA Eli J. STRICKLIN; Eli J. STRICKLIND
Birth: circa 1820; Jasper Co, GA
1860 Location: Dale County, AL
Description: dark complexion, hazel eyes, dark hair
Union Enlistment: 06Apr1864; East Pass, FL; Co E, Private
Died: 18Dec1864; Ft. Barrancas, FL; bounty due $75
Widow's Pension: 13Aug1869; App#178974

STRICKLAND, James Pinckney
AKA: James P. STRICKLIN; James P. STRICKLAND
Birth: circa 1844; Pike Co, AL
Death: 04Jan1906; Washington Co, FL
1860 Location: Henry County, AL
Description: fair complexion, blue eyes, light hair
CSA: 25Jun1863-09Dec1863; 4th Battalion FL Infantry, Co A, Private, deserted, records transferred to 11th FL Infantry, Co C.
Union Enlistment: 30Dec1863; Ft. Barrancas, FL; Co D, Private
Engagements: Montgomery, AL
Union Discharge: 17Nov1865; Tallahassee, FL; bounty due $160
Minor's Pension: 23Mar1909 in FL; App#916213

STRICKLAND, John J.
Birth: circa 1840; Pike Co, AL
Death: 12Feb1916; Los Angeles, Los Angeles Co, CA
1860 Location: Henry County, AL
Description: fair complexion, gray eyes, red hair
CSA: 11May1861 - 31Aug1861; 6th AL Infantry, Co B, Private, estimated desertion date
Union Enlistment: 30Dec1863; Ft. Barrancas, FL; Co D, Private
Engagements: Montgomery, AL
Promotions: 01Apr1864; 8th Sergeant (Quartermaster)
Union Discharge: 17Nov1865; Tallahassee, FL; bounty due $160
Pension: 31Jul1891 in CA; App#1044335, Cert#1114118

STRICKLAND, Reason
AKA: Reason STRICKLIN; Reason STRICKLEN; Reason STRICKLIND

Birth: circa 1838; Macon Co, GA
Death: after 17Nov1865
Description: light complexion, gray eyes, dark hair
CSA: 16May1861 - 30Dec1863; 6th AL Infantry, Co B, Private, deserted
Union Enlistment: 23Mar1864; East Pass, FL; Co E, Private
Engagements: Marianna, FL; Pollard, AL; Blakeley, AL; Greenville, AL; Montgomery, AL
Promotions: 01Apr1865; Corporal
Union Discharge: 17Nov1865; Tallahassee, FL; bounty due $275

SULLIVAN, John
AKA: John SILLIVANT; John SULLIVANT; John SILEVANT
Birth: circa 1834; Putnam Co, GA
Death: before 28Jul1891
Description: fair complexion, hazel eyes, sandy hair
Union Enlistment: 29Apr1864; East Pass, FL; Co F, Private
Promotions: 03Aug1864; Corporal
Military Charges: Jun1865; while on expedition in south AL given leave to visit his house & return to certain place in two days. Gone for 6 months and voluntarily turned himself in.
Demotion: June1865; Private
Union Discharge: 17Nov1865; Tallahassee, FL
Widow's Pension: 28Jul1891 in FL; App#521907, Cert#357570

SUMMERLIN, Lucas
AKA: Lucius SUMMERLIN; Luke SUMMERLIN; Lucas SUMERLIN; Lucas SUNMERLIN
Birth: circa 1834; Madison Co, IL
Death: after 10Dec1883
Description: fair complexion, blue eyes, brown hair
CSA: 30Apr1863 - 11Jul1863; Capt Tanner's Independent Co, FL Infantry, Private, deserted, records transferred to 11th FL Infantry, Co F
Union Enlistment: 12Apr1864; East Pass, FL; Co E, Private
Desertion: 23Mar1865 in Milton, Santa Rosa Co, FL
Military Finding: 03Jan1884; removal of desertion charge denied
Pension: 10Dec1883 in FL; App#501727

SWINNEY, Darby
AKA: Darby SWEENEY; Darby SWENNY; Darby SWEENY
Birth: 17Apr1819; Richmond Co, NC
Death: 18Sept1916; Falco, Covington Co, AL
Burial: Sept2016; Escambia Co, AL; Blackwater Cemetery
1860 Location: Conecuh County, AL
Description: fair complexion, blue eyes, light hair
Union Enlistment: 30Dec1863; Ft. Barrancas, FL; Co F, Private
Desertion: 07Aug1865; Ft. Barrancas, FL
Military Finding: 26Dec1889; desertion charges dropped
Pension: 03Sept1892 in AL; App#1129323, Cert#878144
Widow's Pension: 26Sept1916 in AL; App#1079716, Cert#888252

T

TANNER, John W.
Birth: circa 1845; Randolph Co, AL
Death: after 17Nov1865
1860 Location: Washington County, FL
Description: light complexion, blue eyes, sandy hair
CSA: 25Mar1863 - 30Nov1863; 4th Battalion FL Infantry, Co. C, Private, deserted, records transferred to 11th FL Infantry, Co K.
Union Enlistment: 13Dec1863; Ft. Barrancas, FL; Co C, Private
Promotions: 23Mar1864; Sergeant
Demotion: 7June1864; Private
Promotions: 03Apr1865; Quartermaster Sergeant
Demotion: 12July1865; Private
Union Discharge: 17Nov1865; Tallahassee, FL; bounty due $75

TAYLOR, James W.
AKA: James TAYLOR
Birth: circa 1826; Abbeville Co, SC
Death: before 21May1883
Description: fair complexion, blue eyes, light hair
Union Enlistment: 24Feb1864; Ft. Barrancas, FL; Co C, Private
Promotions: 01Apr1864; Corporal

Promotions: 7Jun1864; Sergeant (Quartermaster)
Desertion: 26Apr1865; Ft. Barrancas, FL
Widow's Pension: 21May1883; App#484319

TAYLOR, Thomas Yancey
Birth: 14Oct1846; Montgomery Co, AL
Death: 17Dec1930; Greenville, Butler Co, AL
Burial: Dec1930; Saville, Crenshaw Co, AL; Sweetwater Church
Description: light complexion, blue eyes, light hair
Union Enlistment: 12Mar1864; East Pass, FL; Co D, Private
Union Discharge: 17Nov1865; Tallahassee, FL; bounty due $120
Pension: 27Nov1895 in AL; App#1172176, Cert#1062979

TAYLOR, William L.
Birth: circa 1841; Macon Co, GA
Death: 01Apr1865; Vernon, Washington Co, FL
Description: dark complexion, blue eyes, dark hair
CSA: 10May1862 - 20Sept1863; 6th FL Infantry, Co K, Private, deserted
Union Enlistment: 27Dec1863; Ft. Barrancas, FL; Co A, Private
Promotions: 01Apr1864; Sergeant
Killed in Action: 1Apr1865; Vernon, FL; on secret service
Military Finding: 12Mar1870; War Dept. statement that he was killed while on secret service in the enemy country
Widow's Pension: 18May1866; App#126840, Cert#150176

TEEL, Henry W.
AKA: Henry TEAL
Birth: Aug1843; Covington Co, AL
Death: 22Oct1924; Saratoga, Hardin Co, TX
Burial: Oct1924; Saratoga, Hardin Co, TX; Teel Cemetery
1860 Location: Covington County, AL
Description: light complexion, blue eyes, light hair
CSA: 31Mar1862 - 10Jul1863; 42nd AL Infantry, Co E, Private, deserted while on parole.
Union Enlistment: 19Jan1864; Ft. Barrancas, FL; Co B, Private
Engagements: Escambia Bay/Milton
Promotions: 01Apr1864; Blacksmith

Union Discharge: 17Nov1865; Tallahassee, FL; bounty due $120
Pension: 06Nov1882 in TX; App#464274

TEEL, John Jr.
AKA: John TEAL
Birth: 8Apr1829; Covington Co, AL
1860 Location: Covington County, Alabama
Description: fair complexion, blue eyes, light hair
Union Enlistment: 24Feb1864; Ft. Barrancas, FL; Co B, Private
Died: 20Apr1865; Ft. Barrancas, FL; bounty due $275
Military Finding: 06Feb1869; War Department statement concerning death date
Minor's Pension: 24May1869; App#175569, Cert#216479

TEMPLERS, William
Death: after 28Jun1865
Union Enlistment: 17Jan1865; Hilton Head Island, SC
Union Discharge: 28Jun1865; mustered out under telegram War Department May 12 1865, POW

TETSON, Jeremiah
AKA: Jeremiah TECHSTONE; Jeremiah TESTON; Jeremiah TESSON
Birth: circa 1820; Barnwell Co, SC
1860 Location: Henry County, AL
Description: fair complexion, blue eyes, brown hair
Union Enlistment: 29Apr1864; East Pass, FL; Co F, Private
Died: 28Nov1864; Ft. Barrancas, Escambia, FL
Widow's Pension: 24Jan1870; App#183581, Cert#239638

THARP, Henry V.
AKA: Henry V. THARPE; Henry V. THORP; Henry W. THORP
Birth: 06Mar1842; Barbour Co, AL
Death: 08Apr1913; Wacissa, Jefferson Co, FL
Burial: Apr1913; Jefferson, FL; Broomsage Cemetery
1860 Location: Barbour County, AL
Description: fair complexion, dark eyes, light hair
CSA: 10Mar1862 - 31Dec1863; 39th AL Infantry, Co C, Private, deserted during sick furlough

Union Enlistment: 05Mar1864; Ft. Barrancas, FL; Co C, Private
Union Discharge: 17Nov1865; Tallahassee, FL; bounty due $120
Pension: 09Oct1897 in FL; App#1199290, Cert#1054845
Widow's Pension: 19Jan1914 in FL; App#1020742
Minor's Pension: 04Apr1914 in FL; Della Tharp, App#1025406

THOMAS, George W. T.
AKA: George S. THOMAS; George T. THAMES
Birth: circa 1835; Randolph Co, GA
Death: 20Nov1931; Dry Prong, Grant Co, LA
1860 Location: Dale County, AL
Description: light complexion, blue eyes, dark hair
CSA: 15May1863 - 31Oct1863; 57th AL Infantry, Co K, Private, deserted
Union Enlistment: 25Dec1863; Ft. Barrancas, FL; Co B, Private
Desertion: 01Aug1865; Ft. Barrancas, FL
Military Finding: 20Oct1884; desertion charges dropped
Pension: 25Aug1897; App#1197372, Cert#1093069
Widow's Pension: 07Jan1932; App#1709221

THOMAS, James W.
Birth: circa 1826; Camden Co, GA
Description: dark complexion, dark eyes, dark hair
Union Enlistment: 09Feb1864; Ft. Barrancas, FL; Co B, Private
Died: 29Oct1864; Ft. Barrancas, FL; bounty due $275

THOMAS, John D. K. P.
Birth: 08Apr1846; Coffee Co, AL
Death: 06Mar1919; Sneads, Jackson Co, FL
Burial: Mar1919; Sneads, Jackson Co, FL; Mill Springs Missionary Baptist Church Cemetery
1860 Location: Dale County, AL
Description: fair complexion, blue eyes, brown hair
Union Enlistment: 31Mar1864; Ft. Barrancas, FL; Co E, Private
Engagements: Blakeley, AL; Greenville, AL; Montgomery, AL
Military Injury: 06May1865; Autauga, AL; wounded in left forearm by bushwhacker
Union Discharge: 17Nov1865; Tallahassee, FL; bounty due $160

Pension: 19Oct1901 in AL; App#1276384, Cert#1065883
Widow's Pension: 27Mar1919 in FL; App#1138396, Cert#875533

THOMAS, Joseph M.
Birth: circa 1840; Coffee Co, AL
1860 Location: Coffee County, AL
Description: light complexion, blue eyes, light hair
Union Enlistment: 30Dec1863; Ft. Barrancas, FL; Co B, Private
Died: 09Aug1864; Ft. Barrancas, FL; bounty due $275
Widow's Pension: 10Feb1871; App#193703, Cert#164499
Minor's Pension: App#200718, Cert#164495

THOMAS, Lawson
Birth: circa 1837; Barbour Co, AL
Death: after 17Nov1865
Description: fair complexion, yellow eyes, brown hair
Union Enlistment: 31Mar1864; Ft. Barrancas, FL; Co E, Private
Union Discharge: 17Nov1865; Tallahassee, FL; bounty due $275

THOMAS, T.
Union Enlistment: before 1864; Co E, Private
Union Discharge: after Jun1864

THOMAS, William J.
Birth: circa 1837; Barbour Co, AL
Death: before 15Feb1894; Alabama
Description: fair complexion, blue eyes, light hair
Union Enlistment: 31Mar1864; Ft. Barrancas, FL; Co E, Private
Union Discharge: 17Nov1865; Tallahassee, FL; bounty due $275
Widow's Pension: 15Feb1894 in AL; App#590343, Cert#612229

THOMPSON, Campbell
Birth: circa 1832; Florida
Death: 30Jun1885 – 1900; Escambia Co, FL
1860 Location: Washington County, FL
Description: fair complexion, brown eyes, light hair
CSA: 08Mar1862 - 14Jun1862; 6th FL Infantry, Co K, Private, deserted

Union Enlistment: 15Feb1864; Ft. Barrancas, FL; Co C, Private
Desertion: 23Jul1864; East Pass, FL

THOMPSON, Enoch
Birth: circa 1825; Barbour Co, AL
Death: 26May1886 – 1890; Texas
1860 Location: Barbour County, AL
Description: dark complexion, blue eyes, black hair
CSA: 21Mar1863 - 13Sept1863; 57th AL Infantry, Co B, Private
Union Enlistment: 20May1864; East Pass, FL; Co F, Private
Engagements: Montgomery, AL
Promotions: 19Jul1865; Corporal
Union Discharge: 17Nov1865; Tallahassee, FL; bounty due $75
Pension: 26May1886; App#574679, Cert#401064

THOMPSON, Jesse
AKA: Jesse THOMAS
Birth: circa 1844; Santa Rosa Co, FL
Death: 12Dec1909; Walton Co, FL
1860 Location: Santa Rosa County, FL
Description: dark complexion, blue eyes, dark hair
CSA: 07Mar1862 - 31Dec1863; 1st FL Reorganized Infantry, Co E, Private, likely deserted from hospital
Union Enlistment: 20Feb1864; Ft. Barrancas, FL; Co B, Private
Engagements: Montgomery, AL
Union Discharge: 17Nov1865; Tallahassee, FL; bounty due $120
Pension: 03Nov1890; App#968486, Cert#1059135
Widow's Pension: 24Jan1910 in FL; App#934527, Cert#703789

THOMPSON, Nelson
Birth: circa 1847; Gadsden Co, FL
Death: Jan1890; Alabama
1860 Location: Henry County, AL
Description: light complexion, blue eyes, light hair
CSA: 01Jun1864 - 07Mar1865; 5th FL Battalion Cavalry, Co E, Private, deserted
Union Enlistment: 20Apr1865; East Pass, FL; Co E, Private
Desertion: 02Jul1865

Widow's Pension: 07May1891 in AL; App#514788

TOLBERT, Hezekiah Jr.
AKA: Ezekiel TALBOT; Hesekiah TALBOT
Birth: circa 1842; Macon Co, AL
Death: after 22Apr1930; Pollard, Escambia Co, AL
Burial: after Apr1930; Pollard, Escambia Co, AL; Pollard Cemetery
1860 Location: Covington County, AL
Description: fair complexion, black eyes, auburn hair
CSA: 09Jul1861 - 31Dec1862; 18th AL Infantry, Co B, Private
Union Enlistment: 1May1864; Ft. Barrancas; FL, Co F, Private
Engagements: Montgomery, AL
Promotions: 07Aug1864; Bugler
Desertion: 22May1865; Montgomery, AL
Military Finding: 19Nov1884; desertion charges dropped
Pension: 30Sep1890 in AL; App#920135, Cert#1051800

TRAMELL, Dawson T.
AKA: Dawson T. TRAMEL; Dorsen TRAMELL
Birth: Jun1836; Lincoln Co, GA
Death: 23Dec1916; Alachua Co, FL
1850 Location: Santa Rosa County, FL
Description: light complexion, blue eyes, light hair
CSA: 29Jan1863 - 09Dec1863; 11th FL Infantry, Co C, Private, deserted
Union Enlistment: 19Dec1863; Ft. Barrancas, FL; Co E, Private
Engagements: Marianna, FL; Pollard, AL
Promotions: 01May1864; Quartermaster Sergeant
Union Discharge: 17Nov1865; Tallahassee, FL; bounty due $75
Pension: 08Feb1896 in FL; App#1090055, Cert#1061124
Widow's Pension: 19Feb1917 in AL; App#1094378

TRUETT, James
AKA: James TREWETT; James TRUWITT
Birth: circa 1834; Darlington Co, SC
Death: after 09Oct1890
1860 Location: Walton County, FL

Description: fair complexion, blue eyes, light hair
CSA: 15Mar1862 - 10Jul1863; 1st FL Reorganized Infantry, Co E, Private, deserted
Union Enlistment: 05Mar1864; Ft. Barrancas, FL; Co C, Private
Promotions: Jan – Feb1865; Blacksmith
Desertion: 02Apr1865; Ft. Barrancas, FL
Pension: 09Oct1890; App#920138

TUCKER, Bartley F.
Birth: Dec1844; Coffee Co, AL
Death: Jun1900 - 24Aug1906; Walton Co, FL
1860 Location: Coffee County, AL
Description: light complexion, blue eyes, light hair
Union Enlistment: 11Mar1864; East Pass, FL; Co D, Private
Promotions: 17Dec1864; Corporal
Demotion: 10Sept1865; Private
Military Confinement: Jun - Sept1865; Ft. Pickens, FL; absent under charges
Union Discharge: 17Nov1865; Tallahassee, FL; bounty due $160
Pension: 13Oct1890 in FL; App#920140, Cert#1009013
Widow's Pension: 24Aug1906 in FL; App#854424, Cert#621471

TUCKER, Robert Garrett
AKA: Robert G. TUCKER
Birth: 14Jun1844; Pike Co, AL
Death: 24Jun1885 - 07Jan1893; McDade's Pond, Walton Co, FL
Burial: 24Jun1885 - 07Jan1893; Florala, Covington Co, AL; Greenwood Memorial Cemetery
1860 Location: Coffee County, AL
Description: fair complexion, blue eyes, light hair
Union Enlistment: 27Aug1864; East Pass, FL; Co D, Private
Desertion: 21Nov1864; Ft. Barrancas, FL
Widow's Pension: 07Jan1893 in AL; App#567819

TURNER, James H.
Birth: 30Jan1830; Pike Co, AL
Death: 08Mar1907; Milligan, Santa Rosa Co, FL
Burial: Mar1907; Milligan, Okaloosa Co, FL; Cobb Cemetery

Description: light complexion, dark eyes, dark hair
Union Enlistment: 25Jan1864; Ft. Barrancas, FL; Co B, Private
Promotions: 01Apr1864; Corporal
Military Confinement: Jul1865 - Sept1865; Ft. Pickens, FL
Union Discharge: 17Nov1865; Tallahassee, FL
Pension: 18Oct1890; App#920141, Cert#1054375
Widow's Pension: 13Apr1928 in FL; App#889229, Cert#670551

TURNER, John E.
Birth: circa 1836; Montgomery, Montgomery Co, AL
Death: before 21Oct1891; Alabama
1860 Location: Covington County, AL
Description: fair complexion, gray eyes, light hair
Union Enlistment: 05Oct1864; Ft. Barrancas, FL; Co D, Private
Union Discharge: 17Nov1865; Tallahassee, FL
Widow's Pension: 21Oct1891 in AL; App#483343, Cert#324105

TURNER, William S.
AKA: William T. TURNER
Birth: circa 1839; Pike Co, AL
Death: 05Sept1864; Ft. Barrancas, Escambia Co, FL
Description: light complexion, gray eyes, brown hair
Union Enlistment: 25Jan1864; Ft. Barrancas, FL; Co B, Private
Died: 05Sep1864; Ft. Barrancas, FL; bounty due $275
Widow's Pension: 15Apr1869; App#174135, Cert#160834

V

VANCE, Francis M. Vance, Francis M.
AKA: Frank M. VANCE
Birth: Feb1845; Washington Co, FL
Death: 20Jan1923; Iola, Grimes Co, TX
Description: fair complexion, blue eyes, dark hair
CSA: 31Mar1863 – 31Dec1863; 2nd Battalion FL Infantry, Co E, Private, deserted
Union Enlistment: 23Mar1864; Ft. Barrancas, FL; Co D, Private
Engagements: Montgomery, AL
Union Discharge: 17Nov1865; Tallahassee, FL; bounty due $120
Pension: 23Aug1903 in TX; App#1303312, Cert#1071856

VELALTO, Unknown
Union Enlistment: date unknown; Co A, Private

VON DER WENSE, August
AKA: August Vonder WENSE
Birth: circa 1825
Death: after 1890
Union Appointment: 05Jul1864; appointed by General Banks from civil life, Co B, 2nd Lt.
Honorable Discharge: 05Dec1864
Pension: 19Aug1890; App#976520, Cert#824110

VON SODEN, Charles
Birth: circa 1821; Hamburg, Germany
Death: before 15Jun1888; Missouri
1860 Location: Cook County, IL
Additional Union Service: 1863; 15th Army Corps, 3rd Division, General and Staff
Union Appointment: 29Mar1864; Co B, 2nd Lt.
Promotions: 29Mar1864; from 2nd Lt to Captain
Honorable Discharge: 15Nov1864; resigned
Widow's Pension: 15Jun1888 in MO; App#374770

VON WESSELY, Joseph W.
AKA: Joseph WESELY; Joseph W. VAN WESSELY; Joseph W. VON WESLEY
Birth: circa 1836; Austria
Death: 15Mar1883; Austria
Additional Union Service: 115th Regiment NY Volunteers, Co K, Private/Sergeant
Union Appointment: 29Mar1864; appointed by General Banks from civil life; Co D, 1st Lt, 3 years
Honorable Discharge: 08Dec1864
Widow's Pension: 21Apr1913 in Austria; App#1006412, Cert#772807

W

WALTERS, George
AKA: George WATERS; George WATTERS
Birth: circa 1844; Alabama
Death: after 27Jun1881
1860 Location: Henry County, AL
Description: fair complexion, blue eyes, light hair
CSA: 25Jun1863 - 23Dec1863; 4th Battalion FL Infantry, Co A, Private, deserted, records transferred to 11th FL Infantry, Co C.
Union Enlistment: 20Apr1864; East Pass, FL; Co E, Private
Disability Discharge: 29May1865; bounty due $75
Pension: 27Jun1881; App#424626, Cert#312521

WARD, Celestine Josiah
AKA: Teen WARD; Celestine WARD; Cilesteen WARD
Birth: 27Mar1829; Euchee Anna, Walton Co, FL
Death: 27Jun1891; Bratt, Escambia Co, FL
Burial: Jun1891; Bratt, Escambia Co, Florida; Godwin Cemetery
1860 Location: Walton County, FL
Description: light complexion, blue eyes, dark hair
CSA: 04Feb - 10May1863; 3rd Battalion FL Cavalry, Co D, Private, deserted; records transferred to 15th Confederate Cavalry, Co I.
Union Enlistment: 19Jan1864; Ft. Barrancas, FL; Co B, Private
Promotions: 01Apr1864; Sergeant
Desertion: 26Feb1865; Ft. Barrancas, FL
Military Finding: 04Apr1888; removal of desertion and request for honorable discharge denied; dishonorable discharge voided 8Apr1901
Pension: 18Oct1890 in AL; App#912659

WARD, Ira Jackson
AKA: Ira J. WARD; I. J. WARD
Birth: May1838; Henry Co, AL
Death: 23Jun1900 - 03Jul1901; Holmes Co, FL
1860 Location: Henry County, AL
Description: dark complexion, gray eyes, dark hair

CSA: 13May1862 - 18Sept1863; 6th FL Infantry, Co I, Private, deserted
Union Enlistment: 02Feb1864; Ft. Barrancas, FL; Co B, Private
Promotions: 01Apr1864; Corporal
Union Discharge: 17Nov1865; Tallahassee, FL; bounty due $160
Pension: 14Jul1890 in FL; App#1038866, Cert#780029
Widow's Pension: 03Jul1901 in FL; App#744455, Cert#544813

WARD, James Madison
Birth: circa 1831; Butler Co, AL
Death: 21Jun1880 - 1900 in Monroe Co, AL
1860 Location: Coffee County, AL
Description: light complexion, gray eyes, dark hair
CSA: 11Feb1862 - 30May1863; 33rd AL Infantry, Co A, Private, deserted
Union Enlistment: 24Mar1864; East Pass, FL; Co E, Private
Desertion: 25Jun1864; Ft. Barrancas, FL

WARD, John
Birth: circa 1828; Robeson Co, NC
Death: after 01May1880
1860 Location: Dale County, AL
Description: dark complexion, gray eyes, dark hair
CSA: 08Mar1862 - 25Aug1862; 33rd AL Infantry, Co G, Private, disability discharge
Union Enlistment: 13Jan1864; Ft. Barrancas, FL; Co A, Private
Military Confinement: 16Apr1865 - Sept1865; Ft. Pickens; by sentence of General Court Martial
Union Discharge: 17Nov1865; Tallahassee, FL; bounty due $275
Pension: 01May1880; App#359412, Cert#788340

WARD, John Brantley
AKA: John B. WARD
Birth: May1846; Henry Co, AL
Death: 1935; Walton Co, FL
1860 Location: Holmes County, FL
Description: dark complexion, brown eyes, dark hair

CSA: 13May1862 - 18Sept1863; 6th FL Infantry, Co I, Private, deserted
Union Enlistment: 25Jan1864; Ft. Barrancas, FL; Co B, Private
Union Discharge: 17Nov1865; Tallahassee, FL; bounty due $120
Pension: 20Apr1890 in FL; App#976511, Cert#786482

WARD, Michael
Birth: circa 1830; Henry Co, AL
Death: after 22Feb1866
1860 Location: Walton County, FL
Description: dark complexion, gray eyes, black hair
CSA: 31May1861 - 30Sept1861; 1st FL Infantry, Co K, Private, discharged. 11Mar1862 – 15Apr1863; 1st FL Reorganized Infantry, Co E, Private, disability discharge.
Union Enlistment: 04Jun1864; Ft. Barrancas, FL; Co F, Private
Promotions: 23Aug1864; Saddler
Union Discharge: 22Feb1866; Jacksonville, FL; arrived in Tallahassee 11Jan1866, sent to Jacksonville & returned, bounty due $100

WARD, William Peter
AKA: William WARD
Birth: circa 1844; Walton Co, FL
Death: 22Jul1887; Walton Co, FL
Description: fair complexion, dark eyes, light hair
Union Enlistment: 28Jan1864; Ft. Barrancas, FL; Co B, Private
Engagements: Expedition up Escambia Bay
Military Confinement: Jul - Sept1865; Ft. Pickens
Union Discharge: 17Nov1865; Tallahassee, FL; bounty due $275
Widow's Pension: 02Sept1914 in FL; App#483962, Cert#418923

WARREN, Andrew J.
Birth: circa 1830; Warren Co, GA
Death: after 25Jun1864
Description: fair complexion, blue eyes, light hair
CSA Service: 22Feb1862 - 30May1863; 33rd AL Infantry, Co A, Private/Corporal, deserted
Union Enlistment: 12Apr1864; East Pass, FL; Co E, Private

Desertion: 25Jun1864; Ft. Barrancas, FL

WATERS, Elisha M.
AKA: Elijah M. WATERS; Elisher WATERS
Birth: 10Dec1845; Escambia Co, FL
Death: 08Aug1930; Muscogee, Escambia Co, FL
Burial: Aug1930; Gateswood, Baldwin Co, AL; Clear Springs UMC Cemetery
1860 Location: Escambia County, FL
Description: dark complexion, blue eyes, dark hair
Union Enlistment: 26Mar1864; Ft. Barrancas, FL; Co A, Private
Military Charges: 29May1865; assault and robbery
Military Confinement: 27Jun1865 - 09Sept1865; Ft. Pickens
Union Discharge: 17Nov1865; Tallahassee, FL; bounty due $275
Pension: 30Oct1891 in AL; App#1069516, Cert# 1146909

WATERS, Jordan L.
Birth: Feb1842; Escambia Co, FL
Death: 01Jan1908 - 04May1908 in Baldwin Co, AL
Burial: 01Jan1908 - 04May1908; Gateswood, Baldwin Co, AL; Clear Springs UMC Cemetery
1860 Location: Escambia County, FL
Description: fair complexion, blue eyes, dark hair
CSA: 24Apr1862 - 24Sept1863; 3rd FL Battalion Cavalry, Co B, Private, transferred. 25Sept1863 – 23Dec1863; 15th Confederate Cavalry, Co D, deserted
Union Enlistment: 07Jan1864; Ft. Barrancas, FL; Co A, Private
Engagements: Marianna, FL; Pollard, AL; Montgomery, AL
Promotions: May - Jun1864; Bugler
Promotions: 1July1865; Corporal
Union Discharge: 17Nov1865; Tallahassee, FL; bounty due $120
Pension: 01Feb1904 in FL; App#1308257, Cert#1092755
Widow's Pension: 04May1908 in FL; App#892370, Cert#673907

WATERS, William H.
Birth: 02Feb1840; Florida
Death: 21Oct1898; Cantonment, Escambia Co, FL

Burial: Oct1898; Cantonment, Escambia Co, FL; Lathram Chapel Cemetery
1860 Location: Escambia County, FL
Description: dark complexion, gray eyes, black hair
CSA: 24Apr1862 - 24Sept1863; 3rd FL Battalion Cavalry, Co B, Sergeant/Private, transferred. 25Sept1863 – 23Dec1863; 15th Confederate Cavalry, Co D, deserted
Union Enlistment: 12Jan1864; Ft. Barrancas, FL; Co A, Private
Engagements: Marianna, FL; Montgomery, AL
Promotions: 01Apr1864; Corporal
Promotions: Sept – Oct1864; Quartermaster Sergeant
Military Confinement: 19Jun1865 - Sept1865; Ft. Pickens
Union Discharge: 17Nov1865; Tallahassee, FL; bounty due $275
Pension: 12Jul1883; App#489806
Widow's Pension: 26Nov1898 in FL; App#687168, Cert#557910
Minor's Pension: circa 1898; App#829648

WATSON, Anderson
Birth: circa 1822; Houston Co, GA
Death: 21Jul1870 - 20Mar1886; Florida
1860 Location: Walton County, FL
Description: dark complexion, hazel eyes, black hair
CSA: 25Mar1863 - 08Jun1863; 4th Battalion FL Infantry, Co C, Private, deserted, records transferred to 11th FL Infantry, Co K.
Union Enlistment: 15Mar1864; East Pass, FL; 1st Co D, Private
Union Discharge: 17Nov1865; Tallahassee, FL; bounty due $160
Minor's Pension: 20Mar1886 in FL; Calvin, App#397135

WATSON, Burton H.
Birth: circa 1845; Carroll Co, GA
Death: 07Jun1880 – 1900; Alabama
1860 Location: Santa Rosa County, FL
Description: light complexion, blue eyes, dark hair
CSA: 16Mar1862 - 29Aug1863; 1st FL Reorganized Infantry, Co E, Private, deserted
Union Enlistment: 07Jan1864; Ft. Barrancas, FL; Co A, Private
Engagements: Marianna, FL; Pollard, AL
Promotions: 01Apr1864; Corporal

Military Charges: 29May1865; assault and robbery of Abram McCloud, a black man with Elisha Waters and Charles Campbell
Military Confinement: 30May1865 - Sept1865; Ft. Pickens
Union Discharge: 17Nov1865; Tallahassee, FL; bounty due $275

WATSON, John W.
Birth: 14Aug1848; Carroll Co, GA
Death: 04Jan1880; Freeport, Walton Co, FL
1860 Location: Santa Rosa County, FL
Description: light complexion, blue eyes, dark hair
CSA: Jul1863 - 21Sept1863; 2nd FL Cavalry, Co G, Private, deserted
Union Enlistment: 24Feb1864; Ft. Barrancas, FL; Co A, Private
Engagements: Marianna, FL; Pollard, AL; Montgomery, AL
Union Discharge: 17Nov1865; Tallahassee, FL; bounty due $120
Widow's Pension: 23Jul1890 in FL; App#453036, Cert#313248

WATSON, William W.
Birth: Jan1840; Chambers Co, AL
Death: 28May1910 – 1920; Shelby Co, TX
1860 Location: Coffee County, AL
Description: light complexion, gray eyes, auburn hair
Union Enlistment: 11Mar1865; East Pass, FL; Co E, Private
Union Discharge: 17Nov1865; Tallahassee, FL; bounty due $100
Military Finding: 18Apr1887; desertion charge dropped
Pension: 30May1884 in AL; App#458685

WEEKS, Benjamin Washington
Birth: circa 1827; Dale Co, AL
Death: 10Sept1897 in Samson, Geneva Co, AL
Burial: Sept1897; Geneva, AL; Piney Grove Cemetery
1860 Location: Coffee County, Alabama
Description: dark complexion, gray eyes, dark hair
CSA: 12Jun1863 - 27Jun1863; 4th Battalion FL Infantry, Co A, Private, deserted, records transferred to 11th FL Infantry, Co C.
Union Enlistment: 24Mar1864; East Pass, FL; Co E, Private
Desertion: 04Apr1865
Military Finding: 31Jul1886; removal of desertion charge denied

Pension: 08Mar1880 in AL; App#377274
Widow's Pension: 29Feb1908 in AL; App#800808

WEEKS, Harmon
Birth: circa 1838; Coffee Co, AL
Description: fair complexion, blue eyes, light hair
Union Enlistment: 08Sept1864; Ft. Barrancas, FL; Co E, Private
Died: 10Oct1864; Ft. Barrancas, FL

WEEKS, Hiram
Birth: circa 1832; Coffee Co, AL
Death: after 31Oct1906; Geneva Co, AL
1850 Location: Coffee County, AL
Description: dark complexion, black eyes, dark hair
Union Enlistment: 10Oct1864; East Pass, FL; Co E, Private
Desertion: 04Apr1865
Pension: 26Apr1893; App#1150126

WEST, Benjamin L.
Birth: 06Oct1845; Pike Co, AL
Death: 14Oct1900; Santa Rosa Co, FL
Burial: Oct1900; Santa Rosa Co, FL; Coldwater RLDS Church
1860 Location: Santa Rosa County, FL
Description: fair complexion, blue eyes, dark hair
CSA: 08May1862 - 29Aug1863; 1st FL Reorganized Infantry, Co G, Private, deserted
Union Enlistment: 26Mar1864; Ft. Barrancas, FL; Co D, Private
Engagements: Montgomery, AL
Military Charges: 11Jul1865; court martial, assault with intent to kill, robbery (found not guilty)
Military Confinement: May1865 - Sept1865; Wetumpka, Elmore Co, AL
Desertion: 21Jul1865
Military Finding: 18Nov1886; desertion charges dropped
Pension: 19Nov1892 in FL; App#1139217
Widow's Pension: 09Aug1902 in FL; App#768289, Cert#586107

WEST, Leonard Frank
AKA: Lenard F. WEST

Birth: 27Jun1847; Pike Co, AL
Death: 07Dec1922 in Milton, Santa Rosa Co, FL
Burial: Dec1922; Santa Rosa Co, FL; Coldwater RLDS Church
1860 Location: Santa Rosa County, FL
Description: fair complexion, brown eyes, dark hair
Union Enlistment: 26Mar1864; Ft. Barrancas, FL; Co D, Private
Engagements: Montgomery, AL
Promotions: 01Apr1864; 5th Corporal
Union Discharge: 17Nov1865; Tallahassee, FL; bounty due $120
Pension: 31Dec1897 in FL; App#1203005, Cert#1156466

WHEELESS, Joshua E.
AKA: Joshua WEELESS; Joshua E. WHEELER; Joshua E. WHEELEES
Birth: May1827; Hancock Co, GA
Death: 26Jun1900 - 1910 in Bradford Co, FL
1860 Location: Coffee County, AL
Description: dark complexion, brown eyes, dark hair
CSA: 13Mar1862 - 31Dec1863; 33rd AL Infantry, Co K, Private, estimated desertion date
Union Enlistment: 06Jul1864; East Pass, FL; Co F, Private
Promotion: 07Aug1864; Bugler
Union Discharge: 17Nov1865; Tallahassee, FL; bounty due $75
Pension: 21Oct1890 in Florida; App#976523, Cert#808422

WHEELESS, Sion A.
AKA: Sion A. WHEELLESS; Sion A. WEELESS
Birth: circa 1849; Macon Co, AL
Death: after 17Nov1865
Description: fair complexion, gray eyes, dark hair
Union Enlistment: 09Jan1865; Ft. Barrancas, FL; Co F, Private
Union Discharge: 17Nov1865; Tallahassee, FL

WHITACRE, Edward
Union Enlistment: unknown place or length of service
Union Discharge: unknown length of service

WHITE, Asa
Birth: circa 1822; Conecuh Co, AL

1860 Location: Baldwin County, AL
Description: light complexion, blue eyes, dark hair
Union Enlistment: 19May1864; Ft. Barrancas, FL; Co A, Private
Died: 25Jun1864; Ft. Barrancas, FL
Widow's Pension: 18Apr1889 in AL; App#393168
Minor's Pension: 27Feb1894 in AL; Cyrus B, App#591155

WHITE, Joseph S.
Death: Jul1864 - 12Feb1867
Union Enlistment: 19May1864: Ft. Barrancas, FL; Co A, Private
Union Discharge: after Jul1864; likely deserted or died
Minor's Pension: 12Feb1867; App#142240, Cert#377922

WHITE, Robert J.
Birth: 25May1826; Conecuh Co, AL
Death: 15Dec1901; Baldwin Co, AL
Burial: Dec1901; Stapleton, Baldwin Co, AL; Stapleton Cemetery
1860 Location: Baldwin County, AL
Description: light complexion, blue eyes, dark hair
Union Enlistment: 19May1864; Ft. Barrancas, FL; Co F, Private
Desertion: 07Aug1865; Ft. Barrancas, FL
Military Finding: 16Dec1884; AWOL/desertion charges dropped
Pension: 26May1884 in AL; App#514137, Cert#1011888

WHITE, Samuel L. Jr.
Birth: circa 1846; Baldwin Co, AL
1860 Location: Baldwin County, AL
Description: fair complexion, blue eyes, light hair
Union Enlistment: 05Feb1864; Ft. Barrancas, FL; Co A, Private
Died: 22Oct1864; Ft. Barrancas, FL

WHITE, William E.
Birth: circa 1823; Henry Co, GA
Death: 20Mar1902 - 21May1909
1860 Location: Pike County, AL
Description: dark complexion, dark eyes, black hair
Union Enlistment: 13Dec1863; Ft. Barrancas, FL; Co A, Private
Engagements: Montgomery, AL
Promotions: 01Apr1864; 1st Sergeant

Military Confinement: 08May - Jun1865; Montgomery, AL
Union Discharge: 17Nov1865; Tallahassee, FL; bounty due $75
Pension: 20Mar1902; App#1282733
Widow's Pension: 21May1909 in AL; App#920497, Cert#705922

WHITTAKER, Elbert David
AKA: Albert D. WHITTAKER; David WHITTAKER; Elbert C. WHITAKER
Birth: Jan1848; Alabama
Death: 02Feb1920 – 1930; Alabama
1860 Location: Henry County, AL
Description: fair complexion, blue eyes, light hair
Union Enlistment: 24Jan1865; Ft. Barrancas, FL; Co C, Private
Desertion: 12Aug1865; Ft. Barrancas, FL

WICKLIFFE, Joseph H.
AKA: James H. WICKLIFFE
Birth: 11Dec1840; Madison Co, IL
Death: 12Jun1880 - 04Jun1900
1860 Location: Madison County, IL
Additional Union Service: 117th Illinois Infantry, Co F, Corporal
Union Appointment: 29Mar1864; Ft. Barrancas, FL; Co C, 1st LT
Engagements: 15 Mile House/Gonzalez House
Honorable Discharge: 22Jun1865; resigned
Widow's Pension: 17Oct1903 in KS; App#793110, Cert#584048

WILCOX, Mark
Birth: Dec1836; Appling Co, GA
Death: 16Ju1909; Holmes Co, FL
Burial: Jul1909; Bonifay, Holmes Co, FL; Wilcox Cemetery
1860 Location: Holmes County, FL
Description: fair complexion, gray eyes, light hair
CSA: 01May1863 - 01Jul1863; 2nd FL Cavalry, Co A, Private, War, transferred. 13Sept1863 – 31Dec1863; 5th FL Battalion Cavalry, Co E, deserted.
Union Enlistment: 30Dec1863; Ft. Barrancas, FL; Co A, Private
Desertion: 10Nov1864; East Pass, FL

Military Finding: 11Apr1893; removal of desertion and an honorable discharge denied
Pension: 23Nov1888; App#679770

WILKINSON, John J.
Birth: Nov1847; Coffee Co, AL
Death: 14Oct1912; Milligan, Santa Rosa Co, FL
Burial: Oct1912; Milligan, Okaloosa Co, FL; Wilkinson-Baggett Cemetery
1860 Location: Santa Rosa County, FL
Description: light complexion, blue eyes, dark hair
Union Enlistment: 25Jan1864; Ft. Barrancas, FL; Co B, Private
Union Discharge: 17Nov1865; Tallahassee, FL; bounty due $120
Pension: 08Nov1890; App#912682, Cert#1041875
Widow's Pension: 18Apr1921; App#1172894, Cert#913328
Minor's Pension: 07Dec1912; App#997656, Cert#779560

WILKINSON, William T. Fletcher
Birth: Apr1845; Coffee Co, AL
Death: 15Nov1921; Milligan, Okaloosa Co, FL
Burial: Nov1921; Milligan, Okaloosa Co, FL; Wilkinson-Baggett Cemetery
1860 Location: Santa Rosa County, FL
Description: light complexion, blue eyes, light hair
Union Enlistment: 25Jan1864; Ft. Barrancas, FL; Co B, Private
Engagements: Montgomery, AL
Union Discharge: 17Nov1865; Tallahassee, FL; bounty due $120
Pension: 08Mar1897; App#1188380, Cert#1045641
Widow's Pension: 09Dec1921; App#1182364, Cert#921277

WILLIAMS, Jeremiah
Birth: circa 1847; Jackson Co, MS
Death: after 17Nov1865
Description: black complexion, black eyes, black hair
Union Enlistment: 15Aug1865; Leon Co, FL; Co C, Under Cook
Union Discharge: 17Nov1865; Tallahassee, FL

WILLIAMS, John C.
AKA: John WILLIAMS

Birth: circa 1841; Barbour Co, AL
Death: 05Oct1891 - 08May1895; Alabama
1860 Location: Barbour County, AL
Description: fair complexion, blue eyes, light hair
Union Enlistment: 27Aug1864; East Pass, FL; Co D, Private
Desertion: 27Aug1865; Ft. Barrancas, FL
Military Finding: 17Oct1884; desertion charges dropped
Pension: 05Oct1891; App#1062265, Cert#836101
Widow's Pension: 08May1895 in AL; App#613671, Cert#486895

WILLIAMS, Wyatt Green
AKA: Wyatt G. WILLIAMS
Birth: 1843; Randolph Co, GA
Death: 1894; Houston Co, AL
Burial: 1894; Grangeburg, Houston Co, AL; Friendship UMC Cemetery
1860 Location: Henry County, AL
Description: light complexion, gray eyes, dark hair
CSA: 04Jun1861 – 02Feb1862; 6th AL Infantry, Co K, Private, transferred. 02 Feb 1862 - 28 Aug 1864; 20th Battalion AL Light Artillery, Co B, Private, deserted
Union Enlistment: 27Mar1865; East Pass, FL; Co A, Private
Desertion: 12Aug1865; Six Mile Camp, Leon Co, FL

WINFIELD, Mathew M.
Birth: circa 1826; Wilcox Co, AL
Burial: Aug1864; Escambia Co, FL; Ft. Barrancas National Cemetery
1860 Location: Walton County, FL
Description: light complexion, blue eyes, dark hair
CSA: 03Apr1863 - 31Oct1863; 6th AL Cavalry, Co K, Private, deserted
Union Enlistment: 02Apr1864; East Pass, FL; Co E, Private
Promotions: 20Jun1864; Sergeant
Died: 10Aug1864; Ft. Barrancas, bounty due $75
Widow's Pension: 06Nov1866; App#136842

WISE, Daniel
Birth: circa 1821; Sumter Co, SC
Death: after 16Aug1864
Description: fair complexion, blue eyes, light hair
Union Enlistment: 16Aug1864; East Pass, FL; not accepted by the Regimental Surgeon

WISE, Hezekiah
AKA: Ezekiel WISE
Birth: circa 1841; Coffee Co, AL
Death: after 08Oct1891
1860 Location: Washington County, FL
Description: fair complexion, blue eyes, light hair
Union Enlistment: 07Apr1864; Ft. Barrancas, FL; Co E, Private
Union Discharge: 17Nov1865; Tallahassee, FL; bounty due $75
Pension: 08Oct1891; App#1062571, Cert#1058986

WOODHAM, James R. N.
Birth: circa 1840; Dale Co, AL
Death: after 22May1865
Description: fair complexion, blue eyes, brown hair
Union Enlistment: 20May1864; East Pass, FL; Co F, Private
Engagements: Pine Barren Creek, FL; Montgomery, AL
Promotions: 03Aug1864; Sergeant
Desertion: 22May1865; Montgomery, AL

WOODHAM, Joseph R.
Birth: circa 1819; Darlington Co, SC
1860 Location: Dale County, AL
Description: fair complexion, blue eyes, dark hair
Union Enlistment: 23Dec1863; Ft. Barrancas, FL; Co A, Private
Died: 02Oct1864; Ft. Barrancas, FL
Widow's Pension: 23Aug1869; App#178996, Cert#151548

WORLEY, Elias S.
AKA: Elias WORLEY
Birth: Sep1845; Pike Co, AL
Death: 12Feb1931; Holmes Co, FL
Burial: 1931; Holmes Co, FL; East Mount Zion Methodist Church

1860 Location: Pike County, AL
Description: light complexion, blue eyes, dark hair
Union Enlistment: 25Jan1864; Ft. Barrancas, FL; Co B, Private
Engagements: Montgomery, AL
Union Discharge: 17Nov1865; Tallahassee, FL; bounty due $120
Pension: 13Jul1896 in FL; App#1179357, Cert#1092912

WORLEY, Peter Coleman
AKA: Coleman P. WORLEY
Birth: circa 1846; Pike Co, AL
1860 Location: Pike County, AL
Description: fair complexion, black eyes, black hair
Union Enlistment: 24Feb1864; Ft. Barrancas, FL; Co B, Private
Died: 10Mar1865; Ft. Barrancas, FL; bounty due $275

WRIGHT, Richard B.
Birth: circa 1824; Lawrence Co, GA
Death: 27Au1890 – 1900; Baldwin Co, AL
Burial: Aug1890–1900; Bay Minette, Baldwin Co, AL; Bay Minette Cemetery
1860 Location: Baldwin County, AL
Description: dark complexion, gray eyes, grey hair
Union Enlistment: 26Apr1864; Ft. Barrancas, FL; Co E, Private
Engagements: Marianna, FL; Pollard, AL; Blakely, AL; Greenville, AL; Montgomery, AL
Promotions: 01Sept1864; Corporal
Promotions: 01May1865; Sergeant
Union Discharge: 17Nov1865; Tallahassee, FL; bounty due $75
Pension: 27Aug1890 in AL; App#974248, Cert#713258

WRIGHT, William
Birth: circa 1844; Alabama
1860 Location: Walton County, FL
Description: fair complexion, blue eyes, light hair
Union Enlistment: 28Jan1864; Ft. Barrancas, FL; Co B, Private
Died: 13Jun1864; Ft. Barrancas, FL; bounty due $275

WYRICK, Samuel
AKA: Samuel WARRICK; Samuel WARIC; Samuel WARICK

Birth: circa 1841; Muscogee Co, GA
Death: after 01Oct1864
1860 Location: Pike County, AL
Description: dark complexion, gray eyes, dark hair
CSA: 29Jan1863 - 23Dec1863; 4th Battalion FL Infantry, Co A, Private, deserted, records transferred to 11th FL Infantry, Co C
Union Enlistment: 05Jan1864; Ft. Barrancas, FL; Co B, Private
Desertion: 01Oct1864; Dale, AL; on secret service

Y

YARBOROUGH, Benjamin A.
Birth: circa 1839; Muscogee Co, GA
Death: after 07Jul1890
1860 Location: Russell County, AL
Description: fair complexion, blue eyes, dark hair
CSA: 10Mar1862 - 31Dec1862; Hardaway's (Hurt's) AL Light Artillery Battery, Private, deserted
Union Enlistment: 05Mar1864; Ft. Barrancas, FL; Co D, Private
Promotions: 01Apr1864; Sergeant
Union Discharge: 17Nov1865; Tallahassee, FL; bounty due $120
Pension: 07Jul1890; App#792074, Cert#1053012

YATES, Jordan
AKA: Gordon YATES
Birth: circa 1838; Jackson Co, FL
1860 Location: Washington County, FL
Description: light complexion, blue eyes, dark hair
Union Enlistment: 03Apr1864; East Pass, FL; Co E, Private
Military Confinement: Oct1864; Ft. Pickens, FL
Died: 09Nov1864; Ft. Pickens, FL; bounty due $75
Military Finding: 11Jun1887; charges of desertion removed
Widow's Pension: 20Jul1869; App#177782, Cert#487498

YATES, Levi
Birth: 11Jul1836; Jackson Co, FL
Death: 28Feb1908; Washington Co, FL
1860 Location: Washington Co, FL
Description: fair complexion, blue eyes, brown hair

CSA: 25Mar1863 - 08Jun1863; 4th Battalion FL Infantry, Co C, Private, deserted, records transferred to 11th FL Infantry, Co K.
Union Enlistment: 12Apr1864; East Pass, FL; Co E, Private
Promotions: 12Apr1864; 7th Sergeant
Military Confinement: 11Sept1864 - Jun1865; Ft. Pickens
Union Discharge: 17Nov1865; Tallahassee, FL; bounty due $75
Pension: 16Jul1890; App#807891, Cert#1015560
Widow's Pension: 26Sept1916; App#1076600, Cert#819902

YON, Darrell
AKA: Derrell YAWN; Derrell YON
Birth: circa 1821; Lawrence Co, GA
1850 Location: Dale Co, AL
Description: dark complexion, blue eyes, dark hair
Union Enlistment: 28Jan1864; Ft. Barrancas, FL; Co B, Private
Died: 27Jul1864; Ft. Barrancas, FL; bounty due $275
Widow's Pension: 13Apr1868; App#159827, Cert#129520
Minor's Pension: after 1865; App#226032, Cert#173840

YON, Joshua A.
AKA: Joshua YAN; Joshua YARN
Birth: circa 1848; Georgia
Death: 24May1915; Lakeland, Polk Co, FL
1860 Location: Coffee County, AL
Description: dark complexion, gray eyes, dark hair
Union Enlistment: 27Aug1864; East Pass, FL; Co D, Private
Engagements: Raid in South Alabama; Montgomery, AL
Union Discharge: 17Nov1865; Tallahassee, FL
Pension: 11Nov1892 in AL; App#1137028, Cert#944432
Widow's Pension: 11Aug1915 in FL; App#1051634, Cert#819026

Known Families in the 1st FCUV

1. **Henry Hilliard and Seaborn S. BAGGETT were brothers**
Both men were born in Alabama. The family was in Coffee County, AL in 1850. Seaborn had moved to Santa Rosa County, FL by 1860. Seaborn joined the 33rd AL Infantry, Co K on 13Mar1862 and likely deserted around 12/31/1863. Seaborn joined the 1st FCUV on 26Apr1864. Henry does not appear to have served in the CSA. He was eighteen on 18August1864 when he joined the 1st FCUV. Both served in the 1st FCUV until mustered out 17Nov1865. Seaborn was a Sergeant from 10Jan1865 until 17Nov1865.

2. **James, Lewis and Joel BAGGETT were brothers**
James was born in Covington County, AL, Lewis was born in Walton County, FL and Joel was born in Santa Rosa County, FL. The family was in Walton County, FL in 1850. James does not appear to have served in the CSA. Lewis and Joel both served in the 24th AL Infantry, Co F. Both joined 14October1861 in Mobile. Lewis received a disability discharge on 10December1861 due to general debility due to prior malarial infection. Joel deserted on 9Feb1863. James enlisted with the 1st FCUV on 9January1864, Joel enlisted on 12January1864 and Lewis enlisted 25January1864. James and Lewis both died during service with the 1st FCUV, James of typhoid fever and Lewis of consumption (TB). Joel deserted 23May1865 and died in Santa Rosa Co, FL on 14Oct1873.

3. **Jacob H. BELL and Francis M. BELL were father and son**
Jacob was born in Duplin County, NC and Francis was born in Dale County, AL. The family was in Walton County, FL in 1850. Based on his discharge papers, Jacob was probably closer to 50 at the time of his enlistment, not the forty-four he indicated on his enlistment papers. He enlisted on 26Mar1864 so it is possible he was trying to avoid a potential draft. The Confederates had extended the upper age for the draft to fifty in February1864. Francis, his son, enlisted with the 1st FCUV on 23Mar1864 at the age of nineteen. There is no evidence that either served with the

Confederacy before enlisting with the Union. Jacob was given a disability discharge on 14Apr1865 after achieving a promotion to Sergeant. Francis was promoted to Corporal in December1864 and completed his service with the Union mustering out on 17November1865.

4. **James Thomas and John Askar BOLTON were brothers**
Both men were born in Pike County, AL. The family was in Pike County, AL in 1850 and Santa Rosa County, FL in 1860. James, the older of the two, was nineteen at his enlistment on 19January1864. There is no evidence that he had served with the Confederacy before joining the 1st FCUV. John was eighteen at his enlistment six days later on 25January1864. Both served their term of service, mustering out on 17November1865.

5. **Elam D., Bailey R., and William B. BOUTWELL were brothers**
All three were born in Pike County, AL. The family was in Pike County, AL in 1850 and 1860. Elam was the oldest of the three brothers being 21 years old at the time of his enlistment with the 1st FCUV. He does not appear to have served with the CSA prior to his enlistment on 16Mar1864 on Santa Rosa Island. He enlisted with his youngest brother, William who appears to have been drafted into the 61st AL Infantry, Co G and has records that have him present with the 61st AL from 6Oct to 31Oct1863. Their brother Bailey, who was 20 years old in March 1864, enlisted six days before his two brothers on 10Mar1864, also on Santa Rosa Island.

6. **Martin, Isom, Benjamin R. and Jasper BRAXTON were brothers**
Martin and Oliver were born in Barbour County, AL. The other three men were born in Henry County, AL. The family was in Henry County, AL in 1850 and except for Martin they were all in Holmes County, FL in 1860. Martin was in Monroe County, AL in 1860. Martin was the oldest of the Braxton brothers and also the first to join the 1st FCUV on 20December1863. Though thirty-four at the time of his enlistment there doesn't appear to be a record of

service with the Confederacy. Next to join were Benjamin and Isom who joined the 1st FCUV ten days later on 30December1863. Both had been drafted into the 4th FL Infantry that was then merged into the 11th FL Infantry with a number of other undermanned regiments. Benjamin's Confederate records indicate he was present from 25Mar to 15May1863 in Company I and Isom was present from 25Mar to 3July1863 in Company K. Jasper was the youngest of the brothers and the next to enlist on 20June1864, likely to avoid being drafted as he was just eighteen. He had no service with the CSA that could be found. Finally, their brother Oliver joined on 8September1864. He had also enlisted on 25Mar1863 in the 4th FL Infantry along with brothers Benjamin and Isom. He appears to have deserted with them but was caught in December 1863, spent some time in the hospital, was returned to the 11th FL Infantry regiment, given a furlough a month later and deserted in September1864. They all mustered out of the 1st FCUV on 17Nov1865 except for possibly Oliver. There is a card in his records indicating he died in December1864 but records have him alive and in the census through 1900. He filed for a pension though he did not receive funds before his death likely due to his confusing records.

7. **John Wesley and George Owen BROWN were brothers**
Both men were born in Walton County, FL. The family was in Walton County, FL in 1850 and George was in Holmes County, FL in 1860. George was the younger of the two brothers, being just eighteen at his enlistment with the 1st FCUV. He enlisted on 3August1864 and deserted on 10July1865. The desertion charge was dropped in February1889. He does not appear to have any Confederate service so he possibly joined the 1st FCUV to avoid being drafted once he was eighteen. His brother John enlisted with the 1st FCUV on 19November1864 and deserted during the Raid on the Florida and Alabama Railroad during the Mobile Campaign on 1April1865. However, he was given a pension in 1890 so his records may be missing some details on the approval of a request to drop desertion charges.

8. **Evan and James D. BUTLER were brothers**
Both men were born in Henry County, AL. The family was in Henry County, AL in 1850 and 1860. Evan enlisted in the 4th FL Battalion Infantry, Co C on 2February1863 and deserted on 12August1863 before his records were transferred to the 11th FL Infantry. He enlisted in the 1st FCUV on 2January1864. James D. served in the 37th AL Infantry, Co E from 2May1862 until he was paroled at Vicksburg, MS on 10July1863. He enlisted in the 1st FCUV on 28November1864. Evan served in the 1st FCUV until the unit was mustered out of service on 17November1865. James D. deserted the 1st FCUV on 4August1865.

9. **James W. and William Henry CARMICHAEL were brothers**
Both men were born in Washington County, FL. The family was in Washington County, FL in 1850. James W. enlisted in the 2nd FL Cavalry, Co G. on 23August1862 and was transferred (unit not provided) and subsequently deserted about 31October1863. He enlisted with the 1st FCUV on 14December1863 and deserted on the Raid to Marianna, FL on 9October1864. His brother William Henry does not appear to have served with the Confederacy. He was eighteen at the time he enlisted with the 1st FCUV on 25January1864. He served until 8May1865. His desertion charge was dropped 20October1884.

10. **William Eli and Daniel Nathaniel CARNLEY were brothers**
Both men were born in Pike County, AL. The family was in Pike County, AL in 1850. Neither man appears to have served with the Confederacy prior to enlistment with the 1st FCUV. They enlisted together on 5March1864 and both served until the regiment was mustered out on 17November1865.

11. **Elijah Gibson, Joseph B., and Frederick D. CARROLL were brothers**
Elijah was born in Twiggs County, GA. Joseph and Frederick were born in Dale County, AL. Elijah was in Barbour County, AL in 1850 and in Coffee County, AL in 1860. Joseph was in Barbour County, AL in both 1850 and 1860. Frederick was in Barbour County, AL in 1850 and Walton County, FL in 1860. Elijah does

not appear to have served with the Confederacy prior to enlistment with the 1st FCUV. Frederick might have served with the Confederacy prior to his Union enlistment but it can't be determined from the records. Joseph did serve with the 4th FL Infantry, Co H as a 2nd Lieutenant from 18September1861 until 31March1863. He resigned his commission due to ill health. He apparently had difficulties in remaining at home due to efforts to draft him into further service. He was enlisted in the 11th FL Infantry, Co C. on 30June1863 and likely deserted on or before 31December1863. Joseph enlisted with the 1st FCUV on 15February1864 and his brothers joined him in early 1865, Frederick on20January1865 and Elijah on 7April1865. Joseph was appointed to 2nd Lieutenant on 29Mar1864 and 1st Lieutenant 8February1865. Frederick deserted on 22May1865. Elijah died on 11November1865. Joseph served until the regiment was mustered out on 17November1865.

12. **Lemuel and William Leonard CARTER were brothers**
Both men were born in Dale County, AL. They were both in Walton County, FL in 1860. Lemuel enlisted in the 57th AL Infantry, Co K on 16March1863 and deserted on 1July1863. Leonard served briefly in the 57th AL Infantry, Co K, enlisting on 21October1863 and deserting ten days later on 31October1863. They enlisted together into the 1st FCUV on 11March1864. Lemuel died two months later on 26May1864. Leonard served with the 1st FCUV until the regiment was mustered out on 17November1865.

13. **John Wesley and James Jackson CHANCEY were father and son**
John Wesley was born in Darlington County, SC. James Jackson was born in Dale County, AL. The family was in Coffee County, AL in 1850 and 1860. Neither appears to have served with the Confederacy. It is possible they joined the Union to avoid being drafted. They joined the 1st FCUV on 27August1864 and both served with the regiment until it was mustered out of the Army on 17November1865.

14. **James Alexander and Micajah Allen COCKCROFT were brothers**

Both men were born in Walton County, FL. The family was in Walton County, FL in both 1850 and 1860. Neither appears to have served with the Confederacy prior to enlistment with the 1st FCUV. They both enlisted with the 1st FCUV on 23March1864 and both served until the regiment was mustered out on 17November1865.

15. **James Jackson and Joseph Jerold COON were father and son**

James was born in Twiggs County, GA. Joseph was born in Coffee County, AL. The family was in Coffee County, AL in 1850 and Covington County, AL in 1860. Neither appears to have served with the Confederacy prior to enlistment with the Union. Both were an age at enlistment that might indicate an effort to avoid the Confederate draft in their enlistment with the 1st FCUV. They both enlisted on 24February1864. James served until he died of cholera on 6September1864. Joseph deserted on 22December1864.

16. **John and Richard CURLEE were brothers**

John was born in Henry County, GA and Richard was born in Stewart County, GA. The family was in Holmes County, FL in 1860. John served with the 4th FL Infantry, Co H from 7September1861 until 31January1864. Richard served with the 6th FL Infantry, Co I from 8May1862 until June1864. From 28April1863 until 11August1863 the muster roll records for Richard indicates he was with the 4th FL Infantry at Vicksburg. Both joined the 1st FCUV on 25September1864. Both deserted on 25February1865. Richard was hanged by Holmes County militia sometime after 25February1865. Richard was reportedly a lieutenant in the notorious "Rhodes Gang", one of a number of gangs who roamed the Florida panhandle during the war.

17. **Hiram D., Daniel Monroe, John and Emanuel G. W. DANSBY were brothers**

All four of the Dansby brothers were born in Barbour County, AL. The family was in Barbour County, AL in both 1850 and 1860. Hiram and Emanuel joined the 39th AL Infantry, Co C on 12May1862. Daniel joined a few months earlier on 10March1862 and John joined a few days before on 10May1862. Hiram received a disability discharge on 12July1862. Emanuel likely deserted after 30June1862. Daniel likely deserted sometime after 31December1862. John likely deserted sometime after 3October1863. They all joined the 1st FCUV on 20May1864. John died of scurvy on 14December1864. The other three all served with the 1st FCUV until it mustered out of service on 17November1865.

18. **Wilson A. and Alexander T. DAVIS were brothers**

Both men were born in Conecuh County, AL. The family was in Conecuh County, AL in 1850 and Monroe County, AL in 1860. It is possible that both men served with the Confederacy but records could not be located with any certainty. Both joined the 1st FCUV on 15March1864. Wilson's only muster record with the 1st FCUV is found in the unassigned section of the microfilm rolls with limited information on his service. Alexander served as a Sergeant from early in his enlistment until the regiment mustered out on 17November1865.

19. **William P., George W., and William C. DOCKINS were father and sons**

William P. was born in Clarke County, AL. His two sons were both born in Butler County, AL. The family was in Butler County, AL in 1850 and Covington County, AL in 1860. None of them appear to have served with the Confederacy prior to enlistment with the 1st FCUV. William C. was the first of the three to enlist with the 1st FCUV, enlisting on 16August1864. William P. and George W. enlisted together on 6October1864. Both boys served until the regiment mustered out on 17November1865. William P. deserted on 8August1865.

20. **James D. and Joseph William DONALDSON were brothers**
Both men were born in Coffee County, AL. The family was in Coffee County, AL in both 1850 and 1860. Joseph does not appear to have served with the Confederacy prior to enlistment with the 1st FCUV. James served with the 57th AL Infantry, Co K from 16March1863 until he deserted on 1September1863. James enlisted with the 1st FCUV on 19January1864 and Joseph enlisted on 25September1864. They both served until the regiment mustered out on 17November1865.

21. **John P., Young R., and Samuel A. ELLISON were brothers**
John was born in Gwinnett County, GA. Young was born in Walton County, GA and Samuel was born in Stewart County, GA. The family was in Early County, GA in 1850 and Henry County, AL in 1860. John does not appear to have served with the Confederacy prior to his enlistment with the 1st FCUV. Young and Samuel both served with the 4th FL Infantry, Co A; Young from 29January1863 and Samuel from November1863. The 4th FL Infantry was consolidated into the 11th FL Infantry in June 1864. However, neither man served with the 11th FL. They had both deserted on 9December1863. Samuel and Young enlisted with the 1st FCUV on 17December1863 and John enlisted on 15February1864. Young died of a liver ailment on 19May1864. John died of diarrhea on 6August1864. Samuel mustered out on 17November1865.

22. **Asa and Phillip FAULK were brothers**
Asa was born in Houston County, GA and Phillip was born in Pike County, AL. The family was in Henry County, AL in 1850 and Santa Rosa County, FL in 1860. Asa served with the 1st FL Reorganized Infantry, Co F from 21March1862 until 1September1863 when he deserted. Phillip does not appear to have served with the Confederacy. He possibly joined the 1st FCUV to avoid being drafted by the Confederacy. He joined the 1st FCUV first, enlisting on 30May1864. Asa enlisted a few days later on 6June1864. Asa served with the 1st FCUV until it mustered out on 17November1865. Phillip was listed as deserting

on 1August1865 but that was dropped in July 1869 and his discharge was set for 17November1865.

23. **Richard and John Franklin FOWLER were brothers**
Both men were born in Henry County, AL. The family was in Henry County, AL in both 1850 and 1860. Both men joined, or was drafted in, Captain Tanner's Company, FL Infantry which would become Company F in the 11th FL Infantry; Richard on 1July1863 and John on 9July1863. Both deserted a month later on 12August1863 before the unit was consolidated with the 11th Florida Infantry. Richard joined the 1st FCUV on 5January1864 and John joined on 15February1864. John deserted on 12January1865 and Richard deserted on 5May1865. Richard's desertion charge was dropped on 10October1884 and his discharge date set as 5May1865.

24. **Silas GAINEY and Silas Jackson Gainey were father and son**
Silas, Sr. was born in Burke County, GA. Silas, Jr. was born in Walton County, FL. The family was in Walton County, FL in both 1850 and 1860. Neither appears to have served in the Confederacy before their enlistment with the Union. They both enlisted with the 1st FCUV on 25September1864. They both served until mustered out on 17November1865.

25. **James Millard and Seth J. GASKIN were brothers**
Both James and Seth were born in Walton County, FL. The family was in Walton County, FL in 1850 and Santa Rosa County, FL in 1860. James enlisted, or was drafted, into the 5th FL Infantry, Co I on 23April1862 but does not appear to have actually served. He was discharged on 9June1862. Seth served in the 3rd FL Battalion Cavalry, Co D from 4October1862 until 12August1863. The 3rd FL Battalion Cavalry was consolidated into the 15th Confederate Cavalry in September1863 and Seth was dropped from the records at the end of December 1863. They both enlisted with the 1st FCUV on 25January1864. They were both promoted to Sergeant. Seth died of diarrhea on 26September1864 while stationed at the Santa Rosa Island recruiting camp. James died

of erysipelas on 14May1865 and is buried at Ft. Barrancas National Cemetery.

26. **Joseph D. and Harmon S. GATLIN were brothers**

Both men were born in Butler County, AL. The family was in Lowndes County, AL in 1850 and Joseph was in Covington County, AL in 1860. Joseph served briefly in the 57th AL Infantry, Co. K from 16March to his desertion on 1July1863. Harmon served with the 1st FL Infantry, Co. A. He enlisted on 22July1861 and received a disability discharge on 16November1861. Joseph enlisted with the 1st FCUV on 3April1864 and Harmon enlisted four days later on 7April1864. Harmon was listed as a deserter on 1May1865 but the charge was dropped in June 1883. Joseph served with the 1st FCUV until it mustered out on 17November1865.

27. **Jordan J. and Sidney GIBSON were brothers**

Both men were born in Henry County, AL. The family was in Henry County, AL in both 1850 and 1860. Sidney doesn't appear to have served with the Confederacy. Jordan served with the 4th FL Battalion Infantry, Co D from 29January1863 until he deserted on 10August1863. His records were transferred to the 11th FL Infantry, Co C but he had already deserted. Sidney enlisted with the 1st FCUV on 29December1863 and Jordan enlisted on 10June1864. They both died while serving with the 1st FCUV. Sidney died on 27September1864 of diarrhea and Jordan died on 18October1864 of inflammation of the bowels.

28. **Albert and Lorenzo Dow GILL were brothers**

Albert was born in Marion County, GA. Lorenzo was born in Georgia but it is unclear in which county. The family was in Dale County, AL in 1850. Both served with the 4th FL Battalion Infantry, Co. A. Lorenzo enlisted, or was drafted, on 29January1863 and Albert enlisted, or was drafted, on 4October1863. Both deserted on 9December1863 and their records were transferred to the 11th FL Infantry, Co C in 1864. They both enlisted with the 1st FCUV on 17December1863. Albert died of unknown causes on

27August1865 and Lorenzo served until mustered out on 17November1865.

29. **John H. and John Daniel GIVENS were father and son**
John H. was born in Barnwell County, SC. John D. was born in Coffee County, AL. The family was in Dale County, AL in 1850 and in Baldwin County, AL in 1860. Neither appears to have served with the Confederacy prior to enlistment with the Union. They both enlisted on 7February1864. John Daniel died of typhoid fever on 2June1864. John H was listed as deserted on 8August1865. The desertion charge was dropped on 5May1885.

30. **William Franklin and William Spencer HARDY were father and son**
William Franklin was born in Montgomery County, GA. William Spencer was born in Shelby County, TN. The family was in Cass County, GA in 1850 and Henry County, AL in 1860. There is no evidence that William Franklin served with the Confederacy prior to Union service. It is possible that William Spencer did but records could not be sufficiently narrowed. William Spencer enlisted with the 1st FCUV on 30March1864 and his father enlisted on 6April1864. William Franklin mustered out on 17November1865. William Spencer died of typhoid fever on 9June1864.

31. **Wiley F. and Jonathan D. HARRISON were father and son**
Wiley F. was born in Jones County, GA. Jonathan D. was born in Henry County, AL. The family was in Henry County, AL in 1860. There is no evidence that either served with the Confederacy prior to enlisting with the 1st FCUV. Wiley F. enlisted on 19January1864 and Jonathan D. enlisted on 27March1865. Both mustered out on 17November1865.

32. **Phillip G. and William J. HATCHER were brothers**
Phillip G. was born in Crawford County, GA. William J. was born in Lee County, GA. The family was in Lee County, GA in 1850 and Decatur County, GA in 1860. There is no evidence that either served in the Confederacy prior to service with the 1st FCUV. They

enlisted together on 29June1864 and deserted together on 16November1864.

33. **John M. L. and James Wilburn HATHAWAY were brothers**
Both men were born in Dale County, AL. The family was in Dale County, AL in both 1850 and 1860. There is no evidence that either served with the Confederacy prior to Union service. John enlisted on 3April1864 and James Wilburn enlisted on 25September1864. They both served until mustered out on 17November1865.

34. **James T. and Thomas O. HATHCOCK were brothers**
Both men were born in Alabama. The family was in Covington County, AL in 1850 and 1860. There is no evidence that either served with the 1st FCUV prior to enlistment with the Union. They enlisted together on 29September1864 and deserted together on 19January1865.

35. **John Wesley and William P. HINOTE were brothers**
Both John Wesley and William P. were born in Henry County, AL. The family was in Dale County, AL in 1850 and Santa Rosa County, FL in 1860. John Wesley is listed with the 6th AL Cavalry, Co I from 29October to 31October1863. He likely deserted after being drafted. There is no evidence that William P. served with the Confederacy prior to enlistment with the Union. They enlisted together in the 1st FCUV on 29April1864 and served until mustered out on 17November1865.

36. **John D., Andrew Lewis (Jr.) and Henry A. HOLMAN were brothers**
All of the Holman brothers were born in Baldwin County, AL. The family was in Baldwin County, AL in 1850 and 1860. John D. served first with the 3rd Battalion FL Cavalry from 24April1862 until it was transferred into the 15th Confederate Cavalry on 24September1863. He deserted on 23December1863. No records were located for either Andrew Lewis or Henry A. with the Confederacy. Andrew Lewis enlisted with the 1st FCUV on 9January1864. John D. joined three days later on 12January1864. Henry A. enlisted on 26July1864. Andrew Lewis

and Henry A. both died while serving. Andrew Lewis died of chronic diarrhea on 28October1864 and Henry A. died of scurvy on 16October1864. John D. served until the regiment mustered out on 17November1865.

37. Thomas J. and George F. HUDSON were brothers

Both men were born in Harris County, GA. The family was in Marion County, GA in 1850. It is possible that both served with the Confederacy prior to enlistment with the 1st FCUV; however, records couldn't be narrowed sufficiently to determine that definitively. They enlisted together in the 1st FCUV on 24February1864. Thomas J. died of typhoid fever on 20June1864. George F. deserted on 22December1864.

38. Bryant and George H. JOHNSON were father and son

Bryant was born in Washington County, GA and George was born in Baker, GA. The family was in Covington County, AL in 1860. No Confederate service records could be located for either man. They enlisted together in the 1st FCUV on 3April1864. Bryant died of typhoid fever on 10July1864. George H served until the regiment was mustered out on 17November1865.

39. John L. and Samuel KENNEDY were brothers

John L. was born in Duplin County, NC and Samuel was born in Barbour County, AL. The family was in Dale County, AL in 1860. There are no records indicating that either man served with the Confederacy. Samuel joined the 1st FCUV on 5March1864 and John L. joined on 3October1864. Both were listed as missing in action on 17December1864 after the Pollard, AL engagement. It appears from descendants' postings on the family that Samuel was shot and mortally wounded at the time of the Pollard engagement, possibly taken home by his brother and died there. His brother, John, was found in census records after the war.

40. Richard and John LEVINS were brothers

Both men were born in Baker County, GA. The family was in Washington County, FL in 1850 and Walton County, FL in 1860. Richard served with the 6th FL Infantry, Co. H from enlistment on 2April to desertion on 14June1862. John enlisted, or was drafted, into the 4th Battalion Florida Infantry, Co C on 25Mar1863 and served until desertion on 20November1863. His records were transferred to the 11th FL Infantry, Co K in 1864. Richard enlisted with the 1st FCUV on 3January1864 and John enlisted on 28January1864. Richard died of typhoid fever on 7July1864 and John died of typho-malaria fever on 29July1864.

41. **James Madison and Benjamin C. MATHEWS were brothers**
Both men were born in Crawford County, GA. The family was in Coffee County, AL in 1850 and Benjamin was in Coffee County, AL in 1860. There is no record that would indicate service with the Confederacy for Benjamin. It is possible that James Madison served with the Confederacy but records could not be eliminated sufficiently to identify the specific record, if any. James Madison enlisted in the 1st FCUV on 16January1864 and Benjamin C. enlisted on 29April1864. Benjamin died of diarrhea on 1August1864. James Madison served the 1st FCUV until the regiment was mustered out on 17November1865.

42. **Joseph P. and Samuel J. MAUND were brothers**
Joseph P. was born in Houston County, GA and Samuel J. was born in Barbour County, AL. The family was in Dale County, AL in 1850 and Joseph P. was in Dale County, AL in 1860. It is possible Joseph P. served in the Confederacy but there isn't enough information to determine the specific record. Samuel J. served with the 39th AL Infantry, Co G. briefly from 6May until 30June1862 when he deserted. Joseph P. enlisted in the 1st FCUV on 29June1864 and Samuel J. enlisted on 22December1864. Joseph P.'s record does not provide an end date in the 1st FCUV. Samuel J. deserted on 30July1865.

43. **Alexander C. and Richard McGEE were brothers**
Both men were born in Baldwin County, AL and were Native Americans, most likely Muskogee/Creek. The family was in Baldwin County, AL in 1850 and 1860. It is possible that Richard served with the Confederacy but there isn't enough information to determine which one is the correct record. It does not appear that

Alexander served with the Confederacy prior to joining the 1st FCUV. Alexander enlisted with the 1st FCUV on 3June1864 and Richard attempted to enlist on 1April1865. He was rejected, likely to the perceived end of the conflict. Alexander served until the regiment was mustered out on 17November1865.

44. Alexander, William M., Angus and Duncan McLELLAN were brothers

All four of the men were born in Cumberland County, NC. They were all in Cumberland County, NC in 1850 and all but William were in Santa Rosa County, FL in 1860. William was in Covington County, AL. It is possible that Alexander served with the Confederacy but records could not be differentiated adequately. Angus did not serve with the Confederacy. Duncan served with the 1st FL Infantry, Co F from 21March1862 until he deserted on 1September1863. William M. served with the 3rd FL Battalion Cavalry, Co D from 1June1863 until he deserted on 11August1863. They all joined the 1st FCUV on 25January1864 and served until the regiment mustered out on 17November1865.

45. Griffin and Daniel V. MELVIN were brothers

Griffin was born in Houston County, GA and Daniel V. was born in Pike County, AL. The family was in Washington County, FL in 1850 and 1860. Both served with the 4th FL Infantry, Co. H, enlisting on 7September1861. Daniel deserted on 3September1863 and Griffin deserted on 5October1863. Daniel joined the 1st FCUV on 2February1864 and Griffin enlisted two months later on 20April1864. They both served until the regiment mustered out on 17November1865.

46. Elias B. and John B. MILLER were brothers

Both men were born in Washington County, FL. The family was in Washington County, FL in both 1850 and 1860. Elias served with the 1st FL Reorganized Infantry, Co D from 28February1862 until he deserted sometime around 28February1864. John served with the 3rd FL Battalion Cavalry, Co D from 4October1862 until 25December1862 when he was listed as a Prisoner of War. On 31December1863 he was listed as deserted after his regiment was transferred into the 15th Confederate Cavalry, Co D. They both enlisted in the 1st FCUV on 15March1864. Both deserted, Elias on 12January1865 and John on 26July1864.

47. **Michael M., James R., and Richard L. MONIAC were brothers**

All three men were born in Baldwin County, AL and were Muskogee/Creek Native Americans. The family was in Baldwin County, AL in 1860. Michael and James served with the 15th Confederate Cavalry, Co C after enlistment in Captain Barlow's Co of the Alabama Cavalry. Michael's initial enlistment was 9April1862 and his estimated desertion date was 1March1864. James enlisted with Captain Barlow's Company on 9April1862 and his estimated desertion date was 30June1864. Richard served with the 23rd AL Infantry, Co I, enlisting on 7October1861 and deserting after being taken a Prisoner of War at Vicksburg on 6July1863. Michael joined the 1st FCUV on 27March1864 and Richard joined two months later on 12May1864. James attempted to join on 1April1865 but his enlistment was canceled, most likely because of the perceived end of the conflict. Michael deserted on 20August1865. Richard served until the regiment mustered out.

48. **Henry and Alexander MORRISON were brothers**

Both men were born in Walton County, FL. The family was in Walton County in both 1850 and 1860. There is no evidence that either served with the Confederacy prior to their enlistment with the1st FCUV. Henry enlisted with the 1st FCUV on 16February1864 and served until the regiment was mustered out on 17November1865. Alexander enlisted on 1October1864. He deserted on 18August1865 but the desertion charge was dropped on 30November1897.

49. **Thomas T., Hansel M., and Silas D. MURPHY were father and sons**

Thomas was born in Charleston, South Carolina. Hansel was born in Georgia and Silas was born in Dale County, AL. The family was in Walton County, FL in 1860. Hansel is the only one that appears to have served with the Confederacy. He served with the

57th AL Infantry, Co. K from 15March to 31December1863. Thomas enlisted first with the 1st FCUV. He enlisted on 24February1864 and deserted on 1August1865. Hansel enlisted on 16August1864 and Silas enlisted two days later on 18August1864. Both served until the regiment mustered out on 17November1865.

50. **William Daniel and Willis W. OWENS were brothers**

Both men were born in Washington County, FL. The family was in Washington County in both 1850 and 1860. There is no evidence that Willis served with the Confederacy. William enlisted in the 4th FL Infantry, Co H on 7September1861 and deserted about March1864. William enlisted with the 1st FCUV on 20April1864. Willis enlisted with the 1st FCUV a month later on 19May1864. They both served until the regiment mustered out on 17November1865.

51. **Richard P. and George W. PARKER were brothers**

Richard was born in Baker County, GA. George was likely born in Covington County, AL. The family was in Covington County, AL in 1850 and Coffee County, AL in 1860. Richard served the Confederacy in the 57th AL Infantry, Co K, enlisting on 16March1863 and deserting on 11August1863. It is possible George also served in the Confederate service but a specific record can't be determined with existing information. They both enlisted with the 1st FCUV on 5March1864. Richard died of what was likely rheumatic fever on 12September1865. George served until the regiment mustered out on 17November1865.

52. **Greenberry G. and John PARKER were brothers**

Both men were born in Butler County, AL. The family was in Conecuh County, AL in 1850 and Baldwin County, AL in 1860. It is possible that John served with the Confederacy but records can't be clearly differentiated given his common name. There are no records indicating that Greenberry served with the Confederacy. John enlisted with the 1st FCUV on 5February1864 and Greenberry enlisted six weeks later on 26March1864. They both served until the regiment was mustered out on 17November1865.

53. Christopher C., George W., Charles W., and Ephraim C. PARRISH were brothers

Christopher was born in Alabama, possibly Henry County. George was born in Henry County, AL, Charles and Ephraim were born in Holmes County, FL. The family was in Holmes County, FL in 1850 and 1860. There is no evidence that Christopher or Ephraim served with the Confederacy but it is possible Charles and George did. There isn't sufficient record detail to make a final determination. Christopher enlisted with the 1st FCUV on 28January1864, Charles enlisted on 26February1864, Ephraim enlisted on 23March1864, and George enlisted on 15April 1864. Everyone served with the 1st FCUV until it mustered out on 17November1865.

54. Owen T. and Robert J. PARRISH were brothers

Both men were born in Henry County, AL. The family was in Holmes County, FL in 1850 and 1860. It is possible that these Parrish brothers are related to the four listed above given their locations prior to the war. There is no evidence that Owen served with the Confederacy. It is possible that Robert did. They both enlisted with the 1st FCUV on 28January1864. Owen was given a medical discharge due to epilepsy on 23December1864. Robert died of diarrhea on 12September1864.

55. Rudolph F. and Joel PATE were brothers

Both men were born in Coffee County, AL. The family was in Washington County, FL in 1850 and Calhoun County, FL in 1860. There is no evidence that either man served with the Confederacy. Rudolph enlisted with the 1st FCUV on 15February1864 and Joel enlisted on 8June1864. Rudolph died of malarial fever on 28June1864. Joel served until the regiment mustered out on 17November1865.

56. John A. and Daniel W. PAUL were brothers

John was born in Barbour County, AL and Daniel was born in Dale County, AL. The family was in Coffee County, AL in 1850 and

1860. John served in the Confederacy with the 57th AL Infantry, Co K from 16March1863 to his desertion about 31October1863. Daniel served in the 33rd AL Infantry, Co A from 22February1862 until sometime near the end of September 1863. They enlisted with the 1st FCUV together on 10October1864. Daniel was listed as deserting on 1August1865 but the desertion charge was dropped on 4August1886. John served with the 1st FCUV until it mustered out on 17November1865.

57. **Lewis, William H., and Isaac P. PITTS were brothers**

Lewis was born in Henry County, AL and William and Isaac were born in Jackson County, FL. The family was in Holmes County, FL in 1850. Lewis was in Washington County, FL in 1860, William was in Holmes County, FL and Isaac was in Walton County, FL. There is no evidence that William served in the Confederacy. Lewis served in the 6th FL Infantry, Co K from 2April1862 until approximately 1June1862. Isaac served in the 1st FL Reorganized Infantry, Co E. from 1March1862 until approximately 31December1863 when he may have deserted while home on sick furlough. Lewis enlisted with the 1st FCUV on 30December1863. William and Isaac enlisted four days later on 3January1864. Lewis died of bilious fever on 13October1864. William deserted on 15January1865. Isaac was listed as deserting on 20May1865 but the charge was dropped on 11July1888.

58. **James J. and Benjamin F. PRIM were brothers**

Both men were born in Stewart County, GA. The family was in Stewart County, GA in 1850 and Barbour County, AL in 1860. Both men served with the Confederacy. James served with the 1st AL Battalion Light Artillery, Co F from 13March1861 until he was discharged on 12March1864. Benjamin served with the 15th AL Infantry, Co E from 3March1862 until he deserted during a sick furlough sometime around 12June1863. Benjamin enlisted with the 1st FCUV on 12May1864 and James enlisted 8 days later on 20May1864. Benjamin was taken prisoner while out on detached service and was killed by Confederates on or about

5December1864. James served with the 1st FCUV until it mustered out on 17November1865.

59. Joseph M., and Akis F. REGISTER were brothers

Both men were born in Washington County, FL. The family was in Washington County in both 1850 and 1860. Joseph served in the Confederacy with the 4th FL Battalion, Co. C. He enlisted with the 4th FL Battalion on 25March1863 and deserted on 30November1863. The regiment was transferred into the 11th FL Infantry in June1864, after Joseph had deserted. There is no evidence that Akis served with the Confederacy. Joseph enlisted with the 1st FCUV on 13December1863 and Akis enlisted a month later on 25January1864. They both served until the regiment mustered out on 17November1865.

60. James F., Thomas F., and George D. ROOKS were brothers

James and Thomas were born in Lowndes County, GA and George was born in Walton County, FL. The family was in Walton County, FL in 1860. There is no evidence that James served with the Confederacy. Thomas served with the 1st FL Infantry, Co D and then the 1st FL Reorganized Infantry, Co D from 20July1861 until he deserted on 28August1863. George served the Confederacy with the 6th AL Infantry, Co K from his enlistment on 3April1863 until he likely deserted on or about 31October1863. George and Thomas enlisted with the 1st FCUV on 21December1863. James enlisted on 14November1864. Thomas was killed by "vigilantes" on 20December1864. James and George served with the 1st FCUV until it mustered out on 17November1865.

61. William R., and Southerd P. SEGARS were brothers

William was born in Gwinnett County, GA and Southerd was born in Marion County, GA. The family was in Early County, GA in 1850 and Southerd was in Henry County, AL in 1860. It is possible that William served with the Confederacy but records can't be differentiated well enough to determine a specific record. Southerd served with the 4th FL Battalion Infantry, Co A, enlisting on 1August1863 and deserting on 9December1863. His records were transferred to the 11th FL Infantry in June1864. Southerd enlisted with the 1st FCUV on 17December1863 and died of an unknown cause on 28July1865. William enlisted with the 1st FCUV on 15February1864. He deserted on 24June1864 and was subsequently killed by Confederates.

62. **John and Thomas SELLERS were brothers**
Both men were born in Brunswick County, NC. The family was in Jackson County, FL in 1850 and John was in Jackson County in 1860. John served the Confederacy with the 4th FL Battalion Infantry, Co C. He enlisted on 25March1863 and deserted on 13Feb1864 before his records were transferred to the 11th FL Infantry, Co K in June1864. It is possible that Thomas also served in the Confederacy but a specific record can't be determined. They both enlisted with the 1st FCUV on 11March1864 and both served until the regiment was mustered out on 17November1865.

63. **John F. and Julius SELLERS were brothers**
John was born in Brunswick County, NC and Julius was born in Jackson County, FL. The family was in Jackson County, FL in 1860. John served the Confederacy with the 5th FL Battalion Cavalry, Co A, enlisting on 11September1863 and likely deserting on or about 29December1863. There is no evidence that Julius served with the Confederacy prior to enlistment with the 1st FCUV. John enlisted on 11March1864 and Julius enlisted on 31March1865. John died of rubella on 18August1864 and Julius served until the regiment was mustered out on 17November 1865. It is possible these two Sellers men are related to the two above, possibly cousins.

64. **Bennett G. SENTERFITT and William L. BARROW were uncle and nephew**
Bennett was born in Pulaski County, GA. William was born in Walton County, FL. Bennett was William's mother's brother. Bennett Senterfitt was in Walton County, FL in 1860. William was in Walton County, FL in 1850 and Santa Rosa County, FL in 1860. Neither man served with the Confederacy before enlistment with

the 1st FCUV. Bennett enlisted with the 1st FCUV on 26March1864 and William enlisted on 10April1864. Both served in the 1st FCUV until it mustered out of service on 17November 1865.

65. Archibald and Derrell M. SMITH were brothers

Archibald was born in Richland County, SC and Derrell was born in Pike County, AL. The family was in Pike County, AL in 1850 and Santa Rosa County, FL in 1860. Archibald served the Confederacy in the 1st FL Reorganized Infantry, Co G from enlistment on 13May1862 until he deserted on 29August1863. There is no evidence that Derrell served in the Confederacy. They both enlisted with the 1st FCUV on 25January1864 and served until the regiment mustered out on 17November1865.

66. Daniel W., John M., and George W. STAGNER were brothers

All three men were born in Pike County, AL. Daniel was in Pike County, AL in 1850 and all three were in Walton County, FL in 1860. Daniel served the Confederacy in the 1st FL Infantry, Co E, enlisting on 21July1861 for 12 months. He was mustered out of the 1st FL Infantry in May 1862 and enlisted, or was drafted, in the 8th FL Infantry, Co E on 13May1862. He deserted 11 days later on 24May1862, which likely indicates he was drafted. John served with the 3rd Battalion FL Cavalry, Co D from 4October1862 until he deserted on 5July1863. His records were transferred to the 15th Confederate Cavalry after he deserted. It doesn't appear that George served with the Confederacy prior to enlistment with the 1st FCUV. George enlisted with the 1st FCUV on 13January1864, John enlisted on 27January1864 and Daniel enlisted on 30January1864. George died of bilious fever on 12August1864, Daniel and John served until the regiment mustered out on 17November1865.

67. Kinion and Joseph S. STANLEY were father and son

Kinion was born in Sampson County, NC and Joseph was born in Barbour County, AL. The family was in Holmes County, FL in 1850. Neither man appears to have served with the Confederacy.

Joseph enlisted with the 1st FCUV on 28December1863 and Kinion enlisted on 29December1863. Both men served until the regiment mustered out on 17November1865.

68. **John J. and James P. STRICKLAND were brothers**
Both men were born in Pike County, AL. James was in Pike County in 1850 and both were in Henry County, AL in 1860. John served with the 6th AL Infantry, Co B. He enlisted on 11May1861 and likely deserted sometime around 31August1861. James served in the 4th Battalion FL Infantry, Co A, enlisting on 25June1863 and deserting on 9December1863. His records were transferred to the 11th FL Infantry, Co C after his desertion. They both enlisted in the 1st FCUV on 30December1863 and served until the regiment mustered out on 17November1865.

69. **John (Jr.) and Henry W. TEEL were brothers**
Both men were born in Covington County, AL. The family was in Covington County in both 1850 and 1860. It is possible John served with the Confederacy but an exact record can't be determined. Henry served the Confederacy in the 42nd AL Infantry, Co E, enlisting on 31March1862 and deserting after parole at Vicksburg. Henry joined the 1st FCUV on 19January1864 and John enlisted on 24February1864. John died of diarrhea on 20April1865. Henry served until the regiment mustered out on 17November1865.

70. **Robert G. and Bartley F. TUCKER were brothers**
Both men were born in Coffee County, AL. The family was in Coffee County in both 1850 and 1860. Neither man appears to have served in the Confederate Army. Bartley joined the 1st FCUV on 11March1864 and Robert joined on 27August1864. Robert deserted on 21November1864. Bartley served until the regiment was mustered out on 17November1865.

71. **William H., Jordan L., and Elisha M. WATERS were brothers**
All three men were born in Escambia County, FL. The family was in Escambia County in both 1850 and 1860. Jordan and William served the Confederacy initially in the 3rd FL Battalion Cavalry, Co

B, both joining on 24April1862. They were transferred around 24September1863 into the 15th Confederate Cavalry, Co D. They both deserted on 23December1863. Elisha does not appear to have served in the Confederate army. Jordan enlisted in the 1st FCUV on 7January1864, Elisha enlisted on 26March1864 and William enlisted on 12January1865. All three served until the regiment was mustered out on 17November1865.

72. Burton H. and John W. WATSON were brothers

Both men were born in Carroll County, GA. The family was in DeKalb County, GA in 1850 and in Santa Rosa County, FL in 1860. Burton served with the 1st FL Reorganized Infantry, Co E before joining the 1st FCUV. He joined the 1st FL Reorganized Infantry, Co E on 16March1862 and deserted on 29August1863. John served the Confederacy in the 2nd FL Cavalry, Co G, joining in July1863 and deserting on 21September1863. Burton joined the 1st FCUV on 7January1864 and John joined on 24February1864. Both men served until the regiment was mustered out on 17November1865.

73. Benjamin W., Hiram and Harmon WEEKS were brothers

All three men were born in Coffee County, AL. The family was in Coffee County in 1850 and Benjamin was there in 1860. Benjamin enlisted in the 4th FL Battalion Infantry, Co A on 12June1863 and deserted a few days later on 27June1863. His records were transferred to the 11th FL Infantry, Co C but he never served with the regiment. Hiram and Harmon do not appear to have served with the Confederacy. Benjamin enlisted with the 1st FCUV on 24March1864 and deserted 4April1865. Hiram enlisted with the 1st FCUV on 10October1864 and also deserted on 4April1865. Harmon enlisted with the 1st FCUV on 8September1864 on died on 10October1864.

74. Benjamin L. and Leonard F. WEST were brothers

Both men were born in Pike County, AL. The family was in Pike County in 1850 and Santa Rosa County, FL in 1860. Benjamin served the Confederacy in the 1st FL Reorganized Infantry, Co G from 8May1862 to his desertion on 29August1863. Leonard did not serve in the Confederacy. Both enlisted with the 1st FCUV on 26March1864. Benjamin deserted on 21July1865 and had his desertion charge dropped on 18November1886. Leonard served until the regiment was mustered out on 17November1865.

75. Joshua E. and Sion A. WHEELESS were father and son

Joshua was born in Hancock County, GA and Sion was born in Macon County, AL. The family was in Coffee County, AL in 1860. Joshua served with the 33rd AL Infantry, Co K from 13March1862 until he deserted about 31December1863. Sion doesn't appear to have served with the Confederacy. Sion joined the 1st FCUV on 9January1864 and Joshua joined 6July1864. Both men served until the regiment mustered out on 17November1865.

76. John J. and William T. F. WILKINSON were brothers

Both men were born in Coffee County, AL. The family was in Santa Rosa County, FL in 1860. It is possible that John served in the Confederacy but records can't be differentiated sufficiently. It does not appear that William served in the Confederacy. Both enlisted in the 1st FCUV on 25January1864 and served until the regiment was mustered out on 17November1865.

77. Elias S. and Peter C. WORLEY were brothers

Both were born in Pike County, AL. They were in Pike County in 1860. Neither appears to have served in the Confederate Army prior to enlistment with the Union. Elias enlisted with the 1st FCUV on 26January1864 and Peter enlisted on 24February1864. Peter died of typhoid fever on 10March1865. Elias served until the regiment mustered out on 17November1865.

78. Levi and Jordan YATES were brothers

Both men were born in Jackson County, FL. The family was in Holmes County, FL in 1850 and in Washington County, FL in 1860. Levi served the Confederacy in the 4th FL Battalion Infantry, Co C from 25March1863 until he deserted on 8June1863. His records were transferred to the 11th FL Infantry, K after his desertion. Jordan does not appear to have served with the Confederate Army. Jordan joined the 1st FCUV on 3April1864 and died of dysentery on 8November1864. Levi enlisted with the 1st

FCUV on 12April1864 and served until the regiment mustered out on 17November1865.

Appendix

Target Counties Military Men to Percent in 1st FCUV

State	County	Men	1860 military age men*	% in 1st FCUV
Alabama	Coffee	53	1827	3%
	Covington	47	1210	4%
	Dale	40	2267	2%
	Henry	39	2447	2%
	Baldwin	32	1140	3%
	Barbour	14	3536	0.4%
	Conecuh	11	1546	0.7%
	Pike	10	3580	0.3%
	Monroe	3		
	Macon	2		
	Mobile	2		
	Bibb	1		
	Blount	1		
	Butler	1		
	Russell	1		
	Walker	1		
Florida	Walton	62	573	11%
	Santa Rosa	58	1038	6%
	Holmes	37	287	13%
	Washington	35	368	10%
	Jackson	10	1270	0.8%
	Escambia	8	1161	0.7%
	Calhoun	4		
	Gadsden	3		
	Franklin	1		
Florida				
	Jefferson	1		
Georgia		8		
South Carolina		1		
Illinois		2		
Louisiana		1		
Massachusetts		2		
Missouri		1		
New York		2		
Pennsylvania		1		
Vermont		1		
Unknown		208		
	Total	704		

Population Data for Target Alabama Counties

Total AL Population	964201	Percent of	Total Whites	Free Colored	Indians	Slaves	Total Slaveholders
Total Free population	529121	55%	526271	2690	160	435080	33730
Total number of families	96603			0%	0%	45%	3%
White men 20-29	47184						
White men 30-39	29425						
White men 40-49	20089						
Total # of white men	270190						
Baldwin County							
Total Population	7530	1%	3585	140	91	3714	289
Total Free Population	3816	51%		2%	1%	49%	4%
Total number of families	653						
White men 20-29	437						
White men 30-39	308						
White men 40-49	203	948					
Total # of white men	2056	54%					
Dale County							
Total Population	12197	1%	10379	7	2	1809	314
Total Free Population	10388	85%		0%	0%	15%	3%
Total number of families	1767						
White men 20-29	815						
White men 30-39	502						
White men 40-49	374	1691					
Total # of white men	5263	43%					

	Total AL Population	964201	Percent of	Total Whites	Free Colored	Indians	Slaves	Total Slaveholders
Henry County								
Total Population	14918	2%	10464	21	0	4433	489	
Total Free Population	10485	70%		0%	0%	30%	3%	
Total number of families	1843							
White men 20-29	964							
White men 30-39	525							
White men 40-49	349	1838						
Total # of white men	5343	36%						
Covington County								
Total Population	6469	1%	5631	17	0	821	144	
Total Free Population	5648	87%		0%	0%	13%	2%	
Total number of families	1045							
White men 20-29	415							
White men 30-39	291							
White men 40-49	201	907						
Total # of white men	2863	44%						
Coffee County								
Total Population	9623	1%	8200	6	0	1417	239	
Total Free Population	8206	85%		0%	0%	15%	2%	
Total number of families	1375							
White men 20-29	636							
White men 30-39	388							
White men 40-49	310	1334						
Total # of white men	4275	44%						

Population Data for Target Florida Counties

Total State Population	140424	Percent of	Total Whites	Free Colored	Indians	Slaves	Total Slaveholders
Total Free population	78679	56%	77747	932	0	61745	5152
Total number of families	15090			1%	0%	44%	4%
White men 20-29	41128						
White men 30-39	7339						
White men 40-49	4912						
Total # of white men	3255						
Walton County							
Total Population	3037	2%	2584	12	0	441	107
Total Free Population	2596	85%		0%	0%	15%	4%
Total number of families	462						
White men 20-29	201						
White men 30-39	126						
White men 40-49	95	422					
Total # of white men	1314	43%					
Santa Rosa County							
Total Population	5480	4%	4048	61	0	1371	166
Total Free Population	4109	75%		1%	0%	25%	3%
Total number of families	720						
White men 20-29	405						
White men 30-39	257						
White men 40-49	169	831					
Total # of white men	2117	39%					

Total State Population	140424	Percent of	Total Whites	Free Colored	Indians	Slaves	Total Slaveholders
Holmes County							
Total Population	1386	1%	1271	3	0	112	29
Total Free Population	1274	92%		0%	0%	8%	2%
Total number of families	235						
White men 20-29	109						
White men 30-39	67						
White men 40-49	44	220					
Total # of white men	619	45%					
Washington County							
Total Population	2154	2%	1670	10	0	474	56
Total Free Population	1680	78%		0%	0%	22%	3%
Total number of families	316						
White men 20-29	126						
White men 30-39	93						
White men 40-49	55	274					
Total # of white men	841	50%					

Economic Data for Nine Counties

	# of farms	Acres Improved land	Cash value of farms	Cash value/farm	Manufacturing Establishments	Capital Invested in Manufacturing
Alabama	5064	6385724	$175,824,622.00	$34,720.50	1459	$9,098,181.00
Baldwin Co	188	10141	$468,090.00	$2,489.84	34	$1,688,640.00
Dale Co	1066	76726	$1,431,122.00	$1,342.52	8	$13,750.00
Henry Co	930	101993	$2,154,860.00	$2,317.05	27	$103,620.00
Covington Co	517	29275	$538,155.00	$1,040.92	4	$21,375.00
Coffee Co	829	56612	$1,004,062.00	$1,211.17	6	$14,550.00
Florida	6396	654213	$16,435,727.00	$2,569.69	185	$1,874,125.00
Walton Co	291	9681	$154,671.00	$531.52	7	$13,425.00
Santa Rosa Co	66	2281	$23,285.00	$352.80	15	$883,200.00
Holmes Co	137	5251	$62,753.00	$458.05	n/a	n/a
Washington Co	219	11245	$86,983.00	$397.18	3	$9,500.00

Map of Route from Milton to Andalusia 1865

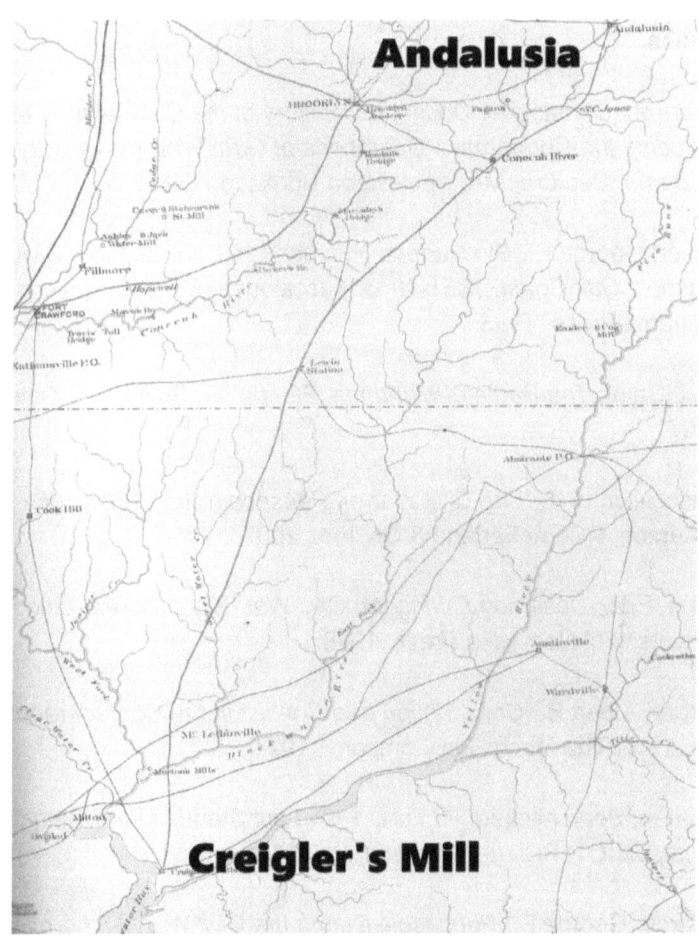

Portion of Plate 110, page 261
The Official Military Atlas of the Civil War
By Major George B. Davis, U.S. Army, Leslie J. Perry, Civilian Expert,
and Joseph W. Kirkley Civilian Expert
Barnes & Noble Books, New York

Resources

Books

Andrews, Christopher Columbus, *History of the Campaign of Mobile: Including the Cooperative Operations of Gen. Wilson's Cavalry in Alabama.* Bedford, MA: Applewood Books, no date

Buker, George E., *Blockaders, Refugees, & Contrabands: Civil War on Florida's Gulf Coast, 1861-1865.* Tuscaloosa, AL: The University of Alabama Press, 1993.

Cox, Dale., *The Battle of Marianna, Florida.* Ft. Smith, AR: Dale Cox, 2007.

Driscoll, John K., *The Civil War on Pensacola Bay, 1861-1862.* Jefferson, NC: McFarland & Co, Inc., 2007.

Lonn, Ella., *Desertion During the Civil War.* Bison Books. Lincoln, NE: University of Nebraska Press, 1998.

Moore, Albert B., *Conscription and Conflict in the Confederacy.* New York, NY: The Macmillan Company, 1924.

O'Brien, Sean Michael, *Mobile, 1865 Last Stand of the Confederacy.* Westport, CT: Praeger Publishers, 2001.

Pearce, George F., *Pensacola During the Civil War: A Thorn in the Side of the Confederacy.* Gainesville, FL: University Press of Florida, 2000.

Roberts, C. C., *General Andrew B. Spurling and Second Maine Cavalry,* 1904.

Online Databases

NARA, "1860 United States Federal Census" [database on-line]. *Ancestry.com.* Images reproduced by FamilySearch. Accessed 2004-2006. http://ancestry.com.

University of Virginia, Geospatial and Statistical Data Center. 1860 census. *Historical Census Browser.* Accessed 2004. http://mapserver.lib.virginia.edu/.

Online Resources

Blount, A. C., "Letter to Governor John Milton.", 1862, Vols. Milton Letterbook, Box 1, Folder 10. Pensacola, FL: Florida Memory: State Library & Archives of FL, April 9th.
https://www.floridamemory.com/items/show/265931.

Inflation Calculator. Accessed 2015. http://www.in2013dollars.com/.

Mobile Campaign Confederate Order of Battle. Accessed 2015.

Mobile Campaign Union Order of Battle. Accessed 2015.

Riley, B. F. (Rev)., "History of Conecuh County, Alabama." 1881, *Genealogy Trails.*
http://genealogytrails.com/ala/conecuh/history_riley.html.

The Southern Star. "Their Raid on Newton and How They Were Put to Flight - A Few Brave and Determined Men Are Powerful in Any Good Cause." 1899, *Battle of Newton.* Accessed 2015.
www.battleofnewton.org/battlehistory.html.

Wikimedia Foundation, Inc. no date, *Alexander Asboth.* Accessed 2015.
https://en.wikipedia.org/wiki/Alexander_Asboth.

CD Databases

Confederate Military History, Carmel, IN: Guild Press of Indiana, 1997.

The War of the Rebellion: A Compilation of the Official Records of the Union and Confederate Armies, Carmel, IN: Guild Press of Indiana, 1997.

Journal Articles

McGee, Val L. "The Confederate Who Switched Sides - The Saga of Captain Joseph G. Sanders." *The Alabama Review: A Quarterly Journal of Alabama History* 1994, 47: 20-28.

Microfilm

Compiled Service Records of Volunteer Union Soldiers Who Served in Organization from the State of Florida, M400, Washington, D.C.: The National Archives and Records Administration, 1994, Rolls 1-6 & 11.

Index

A

Abbott, Robert S., 69, 83
Adams, Ellis W. O., 83
Adams, J. Elijah, 51, 83
Adams, John Quincy, 84
Adams, Larkin A., 84
Alexander, Ezekiel, 84
Allen, Eldred Benjamin, 34, 47, 65, 70, 85
Allen, John Anderson, 57, 70, 85
Allen, Robert J., 85
Alsobrook, Robert A., 30, 86
Alston, John J., 86
Anderson, Willis, 57, 86
Ard, John Wesley, 57, 70, 87
Ard, Zachariah R., 47, 51, 87
Armstrong, James H., 42, 87
Arnold, John T., 88
Atkins, Robert T., 70, 88

B

Baggett, Henry Hilliard, 88, 294
Baggett, Henry L., 70, 89
Baggett, James, 89, 294
Baggett, Joel, 89, 294
Baggett, Lewis, 89, 294
Baggett, Nicholas, 90
Baggett, Seaborn S., 30, 34, 45, 47, 90, 294
Bagwell, Berry E., 51, 91
Bagwell, Curtis G. H., 34, 45, 57, 61, 65, 91
Bagwell, Lewis, 91
Bailey, Arthur, 61, 91

Bailey, John, 92
Baker, Murdock, 92
Banks, Eli Ferguson, 92
Barefield, James J., 93
Barfield, Hugh Huston, 42, 93
Barker, John, 93
Barlow, Lewis Alexander, 93
Barnes, Elias L., 70, 94
Barnes, William, 94
Barnes, William James, 94
Barnes, William W., 51, 95
Barrow, William Lafayette, 70, 95, 314
Barton, Uriah, 70, 95
Basford, Chesterfield, 95
Bass, Holland Middleton, 96
Bass, James W., 96
Bass, Willis T., 96
Bell, Charles P., 34, 47, 65, 70, 97
Bell, Francis M., 97, 294
Bell, Jacob H., 97, 294
Bell, James, 97
Bishop, James M., 70, 98
Black, James M., 98
Blackman, John P., 98
Blake, H., 99
Bohannan, Henry, 57, 65, 70, 99
Bolton, James Thomas, 99, 295
Bolton, John Askar, 70, 99, 295
Boon, Elijah, 70, 100
Bottom, George M. D., 70, 100
Boutwell, Bailey R., 100, 295
Boutwell, Elam D., 101, 295
Boutwell, William B., 101, 295

Braxton, Benjamin R., 57, 101, 295
Braxton, Isom, 102, 295
Braxton, Jasper, 102, 295
Braxton, Martin, 61, 70, 102, 295
Braxton, Oliver O., 102
Brewer, Henry O., 103
Britt, John H., 42, 103
Brown, Allen, 103
Brown, F. M., 103
Brown, George Owen, 104, 296
Brown, George W., 30, 104
Brown, James, 104
Brown, John, 104
Brown, John Wesley, 58, 61, 105, 296
Browning, John, 105
Bullard, James Wilburn, 105
Burdeshaw, Daniel Eli, 70, 106
Burk, Isaac, 106
Burk, Mark, 106
Burleson, Simeon Wilder, 30, 34, 47, 70, 107
Burnham, Francis M., 107
Burnum, Francis, 107
Busbee, William J., 108
Butler, Constantine, 30, 51, 108
Butler, Evan, 108, 297
Butler, James D., 109, 297
Buzbee, Elisha, 109
Buzbee, William H., 47, 109
Byrd, Seaborn J., 110
Byrd, William, 110

C

Cahann, A. J., 110
Callahan, Bethel Haines, 34, 47, 65, 70, 111
Callaway, Elijah Holcomb, 111
Campbell, Allen, 111
Campbell, Charles D., 112
Campbell, Charles M., 112
Campbell, David M., 112
Campbell, Malcolm, 113
Campbell, Thomas, 113
Campbell, William A., 113
Cantaline, Henry, 114
Carlovitz, John, 114
Carmichael, James W., 34, 114, 297
Carmichael, William Henry, 61, 70, 115, 297
Carnley, Daniel Nathaniel, 58, 115, 297
Carnley, William Eli, 115, 297
Carr, W., 116
Carroll, Elijah Gibson, 116, 297
Carroll, Frederick D., 70, 116, 297
Carroll, Joseph B., 58, 70, 116, 297
Carter, Hardy H., 117
Carter, Jasper J., 34, 117
Carter, Lemuel, 117, 298
Carter, William Leonard, 118, 298
Cassida, William, 70, 118
Cassidy, Cornelius, 118
Caswell, William Giles, 34, 47, 65, 70, 119
Cato, Daniel, 51, 119
Cauley, John Richard, 58, 120
Caylor, George Washington, 70, 120
Chancey, James Jackson, 120, 298
Chancey, John Wesley, 121, 298

Chesser, Napoleon Bonaparte, 121
Chestnut, Jasper, 121
Clark, Hamilton, 122
Clark, John H., 122
Clary, William P., 122
Cloud, John, 122
Cobb, Ezekiel M., 123
Cobb, James H., 123
Cockcroft, James Alexander, 58, 70, 123
Cockcroft, Micajah Allen, 58, 70, 123, 299
Cockroft, James Alexander, 299
Coleman, Allen V., 124
Collinsworth, Abraham, 124
Conway, Charles W., 124
Cook, Unknown, 125
Cooley, Gillis, 125
Coon, James Jackson, 125, 299
Coon, Joseph Jerold, 125, 299
Cooper, Thomas Jefferson, 125
Coppahant, James H., 126
Cox, George W., 58, 70, 126
Coxwell, John Thomas, 70, 126
Cravey, Jonas, 126
Creamer, Henry H., 30, 47,
Crenshaw, Aaron, 127
Crews, John, 127
Crider, William R., 30, 34, 47, 58, 61, 70, 127
Crosby, James M., 70, 128
Cuey, William J., 128
Culbreth, Gilmore, 128
Cumbia, Henry M., 129
Curlee, John, 129, 299
Curlee, Richard, 129, 299
Curry, William T., 70, 130
Cutherill, Jasper, 70, 130

Cutts, Zachariah, 130

D

Daniel, Thomas J., 131
Danley, James H., 131
Dansby, Daniel Monroe, 34, 45, 47, 61, 65, 70, 131, 300
Dansby, Emanuel George W., 34, 45, 47, 61, 65, 70, 132, 300
Dansby, Hiram D., 34, 45, 47, 61, 65, 70, 132, 300
Dansby, John, 133, 300
Daughtery, Drew, 133
Daughtery, Joshua S., 133
Daughtry, Joshua, 70, 134
Davis, Alexander T., 134, 300
Davis, Ashley J., 134
Davis, Franklin J., 34, 47, 65, 70, 135
Davis, Harmon, 135
Davis, Leroy, 45, 135
Davis, Samuel, 135
Davis, Thomas, 47, 136
Davis, Wade H., 136
Davis, William A., 136
Davis, William S., 34, 47, 65, 70, 136
Davis, Wilson, 137
Davis, Wilson A., 137, 300
Diamond, Robert W., 137
Dixon, Henry H., 30, 34, 47, 137
Dixon, Washington, 138
Dockins, George W., 138, 300
Dockins, William C., 70, 138, 300
Dockins, William P., 139, 300
Donaldson, Benjamin F., 139
Donaldson, James D., 30, 34, 47, 70, 139, 301

Donaldson, Joseph William, 70, 140, 301
Donaldson, Thomas H., 140
Donelson, John, 51
Dow, John H., 140
Dumont, Charles, 47, 70, 141
Duncan, James M., 141
Dyson, James, 30, 47, 71, 141

E

Early, Thomas J., 142
Easters, John W., 142
Eaton, J. R., 142
Eddin, William H., 142
Eddy, Jefferson H., 58, 71, 142
Ellis, William B., 51, 143
Ellison, John P., 143, 301
Ellison, Samuel A., 143, 301
Ellison, Young R., 143, 301
Elmore, James H., 144
Erickson, John, 144
Evans, Constantine, 51
Evans, James H., 144
Evans, John T., 145

F

Faulk, Alfred J., 145
Faulk, Asa, 71, 145, 301
Faulk, Phillip, 146, 301
Faulkner, Chesley, 146
Flinn, James M., 146
Flowers, Benjamin, 146
Flowers, Thomas, 146
Floyd, Charles J., 147
Forehand, James, 147
Fowler, John Franklin, 147, 302
Fowler, Richard, 71, 148, 302

Franklin, Marion W., 34, 45, 47, 65, 71, 148
Franklin, William H., 148
Freeman, Hardy, 149
French, Robert, 149

G

Gaal, Alexander G., 149
Gainey, Silas, 150, 302
Gainey, Silas Jackson, 150, 302
Galloway, James Levi, 150
Gardner, William D., 150
Garner, Zinamon L., 71, 151
Garrett, George W., 151
Garrett, Joseph, 34, 47, 65, 71, 151
Garrett, Overstreet William, 151
Garrett, Robert, 152
Garrett, William Robert, 152
Gaskin, James Millard, 152, 302
Gaskin, Seth J., 153, 302
Gatewood, Harvey H., 71, 153
Gather, Charles, 153
Gatlin, Harmon S., 154, 303
Gatlin, Joseph D., 51, 154, 303
Gavin, Charles W., 154
George, Moses Andrew, 155
Gibson, John F., 155
Gibson, Jordan J., 156, 303
Gibson, Sidney, 156, 303
Gibson, Stephen D., 156
Gill, Albert, 30, 34, 45, 47, 58, 61, 71, 156, 303
Gill, Lorenzo Dow, 30, 34, 45, 47, 58, 61, 71, 157, 303
Gilmore, Thomas, 157
Givens, John Daniel, 157, 304
Givens, John H., 157, 304
Givens, John W., 71, 158

Givens, Robert J., 71, 158
Glass, James C., 158
Glisson, Henry, 159
Glover, Burrell, 159
Godwin, John S., 71, 159
Goodman, John, 71, 160
Goss, William S., 160
Grant, John B., 160
Graves, Joseph J., 51, 160
Greenwood, Zebedee, 161
Grimes, Felix Kenan, 161
Grimes, Jesse F., 161
Grubbs, Emanuel R., 34, 47, 65, 71, 162
Gunter, Francis Marion, 162

H

Hall, Henry J., 162
Hall, John F., 163
Hall, Louis Marion, 71, 163
Hall, Thomas, 163
Hardy, Patrick, 164
Hardy, Robert, 71, 164
Hardy, William Franklin, 164, 304
Hardy, William Spencer, 165, 304
Harris, John W., 165
Harrison, John A., 165
Harrison, Jonathan D., 165, 304
Harrison, Wiley F., 34, 51, 166, 304
Hart, David Allen, 166
Hatcher, Phillip G., 166, 304
Hatcher, William J., 167, 304
Hathaway, James Marcus Lafayette, 34
Hathaway, James Wilburn, 71, 167, 305

Hathaway, John Marcus Lafayette, 47, 65, 71, 167, 305
Hathcock, James T., 168, 305
Hathcock, Thomas O., 168, 305
Hays, Needham R., 168
Head, John F., 168
Head, Thomas W., 169
Heath, William T., 169
Helf, William, 169
Henderson, John G., 169
Henderson, John L., 71, 170
Hewett, John L., 170
Hewett, Joseph B., 30, 34, 47, 58, 61, 71, 170
Hicks, George, 171
Hicks, James J., 171
Hicks, William, 71, 171
Hinote, John Wesley, 172, 305
Hinote, William P., 172, 305
Hobbs, Benjamin Franklin, 172
Hodge, John Allen, 47, 173
Hodge, McFadden, 173
Holland, Elias, 173
Holley, Godfrey Lee, 34, 47, 65, 71, 173
Holley, William F., 51, 174
Hollinger, Adam Cornelius, 34, 45, 47, 65, 71, 174
Hollis, William, 175
Holly, Calvin H., 175
Holman, Allen, 31
Holman, Andrew Lewis (Jr.), 175, 305
Holman, Henry A., 175, 305
Holman, John D., 176, 305
Holman, Lewis, 176
Hooks, John Franklin, 176
Horton, Hubbard H., 176
Horton, William Wiliford, 71, 177
Howard, Christopher C., 71, 177

Howard, Jefferson H., 177
Howell, Francis, 178
Howell, Thomas, 178
Hubbard, Francis Marion, 71, 178
Huckaby, Andrew J., 71, 178
Hudgens, James J., 179
Hudson, George F., 179, 306
Hudson, James T., 71, 179
Hudson, John G. R., 30, 35, 47, 71, 180
Hudson, Thomas J., 180, 306
Huggins, John, 181
Hughes, John, 181
Hutto, John W., 181

I

Infinger, Absalom, 181

J

Jay, James J., 182
Jerdavil, Unknown, 182
Jernigan, McKay, 182
Johnson, Andrew Jackson, 30, 35, 48, 71, 182
Johnson, Bryant, 183, 306
Johnson, Edmund J., 183
Johnson, George H., 35, 48, 65, 71, 183, 306
Johnson, Jackson, 184
Johnson, Jonathan M., 184
Johnson, William, 184
Jones, Alexander W., 184
Jones, Dixon, 184
Jones, Henry, 185
Jones, James M., 185
Jones, Lionel, 185
Jones, Mathew, 185

Jones, Richard, 71, 186
Jones, Samuel T., 186
Jones, Thomas J., 186
Jones, Wright S., 71, 186
Jordan, Edmond, 51, 187
Jordan, James Monroe, 187
Jordan, William M., 187
Jost, Frederick C., 71, 188

K

Kelley, William A., 188
Kemp, James B., 51, 188
Kemp, William T., 189
Kennedy, John L., 48, 189, 306
Kennedy, Samuel, 189, 306
Kielmansegge, Eugene, 189
Kilpatrick, Noah Powell, 61, 190
Kimmons, John, 190
King, Angus, 71, 190
King, Benjamin, 191
King, William, 191
King, William Johnson, 191
Kirkland, Emanuel, 191
Kittrell, Zenith Andrew, 191
Knowles, James H., 192
Krimminger, John N., 192

L

Langford, Jesse, 192
Langley, Levi, 193
Lee, George W., 193
Lee, Johnson, 193
Levins, Alexander C., 35, 193
Levins, John, 194, 306
Levins, Richard, 194, 306
Levins, William Jackson, 194
Lewis, Alia, 195
Lewis, James M., 195

Lisenby, William, 195
Little, James P., 195
Locklin, Erastus Martin, 196
Love, James, 196
Love, James Samuel, 196
Love, William H., 196
Lowery, Joel H., 196
Lowery, William D., 197
Ludlam, Samuel P., 71, 197
Lyons, Francis, 30, 35, 48, 198

M

Main, Travis, 198
Malloy, James E., 51, 198
Maloy, John E., 199
Maloy, William H., 199
Mann, John T., 199
Manning, William Thomas, 71, 199
Marshall, John Thomas, 200
Martin, Burrell, 200
Martin, John Thomas, 71, 200
Martin, Jonathan F., 71, 201
Mathews, Benjamin C., 201, 307
Mathews, James H., 201
Mathews, James Madison, 201, 307
Mathis, Samuel Wesley, 202
Maund Samuel J., 307
Maund, Joseph P., 202, 307
Maund, Samuel J., 202
McArthur, Charles Columbus, 203
McCuller, David, 71, 203
McCurley, Joseph, 71, 204
McDaniel, Randal K., 51, 204
McGee, Alexander C., 72, 204, 307
McGee, Richard, 204, 307

McKiney, John R., 205
McLean, William F., 205
McLellan, Alexander, 205, 308
McLellan, Angus, 205, 308
McLellan, Duncan, 206, 308
McLellan, William M., 206, 308
McLendon, John A., 206
McMillan, Jackson, 207
McMillan, Thomas B., 207
McMillion, Alfred C., 51, 207
Meadows, William H., 208
Medlock, Robert Lewis, 72, 208
Melvin, Daniel V., 72, 208, 308
Melvin, Griffin, 35, 48, 65, 72, 209, 308
Merritt, Henry, 209
Merritt, Leroy R., 209
Merritt, William, 210
Meszaros, Emeric, 210
Miller, Abraham L., 210
Miller, Elias B., 211, 308
Miller, Henry J., 211
Miller, James L., 72, 211
Miller, James W., 211
Miller, John, 212
Miller, John B., 212, 308
Miller, John M., 212
Miller, William, 212
Mills, Warren, 35, 48, 66, 72, 213
Mills, William, 213
Milton, Andrew H., 213
Mims, Columbus C., 213
Mims, Nathan K., 72, 214
Mitchem, Joseph, 214
Moniac, James R., 214, 309
Moniac, Michael M., 35, 48, 66, 72, 215, 309
Moniac, Richard L., 72, 215, 309
Monten, Christian, 216
Mooney, Isaac P., 48, 216

Morgan, Isaiah M., 45, 216
Morris, Eli, 216
Morrison, Alexander, 217, 309
Morrison, Henry, 217, 309
Morrison, John, 217
Morrison, Robert, 218
Moses, Dennis F., 218
Murphy, Hansel M., 72, 218, 309
Murphy, Silas D., 72, 218, 309
Murphy, Thomas T., 51, 219, 309

N

Neal, Hugh William, 219
Nelson, Jonah, 219
Nettles, Adam Wyrick, 220
Nettles, Alexander (Adam) Wyrick, 72
Newberry, Nathaniel, 220
Newsom, James M., 220
Nichols, Elias, 221
Nobles, Andrew J., 30, 72, 221
Norris, Alvah Colby, 72, 221
Norris, Green, 58, 72, 222
Norris, James I., 66, 222
Norris, Joel B., 222
Norton, William A. C., 48, 223
Nowland, Henry, 223

O

Oglesbee, Benjamin, 223
Oglesbee, George W., 223
Omosro, David, 224
Overstreet, Henry, 224
Owens, Franklin, 72, 224
Owens, William Daniel, 224, 310
Owens, Willis W., 225, 310

P

Parker, George W., 30, 225, 310
Parker, Greenberry G., 226, 310
Parker, John, 226, 310
Parker, Richard P., 30, 226, 310
Parker, William, 31, 227
Parrish, Charles Wesley, 227, 311
Parrish, Christopher Columbus, 227, 311
Parrish, Ephraim C., 58, 72, 227, 311
Parrish, George W., 228, 311
Parrish, Owen T., 228, 311
Parrish, Robert J., 228, 311
Pate, David, 229
Pate, Joel, 72, 229, 311
Pate, Mathew, 229
Pate, Rudolph F., 229, 311
Paul, Daniel William, 51, 230, 311
Paul, David Enoch, 230
Paul, John A., 51, 230, 311
Paulk, Jonathan, 35, 48, 66, 72, 231
Peacock, John, 58, 231
Penton, John T., 232
Peterson, William J., 232
Phillips, William, 232
Philmon, Jesse, 232
Pickard, Cyrus P., 232
Pickron, William W., 51, 233
Pippin, Griffin Lambert, 233
Pitman, George Washington, 233
Pittman, Thomas H., 72, 234
Pitts, Isaac Porter, 234, 312
Pitts, Lewis, 235, 312
Pitts, William Henry, 235, 312

Poe, Aaron, 235
Polatta, John M., 235
Polatta, William, 236
Pompey, Jackson, 236
Potter, Andrew J., 72, 236
Potter, George, 236
Potts, Alexander Dunbar, 237
Powell, John W., 237
Powell, Joseph, 237
Price, Andrew J., 237
Prim, Benjamin Franklin, 238, 312
Prim, D. J., 238
Prim, James Jordan, 72, 238, 312
Provost, Richard V., 238
Pullum, Thomas, 35, 48, 239

R

Ramer, Elias J., 239
Ray, Jesse, 31, 239
Ray, Soverign Frederick, 30, 35, 48, 240
Rayburn, Ira W., 240
Register, Akis F., 313
Register, Akis Franklin, 58, 72, 240
Register, Joseph M., 72, 241, 313
Rhodes, John M., 241
Richards, John S., 241
Richardson, Francis M., 242
Richardson, George M., 51, 242
Richardson, Wade H., 242
Richbourg, William L., 243
Riley, Daniel, 243
Roberson, Benjamin, 35
Roberson, Daniel L., 35

Roberson, Samuel Benjamin, 48, 66, 72, 243
Roberts, Daniel D., 244
Roberts, Francis M., 244
Roberts, Gray S., 244
Robinson, Daniel L., 48, 66, 72, 244
Rogers, James W., 72, 245
Roland, John, 245
Rombauer, Roland T., 245
Rooks, George Daniel, 246, 313
Rooks, Isaac, 246
Rooks, James Franklin, 246, 313
Rooks, Thomas F., 247, 313
Rossvalley, Max L., 247
Rouse, Charles A., 247
Rowley, Lyman W., 247
Russ, Robert S., 248
Russell, Henry, 248
Ruttkay, Albert, 249

S

Sanders, Joseph Ganes, 45, 48, 249
Sanders, William, 249
Sarris, William V., 249
Scammell, William, 250
Scroggins, Richard Wesley, 72, 250
Seagers, William, 250
Segars, Southerd P., 251, 313
Segars, William R., 251, 313
Sellers, Henry T., 251
Sellers, John, 252, 314
Sellers, John F., 252, 314
Sellers, Julius, 252, 314
Sellers, Norman L., 252

Sellers, Thomas, 58, 72, 253, 314
Sellers, Thomas L., 253
Senterfitt, Bennett G., 58, 72, 253, 314
Sessions, James A., 254
Settles, Samuel C., 51, 254
Sheffield, Joseph, 254
Shellhouse, Sampson J., 51, 254
Sikes, James E., 255
Simmons, James A., 255
Singletary, Elijah, 255
Singletary, William L., 255
Skinner, John W., 72, 256
Smith, Archibald, 256, 315
Smith, Derrell Malcolm, 256, 315
Smith, Dred H., 257
Smith, Isaac, 58, 257
Smith, Jacob, 257
Smith, Thomas, 257
Smith, William, 72, 257
Smith, William J., 258
Snell, James Barnett, 258
Snowden, James M., 258
Snowden, Josiah H., 58, 72, 259
Sowell, Abijah Lewis, 58, 72, 259
Sowell, John W., 259
Spears, John, 260
Spence, Joshua, 260
Spurlock, Samuel H., 261
Stagner, Daniel W., 72, 261, 315
Stagner, Elias, 51
Stagner, George W., 261, 315
Stagner, John M., 72, 261, 315
Stanley, Garrett S., 72, 262
Stanley, Joseph S., 72, 262, 315
Stanley, Kinion, 263, 315

Stearns, Benjamin F., 30, 35, 48, 72, 263
Steel, William C., 263
Steele, Henry William, 264
Stegall, Reuben N., 72, 264
Stephens, Benjamin F., 72, 264
Stewart, George W., 35, 48, 66, 72, 264
Stewart, James H., 35, 48, 66, 73, 265
Stokes, John O., 265
Streets, Hugh, 265
Strickland, Eli J., 266
Strickland, James Pinckney, 73, 266, 316
Strickland, John J., 73, 266, 316
Strickland, Reason, 35, 48, 66, 73, 266
Sullivan, John, 267
Summerlin, Lucas, 267
Swinney, Darby, 268

T

Tanner, John W., 268
Taylor, James W., 268
Taylor, Thomas Yancey, 269
Taylor, William L., 269
Teel, Henry W., 42, 269, 316
Teel, John (Jr.), 270, 316
Templers, William, 270
Tetson, Jeremiah, 270
Tharp, Henry V., 270
Thomas, George W. T., 271
Thomas, James W., 271
Thomas, John D. K. P., 66, 73, 271
Thomas, Joseph M., 272
Thomas, Lawson, 272
Thomas, T., 272

Thomas, William J., 272
Thompson, Campbell, 272
Thompson, Enoch, 73, 273
Thompson, Jesse, 73, 273
Thompson, Nelson, 273
Tolbert, Hezekiah (Jr.), 73, 274
Tramell, Dawson T., 35, 48, 274
Truett, James, 274
Tucker, Bartley F., 275, 316
Tucker, Robert Garrett, 275, 316
Turner, James H., 275
Turner, John E., 276
Turner, William S., 276

V

Vance, Francis M., 73, 276
Velalto, Unknown, 277
Von Der Wense, August, 277
Von Soden, Charles, 277
Von Wessely, Joseph W., 277

W

Walters, George, 278
Ward, Celestine Josiah, 51, 278
Ward, Ira Jackson, 278
Ward, James Madison, 279
Ward, John, 279
Ward, John Brantley, 279
Ward, Michael, 280
Ward, William Peter, 42, 280
Warren, Andrew J., 280
Waters, Elisha M., 281, 316
Waters, Jordan L., 35, 48, 73, 281, 316
Waters, William H., 35, 73, 281, 316
Watson, Anderson, 282
Watson, Burton H., 35, 48, 282, 317
Watson, John W., 35, 48, 73, 283, 317
Watson, William W., 283
Weeks, Benjamin W., 317
Weeks, Benjamin Washington, 283
Weeks, Harmon, 284, 317
Weeks, Hiram, 284, 317
West, Benjamin L., 73, 284, 317
West, Leonard Frank, 73, 284, 317
Wheeless, Joshua E., 51, 285, 318
Wheeless, Sion A., 285, 318
Whitacre, Edward, 285
White, Asa, 285
White, Joseph S., 286
White, Robert J., 286
White, Samuel L. (Jr.), 286
White, William E., 73, 286
Whittaker, Elbert David, 287
Wickliffe, Joseph H., 30, 287
Wilcox, Mark, 287
Wilkinson, John J., 288, 318
Wilkinson, William T. Fletcher, 73, 288, 318
Williams, Jeremiah, 288
Williams, John C., 288
Williams, Wyatt Green, 289
Winfield, Mathew M., 289
Wise, Daniel, 290
Wise, Hezekiah, 290
Woodham, James R. N., 45, 73, 290
Woodham, Joseph R., 290
Worley, Elias S., 73, 290, 318
Worley, Peter Coleman, 291, 318

Wright, Richard B., 35, 48, 66, 73, 291
Wright, William, 291
Wyrick, Samuel, 291

Y

Yarborough, Benjamin A., 292
Yates, Jordan, 292, 318
Yates, Levi, 292, 318
Yon, Darrell, 293
Yon, Joshua A., 58, 73, 293

www.ingramcontent.com/pod-product-compliance
Lightning Source LLC
Chambersburg PA
CBHW021800220426
43662CB00006B/133